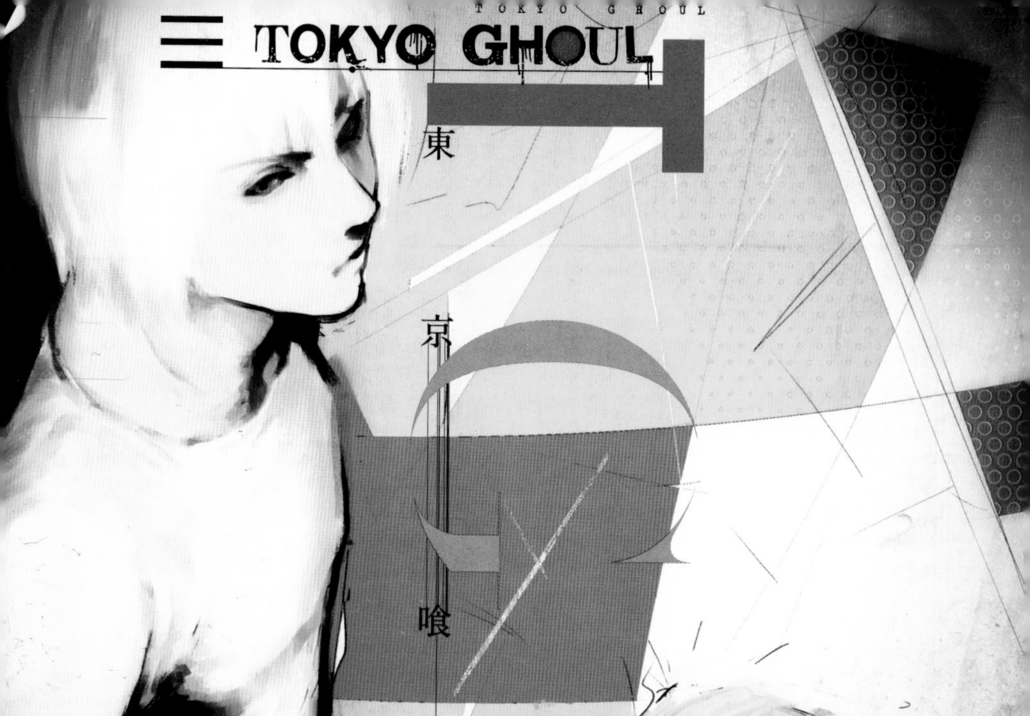
TOKYO GHOUL
TOKYO GHOUL
東京喰種
III SUI ISHIDA
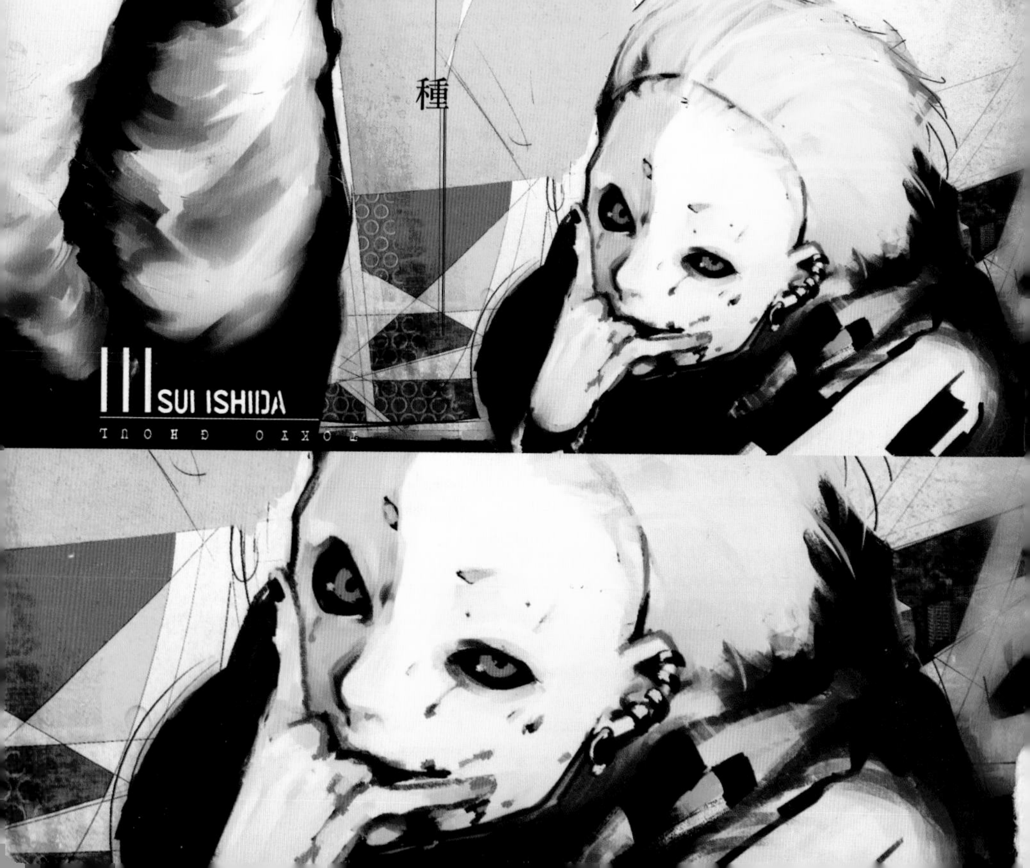

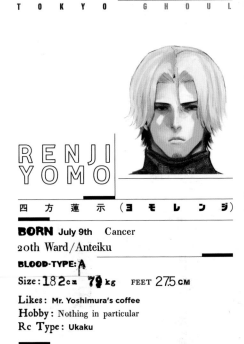

R E N J I
Y O M O

四 方 蓮 示 (ヨ モ レ ン ジ)

BORN July 9th   Cancer

20th Ward/Anteiku

BLOOD-TYPE: A

Size: 182cm 79 kg   FEET 27.5 CM

Likes : **Mr. Yoshimura's coffee**

Hobby : Nothing in particular

Rc Type : **Ukaku**

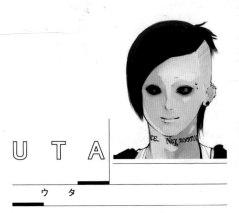

U T A

ウ タ

BORN December 2nd   Sagittarius

4th Ward/HySy Art Mask Studio Owner

BLOOD-TYPE: B

Size: 177cm 57 kg   FEET 25.0 CM

Likes : Making masks, music, **humans**, art

Hobby : Various

Rc Type : **?**

SUI ISHIDA was born in Fukuoka, Japan. He is the author of **Tokyo Ghoul** and several **Tokyo Ghoul** one-shots, including one that won him second place in the *Weekly Young Jump* 113th Grand Prix award in 2010. **Tokyo Ghoul** began serialization in *Weekly Young Jump* in 2011 and was adapted into an anime series in 2014.

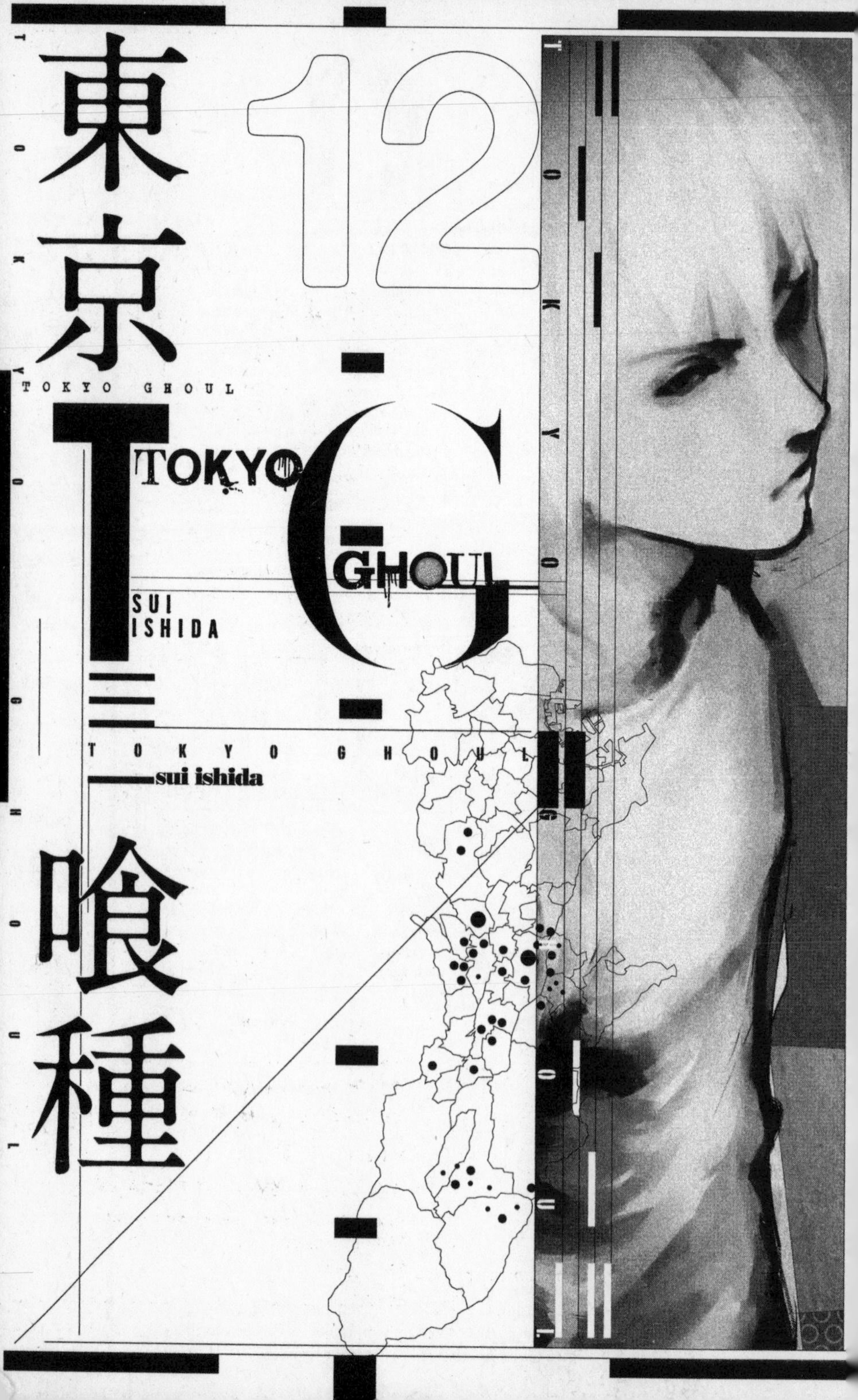
東京喰種
12
TOKYO GHOUL
TOKYO
GHOUL
SUI
ISHIDA
TOKYO GHOUL
sui ishida

TOKYO GHOUL SO FAR

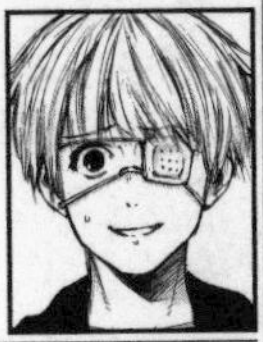

KEN KANEKI

An ordinary young man with a fondness for literature who meets with an accident, has Rize's organs transplanted into him and becomes a half-Ghoul. Struggling to find his place in the world. After being abducted by the Aogiri Tree and enduring Yamori's torture, the Ghoul inside him awakens.

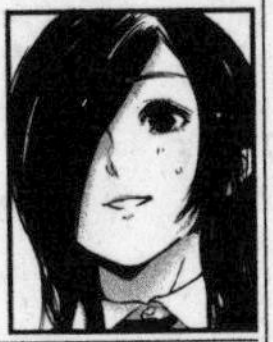

TOUKA KIRISHIMA

A conflicted heroine with two sides, rage and kindness. Ayato's older sister. Lives with the conflict of longing to be human. Hated investigators in the past…?

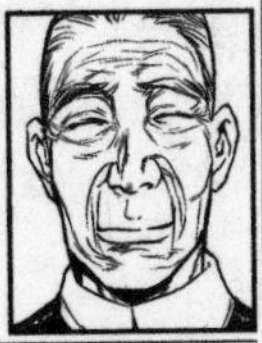

YOSHIMURA

Owner of Anteiku. Guides Kaneki so he can live as a Ghoul. Often works with Yomo. Shrouded in mystery.

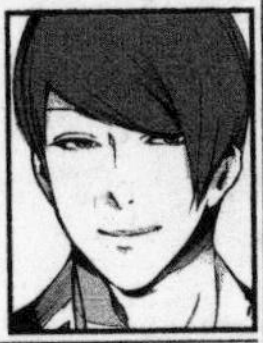

SHU TSUKIYAMA

A Gourmet who seeks the taste of the unknown. Obsessed with Kaneki, who is a half-Ghoul.

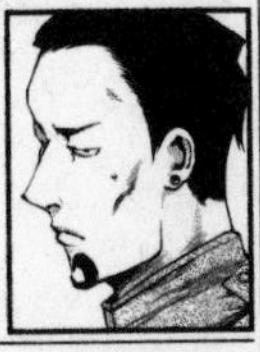

KAZUICHI BANJO

Former leader of the 11th Ward who admires Rize. Former member of the Aogiri Tree, but joins Kaneki after the fall of the 11th Ward.

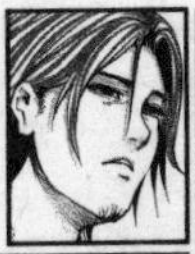

RENJI YOMO

Does not appear out in the open that often. Taciturn and unfriendly, but is trusted by many. Frequently acts together with Yoshimura. Concerned about Kaneki's condition.

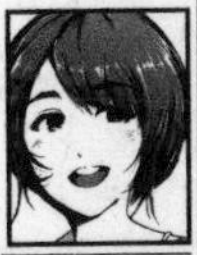

HINAMI FUEGUCHI

An orphan whose parents were killed by the CCG. Admires Kaneki like an older brother.

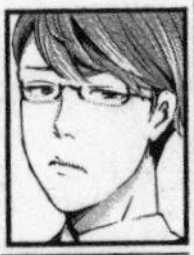

NISHIKI NISHIO

Studious. Adept at blending in with humans. Has a human girlfriend and a compassionate side.

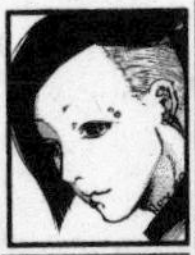

UTA

Owner of HySy Art-Mask Studio, a mask shop in the 4th Ward. Looks out for Kaneki.

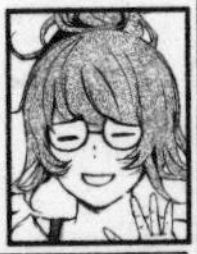

SEN TAKATSUKI

A brilliant novelist who is popular both as a person and as a writer. Author of *The Black Goat's Egg*, which led to Kaneki meeting Rize.

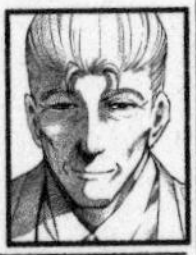

DOCTOR KANO

HUMAN

Kaneki's operating surgeon after the 20th Ward accident and the man responsible for turning him into a Ghoul. Ex-CCG medical examiner.

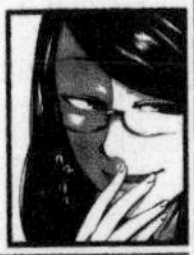

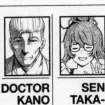

RIZE KAMISHIRO

Freewheeling Binge Eater who despised boredom. Previously lived in the 11th Ward. Met Kaneki in the 20th Ward and then had an accident. There are rumors she used an alias to hide her true identity.

[GHOUL]

A creature that appears human yet consumes humans. The top of the food chain. Finds anything other than humans and coffee unpleasant. Releases a highly lethal natural weapon unique to Ghouls, known as Kagune, from their body to prey on humans. Can be cannibalistic. Only sustains damage from Kagune or Quinques that are made from Kagune.

AOGIRI TREE 11TH WARD

A group of Ghouls formed with the ambition of ruling Ghouls and humans with force. Lures the CCG to their 11th Ward hideout and then attacks the 23rd Ward Ghoul Detention Center. Appoints a Ghoul called the One-Eyed King as their leader.

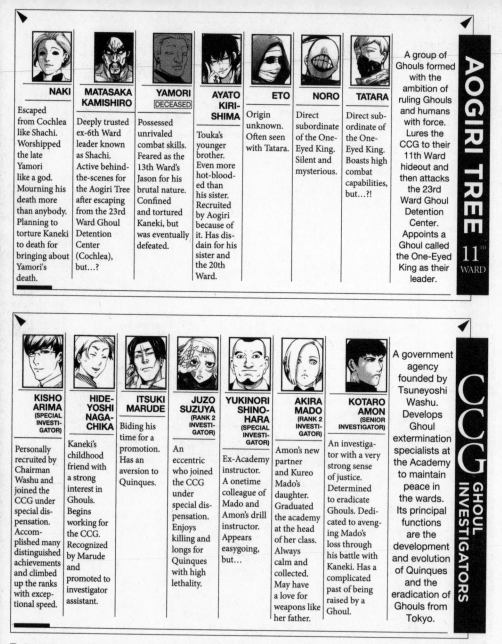

NAKI

Escaped from Cochlea like Shachi. Worshipped the late Yamori like a god. Mourning his death more than anybody. Planning to torture Kaneki to death for bringing about Yamori's death.

MATASAKA KAMISHIRO

Deeply trusted ex-6th Ward leader known as Shachi. Active behind-the-scenes for the Aogiri Tree after escaping from the 23rd Ward Ghoul Detention Center (Cochlea), but…?

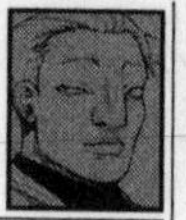

YAMORI

DECEASED

Possessed unrivaled combat skills. Feared as the 13th Ward's Jason for his brutal nature. Confined and tortured Kaneki, but was eventually defeated.

AYATO KIRISHIMA

Touka's younger brother. Even more hot-blooded than his sister. Recruited by Aogiri because of it. Has disdain for his sister and the 20th Ward.

ETO

Origin unknown. Often seen with Tatara.

NORO

Direct subordinate of the One-Eyed King. Silent and mysterious.

TATARA

Direct subordinate of the One-Eyed King. Boasts high combat capabilities, but…?!

CCG GHOUL INVESTIGATORS

A government agency founded by Tsuneyoshi Washu. Develops Ghoul extermination specialists at the Academy to maintain peace in the wards. Its principal functions are the development and evolution of Quinques and the eradication of Ghouls from Tokyo.

KISHO ARIMA (SPECIAL INVESTIGATOR)

Personally recruited by Chairman Washu and joined the CCG under special dispensation. Accomplished many distinguished achievements and climbed up the ranks with exceptional speed.

HIDEYOSHI NAGACHIKA

Kaneki's childhood friend with a strong interest in Ghouls. Begins working for the CCG. Recognized by Marude and promoted to investigator assistant.

ITSUKI MARUDE

Biding his time for a promotion. Has an aversion to Quinques.

JUZO SUZUYA (RANK 2 INVESTIGATOR)

An eccentric who joined the CCG under special dispensation. Enjoys killing and longs for Quinques with high lethality.

YUKINORI SHINOHARA (SPECIAL INVESTIGATOR)

Ex-Academy instructor. A onetime colleague of Mado and Amon's drill instructor. Appears easygoing, but…

AKIRA MADO (RANK 2 INVESTIGATOR)

Amon's new partner and Kureo Mado's daughter. Graduated the academy at the head of her class. Always calm and collected. May have a love for weapons like her father.

KOTARO AMON (SENIOR INVESTIGATOR)

An investigator with a very strong sense of justice. Determined to eradicate Ghouls. Dedicated to avenging Mado's loss through his battle with Kaneki. Has a complicated past of being raised by a Ghoul.

Summary

Kaneki, an average college student, is fated to live as a Ghoul when Rize's organs are transplanted into him. While questioning and struggling with the existence of creatures that take human lives to survive, he searches for how the world should be. One day while at Anteiku, he is abducted by the Aogiri Tree. While being held captive and viciously tortured by Yamori, he accepts that he is a Ghoul. He later relocates to the 6th Ward with Tsukiyama and Banjo in pursuit of Dr. Kano. They arrive at Kano's underground lab and face a series of startling revelations that transform Kaneki into a half-Kakuja. Unable to control his power, he wounds a friend.

東

京

喰

種

TOKYO GHOUL

TOKYO GHOUL

TOKYO GHOUL

SUI
ISHIJA

C O N T E N T S

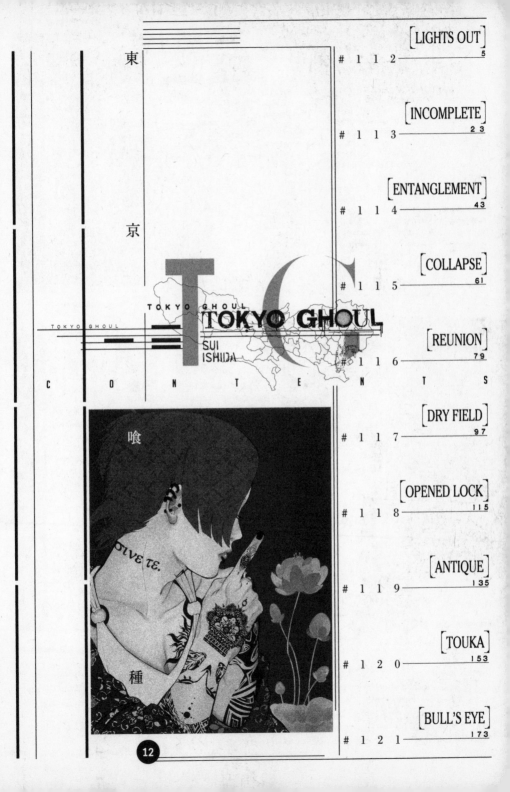

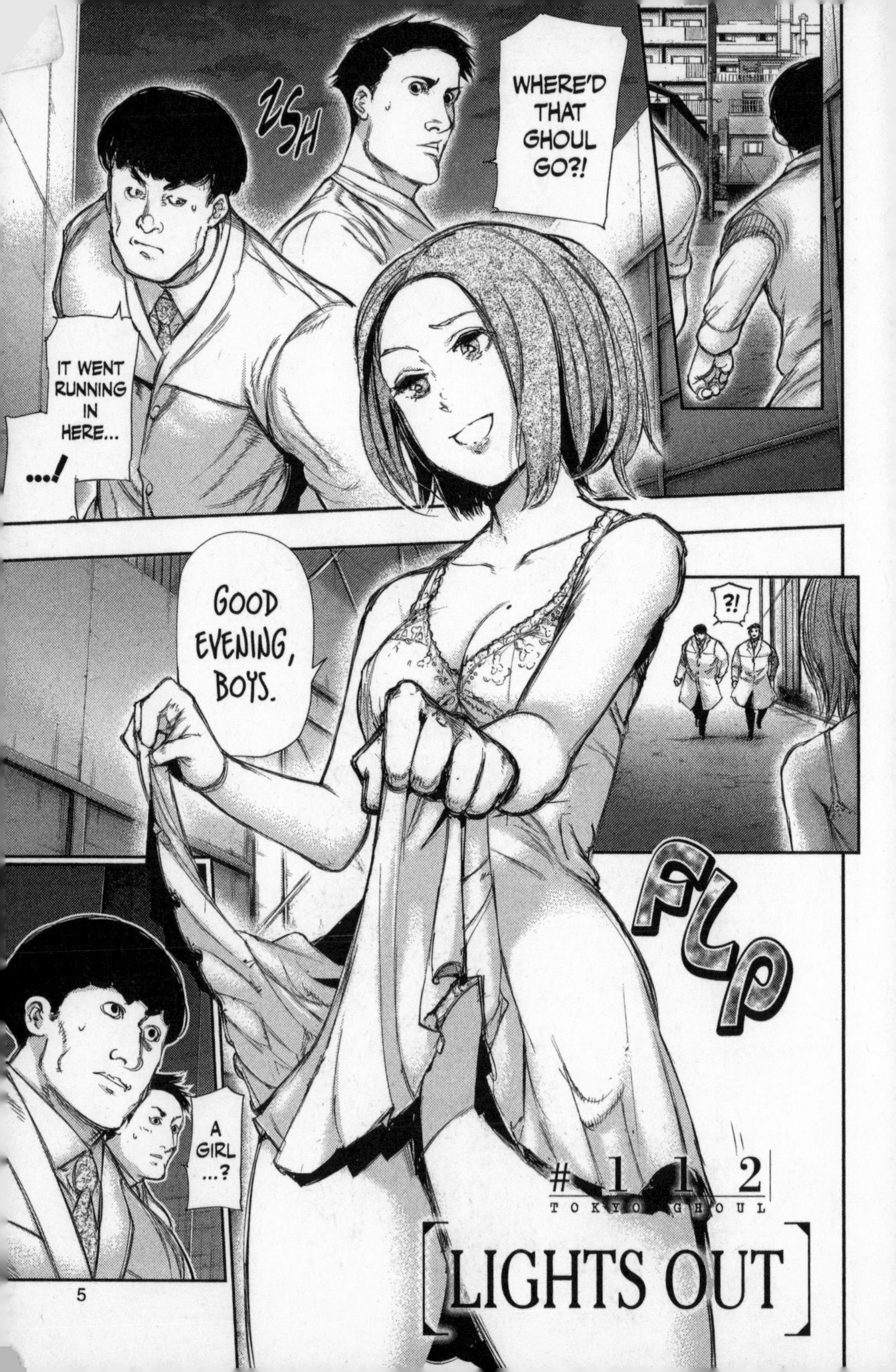
WHERE'D THAT GHOUL GO?!
ZSH
IT WENT RUNNING IN HERE...
...!
?!
FLP
GOOD EVENING, BOYS.
A GIRL ...?
#112
TOKYO GHOUL
LIGHTS OUT

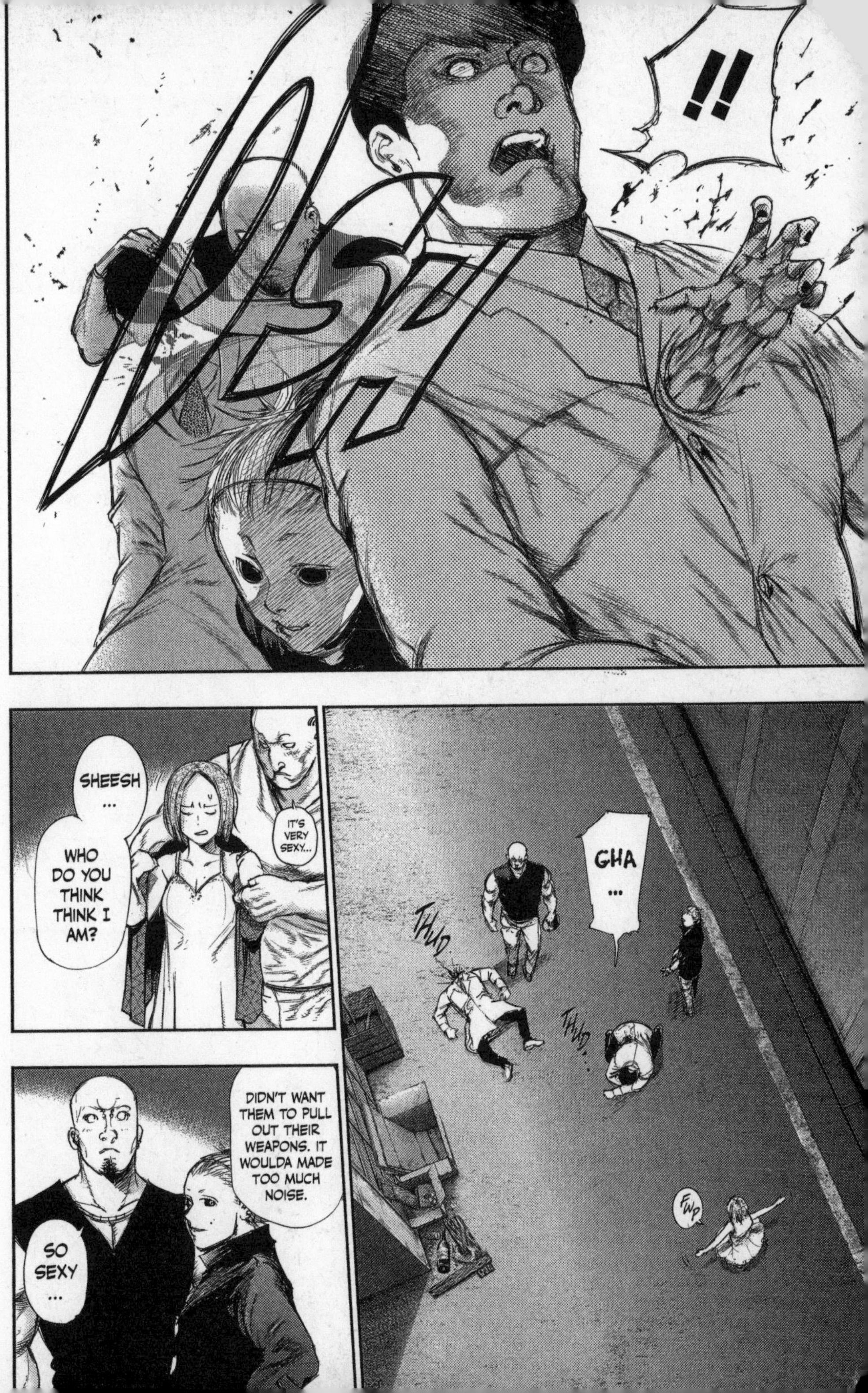
DSH
!!
GHA ...
THUD
THUD
FWP
SHEESH ...
WHO DO YOU THINK THINK I AM?
IT'S VERY SEXY...
DIDN'T WANT THEM TO PULL OUT THEIR WEAPONS. IT WOULDA MADE TOO MUCH NOISE.
SO SEXY ...

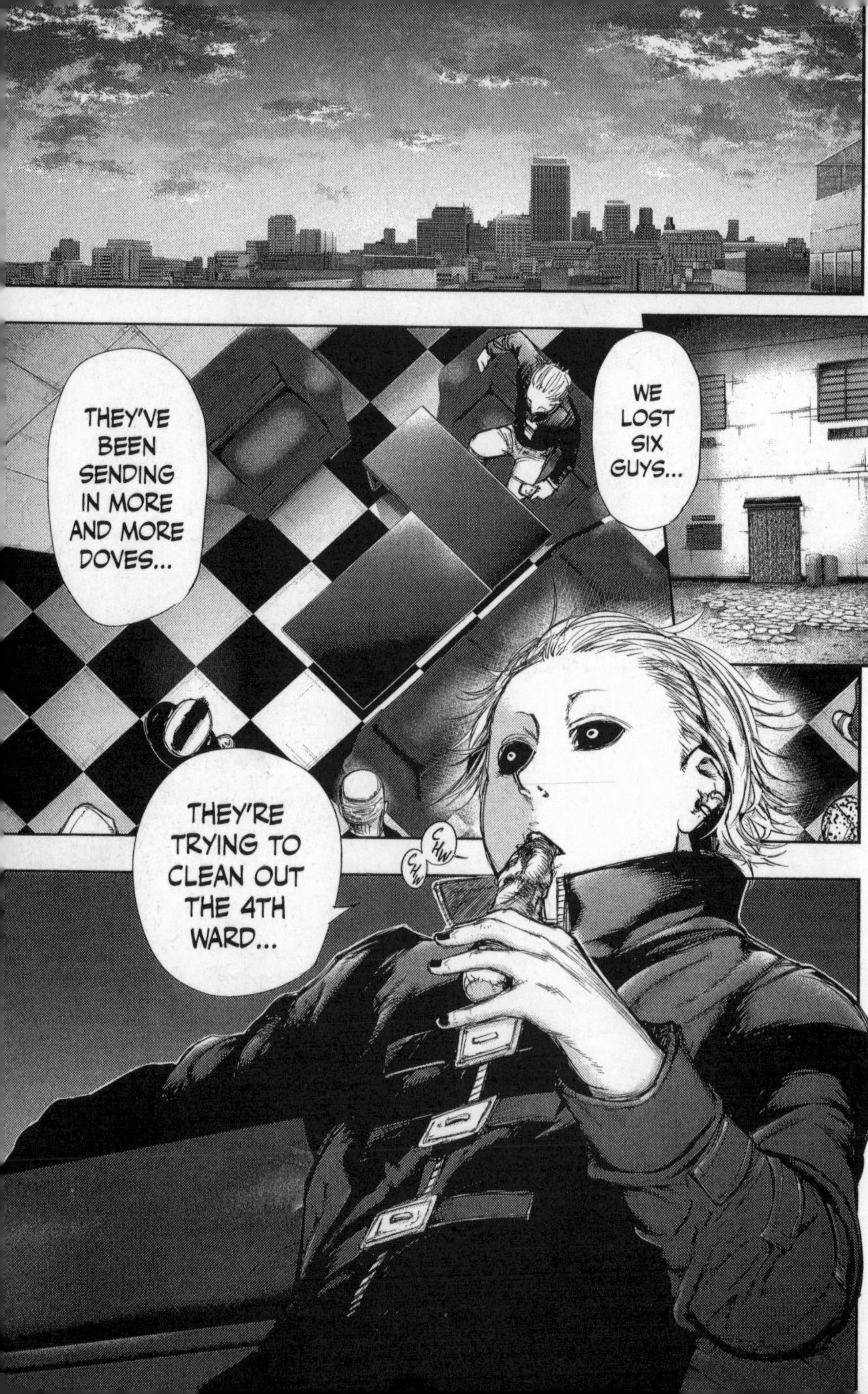

WE LOST SIX GUYS...
THEY'VE BEEN SENDING IN MORE AND MORE DOVES...
CHW CHW
THEY'RE TRYING TO CLEAN OUT THE 4TH WARD...

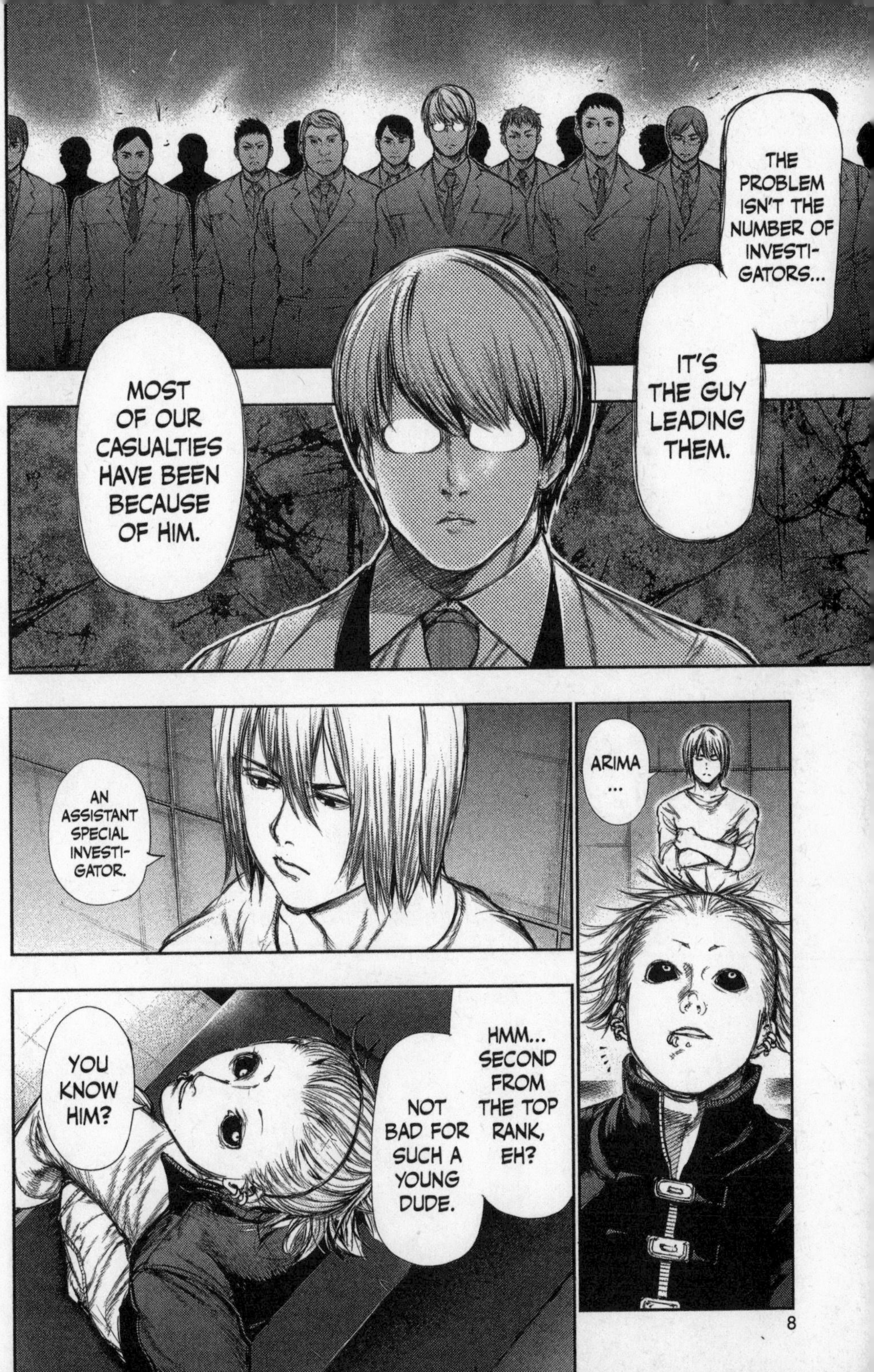
THE PROBLEM ISN'T THE NUMBER OF INVESTI-GATORS...
IT'S THE GUY LEADING THEM.
MOST OF OUR CASUALTIES HAVE BEEN BECAUSE OF HIM.
ARIMA ...
AN ASSISTANT SPECIAL INVESTI-GATOR.
HMM... SECOND FROM THE TOP RANK, EH?
NOT BAD FOR SUCH A YOUNG DUDE.
YOU KNOW HIM?

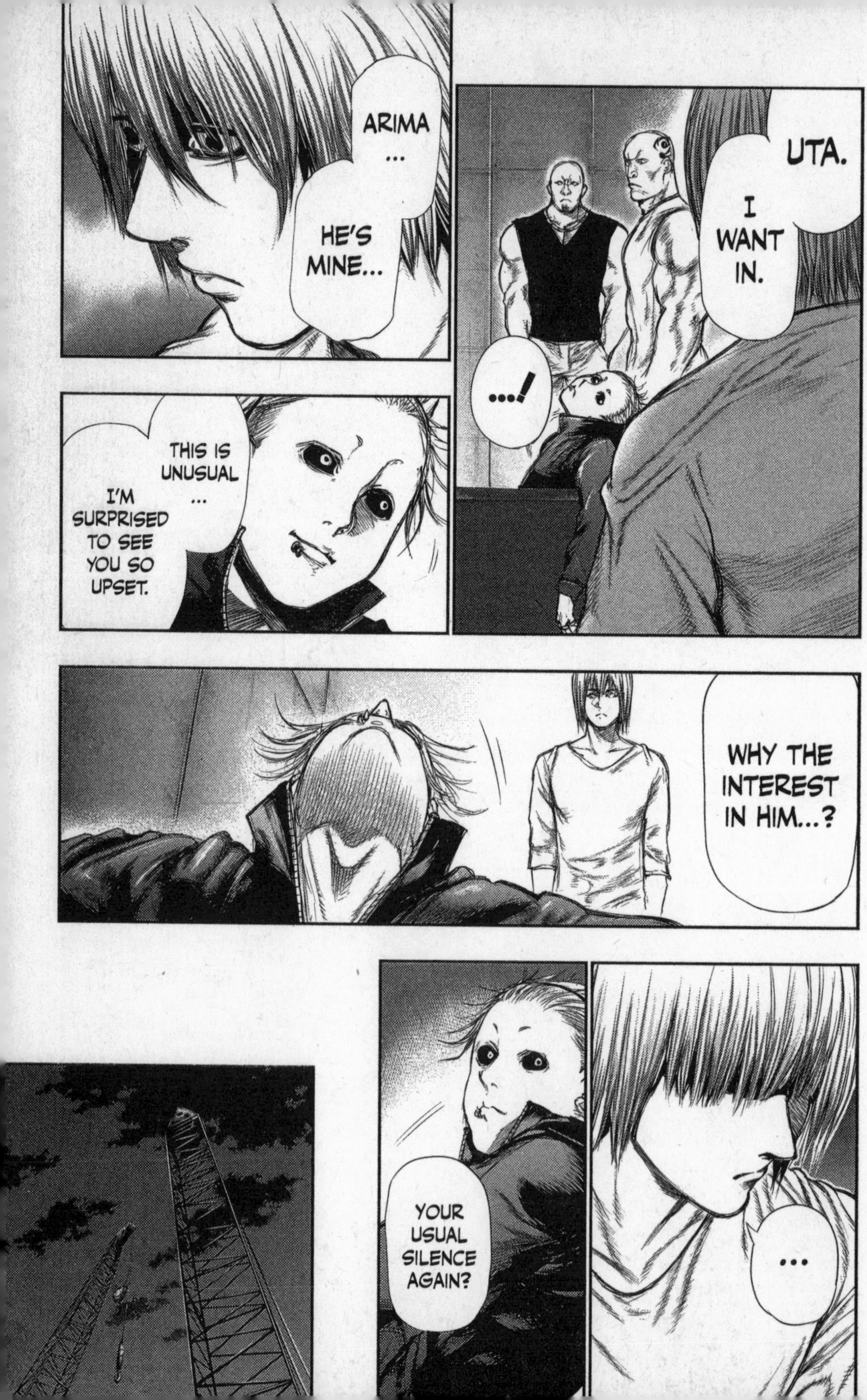
UTA.
I WANT IN.
...!
ARIMA ...
HE'S MINE...
THIS IS UNUSUAL ...
I'M SURPRISED TO SEE YOU SO UPSET.
WHY THE INTEREST IN HIM...?
...
YOUR USUAL SILENCE AGAIN?

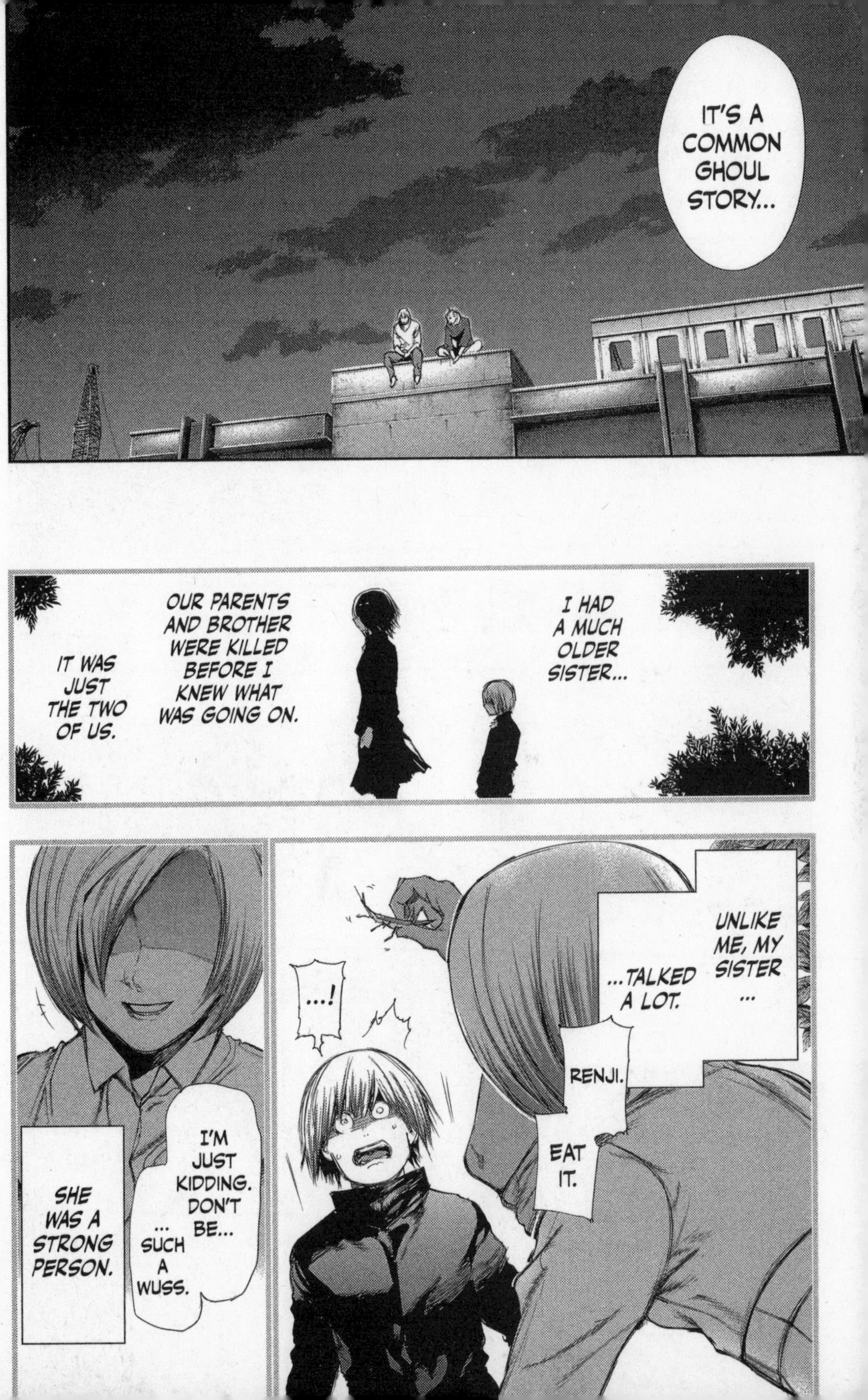
IT'S A COMMON GHOUL STORY...
I HAD A MUCH OLDER SISTER...
OUR PARENTS AND BROTHER WERE KILLED BEFORE I KNEW WHAT WAS GOING ON.
IT WAS JUST THE TWO OF US.
UNLIKE ME, MY SISTER ...
...TALKED A LOT.
RENJI.
EAT IT.
...!
I'M JUST KIDDING. DON'T BE... ...SUCH A WUSS.
SHE WAS A STRONG PERSON.

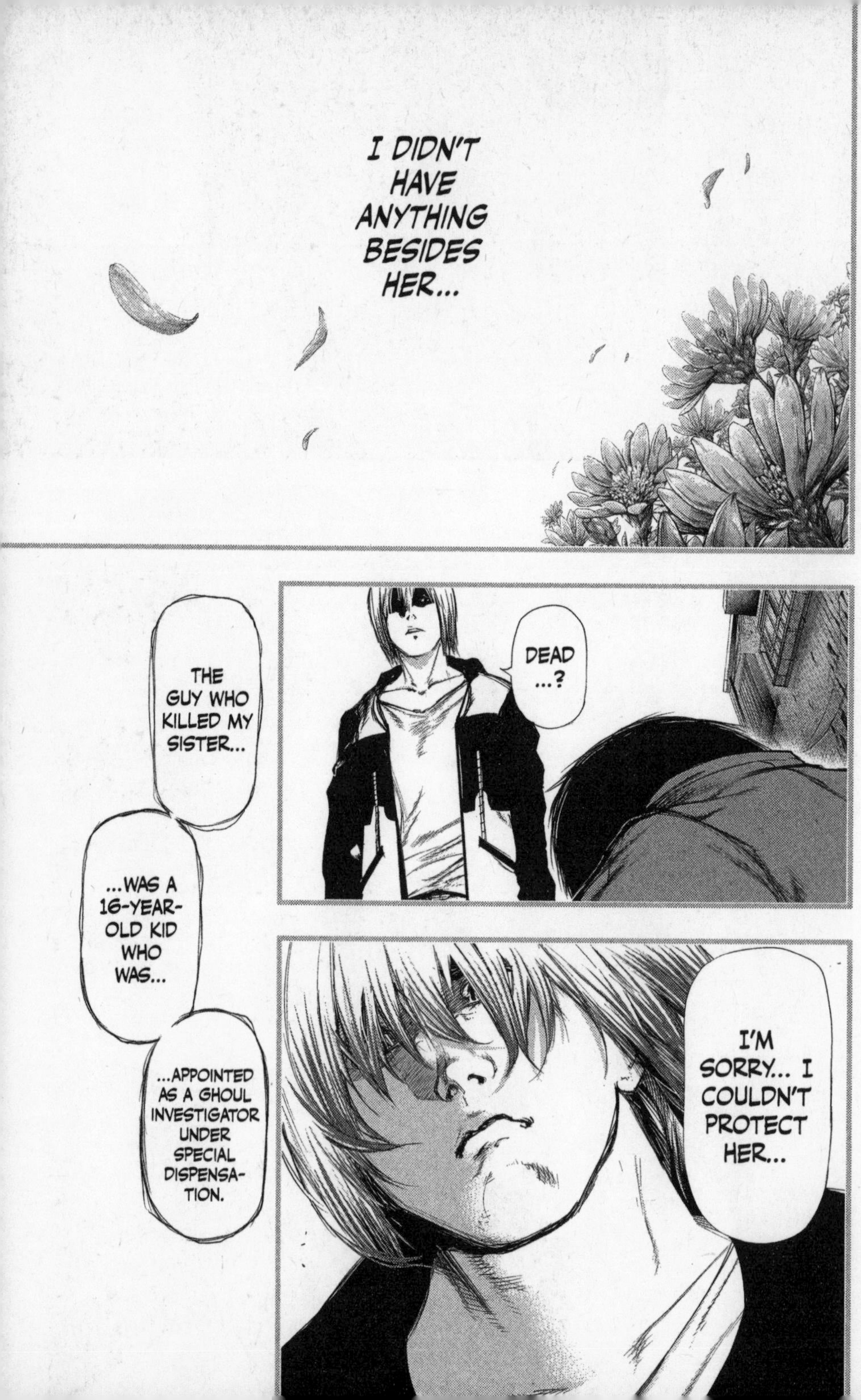
I DIDN'T HAVE ANYTHING BESIDES HER...
DEAD ...?
THE GUY WHO KILLED MY SISTER...
...WAS A 16-YEAR-OLD KID WHO WAS...
I'M SORRY... I COULDN'T PROTECT HER...
...APPOINTED AS A GHOUL INVESTIGATOR UNDER SPECIAL DISPENSA-TION.

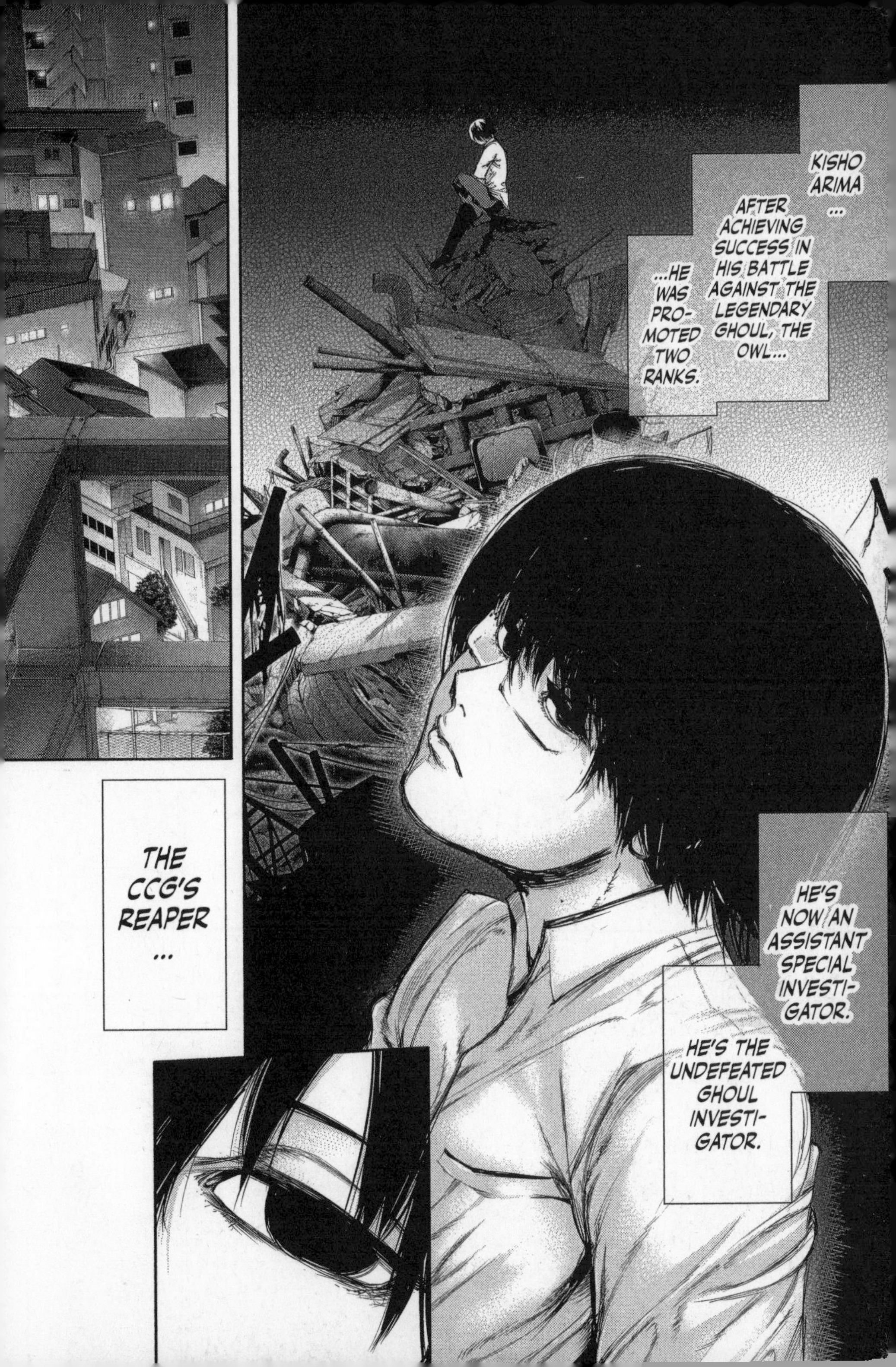
KISHO ARIMA ...
AFTER ACHIEVING SUCCESS IN HIS BATTLE AGAINST THE LEGENDARY GHOUL, THE OWL...
...HE WAS PRO-MOTED TWO RANKS.
HE'S NOW AN ASSISTANT SPECIAL INVESTI-GATOR.
HE'S THE UNDEFEATED GHOUL INVESTI-GATOR.
THE CCG'S REAPER ...

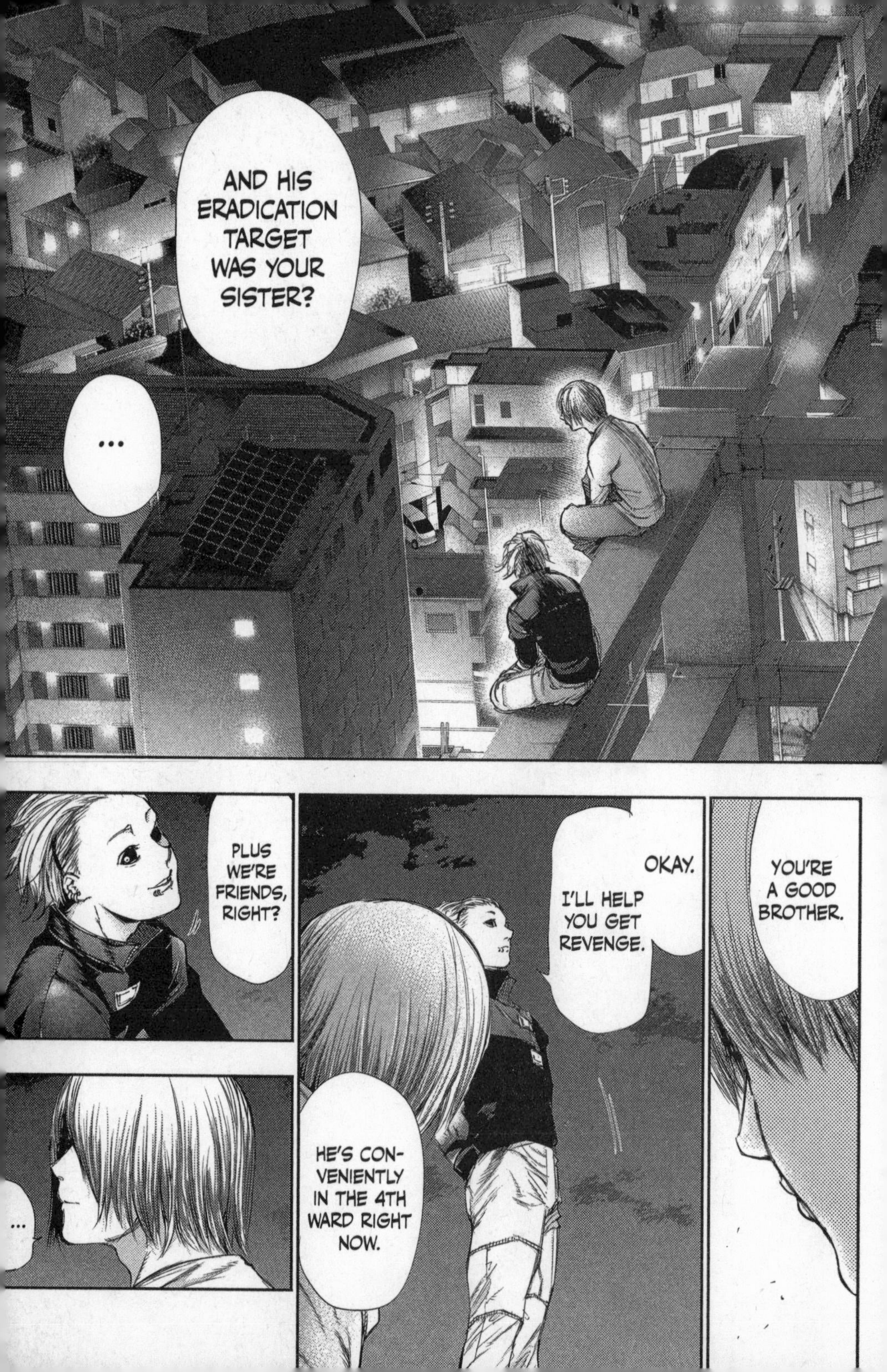
AND HIS ERADICATION TARGET WAS YOUR SISTER?
...
YOU'RE A GOOD BROTHER.
OKAY.
I'LL HELP YOU GET REVENGE.
HE'S CON-VENIENTLY IN THE 4TH WARD RIGHT NOW.
PLUS WE'RE FRIENDS, RIGHT?
...

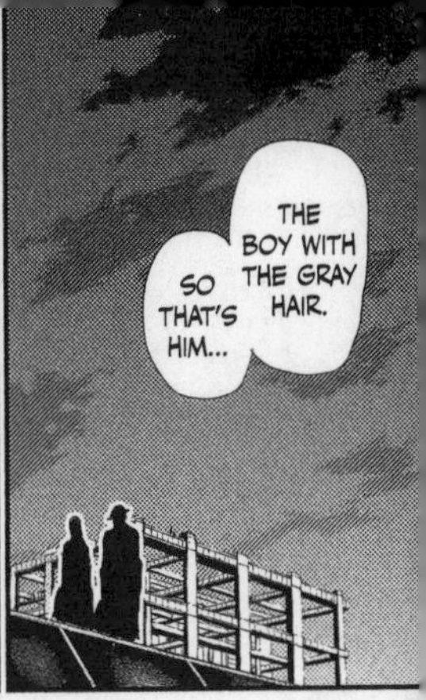
THE BOY WITH THE GRAY HAIR.
SO THAT'S HIM...
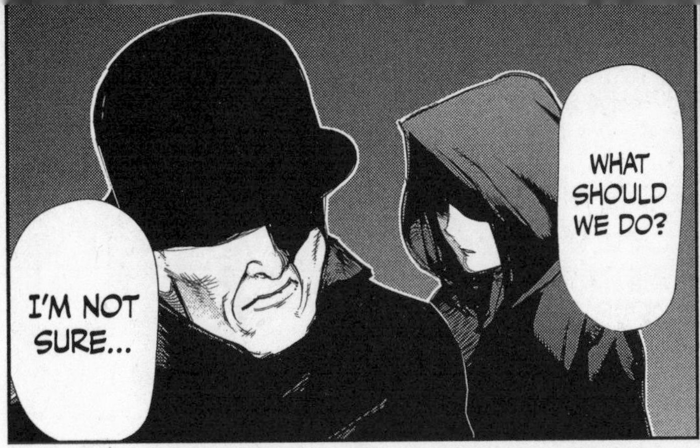
WHAT SHOULD WE DO?
I'M NOT SURE...
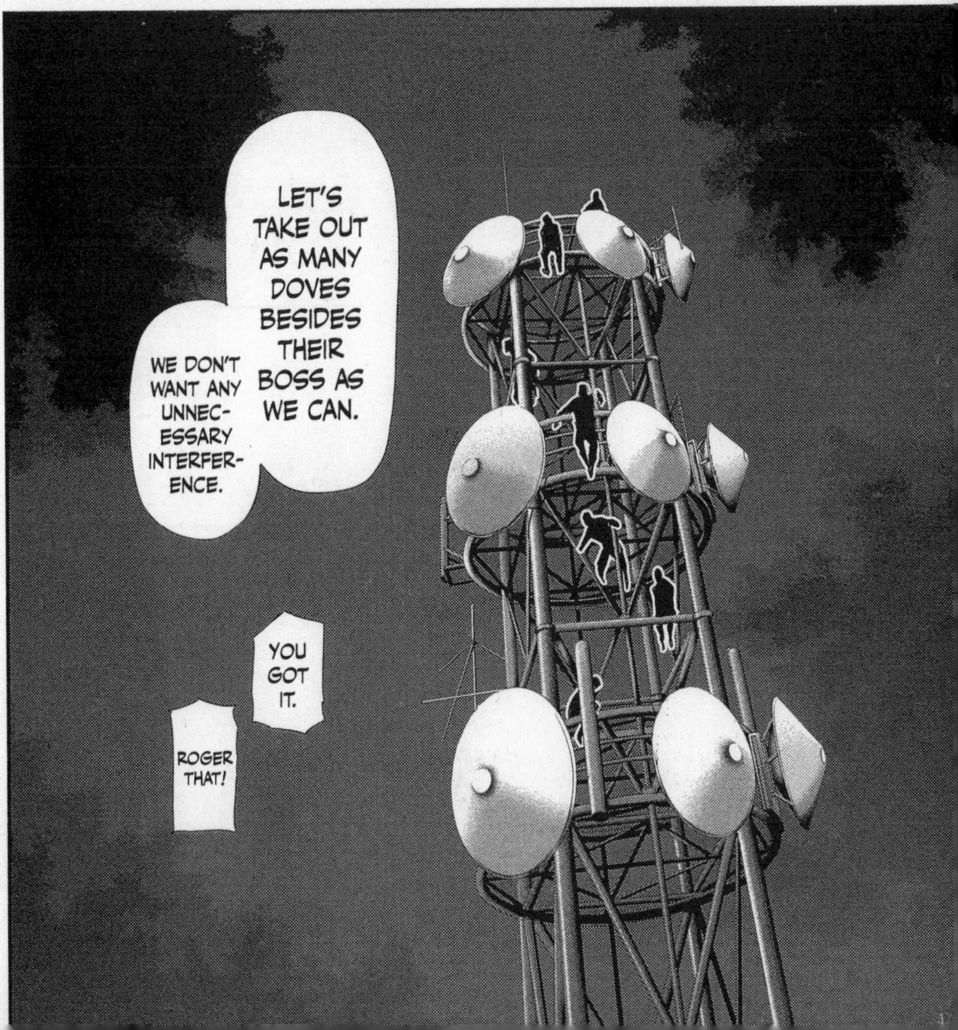
LET'S TAKE OUT AS MANY DOVES BESIDES THEIR BOSS AS WE CAN.
WE DON'T WANT ANY UNNEC-ESSARY INTERFER-ENCE.
YOU GOT IT.
ROGER THAT!

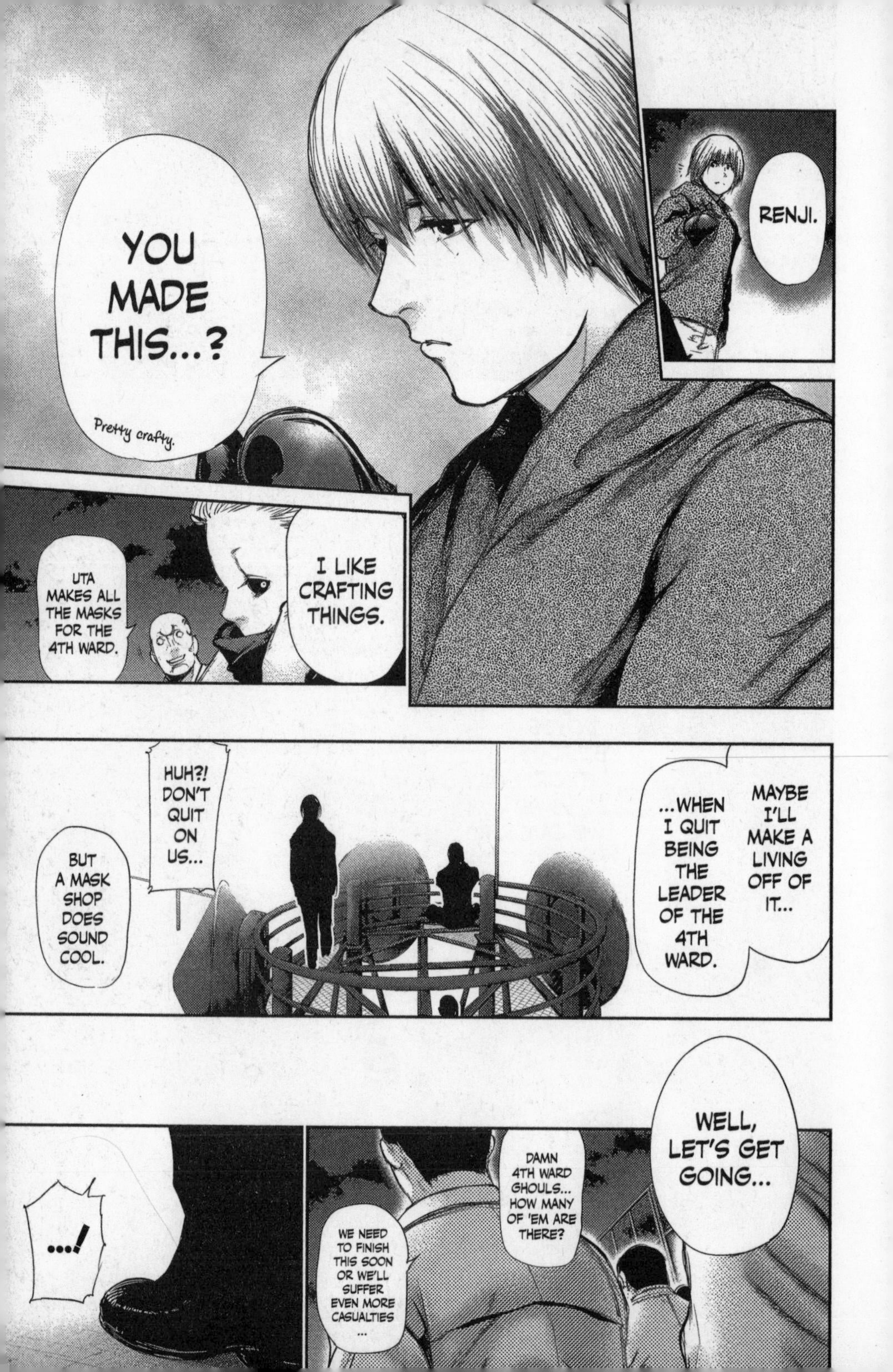
RENJI.
YOU MADE THIS...?
Pretty crafty.
I LIKE CRAFTING THINGS.
UTA MAKES ALL THE MASKS FOR THE 4TH WARD.
MAYBE I'LL MAKE A LIVING OFF OF IT...
...WHEN I QUIT BEING THE LEADER OF THE 4TH WARD.
HUH?! DON'T QUIT ON US...
BUT A MASK SHOP DOES SOUND COOL.
WELL, LET'S GET GOING...
DAMN 4TH WARD GHOULS... HOW MANY OF 'EM ARE THERE?
WE NEED TO FINISH THIS SOON OR WE'LL SUFFER EVEN MORE CASUALTIES ...
...!

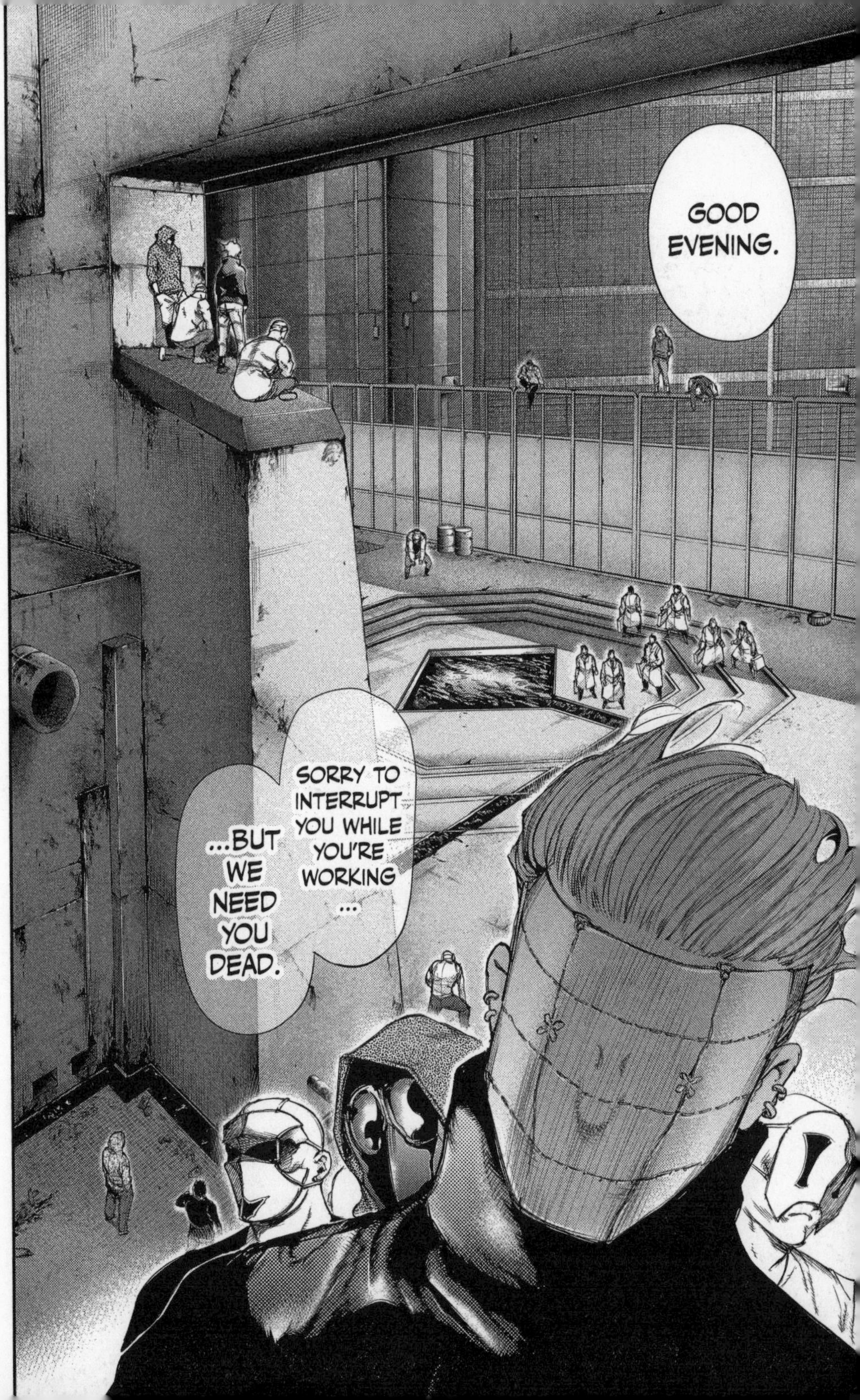

GOOD EVENING.
SORRY TO INTERRUPT YOU WHILE YOU'RE WORKING ...
...BUT WE NEED YOU DEAD.

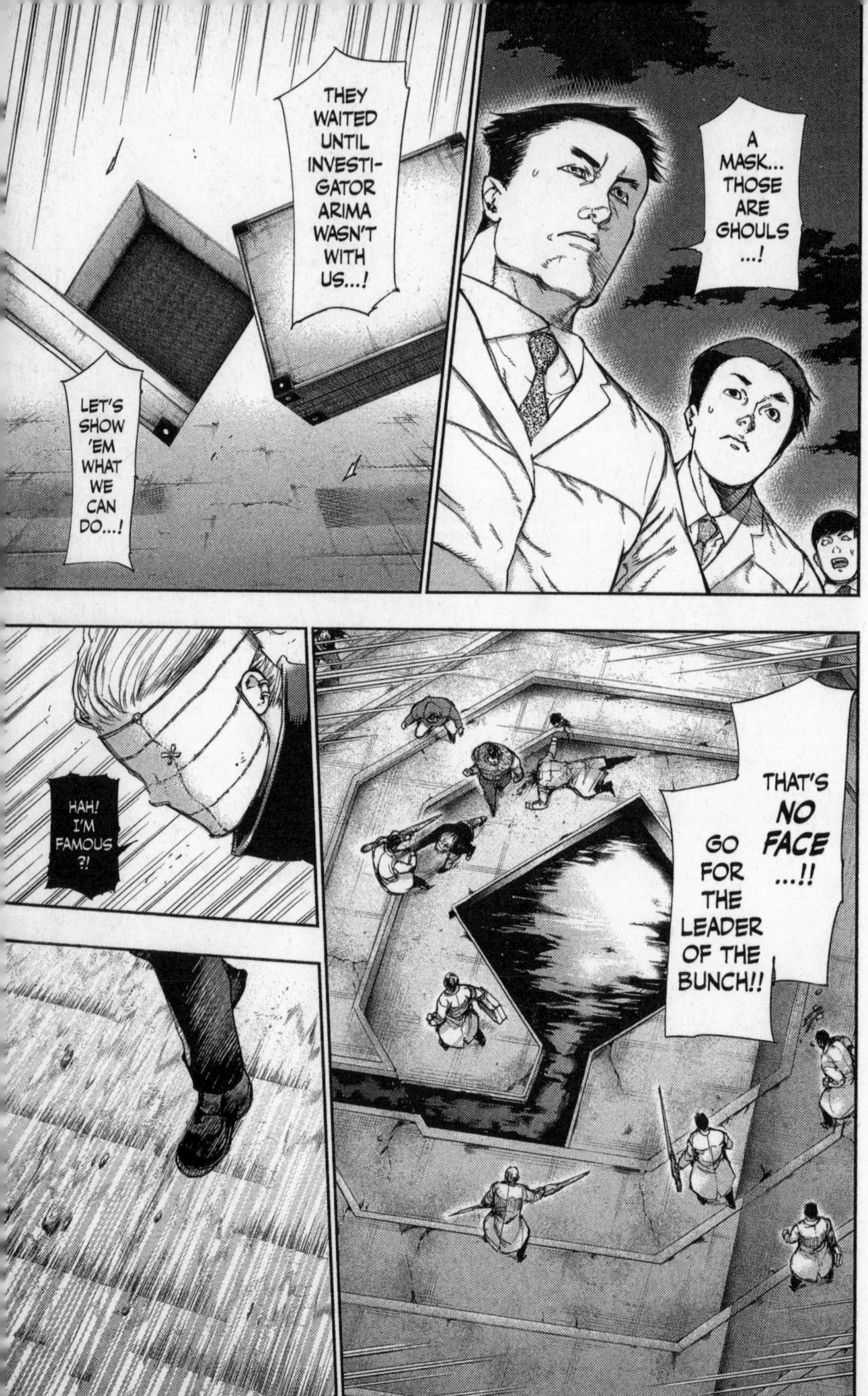
A MASK... THOSE ARE GHOULS ...!
THEY WAITED UNTIL INVESTI-GATOR ARIMA WASN'T WITH US...!
LET'S SHOW 'EM WHAT WE CAN DO...!
THAT'S NO FACE ...!!
GO FOR THE LEADER OF THE BUNCH!!
HAH! I'M FAMOUS ?!

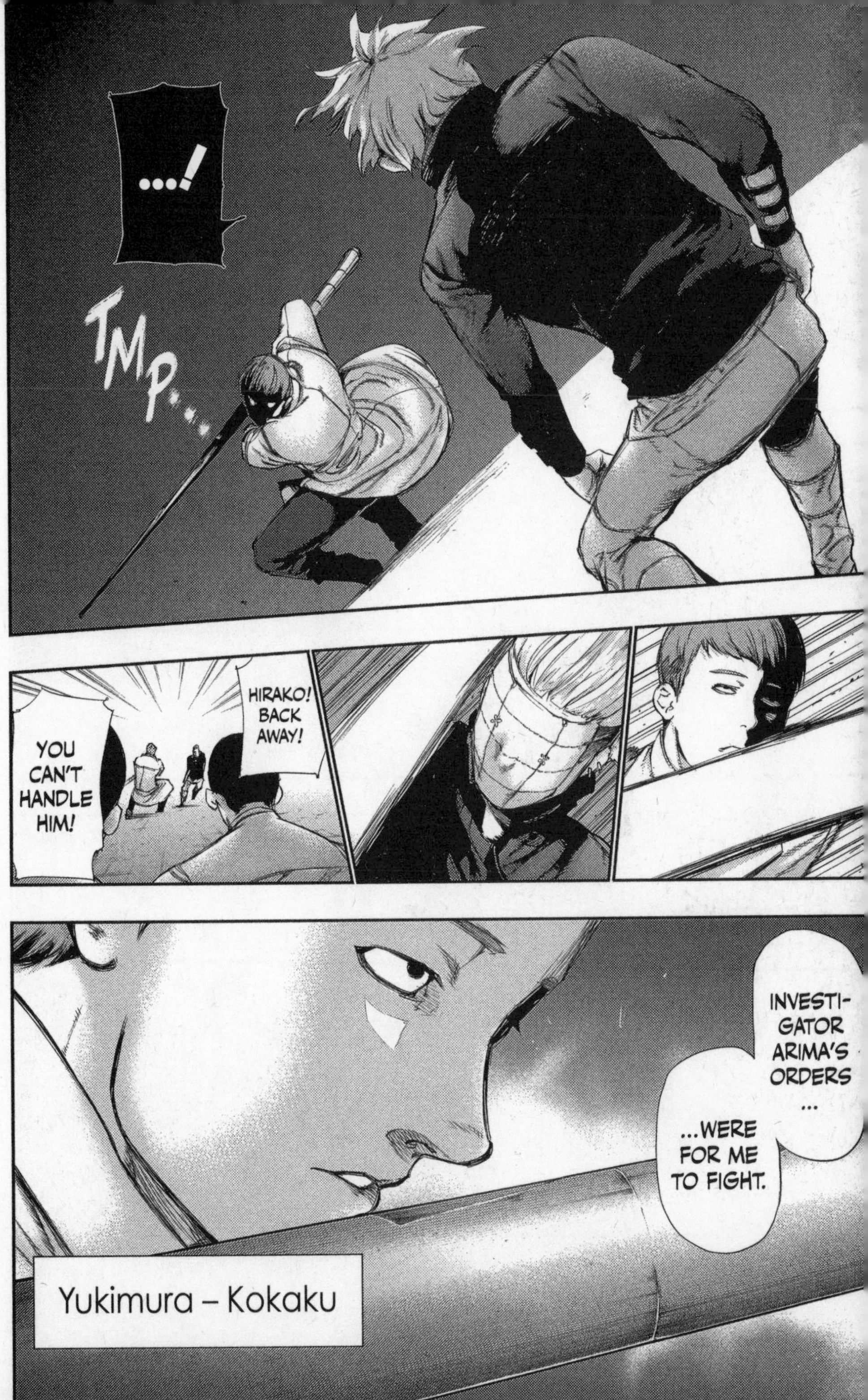
...!
TMP...
HIRAKO! BACK AWAY!
YOU CAN'T HANDLE HIM!
INVESTIGATOR ARIMA'S ORDERS...
...WERE FOR ME TO FIGHT.
Yukimura – Kokaku

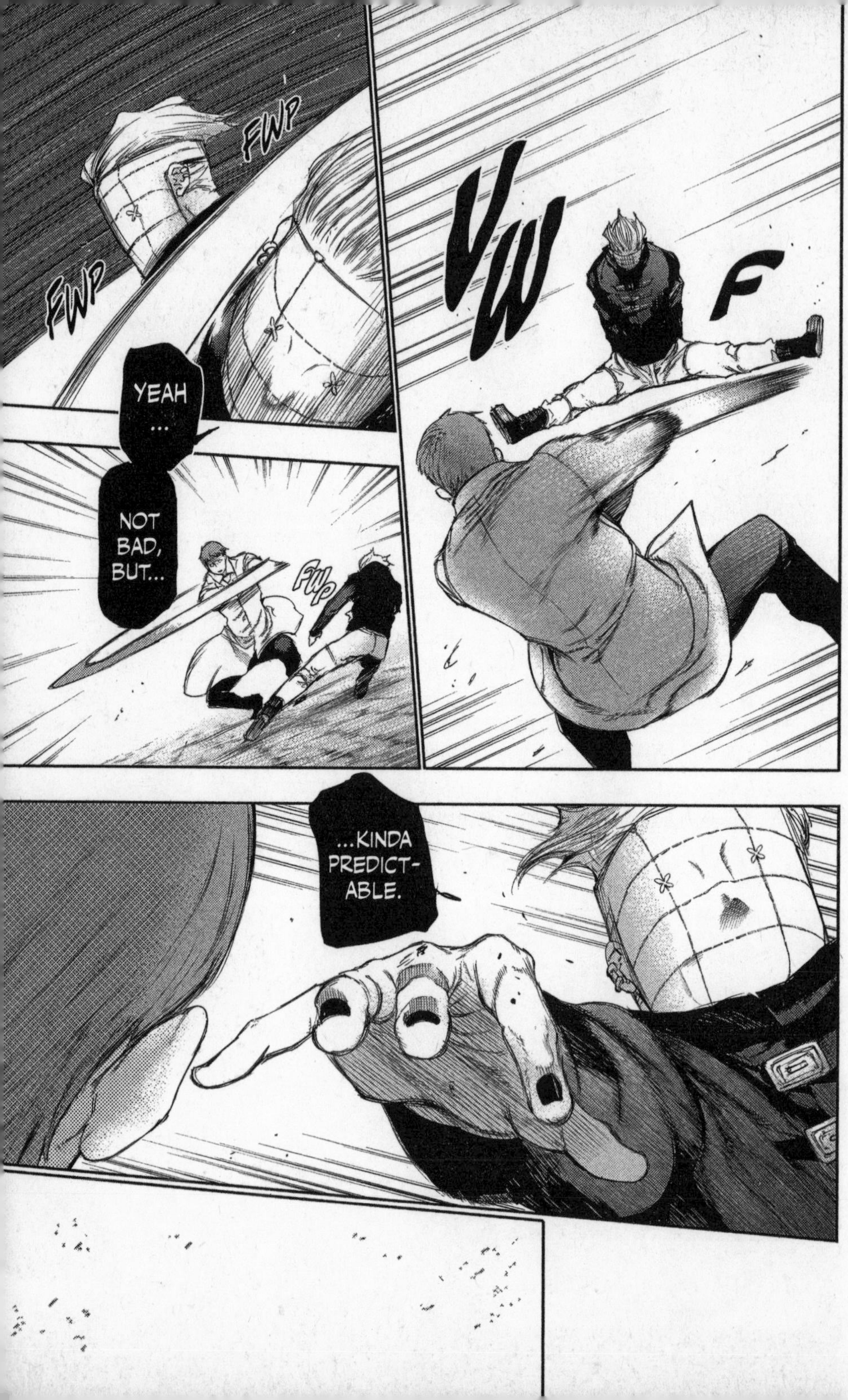
VW
F
FWP
FWP
YEAH...
NOT BAD, BUT...
FWP
...KINDA PREDICT-ABLE.

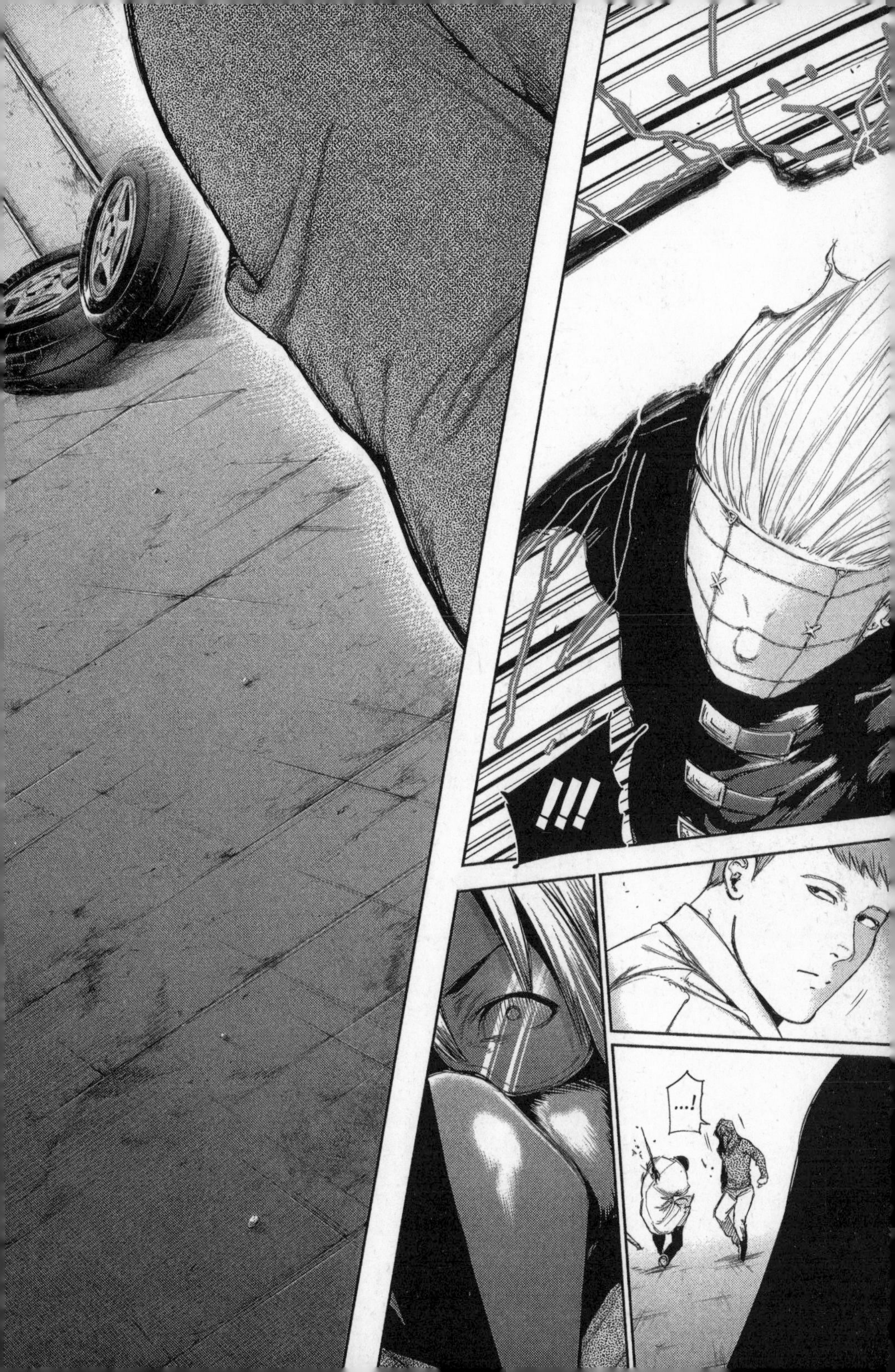
!!!
...!

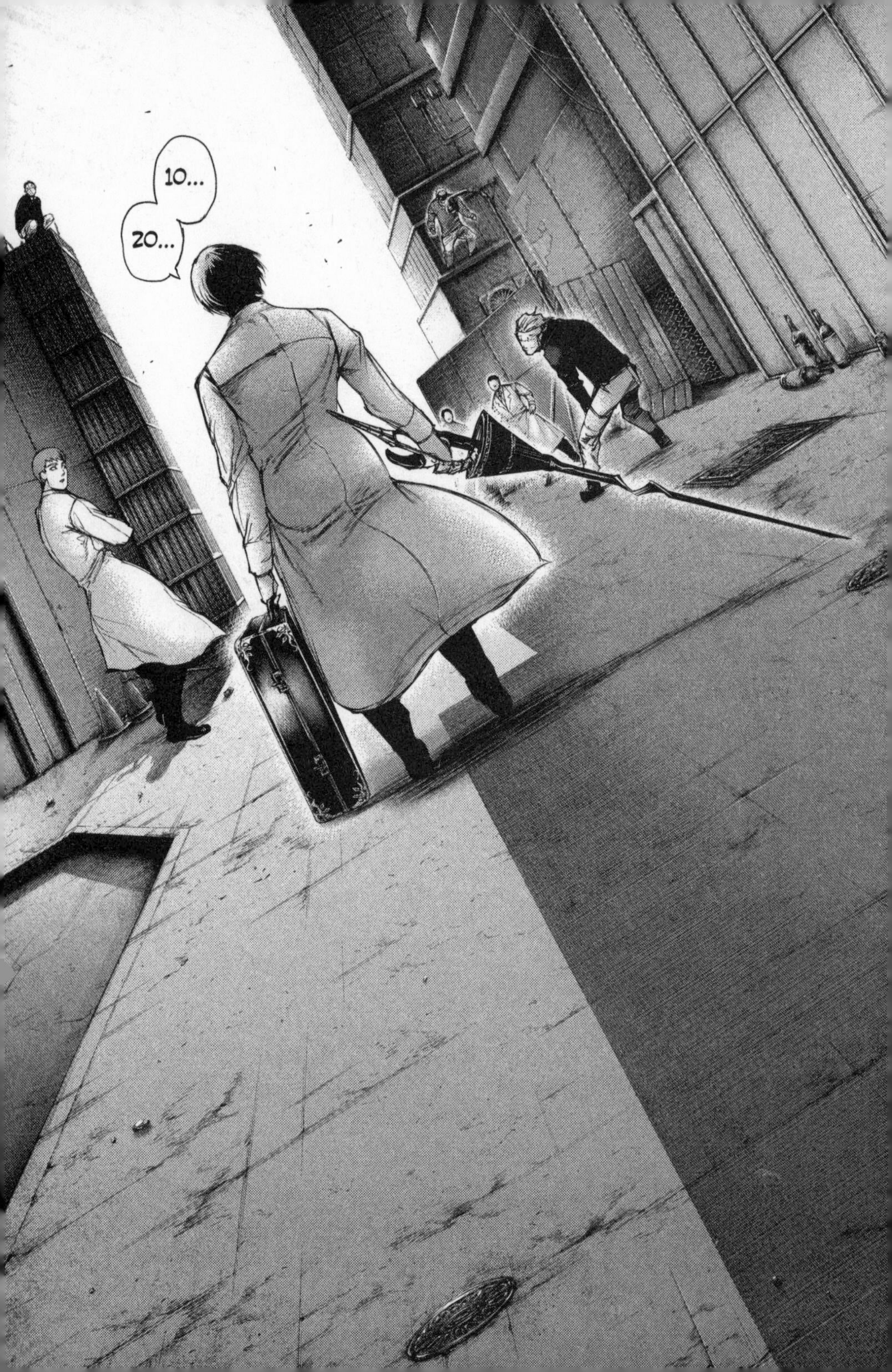
10...
20...

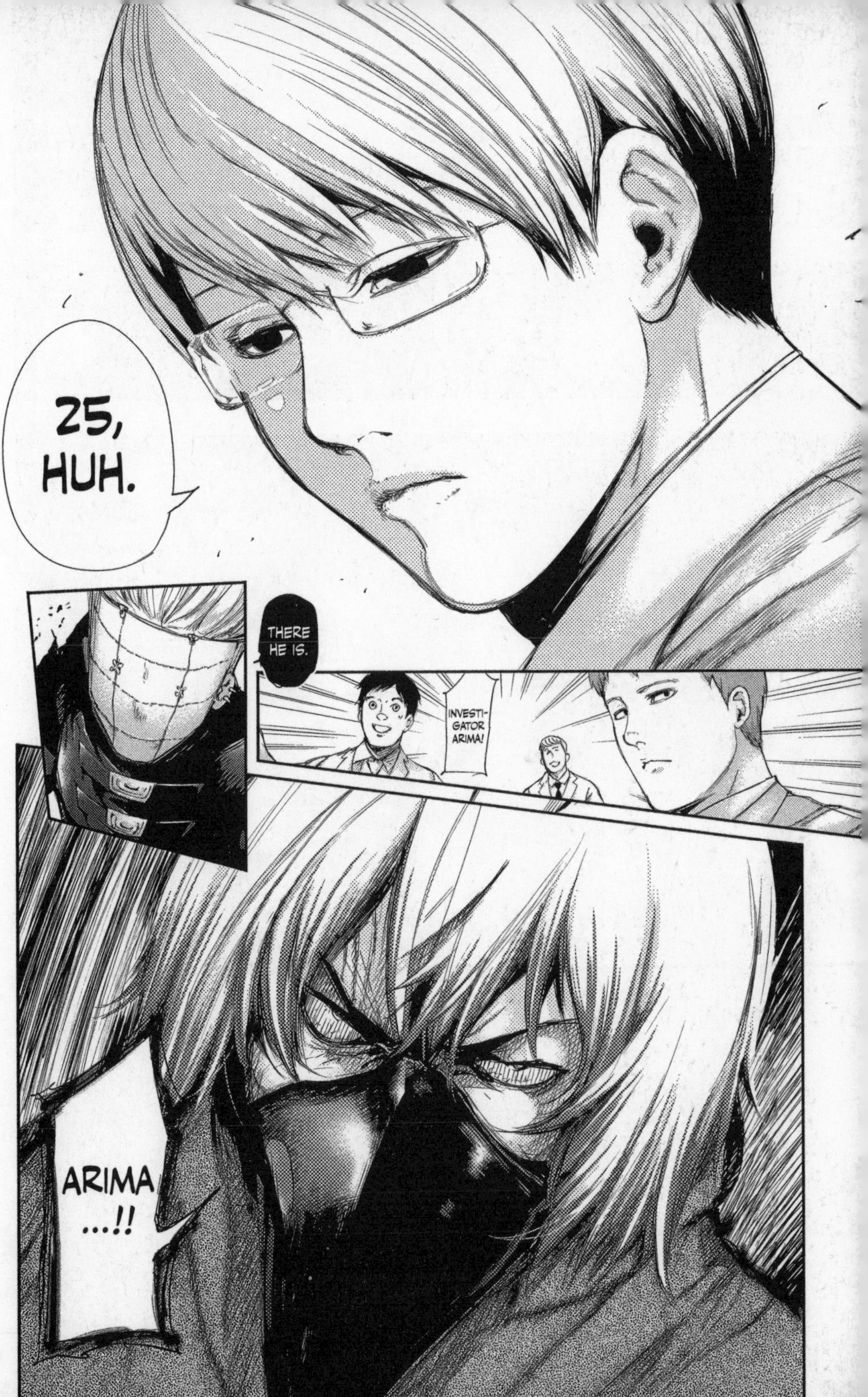
25, HUH.
THERE HE IS.
INVESTI-GATOR ARIMA!
ARIMA ...!!

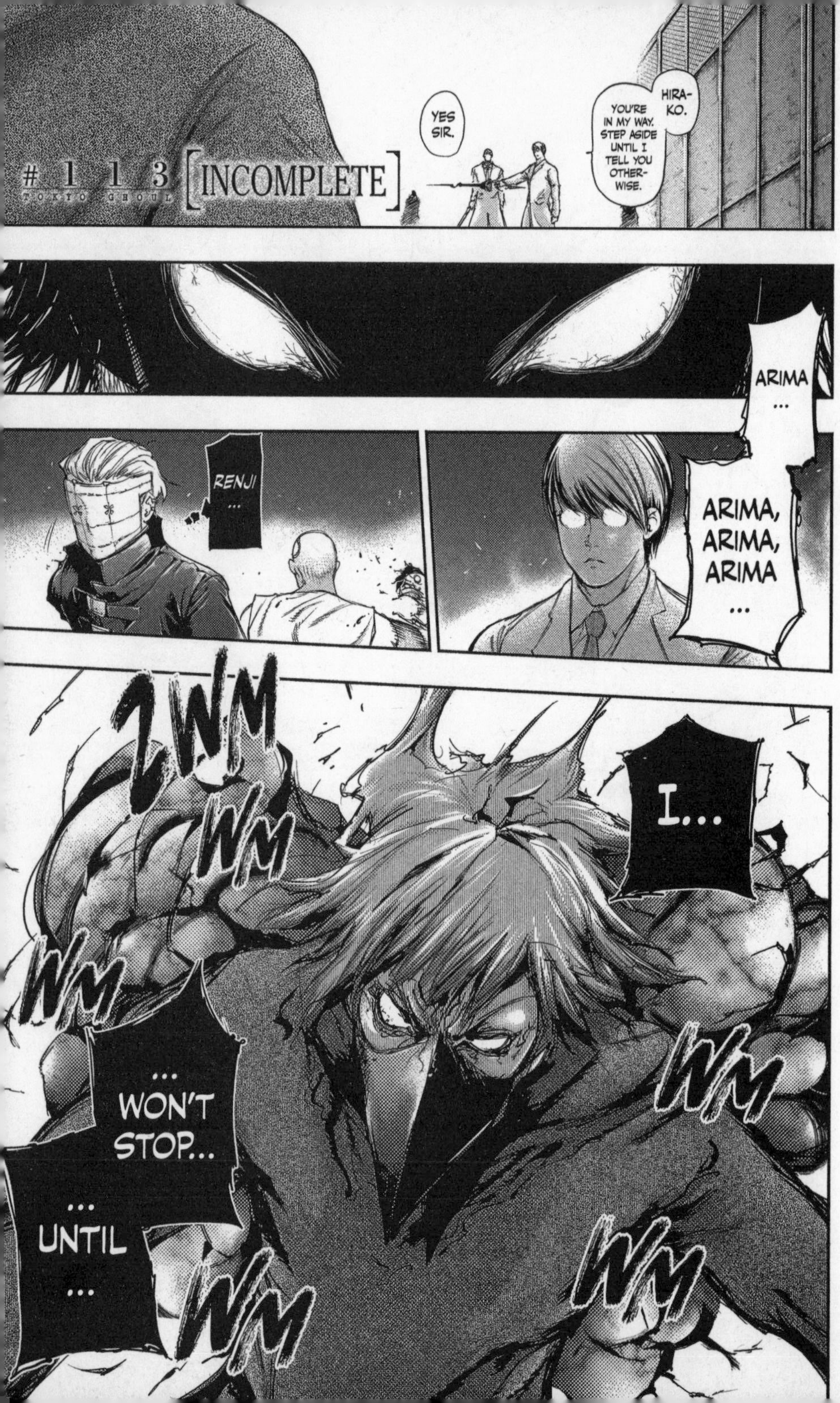
#113 [INCOMPLETE]
TOKYO GHOUL
HIRA-KO.
YOU'RE IN MY WAY. STEP ASIDE UNTIL I TELL YOU OTHER-WISE.
YES SIR.
ARIMA ...
ARIMA, ARIMA, ARIMA ...
RENJI ...
I...
ZWM
WM
WM
WM
... WON'T STOP...
... UNTIL ...
WM
WM

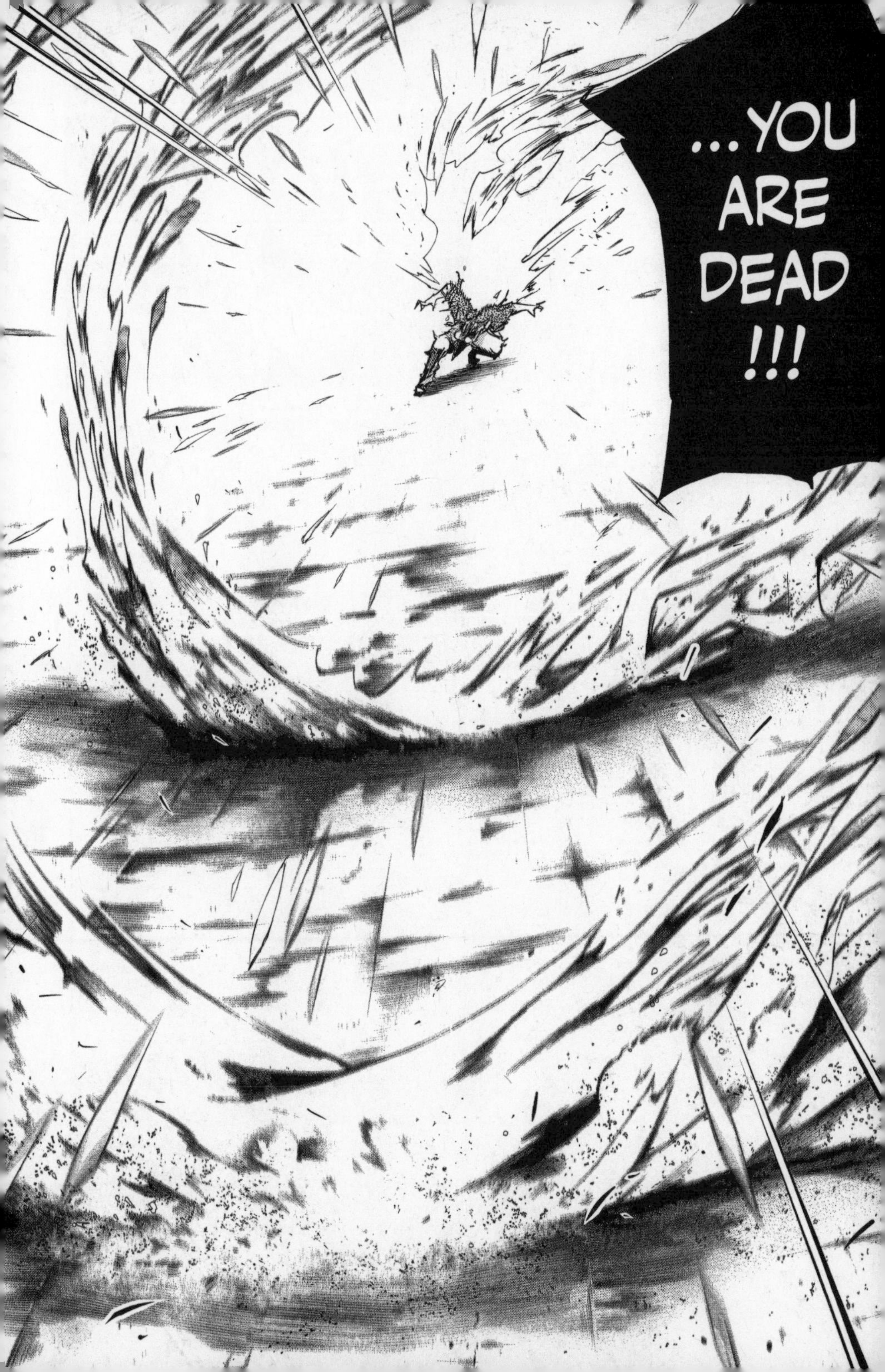
...YOU ARE DEAD !!!

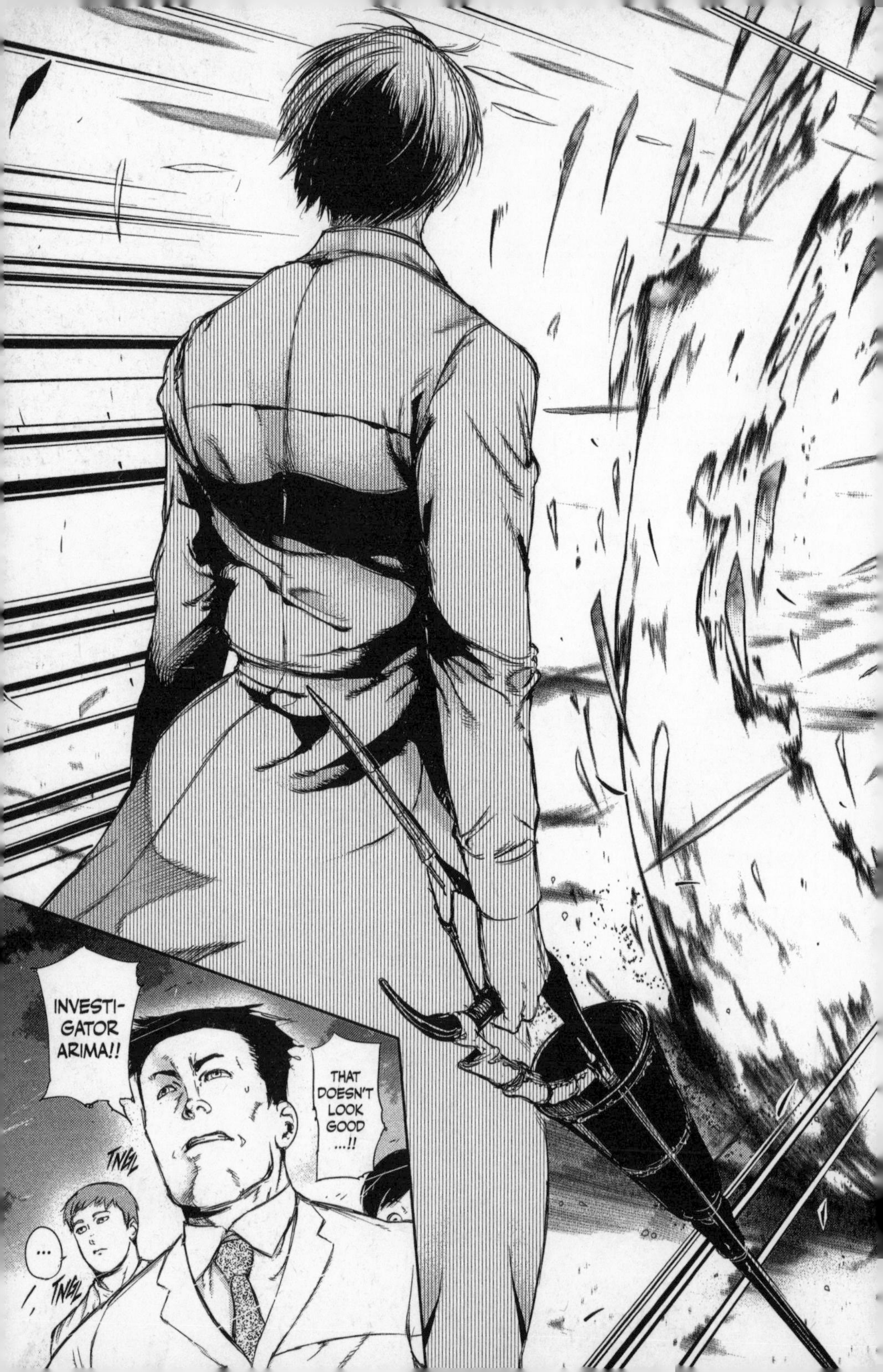
INVESTI-GATOR ARIMA!!
THAT DOESN'T LOOK GOOD ...!!
TNGL
...
TNGL

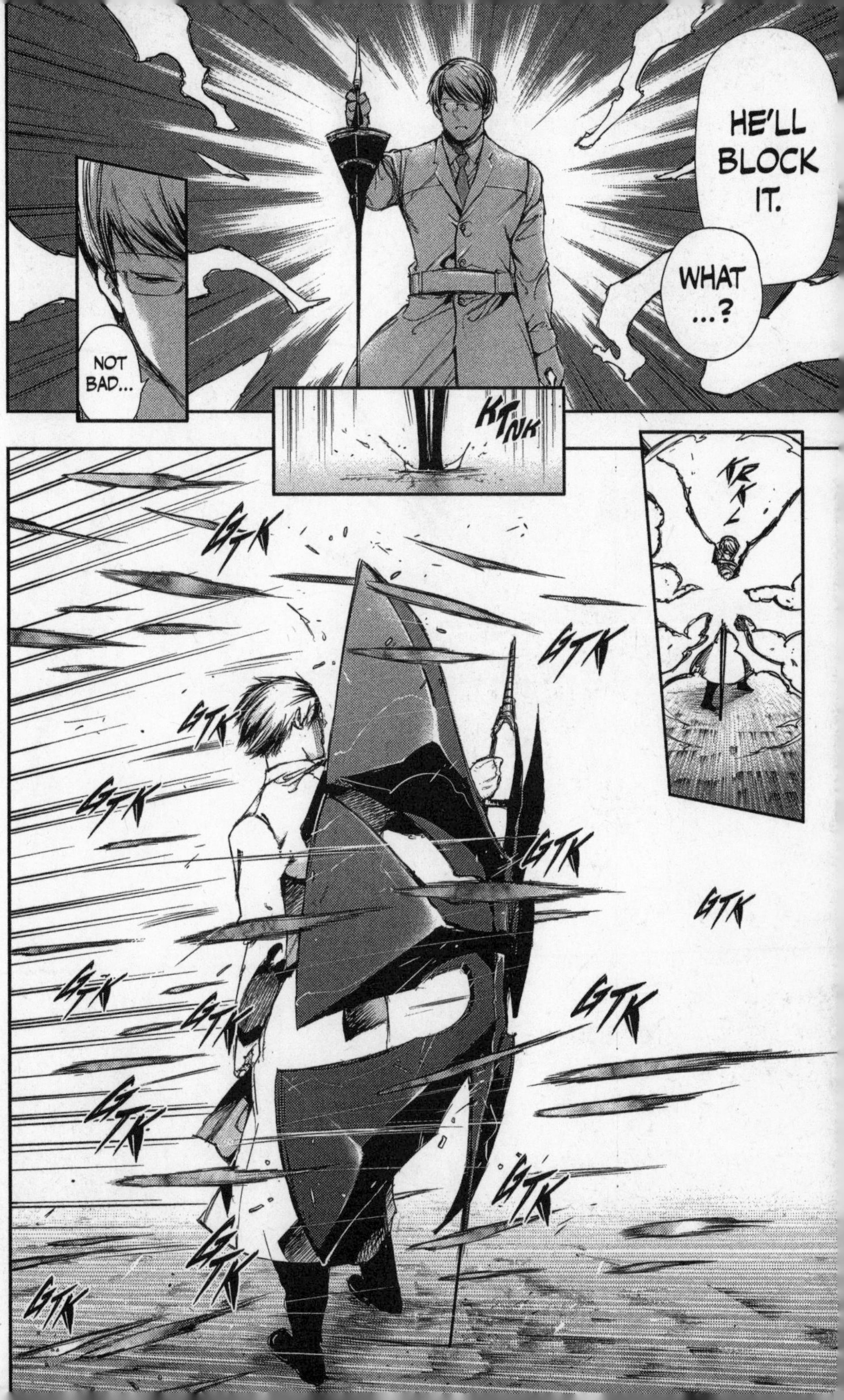
HE'LL BLOCK IT.
WHAT ...?
NOT BAD...
KTNK
GTK
GTK
GTK
GTK
GTK
GTK
GTK
GTK
GTK
GTK
GTK
GTK
GTK

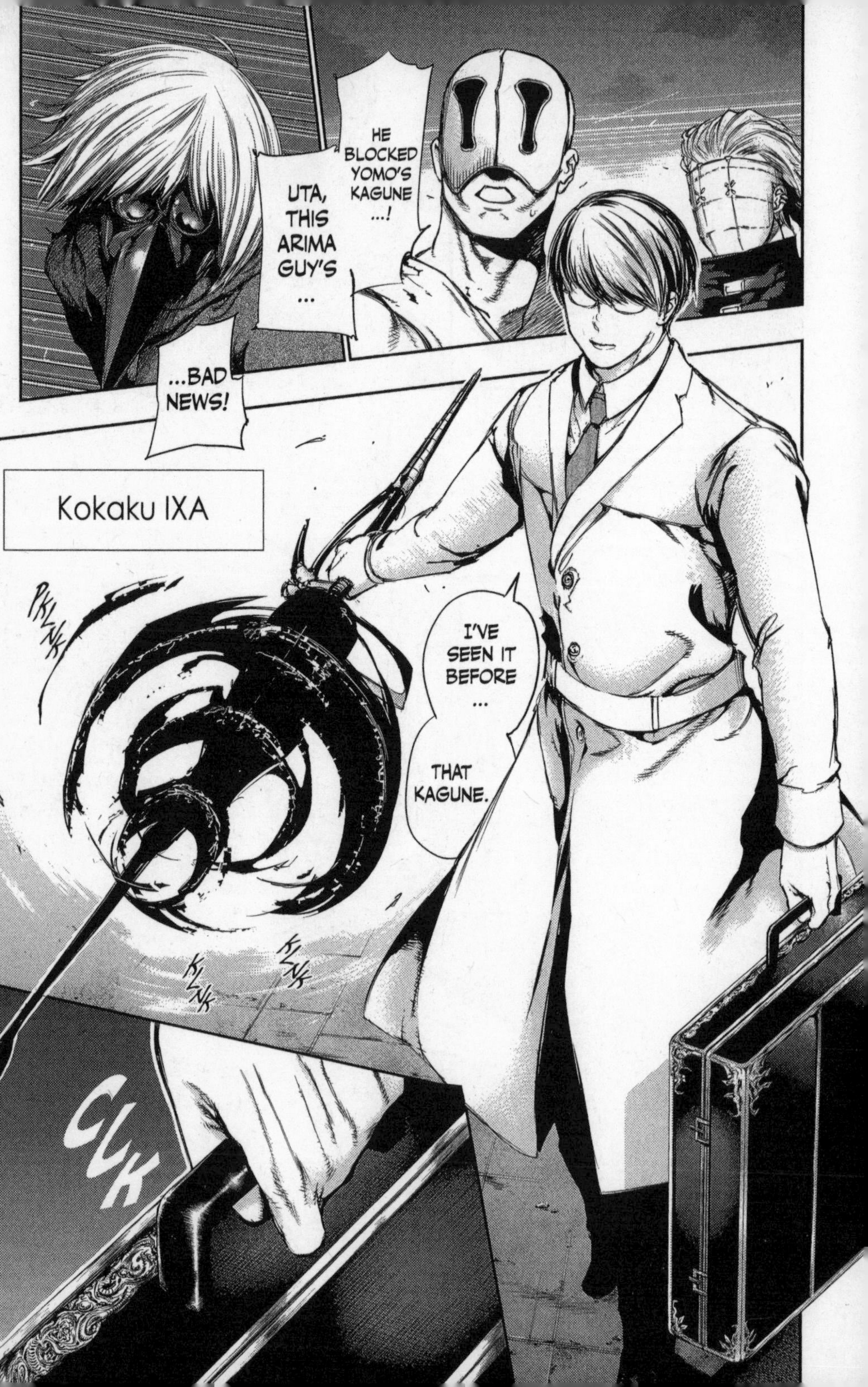
HE BLOCKED YOMO'S KAGUNE ...!
UTA, THIS ARIMA GUY'S ...
...BAD NEWS!
Kokaku IXA
PKLNK
I'VE SEEN IT BEFORE ...
THAT KAGUNE.
KLNK
KLNK
CLK

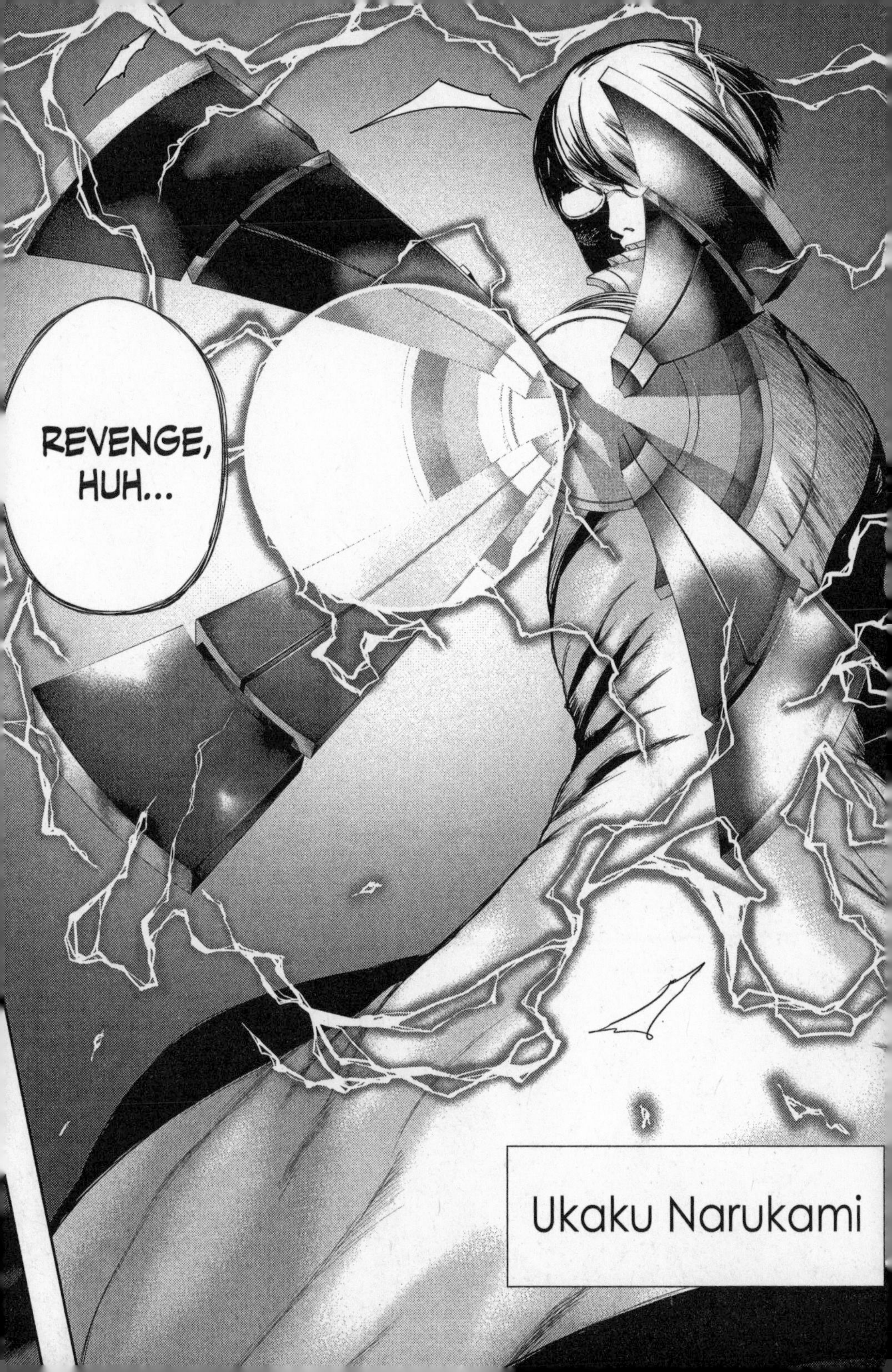
REVENGE, HUH...
Ukaku Narukami

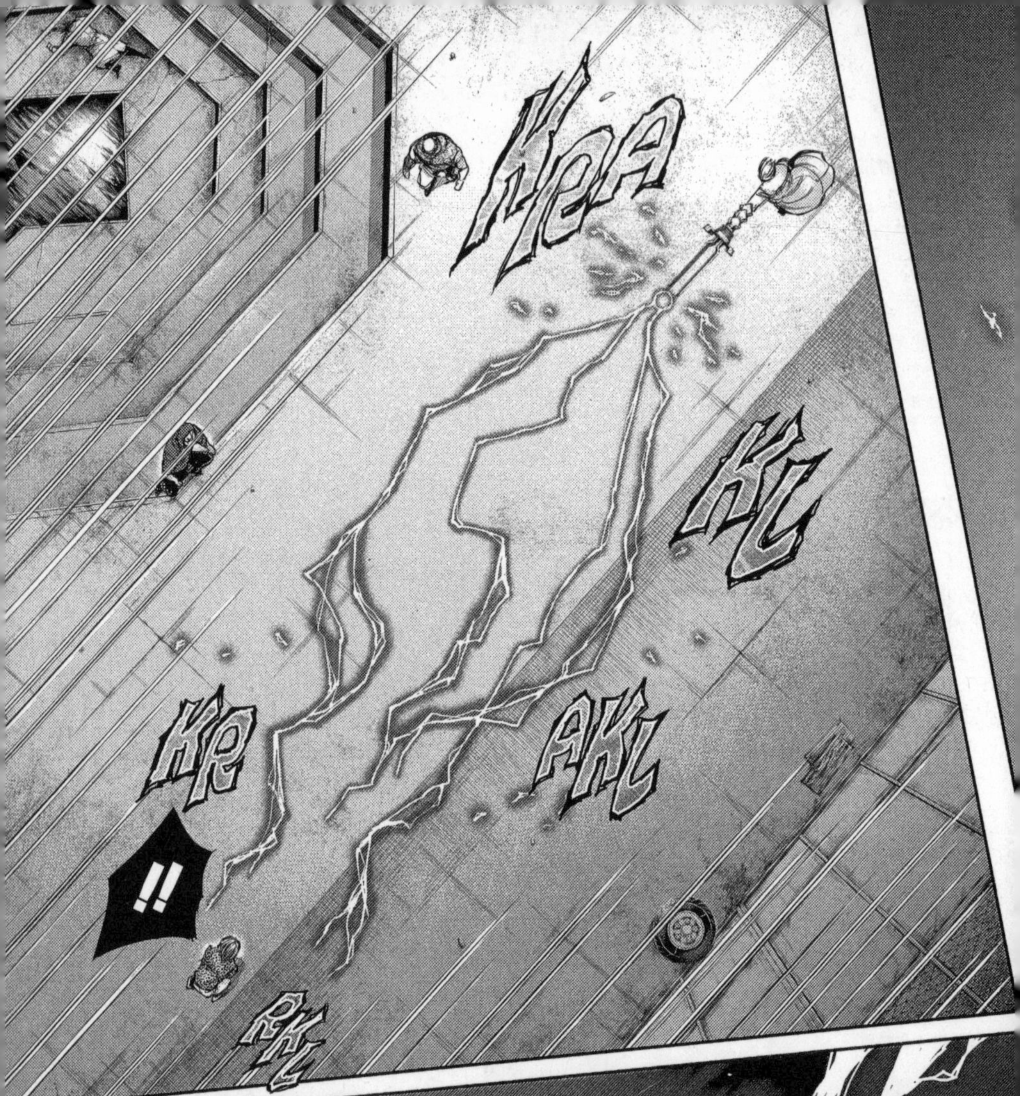
KRA
KL
AKL
KR
!!
RKL
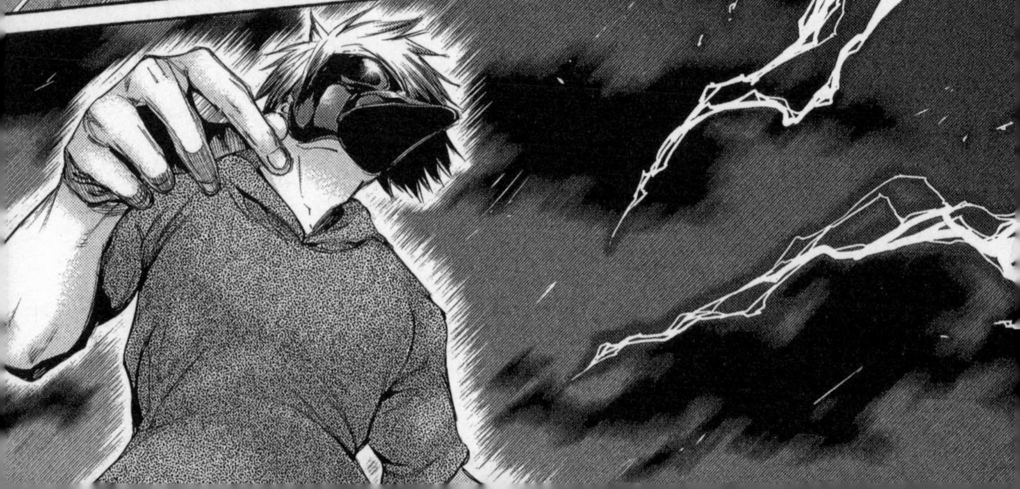

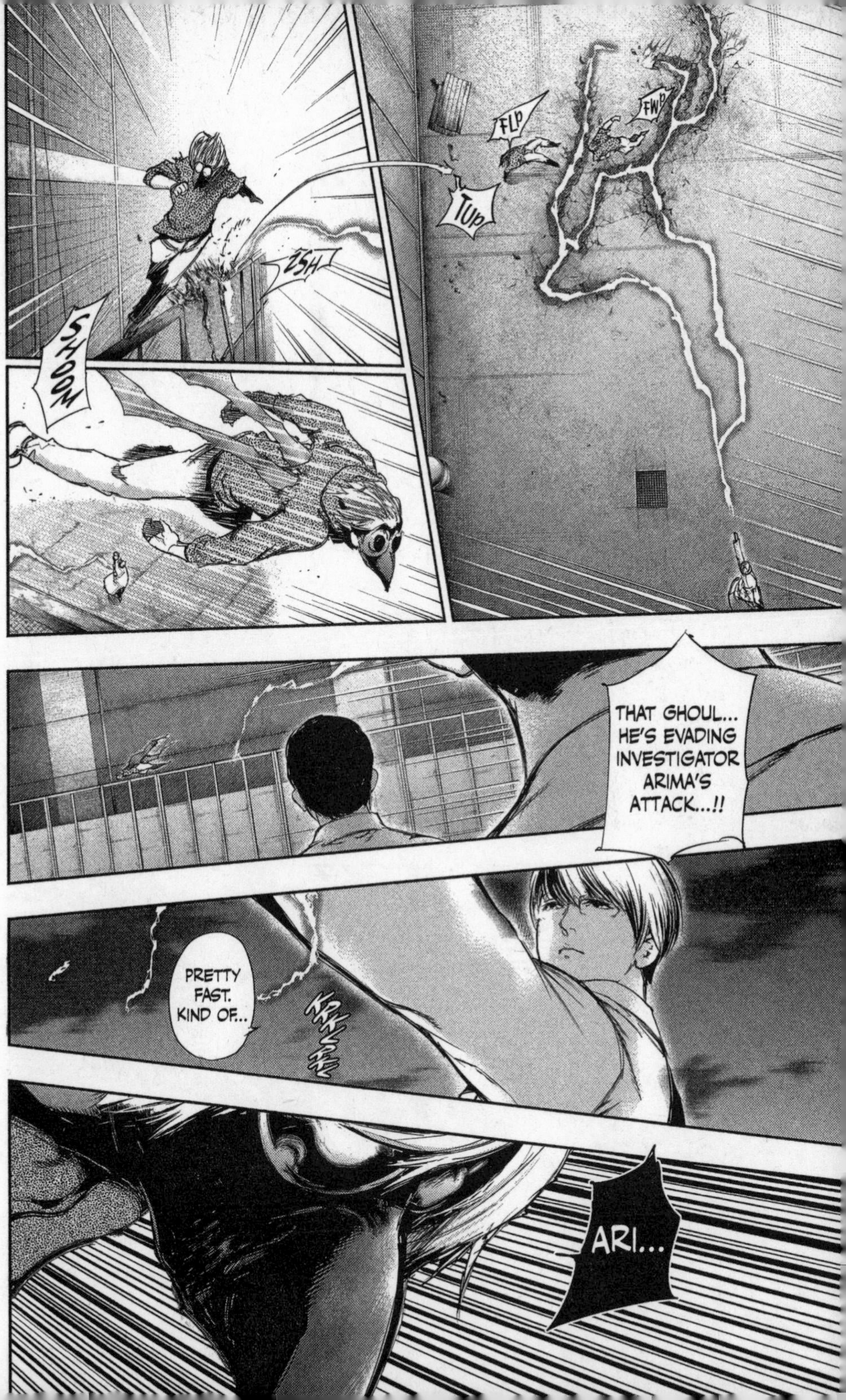
FLP
FWP
TUP
ZSH
SHOOM
THAT GHOUL... HE'S EVADING INVESTIGATOR ARIMA'S ATTACK...!!
PRETTY FAST. KIND OF...
KRNCH
ARI...

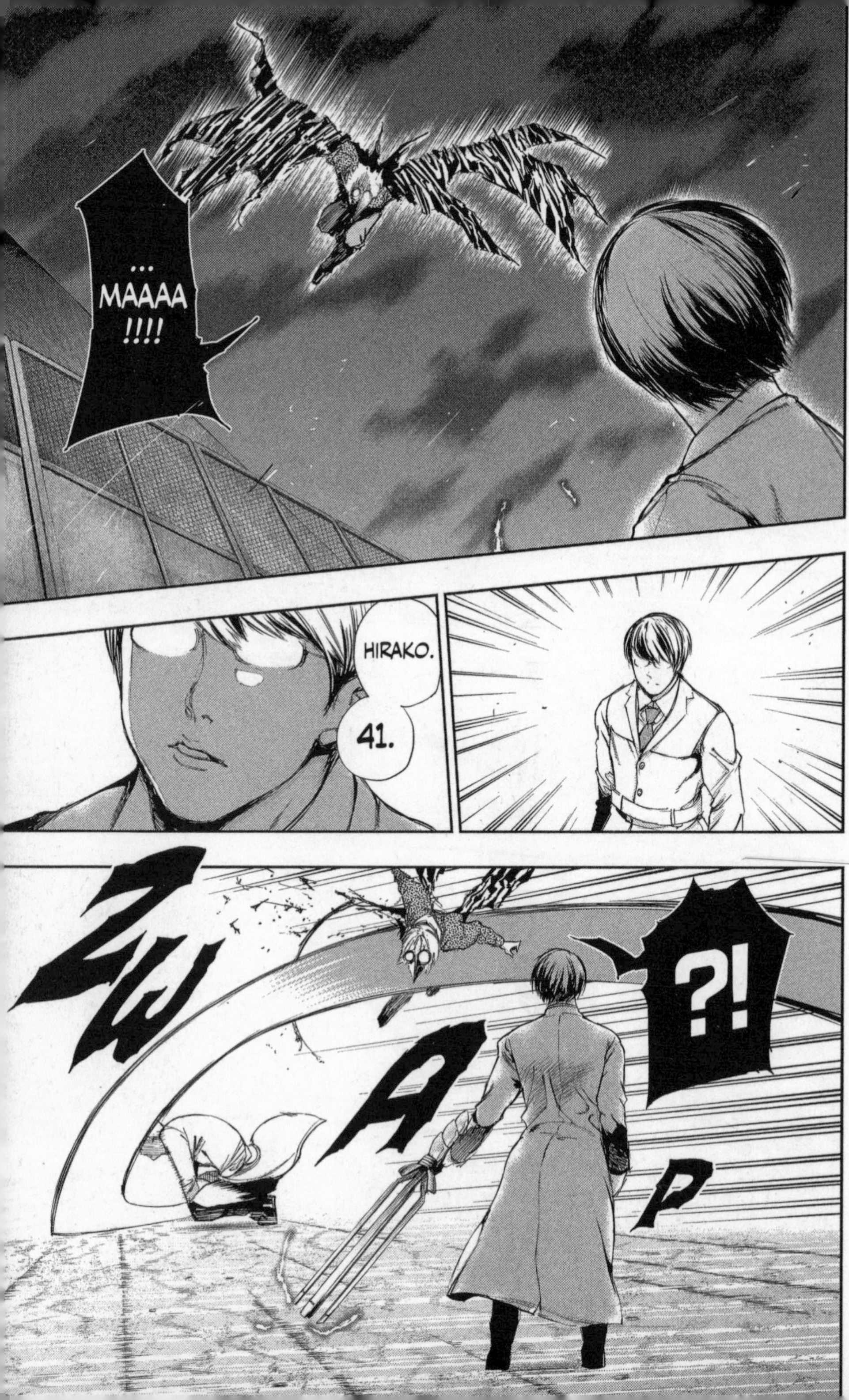
... MAAAA !!!!
HIRAKO.
41.
ZWAP
?!

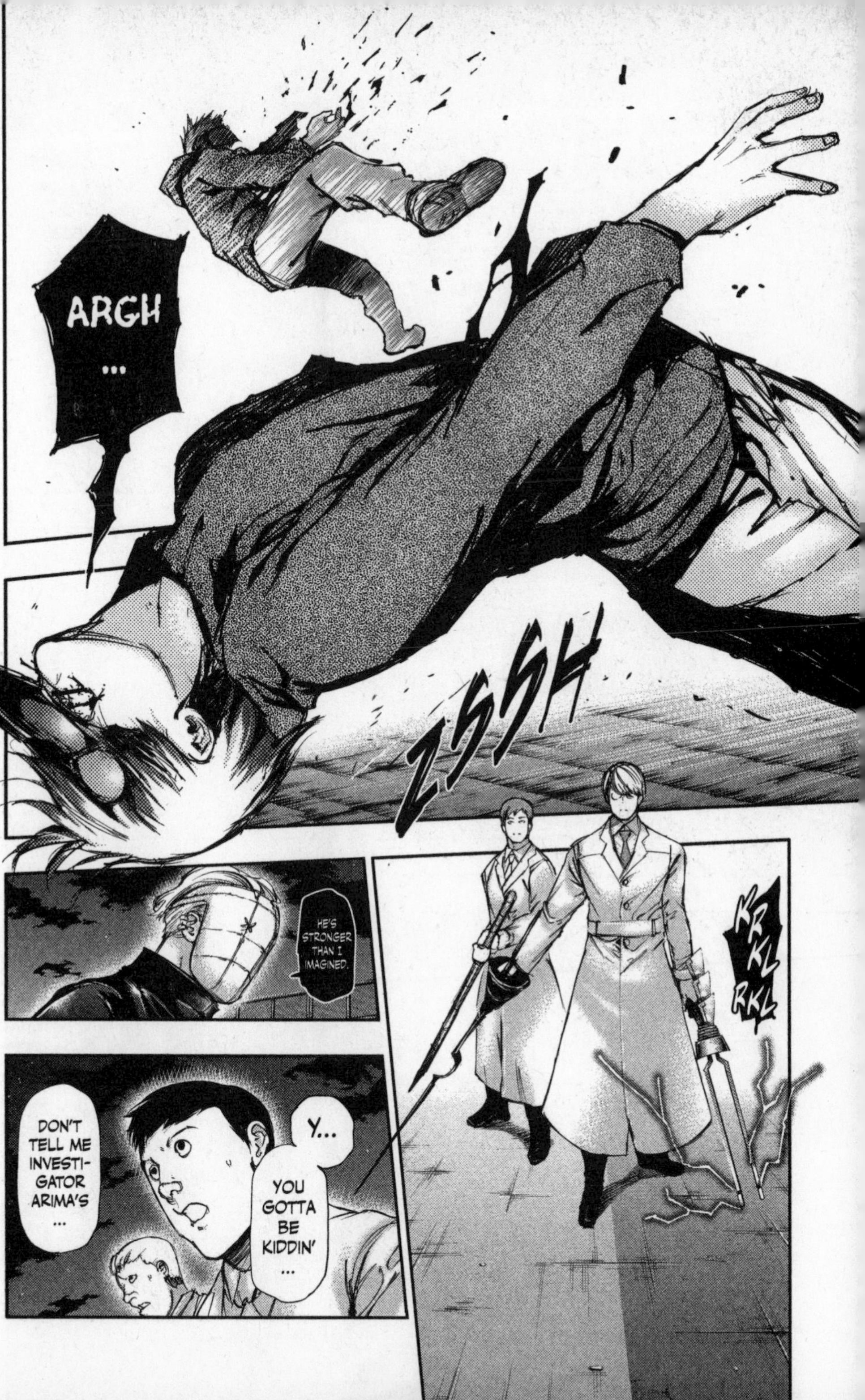
ARGH...
ZSSH
KRKL RKL
HE'S STRONGER THAN I IMAGINED.
Y...
YOU GOTTA BE KIDDIN'...
DON'T TELL ME INVESTIGATOR ARIMA'S...

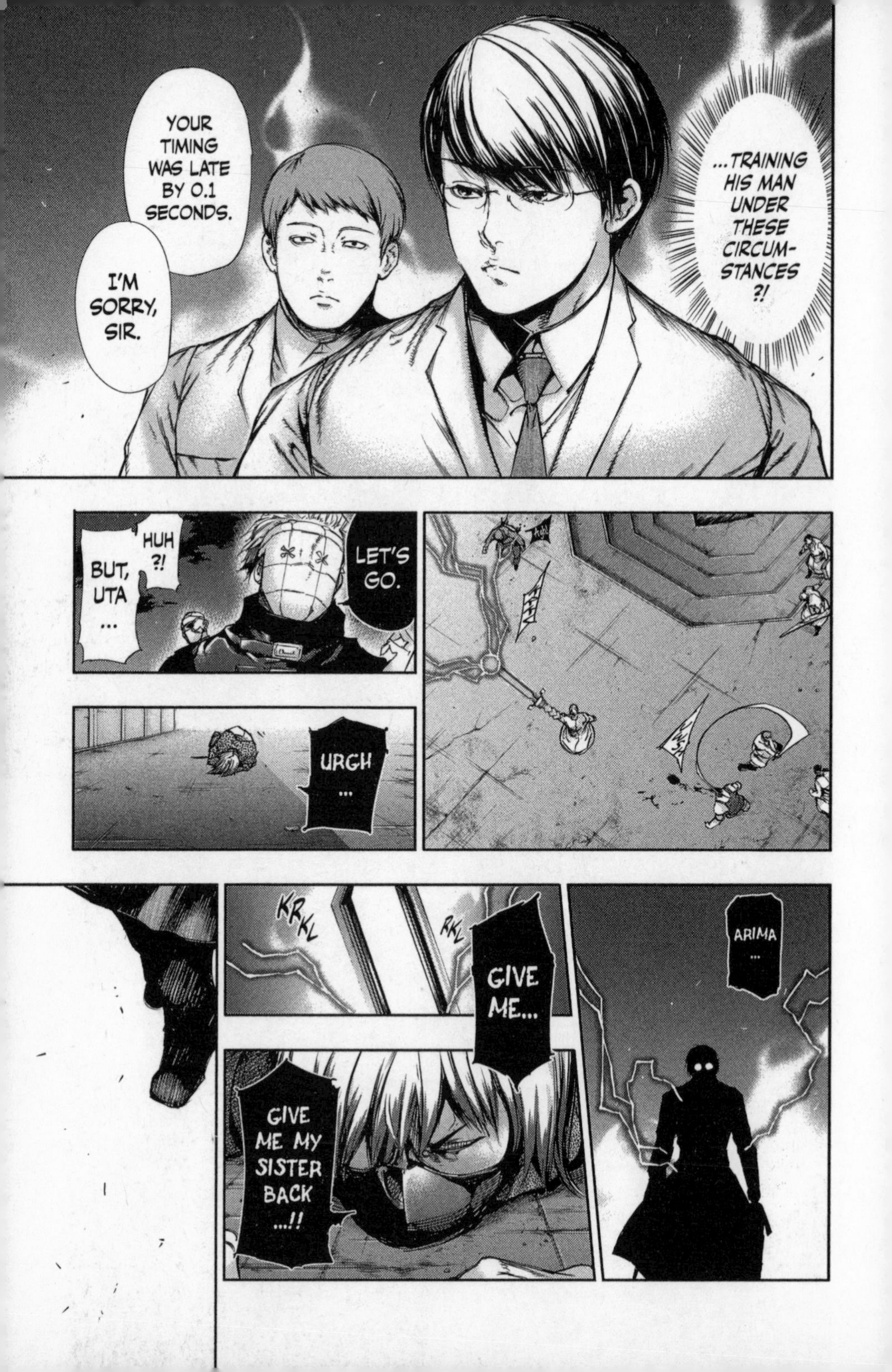
...TRAINING HIS MAN UNDER THESE CIRCUM-STANCES?!
YOUR TIMING WAS LATE BY 0.1 SECONDS.
I'M SORRY, SIR.
LET'S GO.
HUH?!
BUT, UTA ...
URGH ...
ARIMA ...
KRKL
RKL
GIVE ME...
GIVE ME MY SISTER BACK ...!!

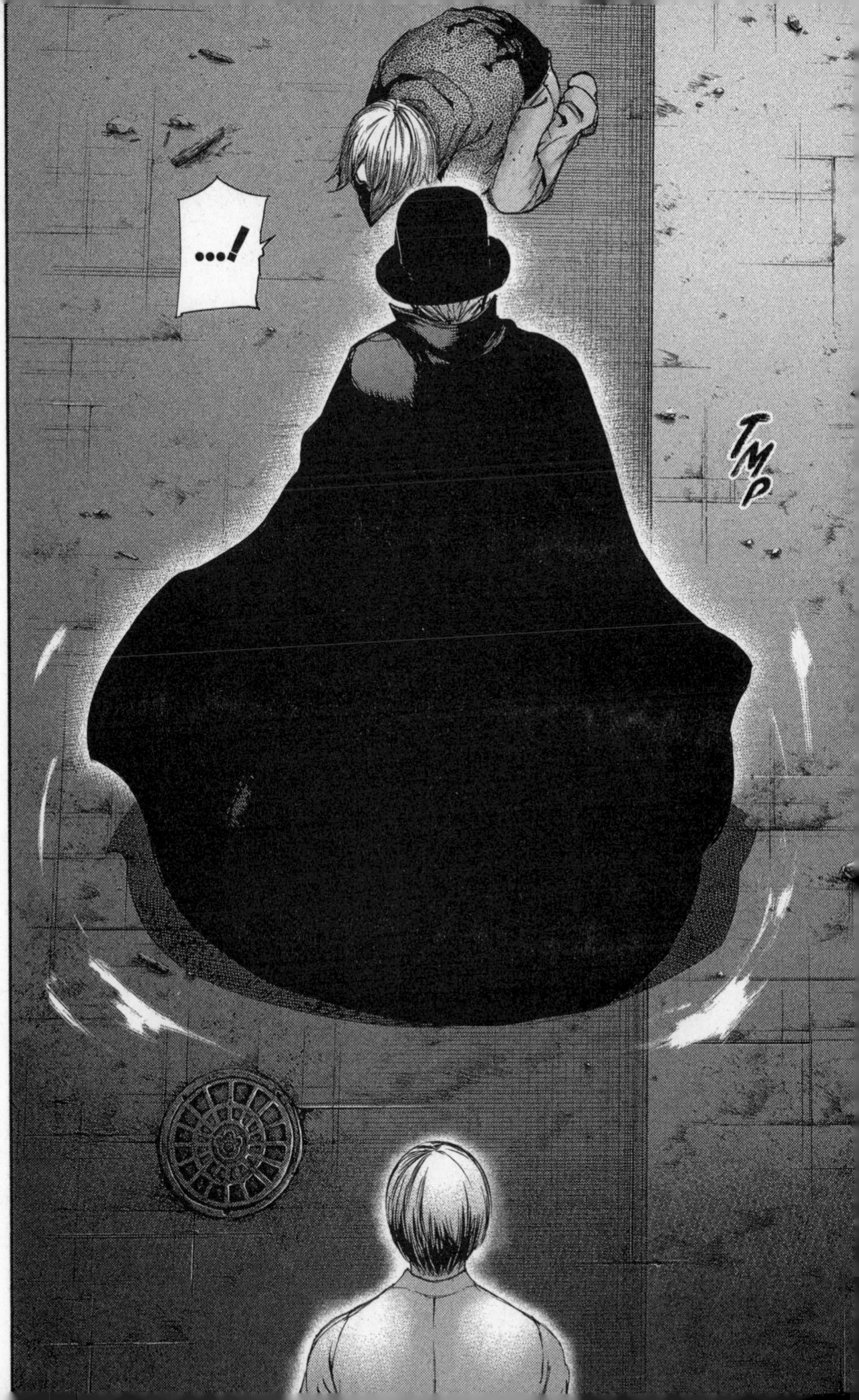
...!
TMP

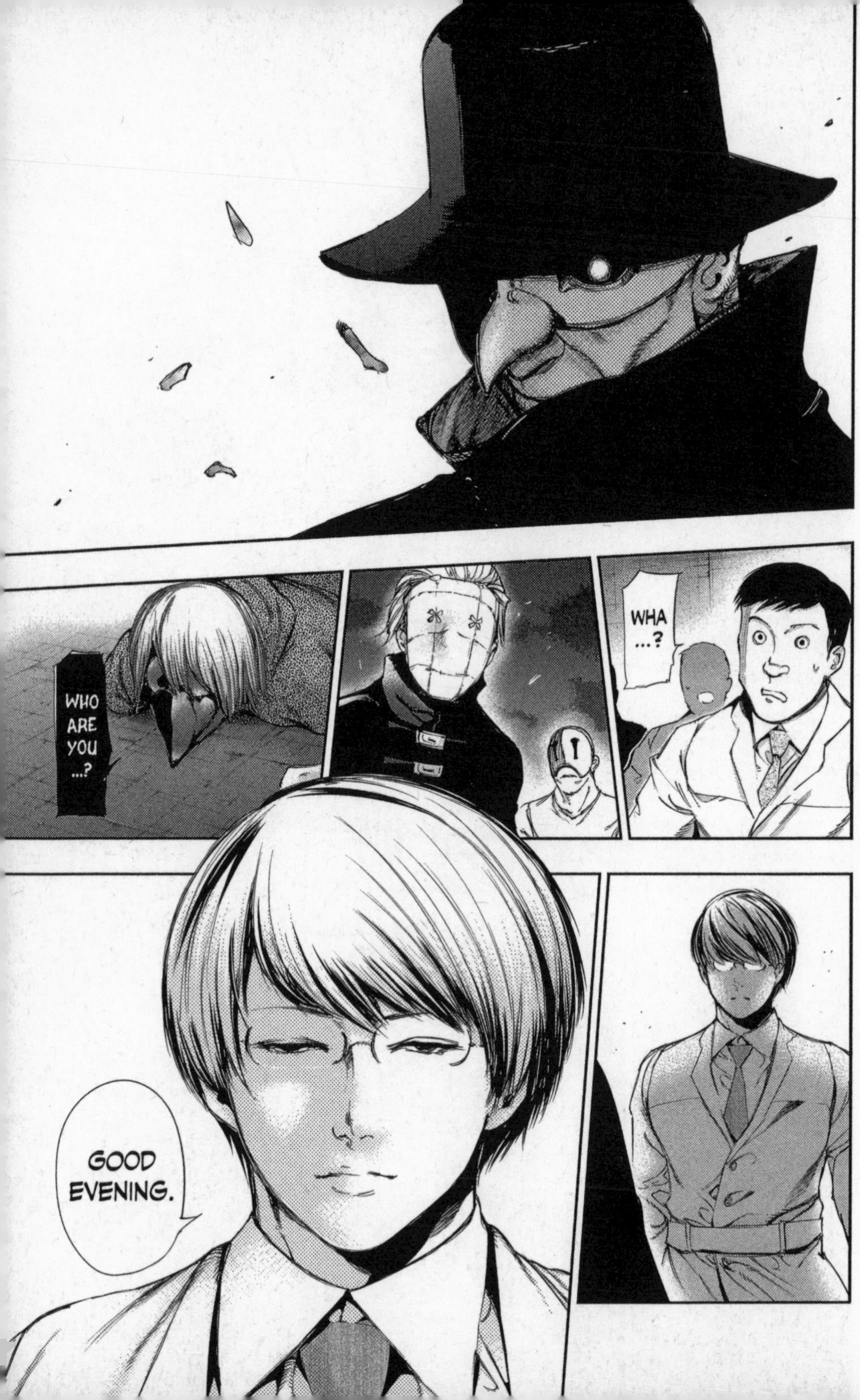
WHA ...?
WHO ARE YOU ...?
GOOD EVENING.

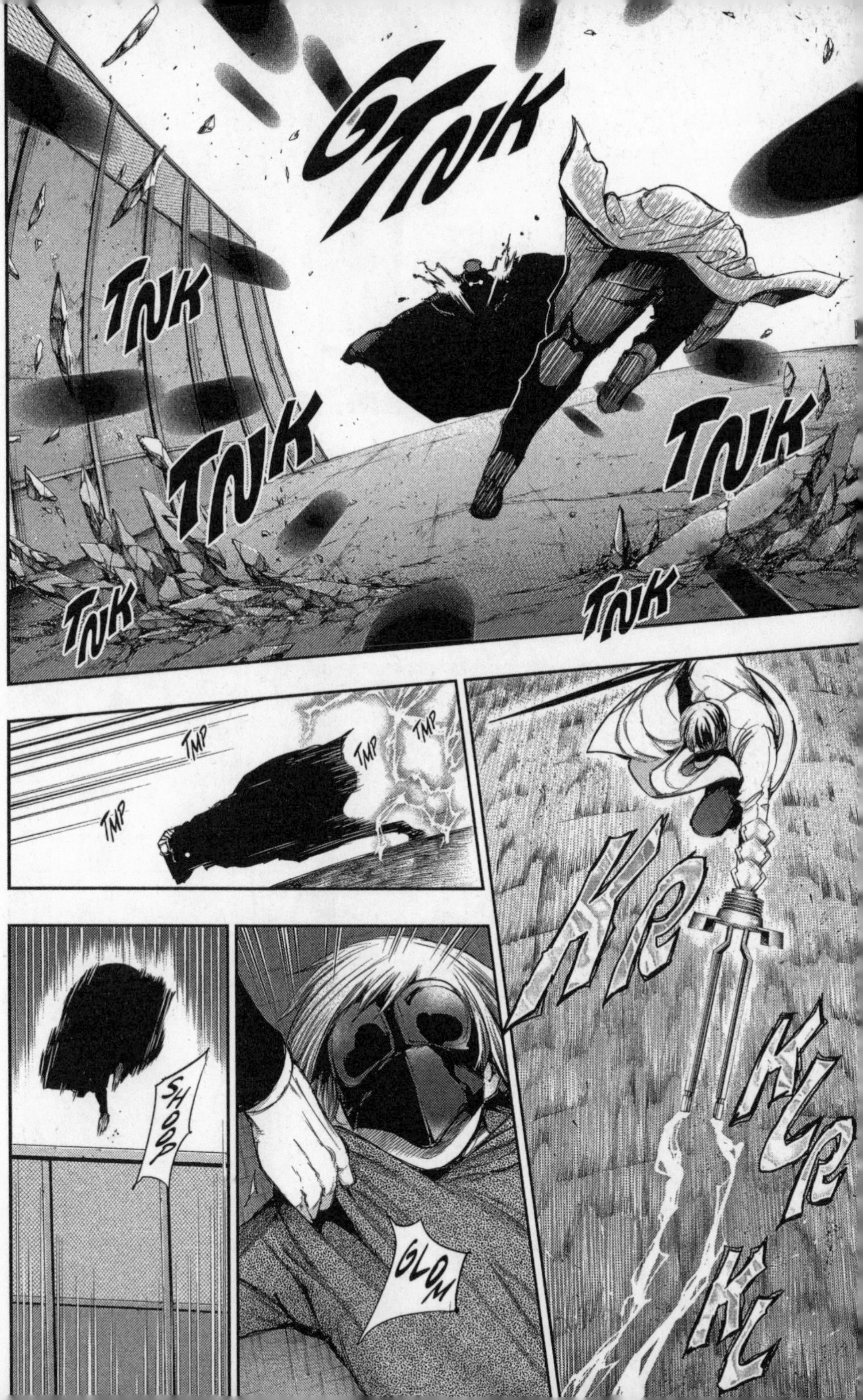
GTNK
TNK
TNK
TNK
TNK
TNK
KR
KLR
KL
TMP
TMP
TMP
TMP
GLOM
SHOOP

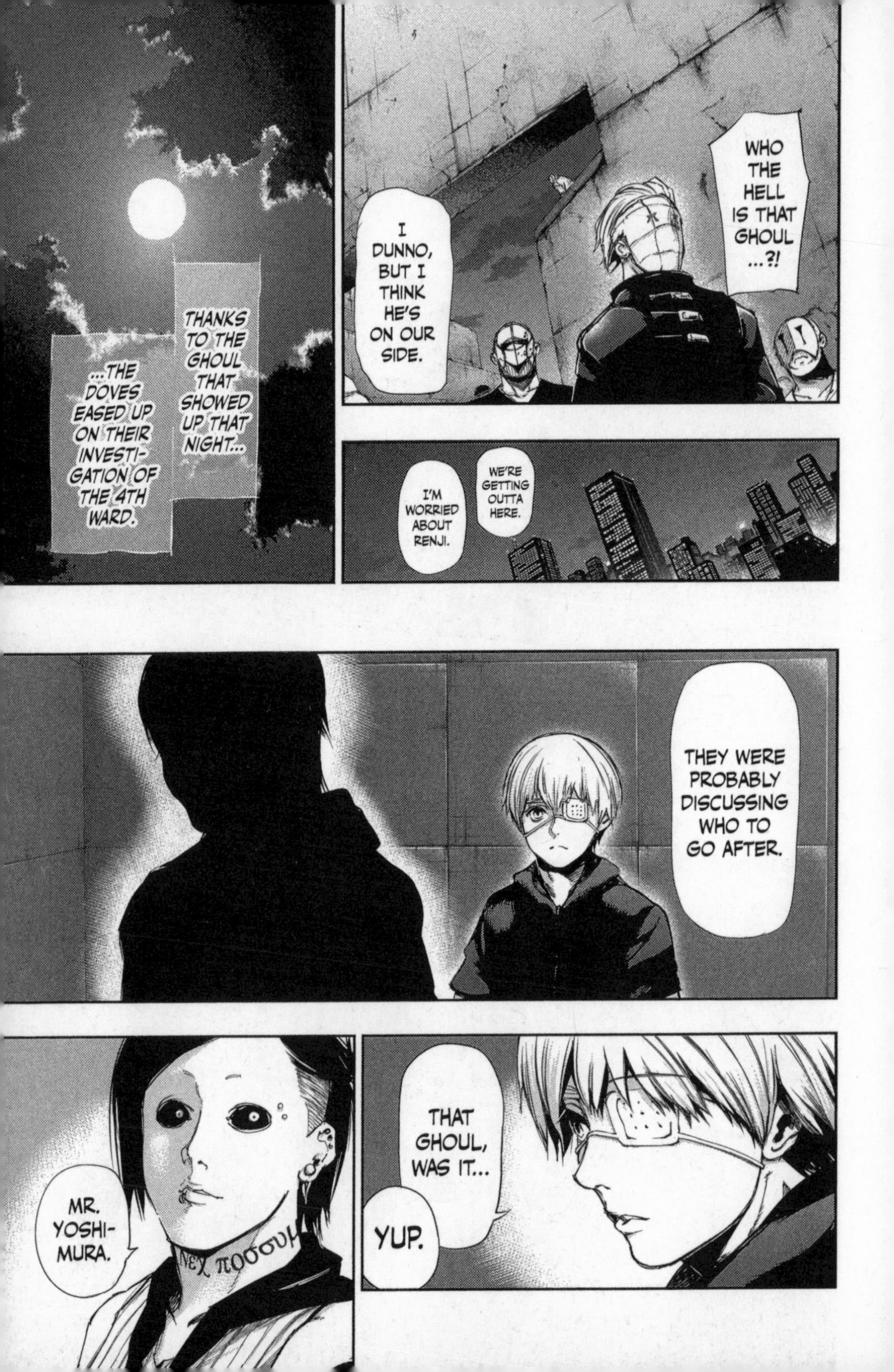
WHO THE HELL IS THAT GHOUL ...?!
I DUNNO, BUT I THINK HE'S ON OUR SIDE.
WE'RE GETTING OUTTA HERE.
I'M WORRIED ABOUT RENJI.
THANKS TO THE GHOUL THAT SHOWED UP THAT NIGHT...
...THE DOVES EASED UP ON THEIR INVESTIGATION OF THE 4TH WARD.
THEY WERE PROBABLY DISCUSSING WHO TO GO AFTER.
THAT GHOUL, WAS IT...
YUP.
MR. YOSHIMURA.

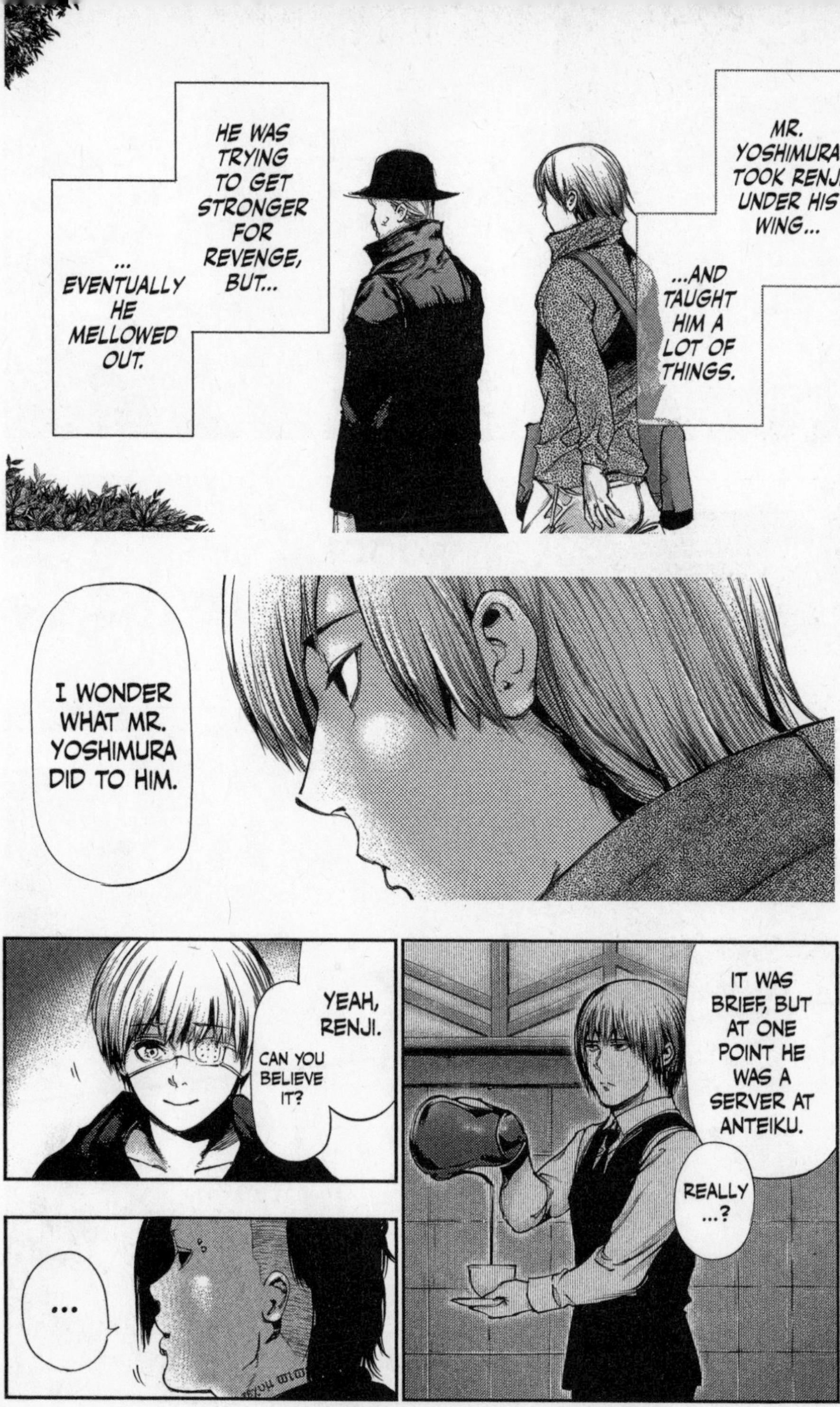
MR. YOSHIMURA TOOK RENJI UNDER HIS WING...
...AND TAUGHT HIM A LOT OF THINGS.
HE WAS TRYING TO GET STRONGER FOR REVENGE, BUT...
...EVENTUALLY HE MELLOWED OUT.
I WONDER WHAT MR. YOSHIMURA DID TO HIM.
IT WAS BRIEF, BUT AT ONE POINT HE WAS A SERVER AT ANTEIKU.
REALLY...?
YEAH, RENJI.
CAN YOU BELIEVE IT?
...

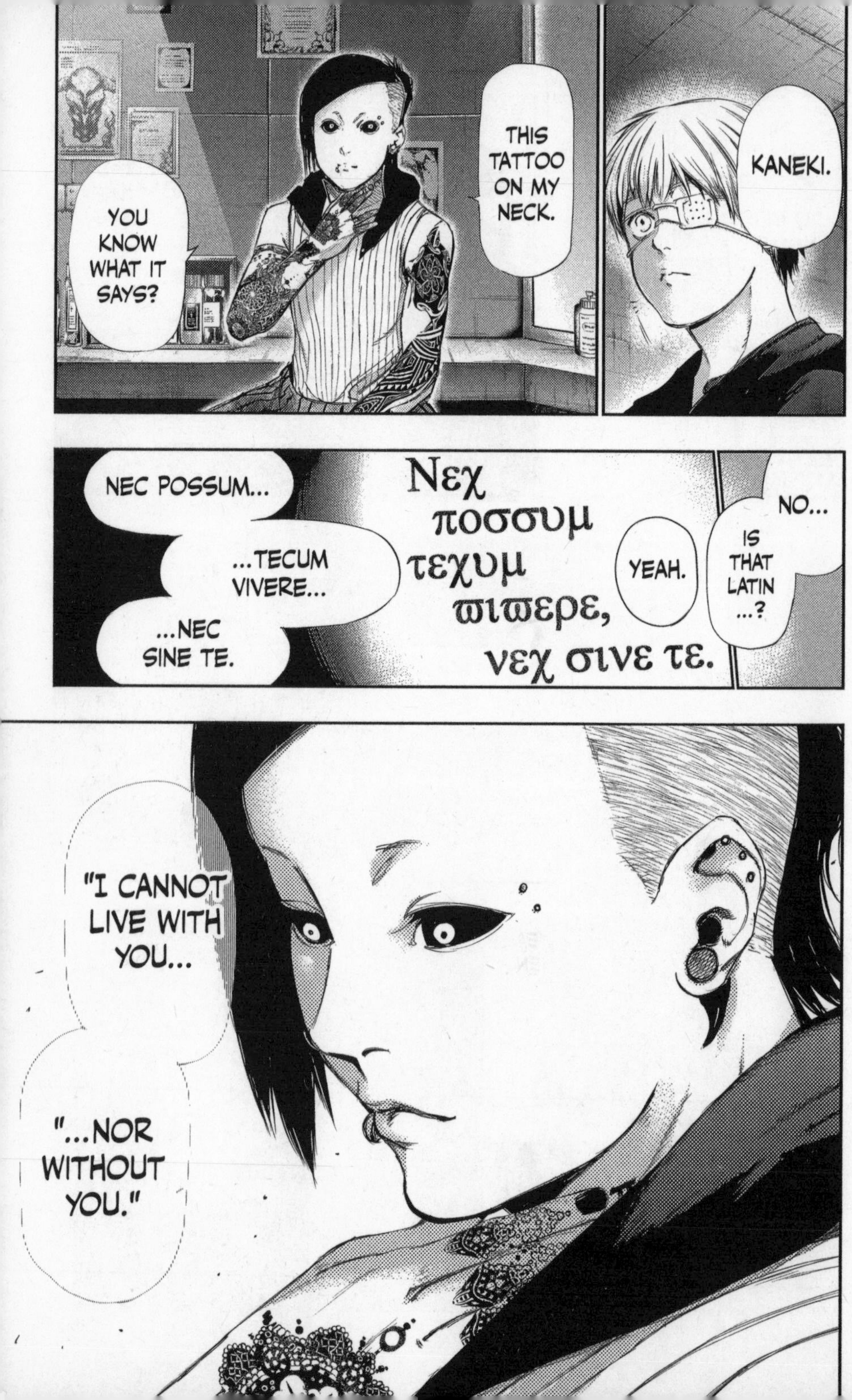
KANEKI.
THIS TATTOO ON MY NECK.
YOU KNOW WHAT IT SAYS?
NO...
IS THAT LATIN ...?
YEAH.
Νεχ ποσσυμ τεχυμ ϖιϖερε, νεχ σινε τε.
NEC POSSUM...
...TECUM VIVERE...
...NEC SINE TE.
"I CANNOT LIVE WITH YOU...
"...NOR WITHOUT YOU."

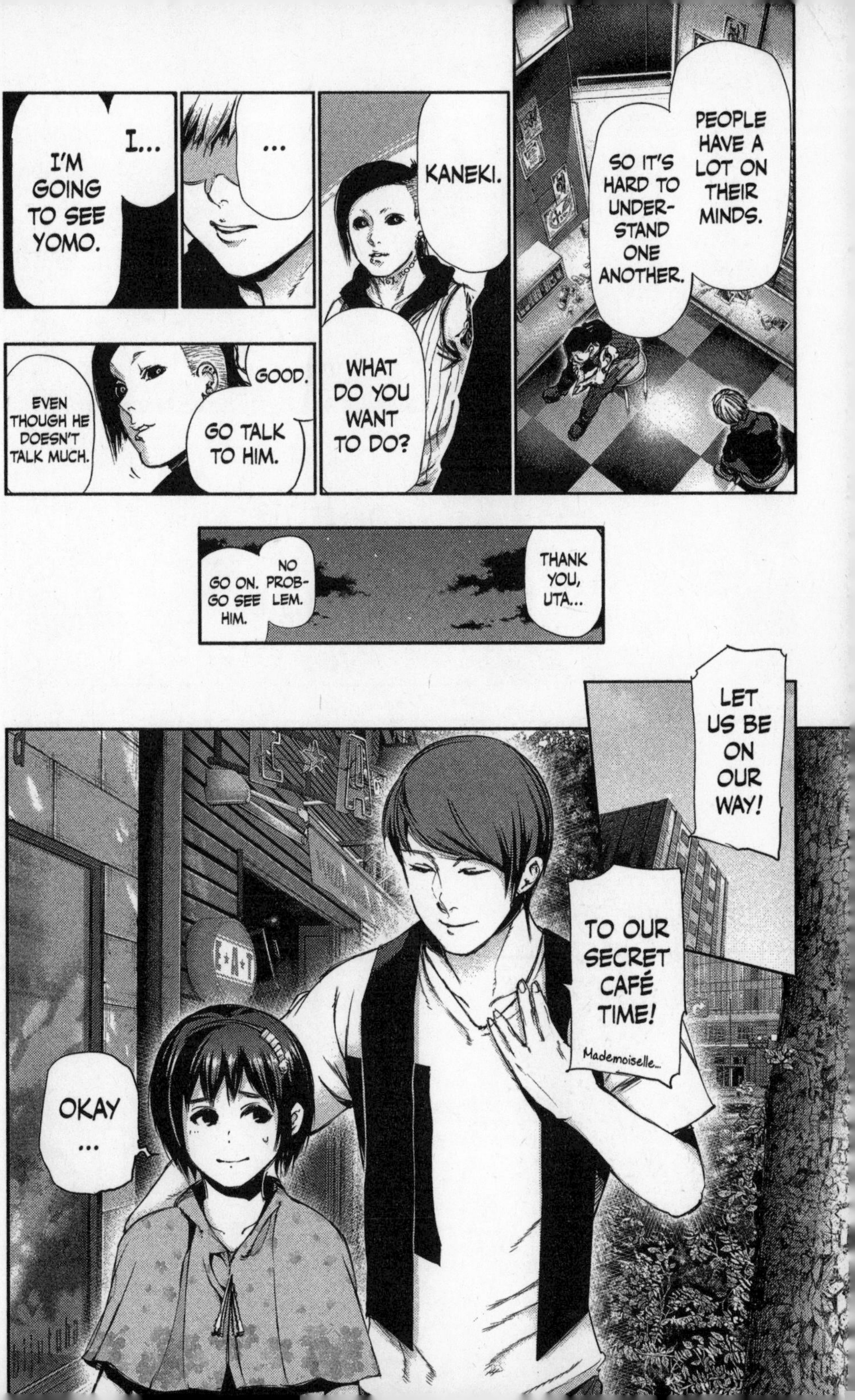
PEOPLE HAVE A LOT ON THEIR MINDS.
SO IT'S HARD TO UNDER-STAND ONE ANOTHER.
KANEKI.
WHAT DO YOU WANT TO DO?
...
I...
I'M GOING TO SEE YOMO.
GOOD.
GO TALK TO HIM.
EVEN THOUGH HE DOESN'T TALK MUCH.
THANK YOU, UTA...
NO PROB-LEM.
GO ON. GO SEE HIM.
LET US BE ON OUR WAY!
TO OUR SECRET CAFÉ TIME!
Mademoiselle...
OKAY ...

東京
トーキョーグール
喰種
Tokyo
Ghoul

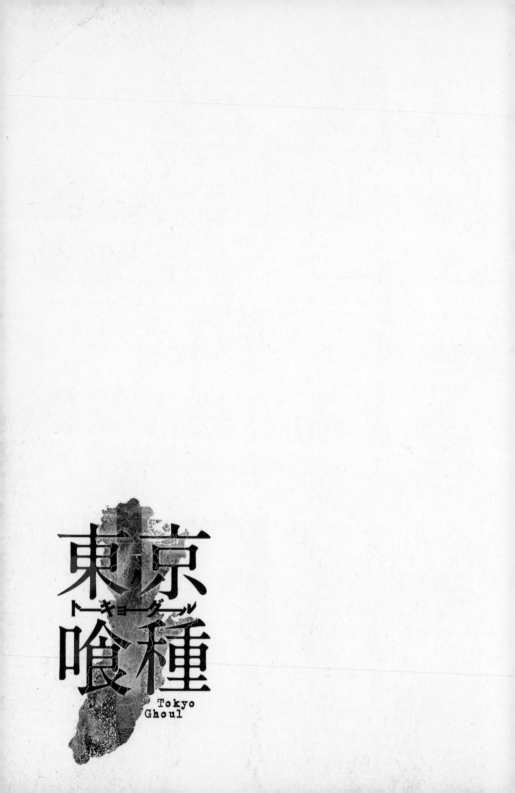

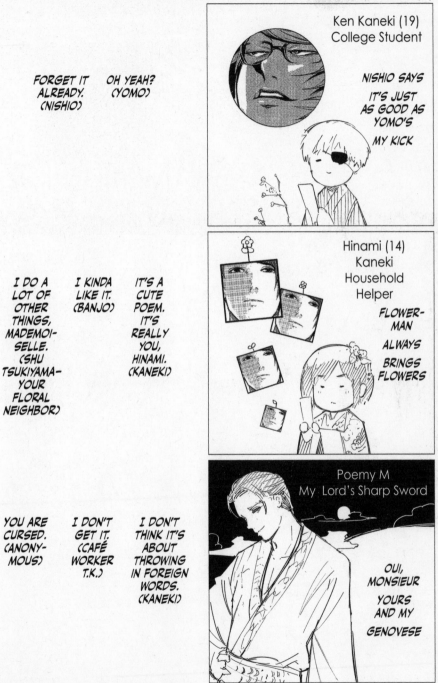

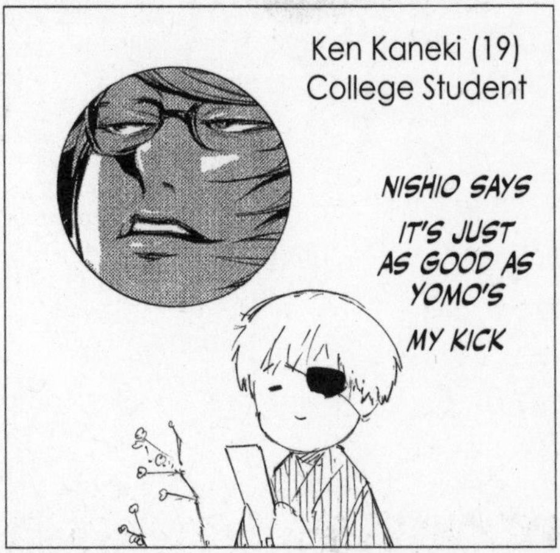
Ken Kaneki (19)
College Student
NISHIO SAYS
IT'S JUST AS GOOD AS YOMO'S
MY KICK

OH YEAH? (YOMO)

FORGET IT ALREADY. (NISHIO)

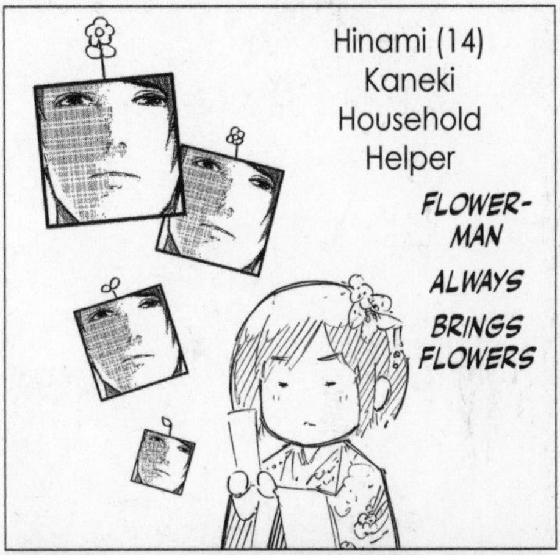
Hinami (14)
Kaneki Household Helper
FLOWER-MAN
ALWAYS
BRINGS FLOWERS

IT'S A CUTE POEM. IT'S REALLY YOU, HINAMI. (KANEKI)

I KINDA LIKE IT. (BANJO)

I DO A LOT OF OTHER THINGS, MADEMOISELLE. (SHU TSUKIYAMA-YOUR FLORAL NEIGHBOR)

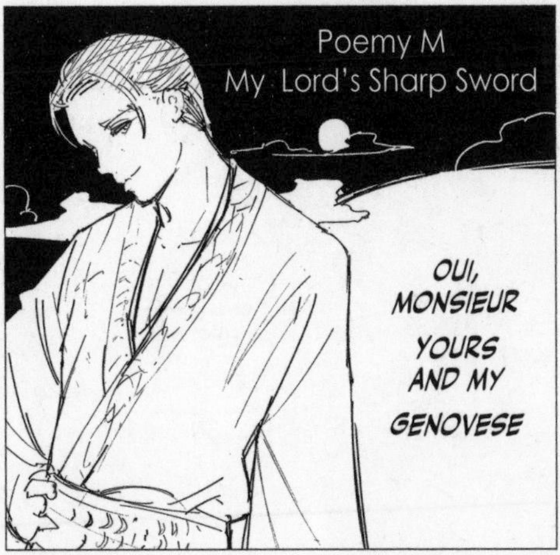
Poemy M
My Lord's Sharp Sword
OUI, MONSIEUR
YOURS AND MY
GENOVESE

I DON'T THINK IT'S ABOUT THROWING IN FOREIGN WORDS. (KANEKI)

I DON'T GET IT. (CAFÉ WORKER T.K.)

YOU ARE CURSED. (ANONYMOUS)

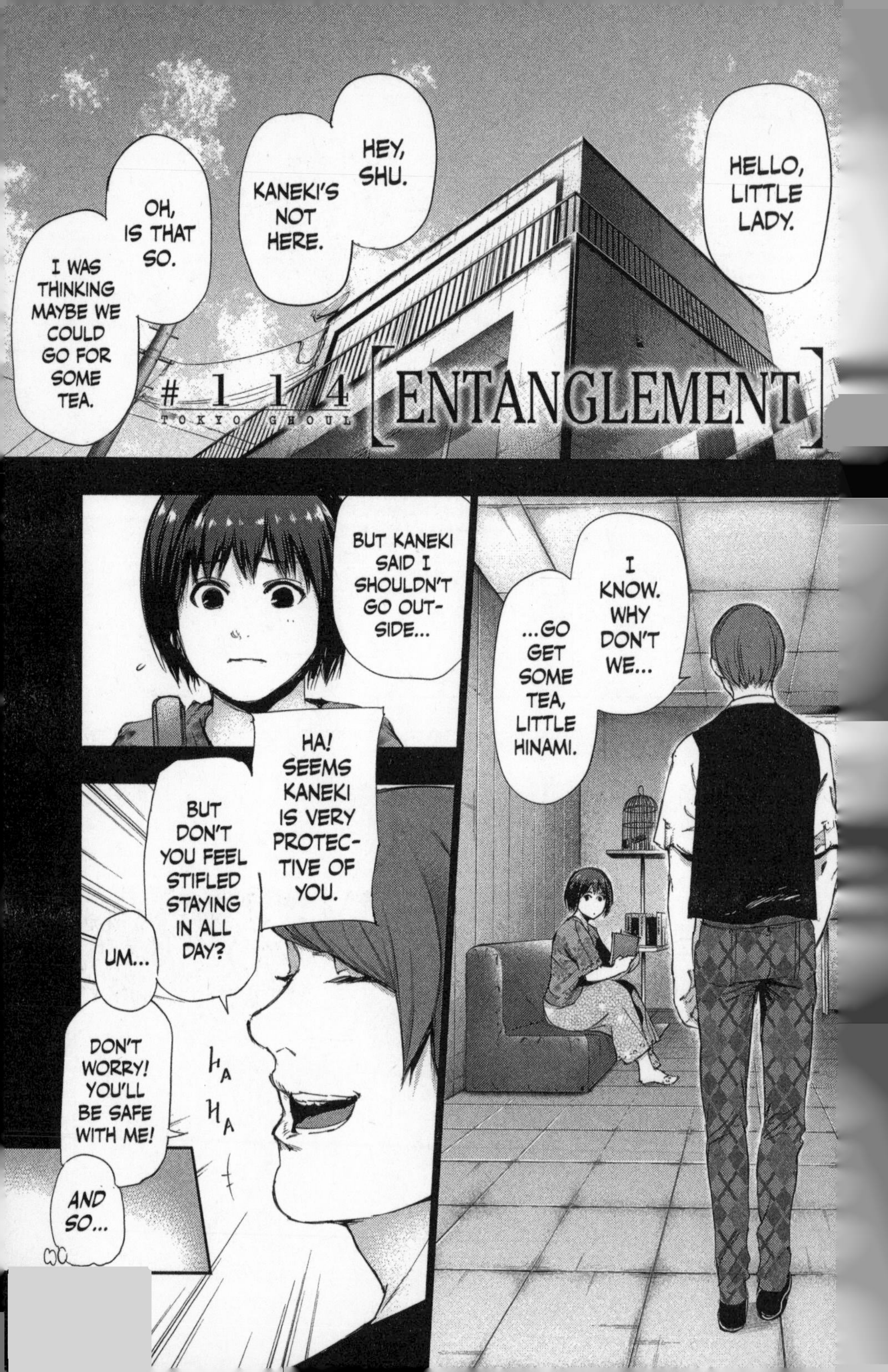
HELLO, LITTLE LADY.
HEY, SHU.
KANEKI'S NOT HERE.
OH, IS THAT SO.
I WAS THINKING MAYBE WE COULD GO FOR SOME TEA.
#114 [ENTANGLEMENT]
TOKYO GHOUL
I KNOW. WHY DON'T WE...
...GO GET SOME TEA, LITTLE HINAMI.
BUT KANEKI SAID I SHOULDN'T GO OUT-SIDE...
HA! SEEMS KANEKI IS VERY PROTEC-TIVE OF YOU.
BUT DON'T YOU FEEL STIFLED STAYING IN ALL DAY?
UM...
HA HA
DON'T WORRY! YOU'LL BE SAFE WITH ME!
AND SO...

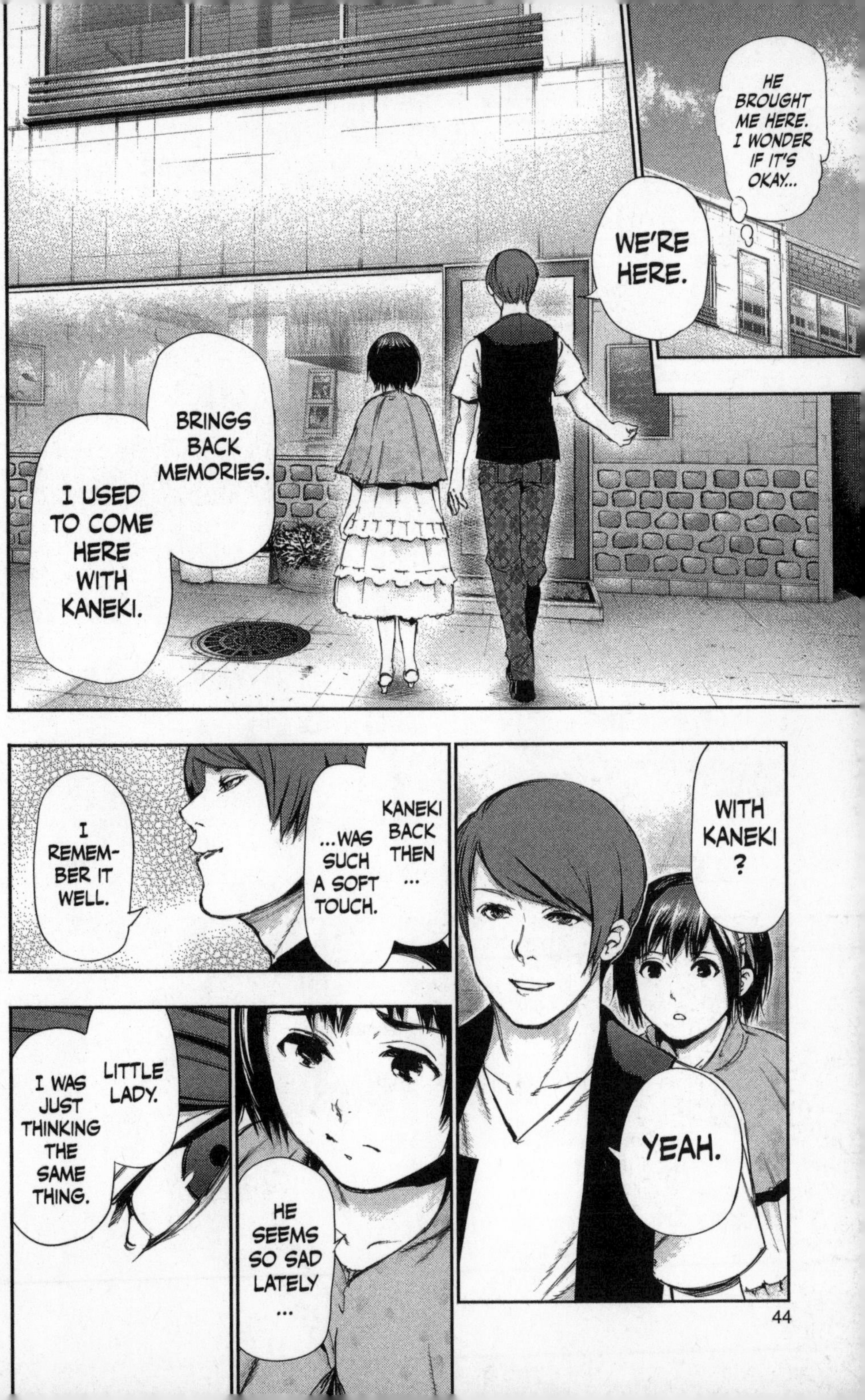
HE BROUGHT ME HERE. I WONDER IF IT'S OKAY...
WE'RE HERE.
BRINGS BACK MEMORIES.
I USED TO COME HERE WITH KANEKI.
WITH KANEKI?
YEAH.
KANEKI BACK THEN...
...WAS SUCH A SOFT TOUCH.
I REMEMBER IT WELL.
LITTLE LADY.
I WAS JUST THINKING THE SAME THING.
HE SEEMS SO SAD LATELY...

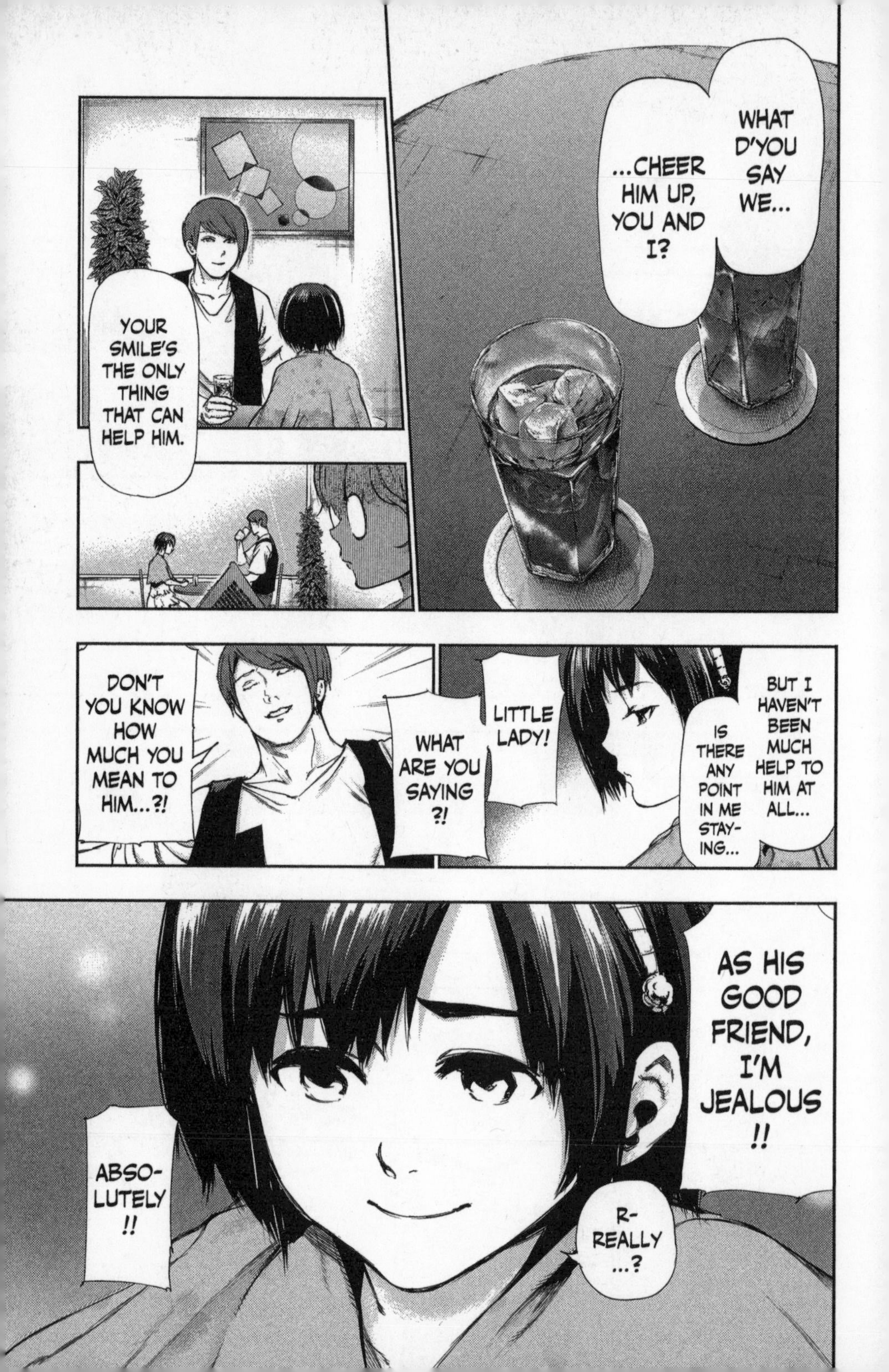
WHAT D'YOU SAY WE...
...CHEER HIM UP, YOU AND I?
YOUR SMILE'S THE ONLY THING THAT CAN HELP HIM.
BUT I HAVEN'T BEEN MUCH HELP TO HIM AT ALL...
IS THERE ANY POINT IN ME STAY-ING...
LITTLE LADY!
WHAT ARE YOU SAYING?!
DON'T YOU KNOW HOW MUCH YOU MEAN TO HIM...?!
AS HIS GOOD FRIEND, I'M JEALOUS!!
R-REALLY...?
ABSO-LUTELY!!

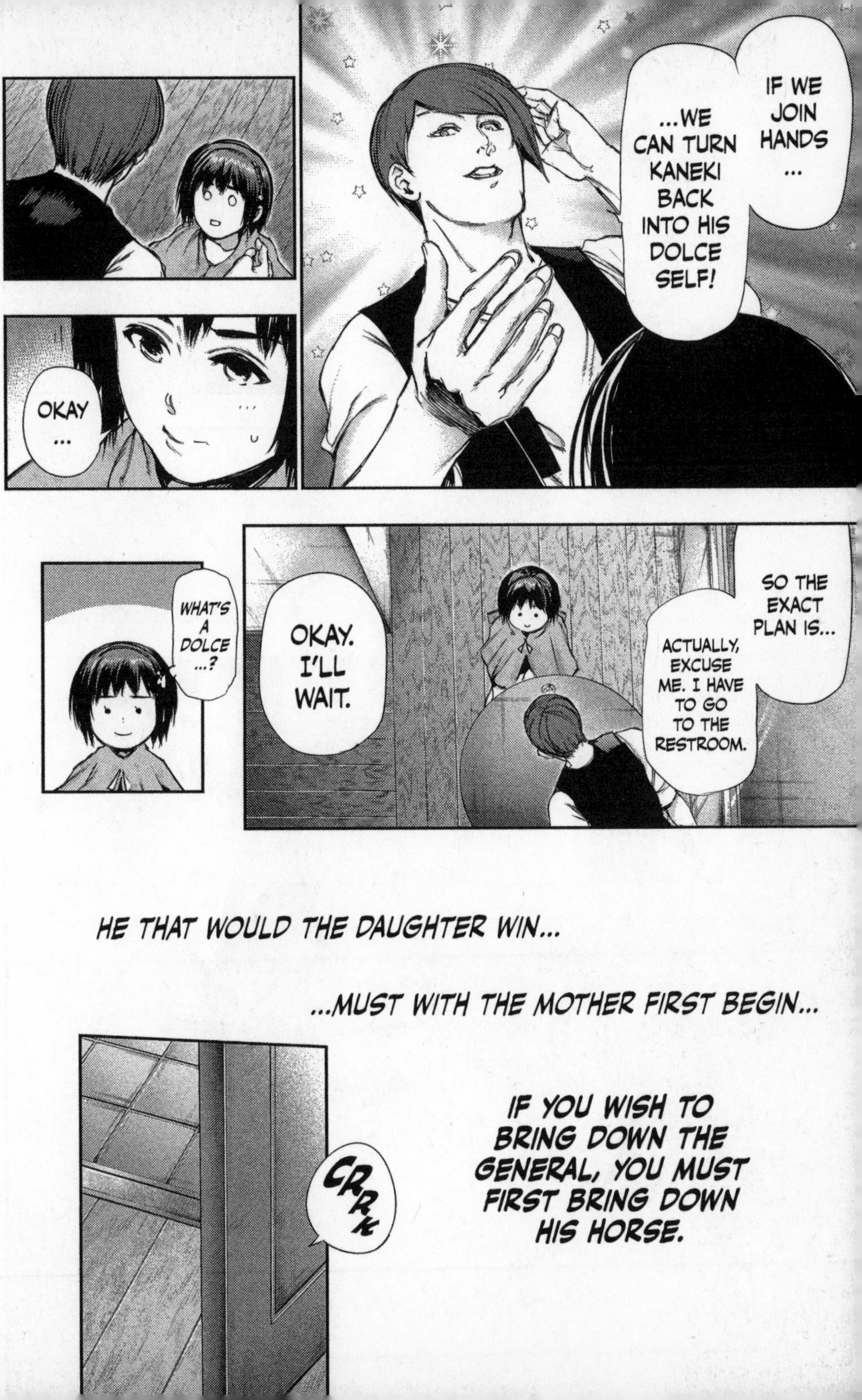
IF WE JOIN HANDS ...
...WE CAN TURN KANEKI BACK INTO HIS DOLCE SELF!
OKAY ...
SO THE EXACT PLAN IS...
ACTUALLY, EXCUSE ME. I HAVE TO GO TO THE RESTROOM.
OKAY. I'LL WAIT.
WHAT'S A DOLCE ...?
HE THAT WOULD THE DAUGHTER WIN...
...MUST WITH THE MOTHER FIRST BEGIN...
IF YOU WISH TO BRING DOWN THE GENERAL, YOU MUST FIRST BRING DOWN HIS HORSE.
CRRK

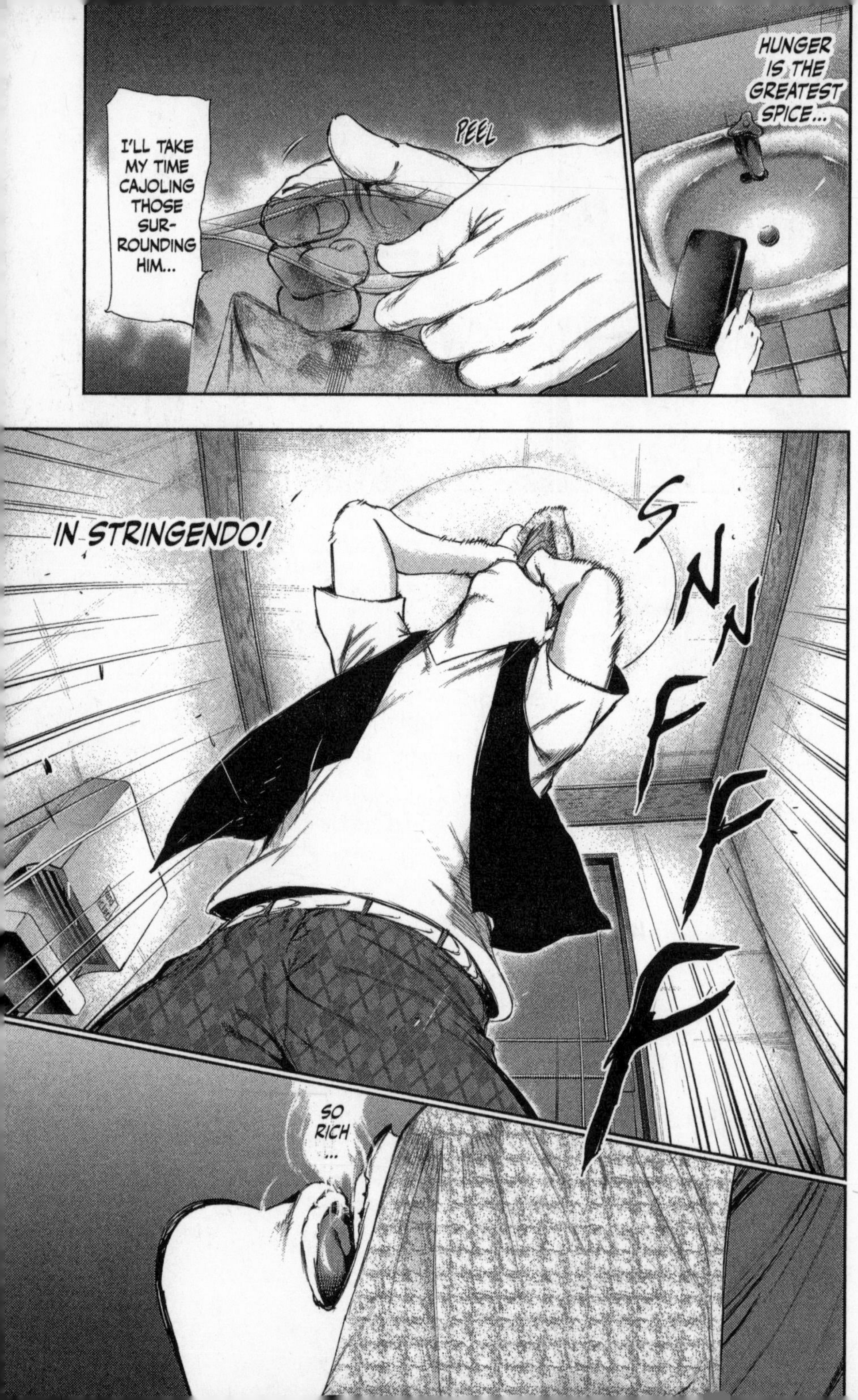
HUNGER IS THE GREATEST SPICE...
I'LL TAKE MY TIME CAJOLING THOSE SUR-ROUNDING HIM...
PEEL
SNNFFFF
IN STRINGENDO!
SO RICH ...

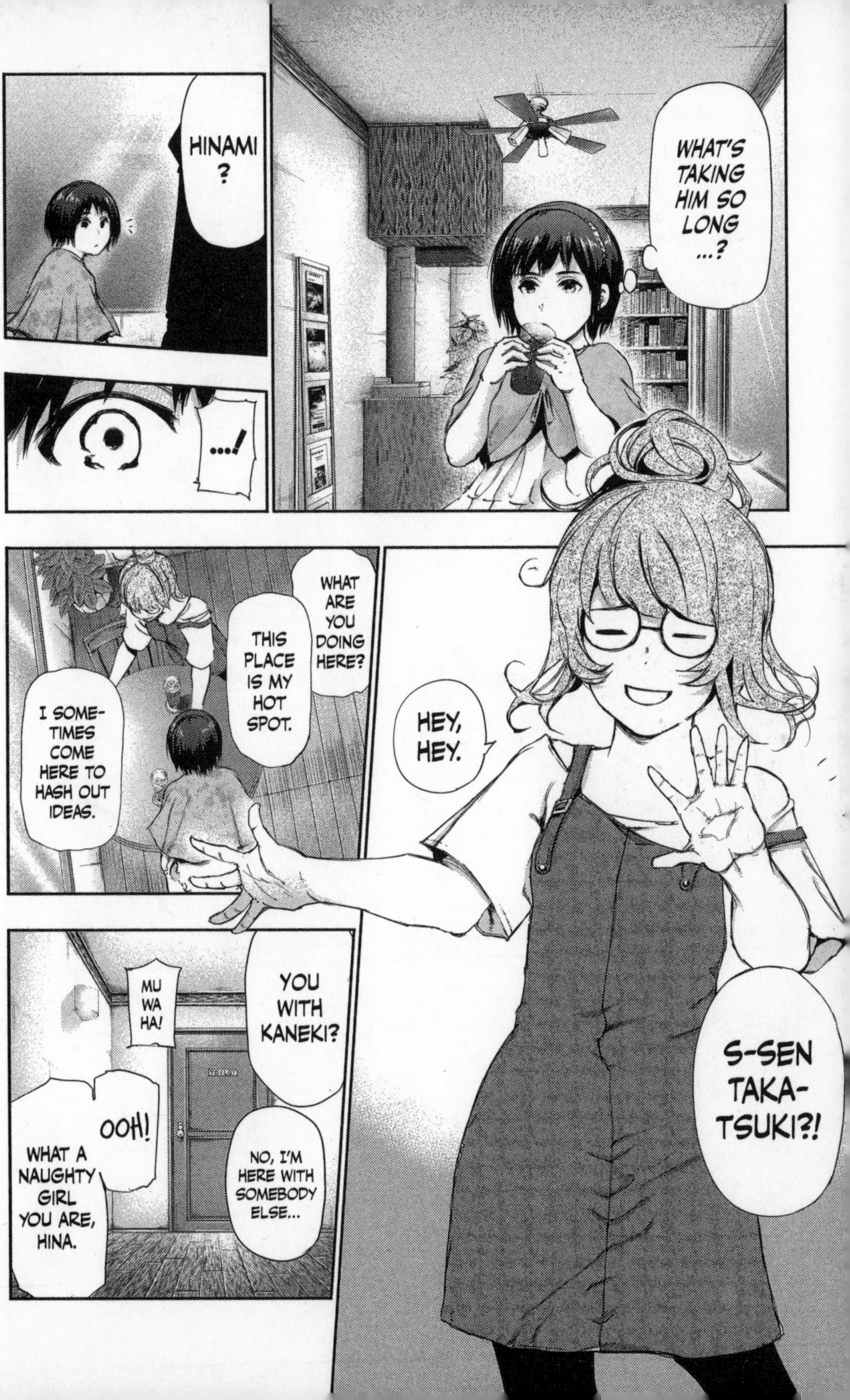
WHAT'S TAKING HIM SO LONG ...?
HINAMI ?
...!
HEY, HEY.
S-SEN TAKA-TSUKI?!
WHAT ARE YOU DOING HERE?
THIS PLACE IS MY HOT SPOT.
I SOME-TIMES COME HERE TO HASH OUT IDEAS.
YOU WITH KANEKI?
MU WA HA!
NO, I'M HERE WITH SOMEBODY ELSE...
OOH!
WHAT A NAUGHTY GIRL YOU ARE, HINA.

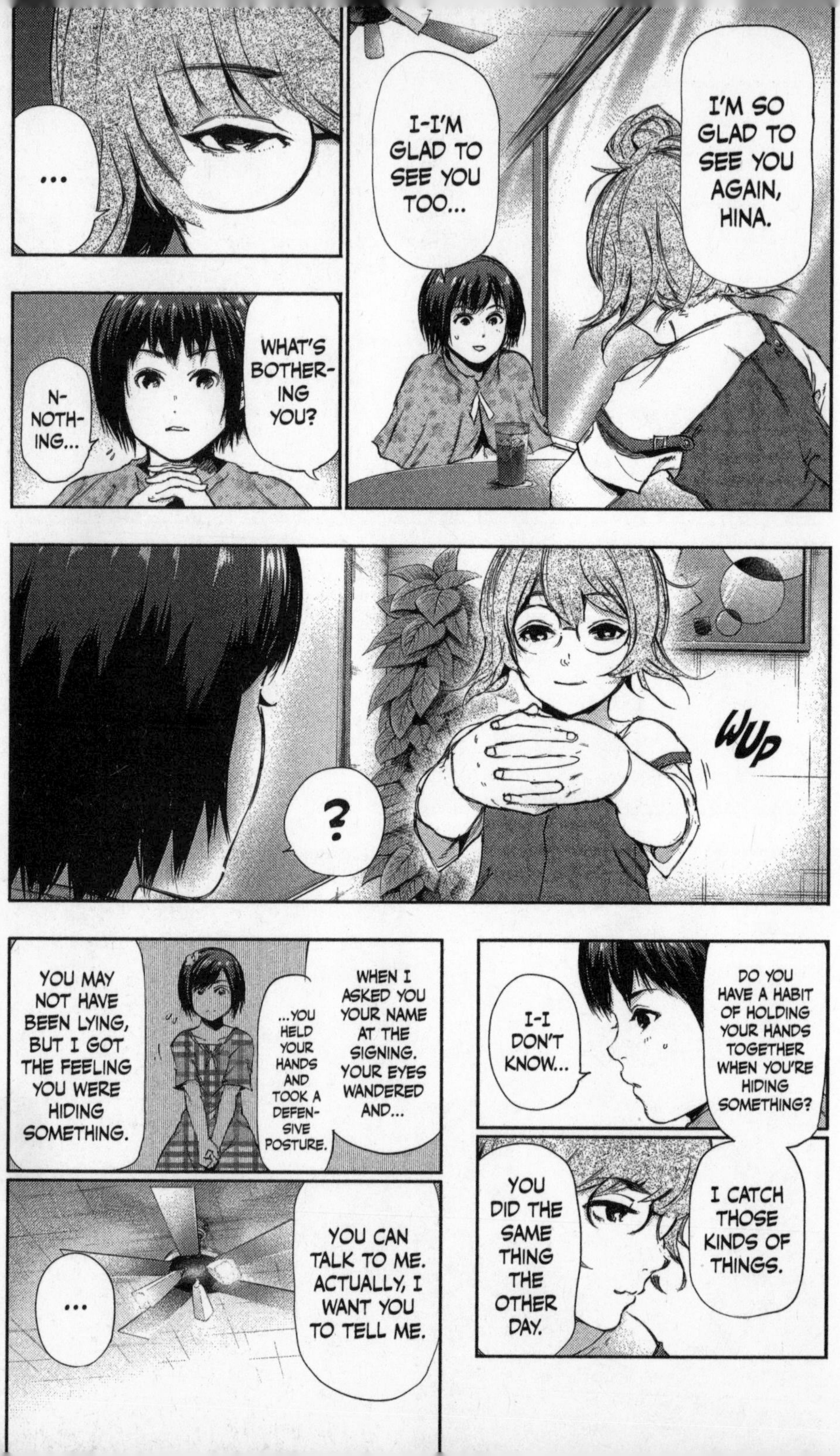

I'M SO GLAD TO SEE YOU AGAIN, HINA.
I-I'M GLAD TO SEE YOU TOO...
...
WHAT'S BOTHERING YOU?
N-NOTHING...
WUP
?
DO YOU HAVE A HABIT OF HOLDING YOUR HANDS TOGETHER WHEN YOU'RE HIDING SOMETHING?
I-I DON'T KNOW...
I CATCH THOSE KINDS OF THINGS.
YOU DID THE SAME THING THE OTHER DAY.
WHEN I ASKED YOU YOUR NAME AT THE SIGNING. YOUR EYES WANDERED AND...
...YOU HELD YOUR HANDS AND TOOK A DEFENSIVE POSTURE.
YOU MAY NOT HAVE BEEN LYING, BUT I GOT THE FEELING YOU WERE HIDING SOMETHING.
YOU CAN TALK TO ME. ACTUALLY, I WANT YOU TO TELL ME.
...

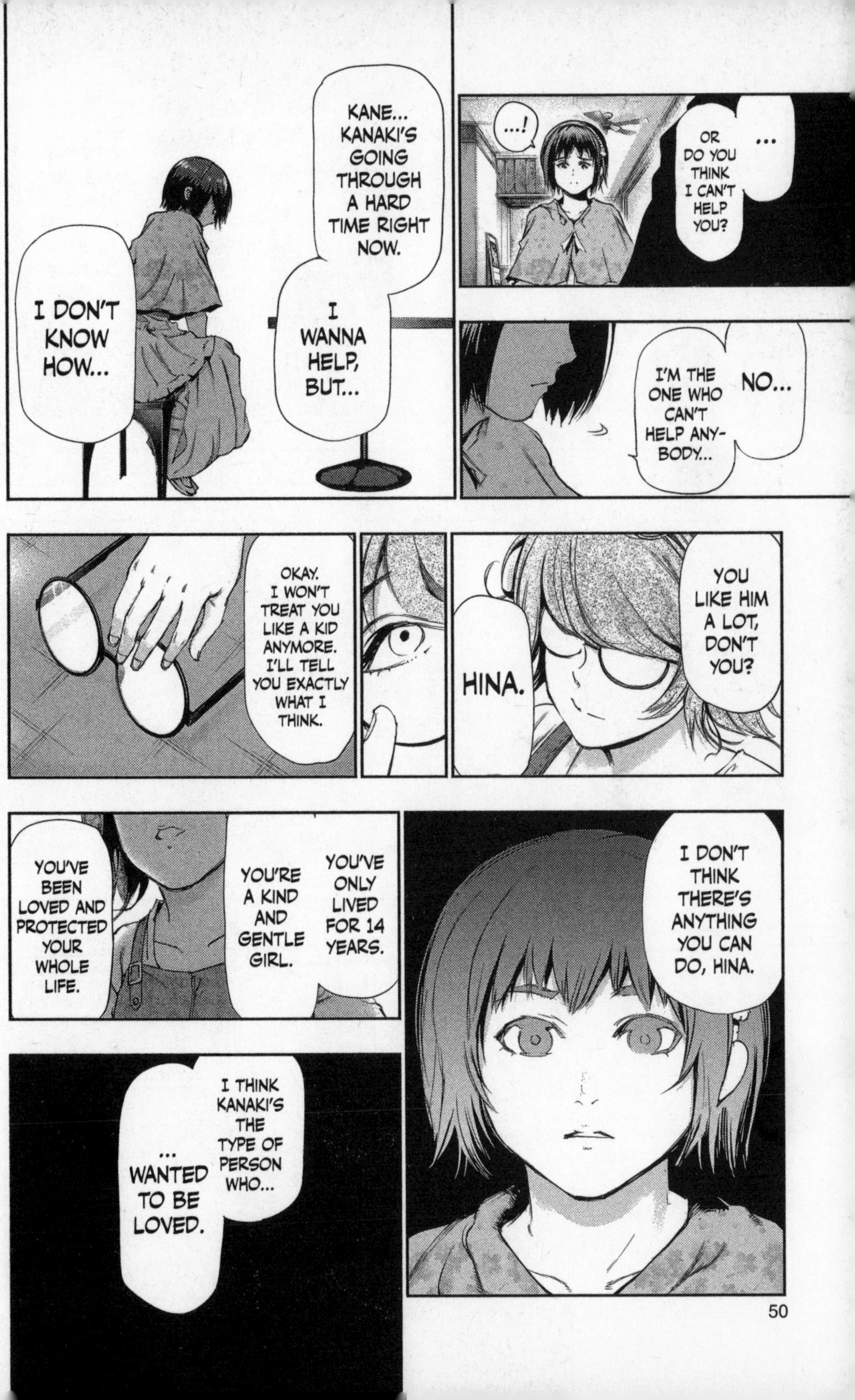
...
OR DO YOU THINK I CAN'T HELP YOU?
...!
NO...
I'M THE ONE WHO CAN'T HELP ANY-BODY...
KANE... KANAKI'S GOING THROUGH A HARD TIME RIGHT NOW.
I WANNA HELP, BUT...
I DON'T KNOW HOW...
YOU LIKE HIM A LOT, DON'T YOU?
HINA.
OKAY. I WON'T TREAT YOU LIKE A KID ANYMORE. I'LL TELL YOU EXACTLY WHAT I THINK.
I DON'T THINK THERE'S ANYTHING YOU CAN DO, HINA.
YOU'VE ONLY LIVED FOR 14 YEARS.
YOU'RE A KIND AND GENTLE GIRL.
YOU'VE BEEN LOVED AND PROTECTED YOUR WHOLE LIFE.
I THINK KANAKI'S THE TYPE OF PERSON WHO...
...WANTED TO BE LOVED.

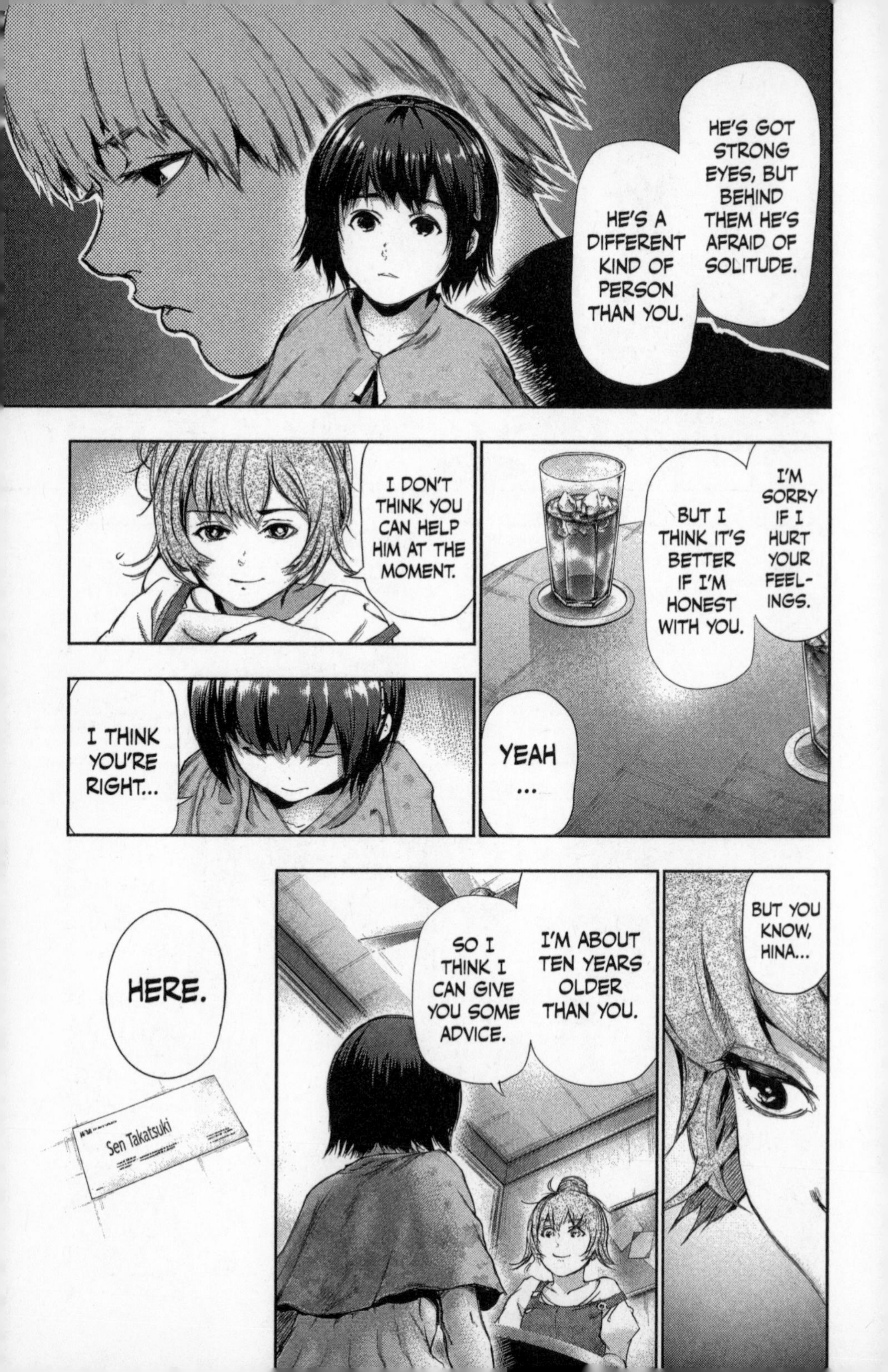
HE'S GOT STRONG EYES, BUT BEHIND THEM HE'S AFRAID OF SOLITUDE.
HE'S A DIFFERENT KIND OF PERSON THAN YOU.
I'M SORRY IF I HURT YOUR FEEL-INGS.
BUT I THINK IT'S BETTER IF I'M HONEST WITH YOU.
YEAH ...
I DON'T THINK YOU CAN HELP HIM AT THE MOMENT.
I THINK YOU'RE RIGHT...
BUT YOU KNOW, HINA...
I'M ABOUT TEN YEARS OLDER THAN YOU.
SO I THINK I CAN GIVE YOU SOME ADVICE.
HERE.
Sen Takatsuki

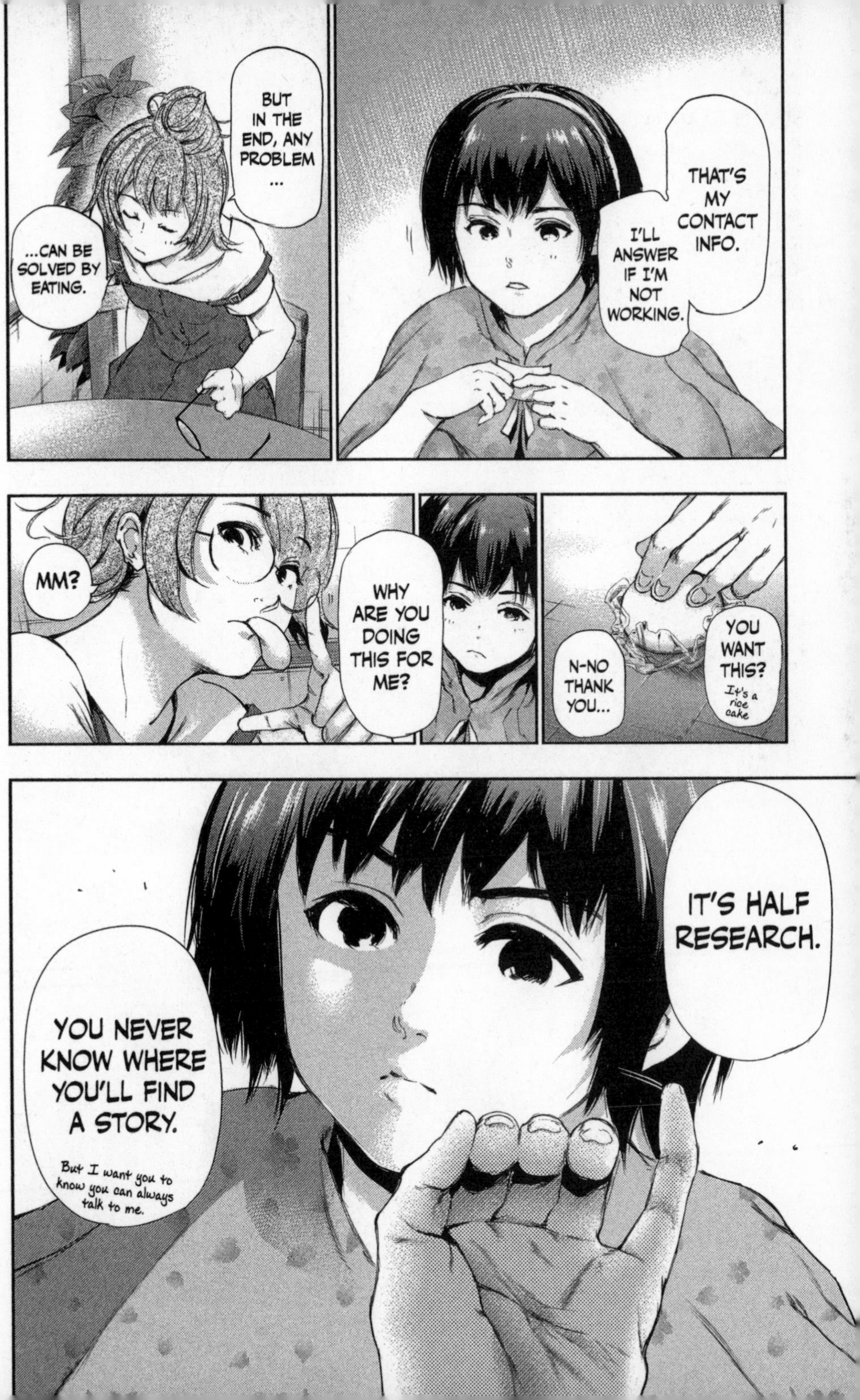
THAT'S MY CONTACT INFO.
I'LL ANSWER IF I'M NOT WORKING.
BUT IN THE END, ANY PROBLEM ...
...CAN BE SOLVED BY EATING.
YOU WANT THIS?
It's a rice cake
N-NO THANK YOU...
WHY ARE YOU DOING THIS FOR ME?
MM?
IT'S HALF RESEARCH.
YOU NEVER KNOW WHERE YOU'LL FIND A STORY.
But I want you to know you can always talk to me.

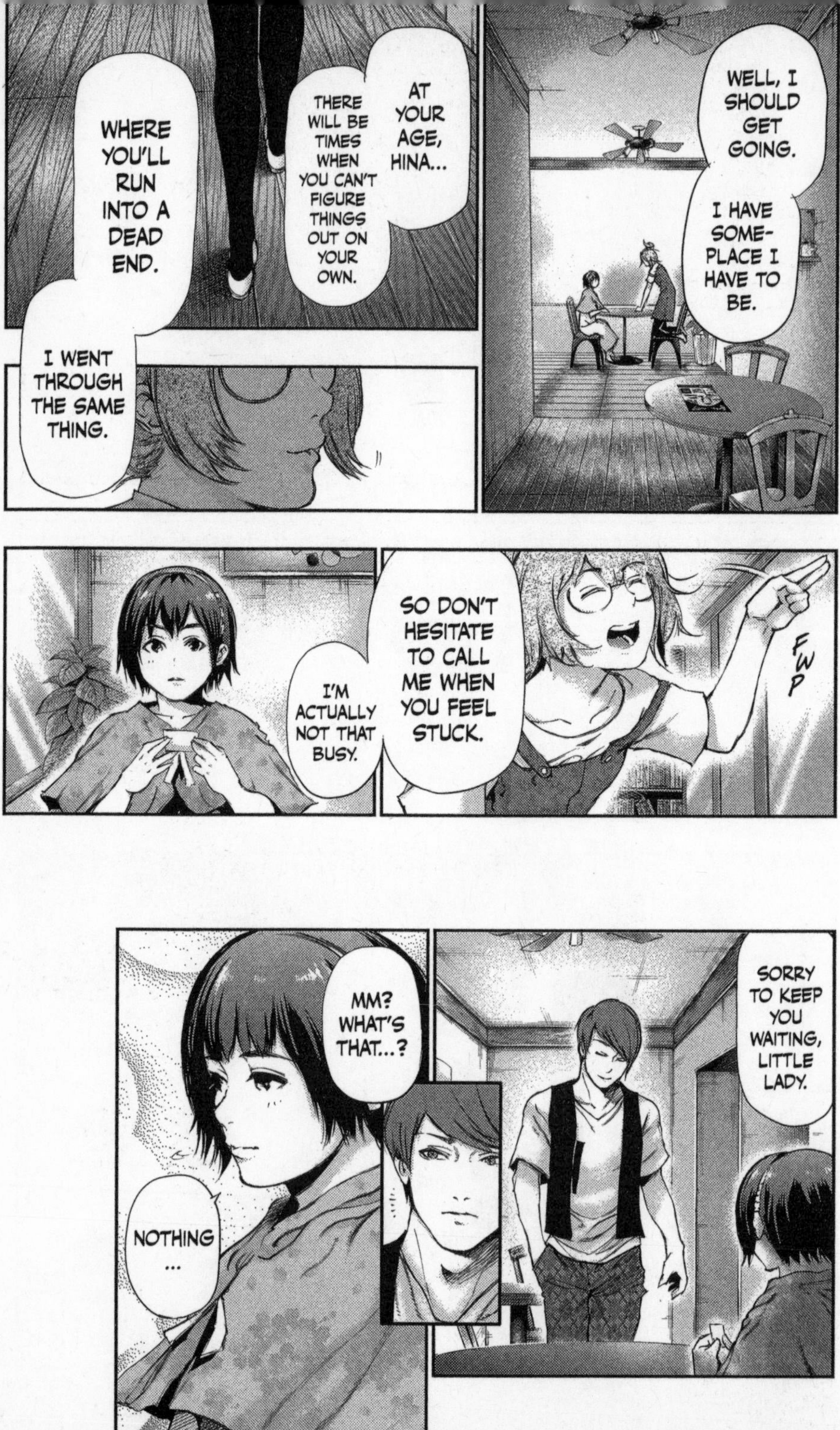
WELL, I SHOULD GET GOING.
I HAVE SOME-PLACE I HAVE TO BE.
AT YOUR AGE, HINA...
THERE WILL BE TIMES WHEN YOU CAN'T FIGURE THINGS OUT ON YOUR OWN.
WHERE YOU'LL RUN INTO A DEAD END.
I WENT THROUGH THE SAME THING.
SO DON'T HESITATE TO CALL ME WHEN YOU FEEL STUCK.
FWP
I'M ACTUALLY NOT THAT BUSY.
SORRY TO KEEP YOU WAITING, LITTLE LADY.
MM? WHAT'S THAT...?
NOTHING...

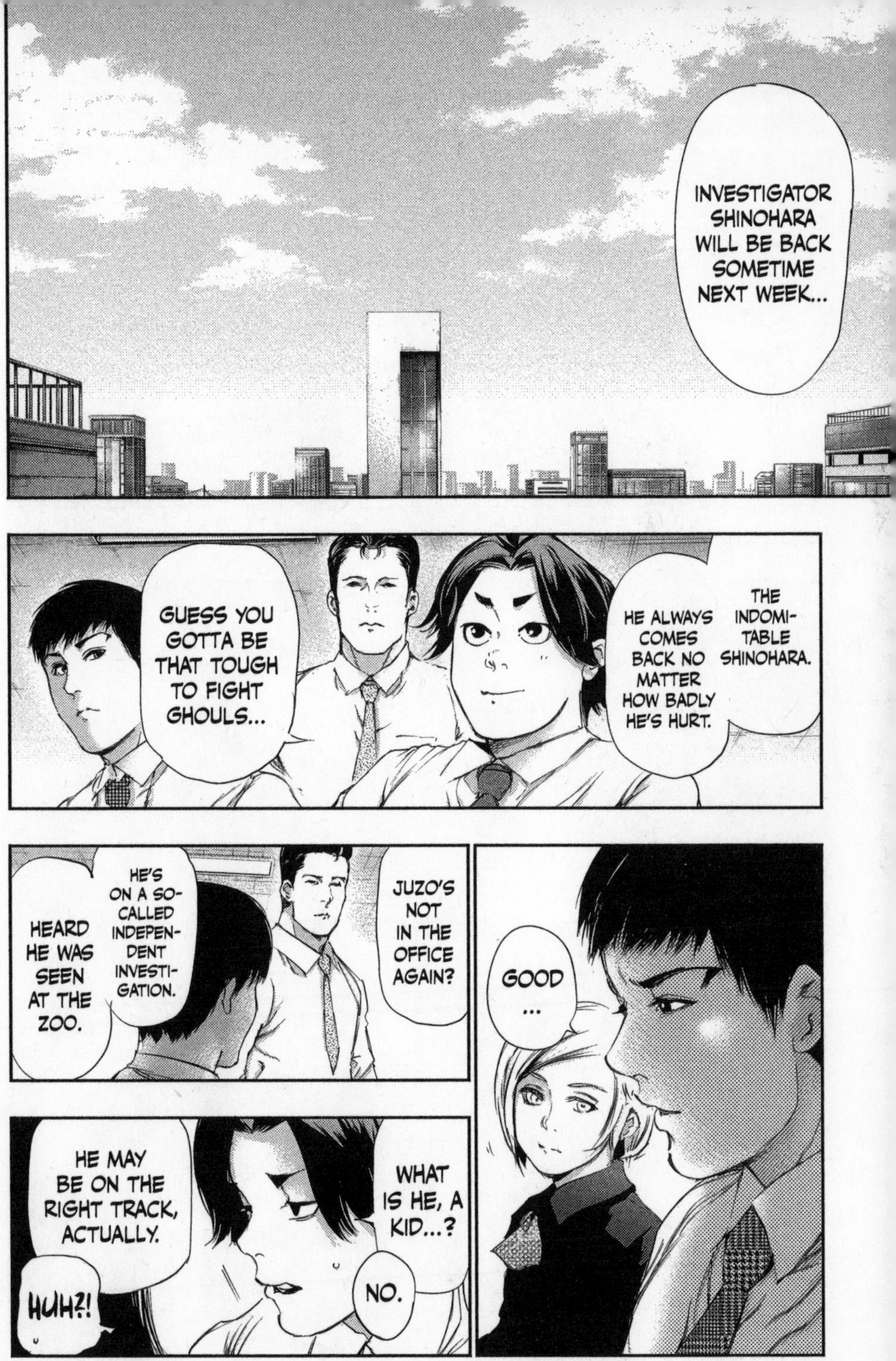
INVESTIGATOR SHINOHARA WILL BE BACK SOMETIME NEXT WEEK...
THE INDOMITABLE SHINOHARA.
HE ALWAYS COMES BACK NO MATTER HOW BADLY HE'S HURT.
GUESS YOU GOTTA BE THAT TOUGH TO FIGHT GHOULS...
GOOD ...
JUZO'S NOT IN THE OFFICE AGAIN?
HE'S ON A SO-CALLED INDEPENDENT INVESTIGATION.
HEARD HE WAS SEEN AT THE ZOO.
WHAT IS HE, A KID...?
NO.
HE MAY BE ON THE RIGHT TRACK, ACTUALLY.
HUH?!

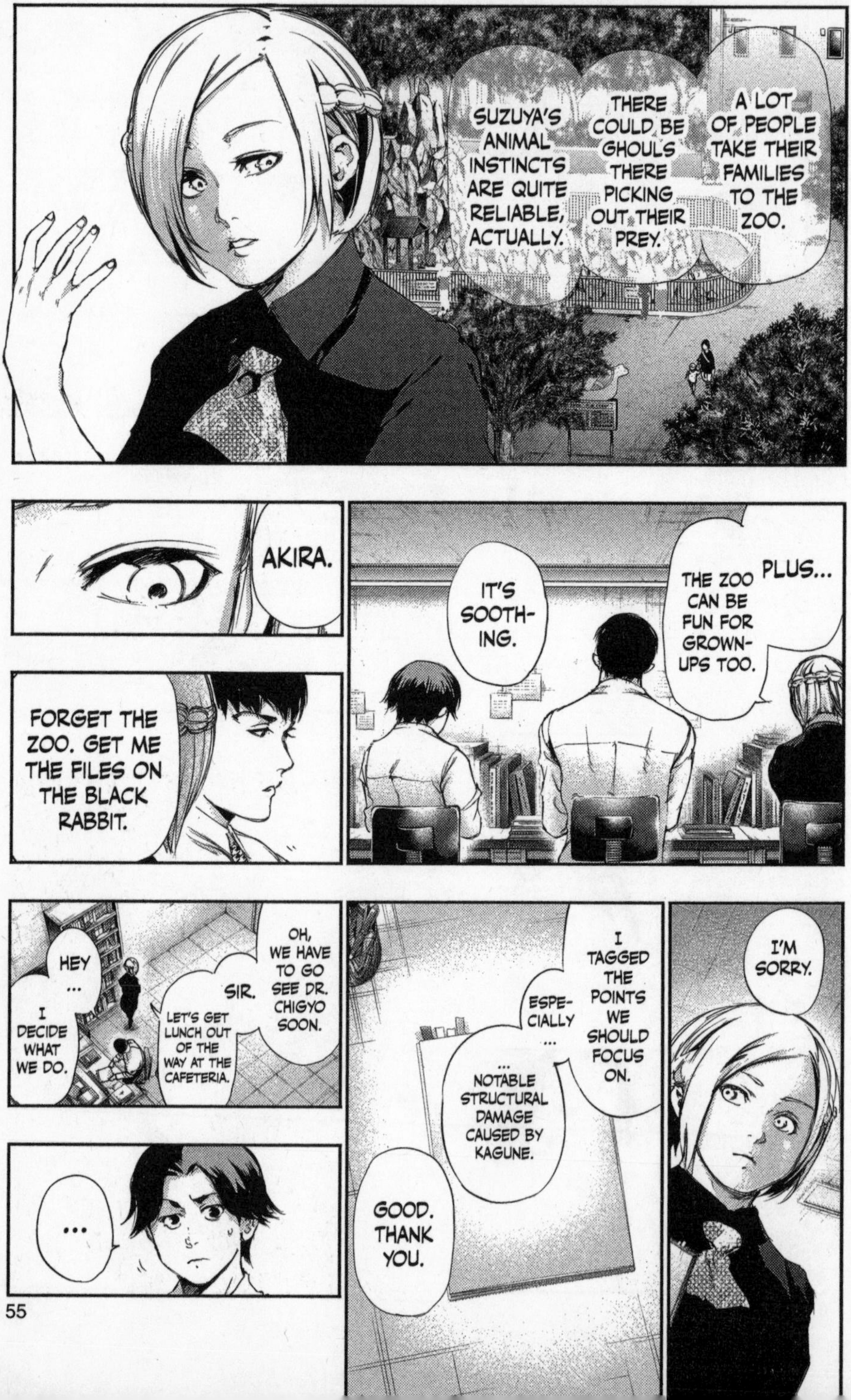
A LOT OF PEOPLE TAKE THEIR FAMILIES TO THE ZOO.
THERE COULD BE GHOULS THERE PICKING OUT THEIR PREY.
SUZUYA'S ANIMAL INSTINCTS ARE QUITE RELIABLE, ACTUALLY.
PLUS...
THE ZOO CAN BE FUN FOR GROWN-UPS TOO.
IT'S SOOTHING.
AKIRA.
FORGET THE ZOO. GET ME THE FILES ON THE BLACK RABBIT.
I'M SORRY.
I TAGGED THE POINTS WE SHOULD FOCUS ON.
ESPECIALLY ...
... NOTABLE STRUCTURAL DAMAGE CAUSED BY KAGUNE.
GOOD. THANK YOU.
OH, WE HAVE TO GO SEE DR. CHIGYO SOON.
SIR.
LET'S GET LUNCH OUT OF THE WAY AT THE CAFETERIA.
HEY ...
I DECIDE WHAT WE DO.
...

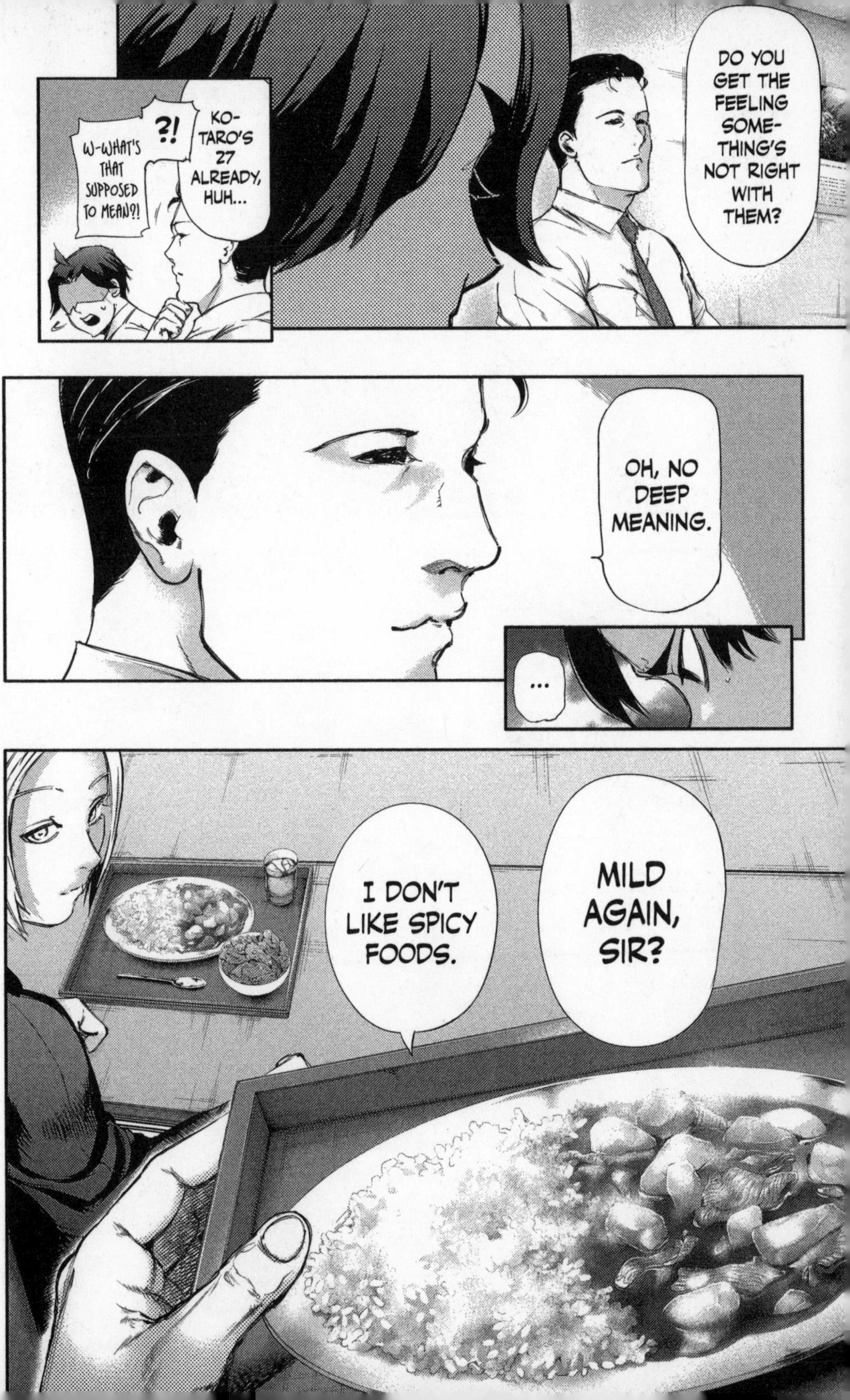
DO YOU GET THE FEELING SOME-THING'S NOT RIGHT WITH THEM?
KO-TARO'S 27 ALREADY, HUH...
?!
W-WHAT'S THAT SUPPOSED TO MEAN?!
OH, NO DEEP MEANING.
...
MILD AGAIN, SIR?
I DON'T LIKE SPICY FOODS.

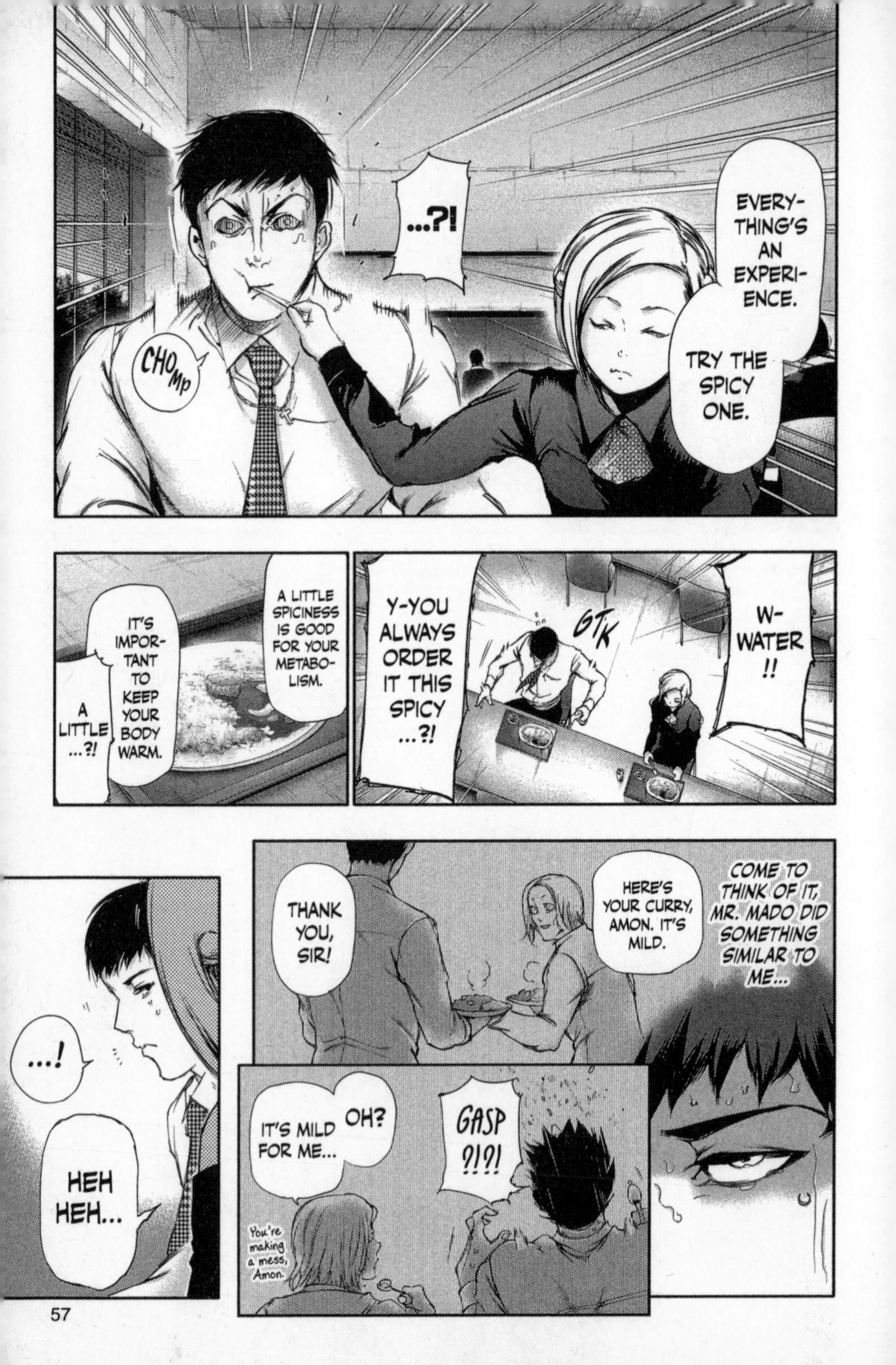
EVERYTHING'S AN EXPERIENCE.
TRY THE SPICY ONE.
...?!
CHOMP
W-WATER!!
GTK
Y-YOU ALWAYS ORDER IT THIS SPICY...?!
A LITTLE SPICINESS IS GOOD FOR YOUR METABOLISM.
IT'S IMPORTANT TO KEEP YOUR BODY WARM.
A LITTLE...?!
COME TO THINK OF IT, MR. MADO DID SOMETHING SIMILAR TO ME...
HERE'S YOUR CURRY, AMON. IT'S MILD.
THANK YOU, SIR!
GASP ?!?!
OH?
IT'S MILD FOR ME...
You're making a mess, Amon.
...!
HEH HEH...

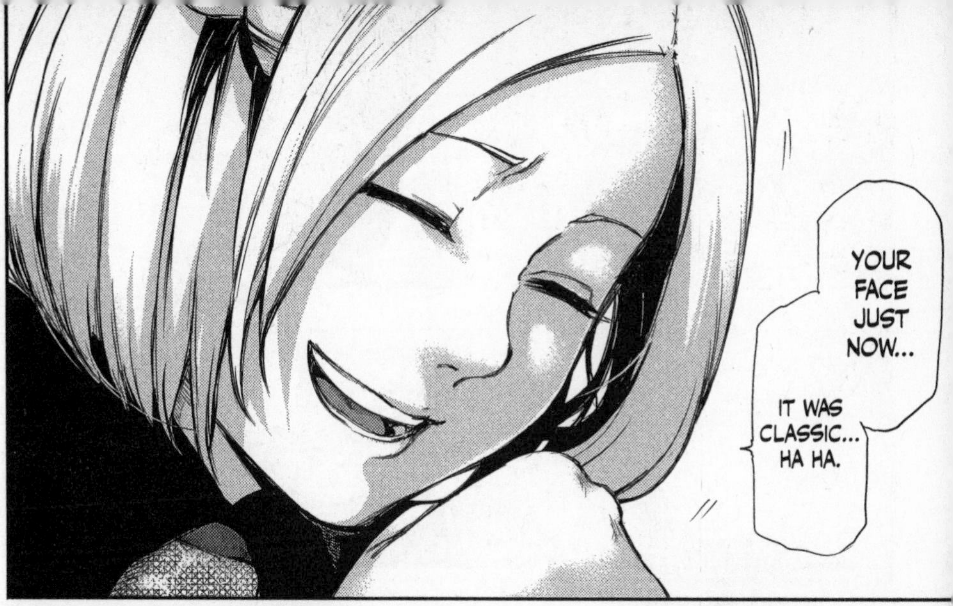
YOUR FACE JUST NOW...
IT WAS CLASSIC... HA HA.

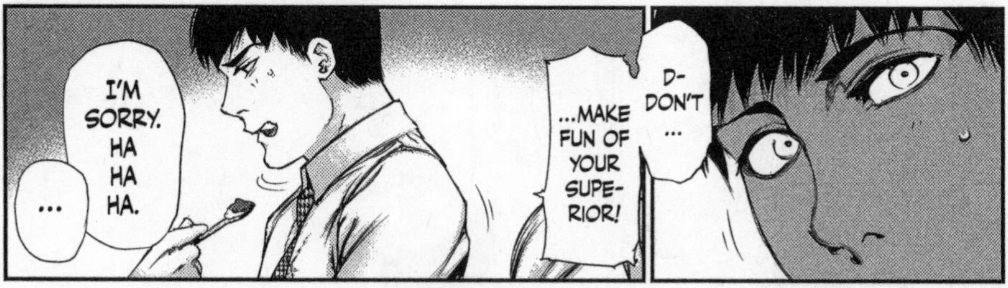
D-DON'T...
...MAKE FUN OF YOUR SUPERIOR!
I'M SORRY. HA HA HA.
...

SO SHE CAN LAUGH...

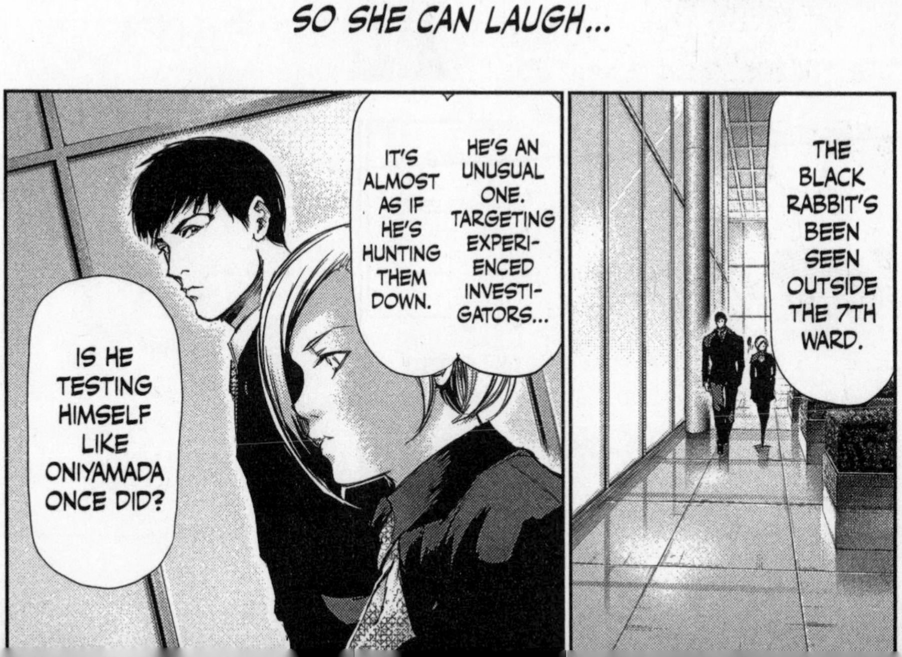
THE BLACK RABBIT'S BEEN SEEN OUTSIDE THE 7TH WARD.
HE'S AN UNUSUAL ONE. TARGETING EXPERIENCED INVESTIGATORS...
IT'S ALMOST AS IF HE'S HUNTING THEM DOWN.
IS HE TESTING HIMSELF LIKE ONIYAMADA ONCE DID?

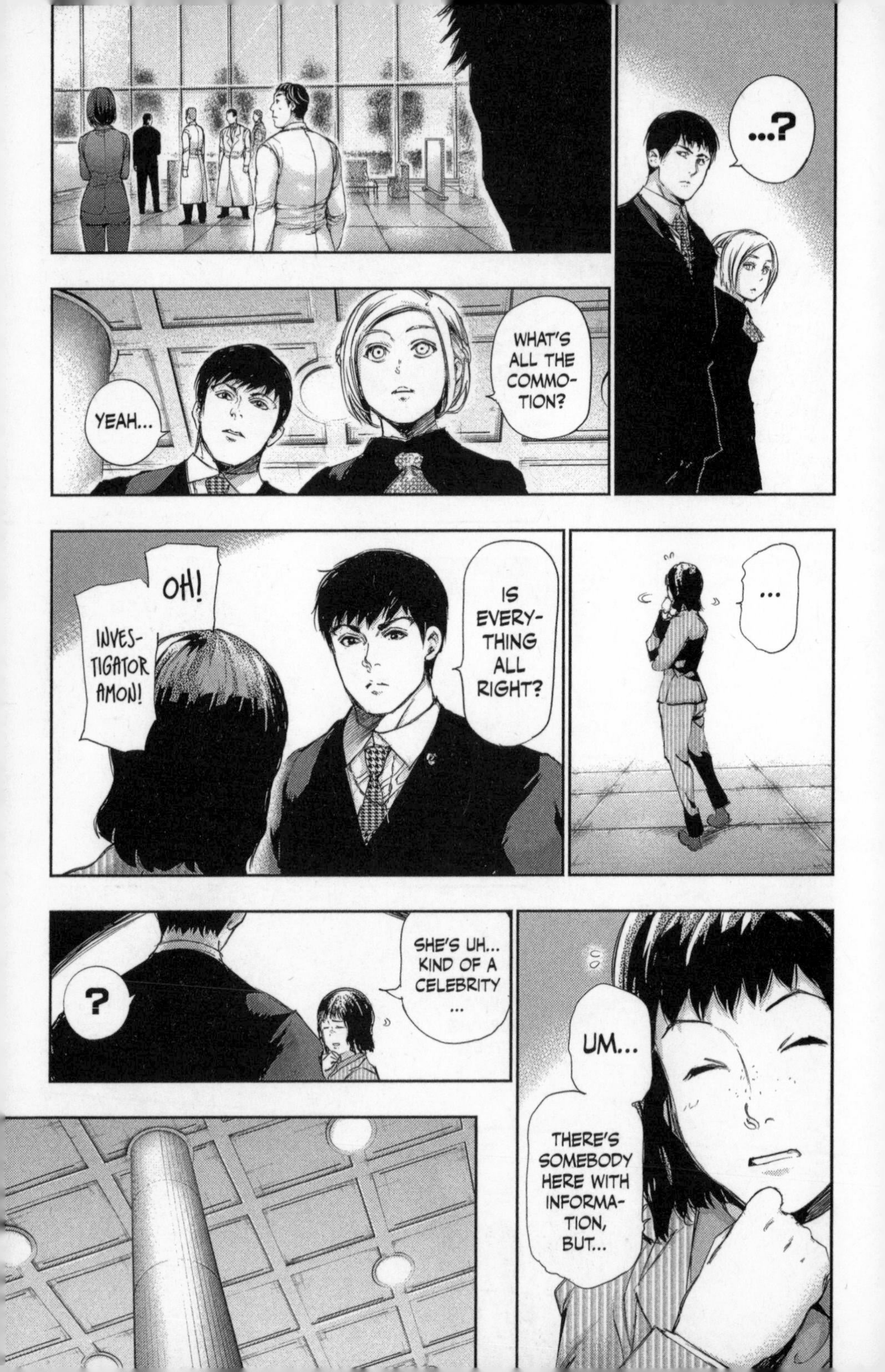
...?
WHAT'S ALL THE COMMOTION?
YEAH...
...
IS EVERYTHING ALL RIGHT?
OH!
INVESTIGATOR AMON!
UM...
THERE'S SOMEBODY HERE WITH INFORMATION, BUT...
SHE'S UH... KIND OF A CELEBRITY...
?

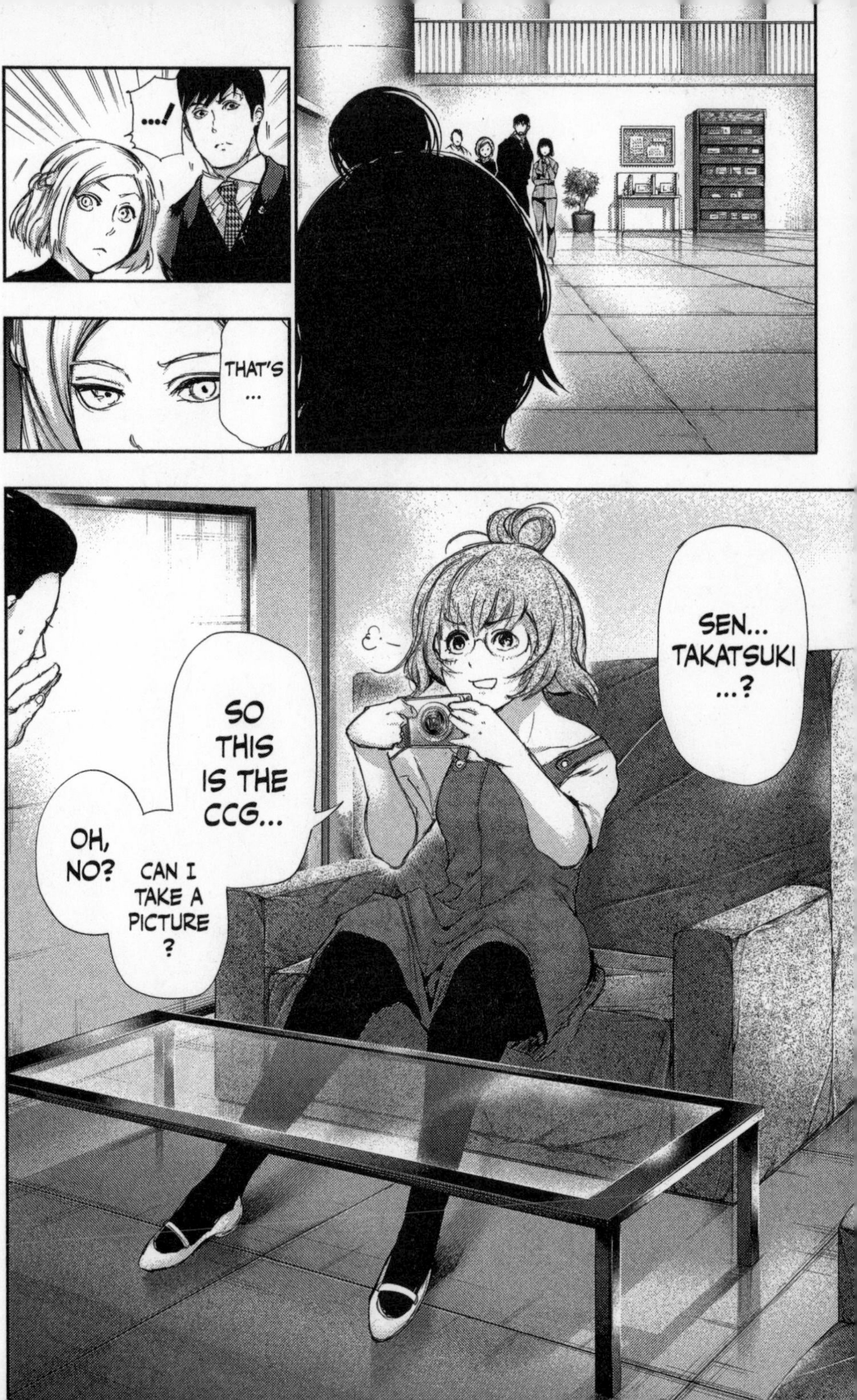
...!
THAT'S ...
SEN... TAKATSUKI ...?
SO THIS IS THE CCG...
OH, NO?
CAN I TAKE A PICTURE ?

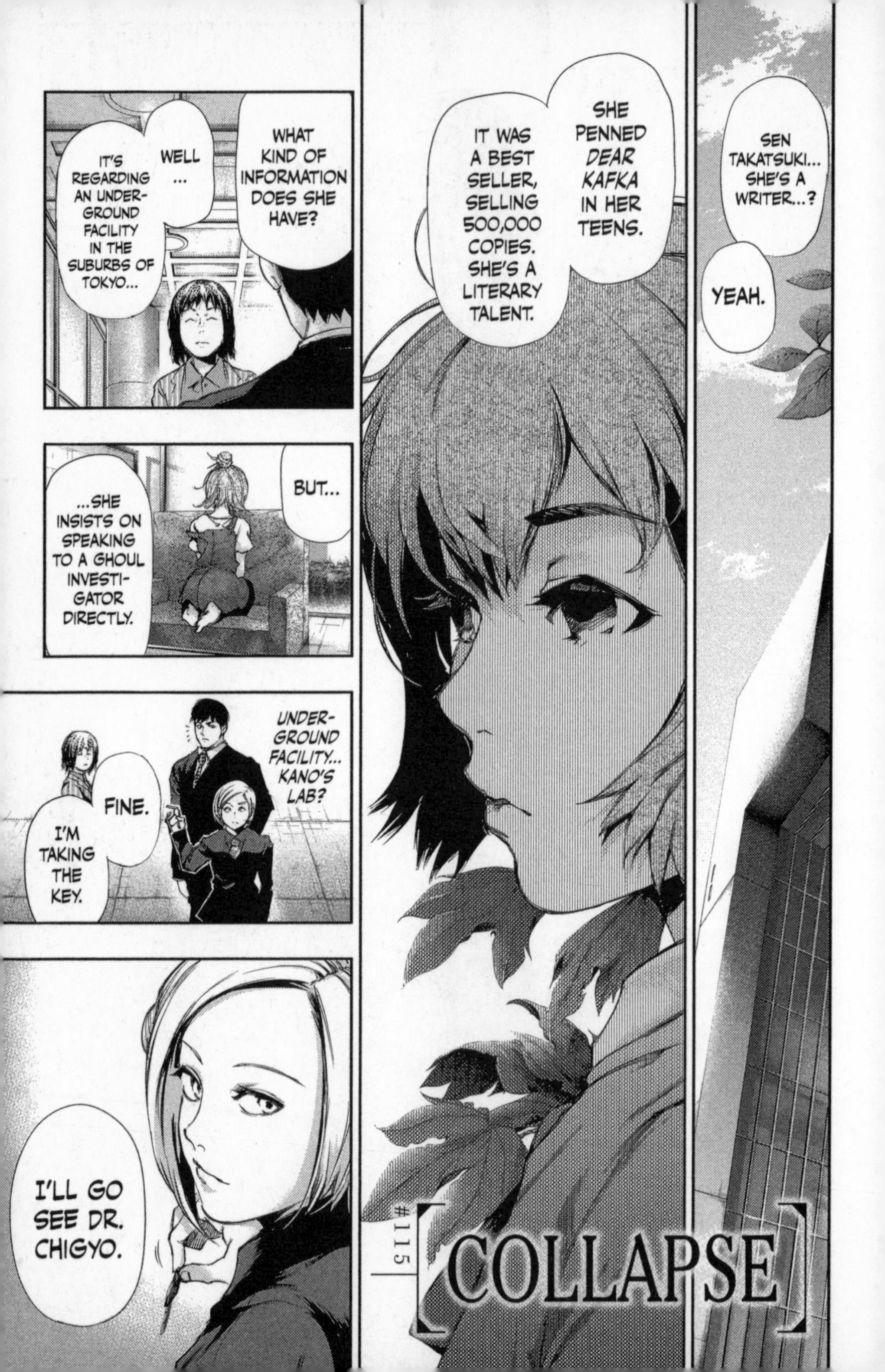
SEN TAKATSUKI... SHE'S A WRITER...?
YEAH.
SHE PENNED DEAR KAFKA IN HER TEENS.
IT WAS A BEST SELLER, SELLING 500,000 COPIES. SHE'S A LITERARY TALENT.
#115 [COLLAPSE]
WHAT KIND OF INFORMATION DOES SHE HAVE?
WELL ...
IT'S REGARDING AN UNDER-GROUND FACILITY IN THE SUBURBS OF TOKYO...
BUT...
...SHE INSISTS ON SPEAKING TO A GHOUL INVESTI-GATOR DIRECTLY.
UNDER-GROUND FACILITY... KANO'S LAB?
FINE.
I'M TAKING THE KEY.
I'LL GO SEE DR. CHIGYO.

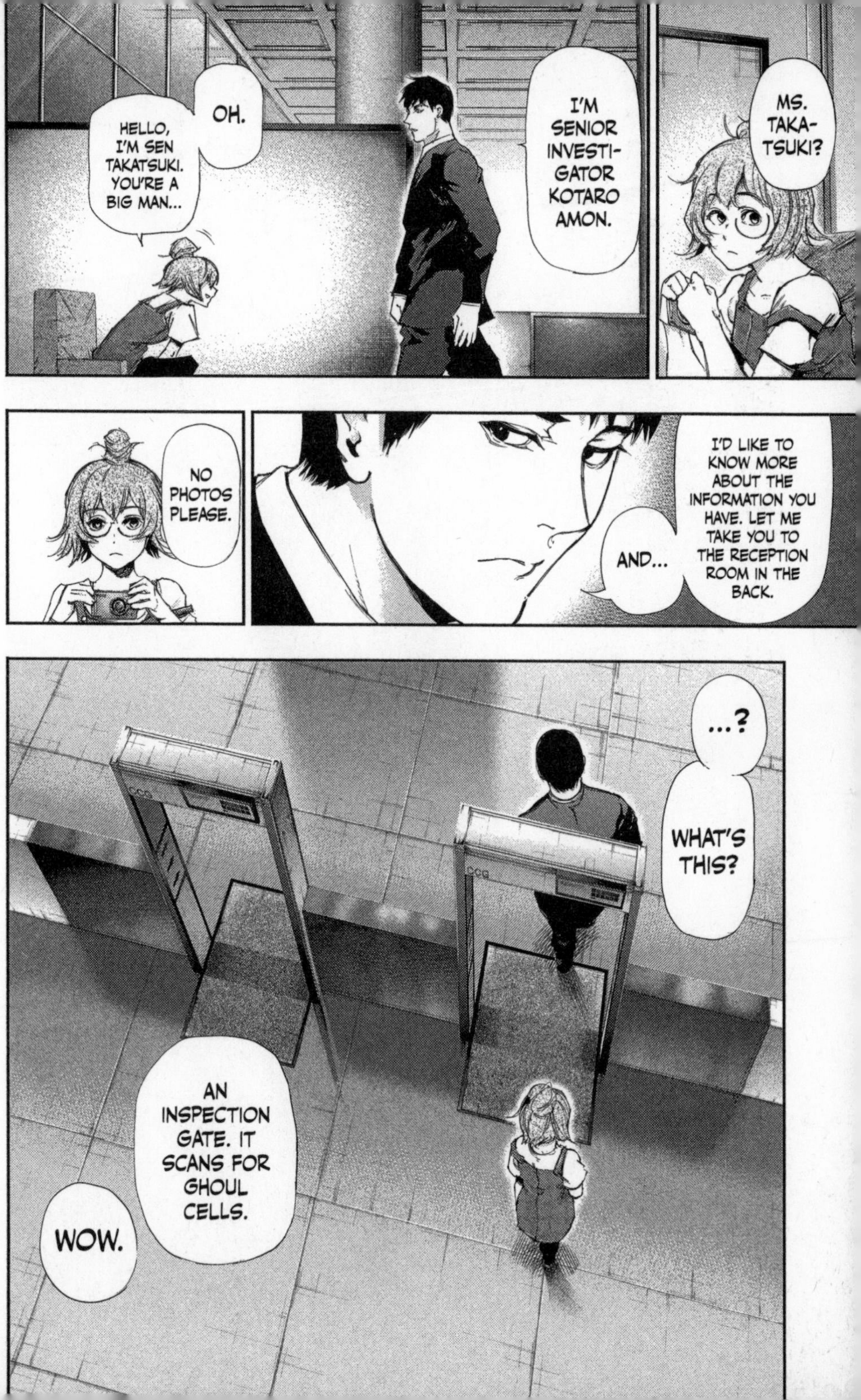
MS. TAKATSUKI?
I'M SENIOR INVESTIGATOR KOTARO AMON.
OH.
HELLO, I'M SEN TAKATSUKI. YOU'RE A BIG MAN...
I'D LIKE TO KNOW MORE ABOUT THE INFORMATION YOU HAVE. LET ME TAKE YOU TO THE RECEPTION ROOM IN THE BACK.
AND...
NO PHOTOS PLEASE.
...?
WHAT'S THIS?
AN INSPECTION GATE. IT SCANS FOR GHOUL CELLS.
WOW.

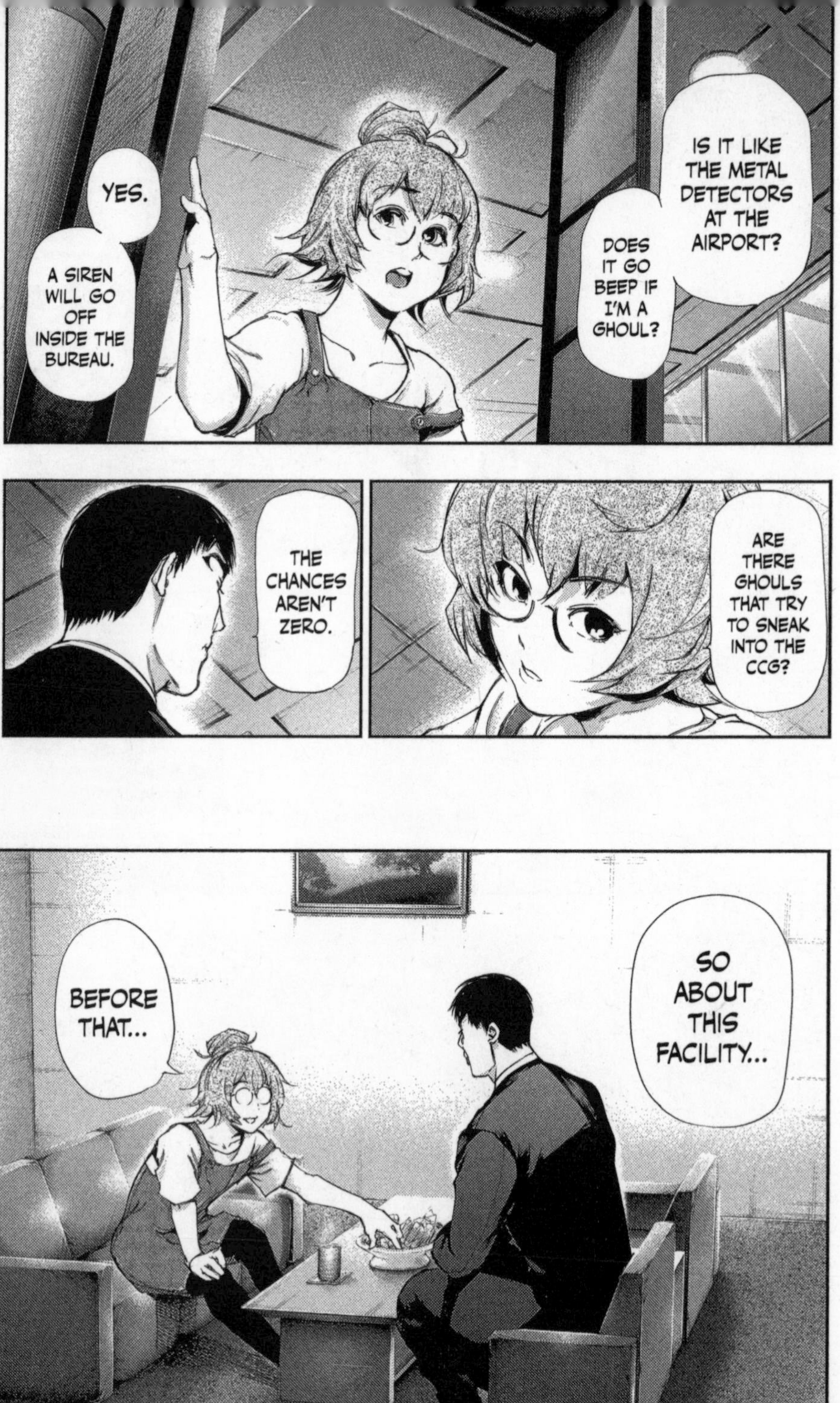
IS IT LIKE THE METAL DETECTORS AT THE AIRPORT?
DOES IT GO BEEP IF I'M A GHOUL?
YES.
A SIREN WILL GO OFF INSIDE THE BUREAU.
ARE THERE GHOULS THAT TRY TO SNEAK INTO THE CCG?
THE CHANCES AREN'T ZERO.
SO ABOUT THIS FACILITY...
BEFORE THAT...

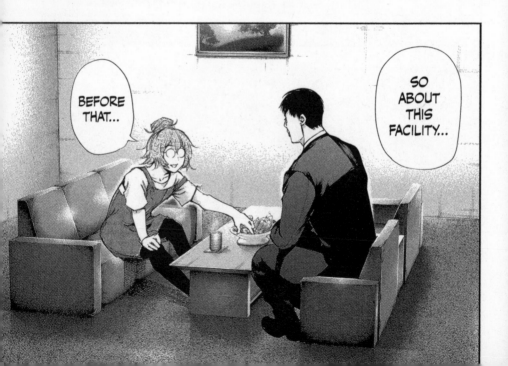

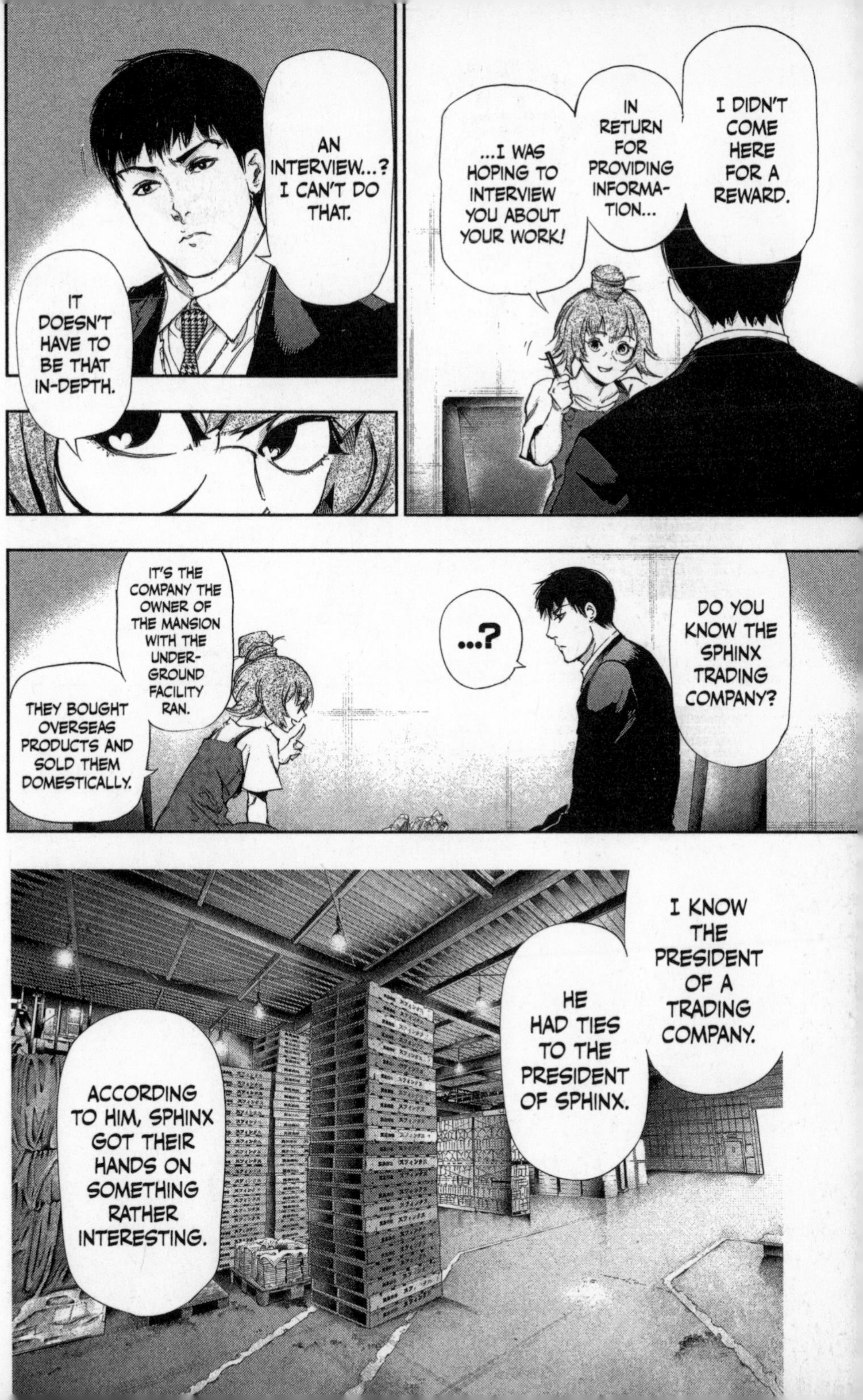
I DIDN'T COME HERE FOR A REWARD.
IN RETURN FOR PROVIDING INFORMA-TION...
...I WAS HOPING TO INTERVIEW YOU ABOUT YOUR WORK!
AN INTERVIEW...? I CAN'T DO THAT.
IT DOESN'T HAVE TO BE THAT IN-DEPTH.
DO YOU KNOW THE SPHINX TRADING COMPANY?
...?
IT'S THE COMPANY THE OWNER OF THE MANSION WITH THE UNDER-GROUND FACILITY RAN.
THEY BOUGHT OVERSEAS PRODUCTS AND SOLD THEM DOMESTICALLY.
I KNOW THE PRESIDENT OF A TRADING COMPANY.
HE HAD TIES TO THE PRESIDENT OF SPHINX.
ACCORDING TO HIM, SPHINX GOT THEIR HANDS ON SOMETHING RATHER INTERESTING.

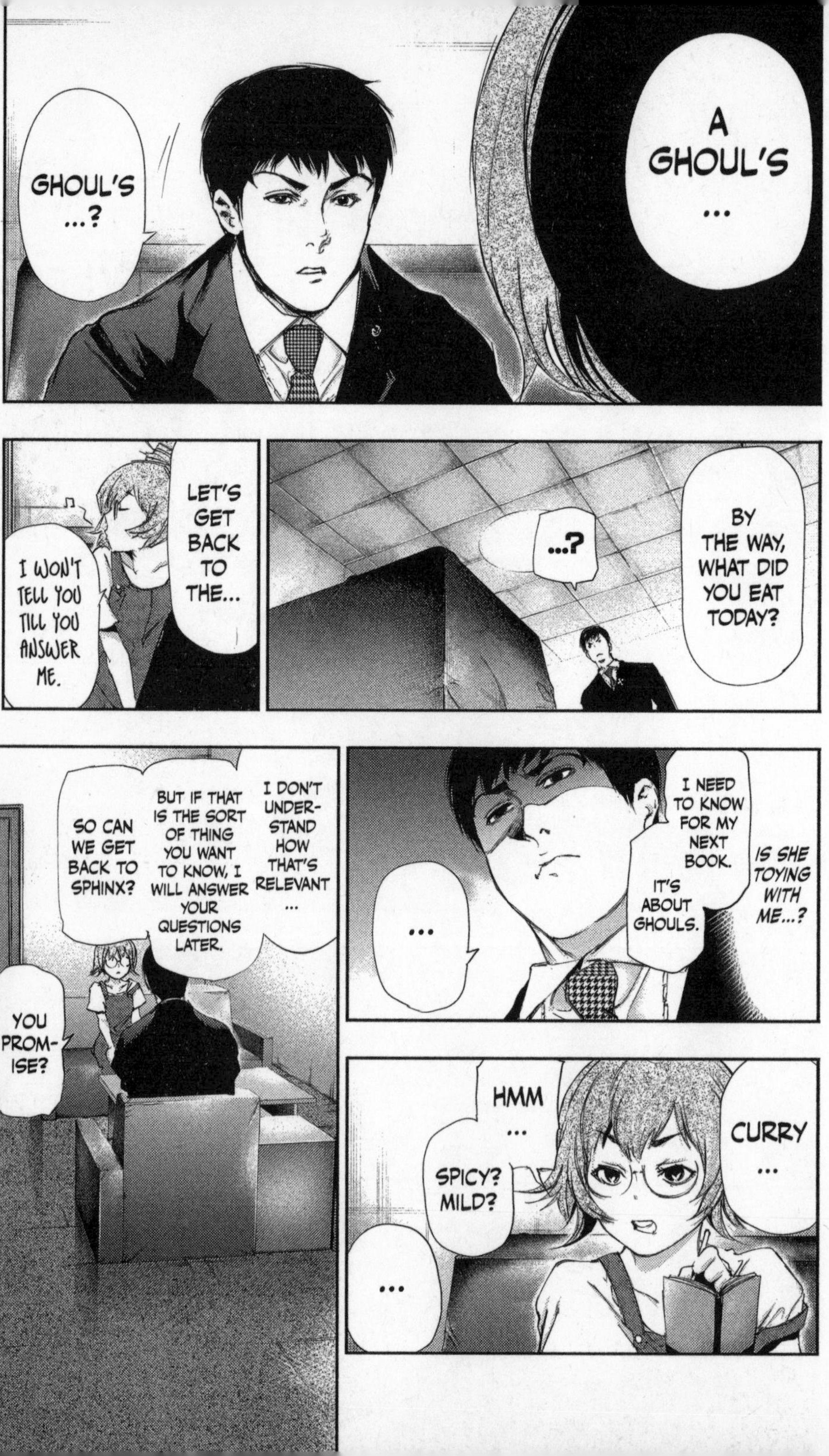
A GHOUL'S ...
GHOUL'S ...?
BY THE WAY, WHAT DID YOU EAT TODAY?
...?
LET'S GET BACK TO THE...
I WON'T TELL YOU TILL YOU ANSWER ME.
IS SHE TOYING WITH ME...?
I NEED TO KNOW FOR MY NEXT BOOK.
IT'S ABOUT GHOULS.
...
CURRY ...
HMM ...
SPICY? MILD?
...
I DON'T UNDER-STAND HOW THAT'S RELEVANT ...
BUT IF THAT IS THE SORT OF THING YOU WANT TO KNOW, I WILL ANSWER YOUR QUESTIONS LATER.
SO CAN WE GET BACK TO SPHINX?
YOU PROM-ISE?

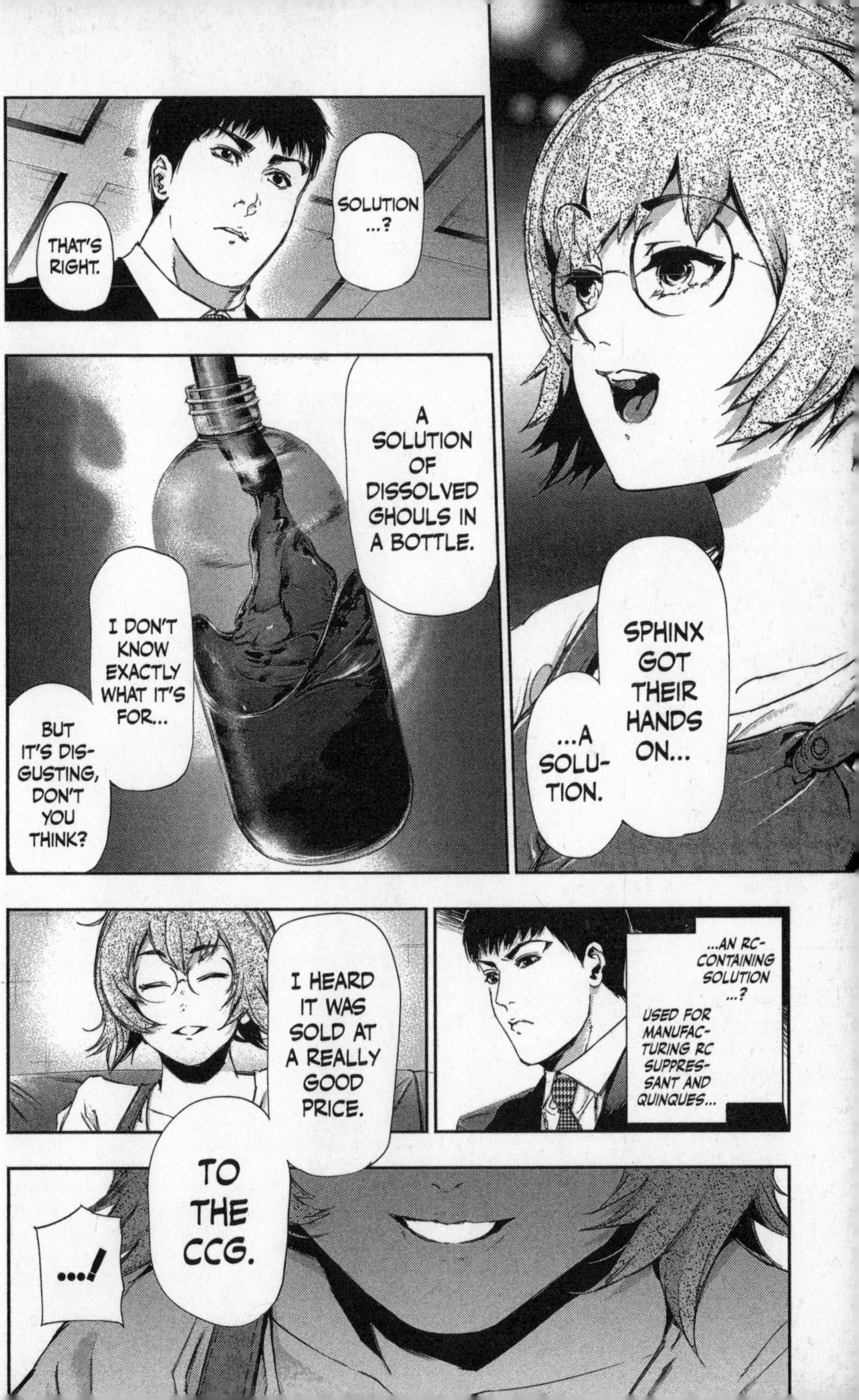
SPHINX GOT THEIR HANDS ON...
...A SOLUTION.
SOLUTION...?
THAT'S RIGHT.
A SOLUTION OF DISSOLVED GHOULS IN A BOTTLE.
I DON'T KNOW EXACTLY WHAT IT'S FOR...
BUT IT'S DISGUSTING, DON'T YOU THINK?
...AN RC-CONTAINING SOLUTION...?
USED FOR MANUFACTURING RC SUPPRESSANT AND QUINQUES...
I HEARD IT WAS SOLD AT A REALLY GOOD PRICE.
TO THE CCG.
...!

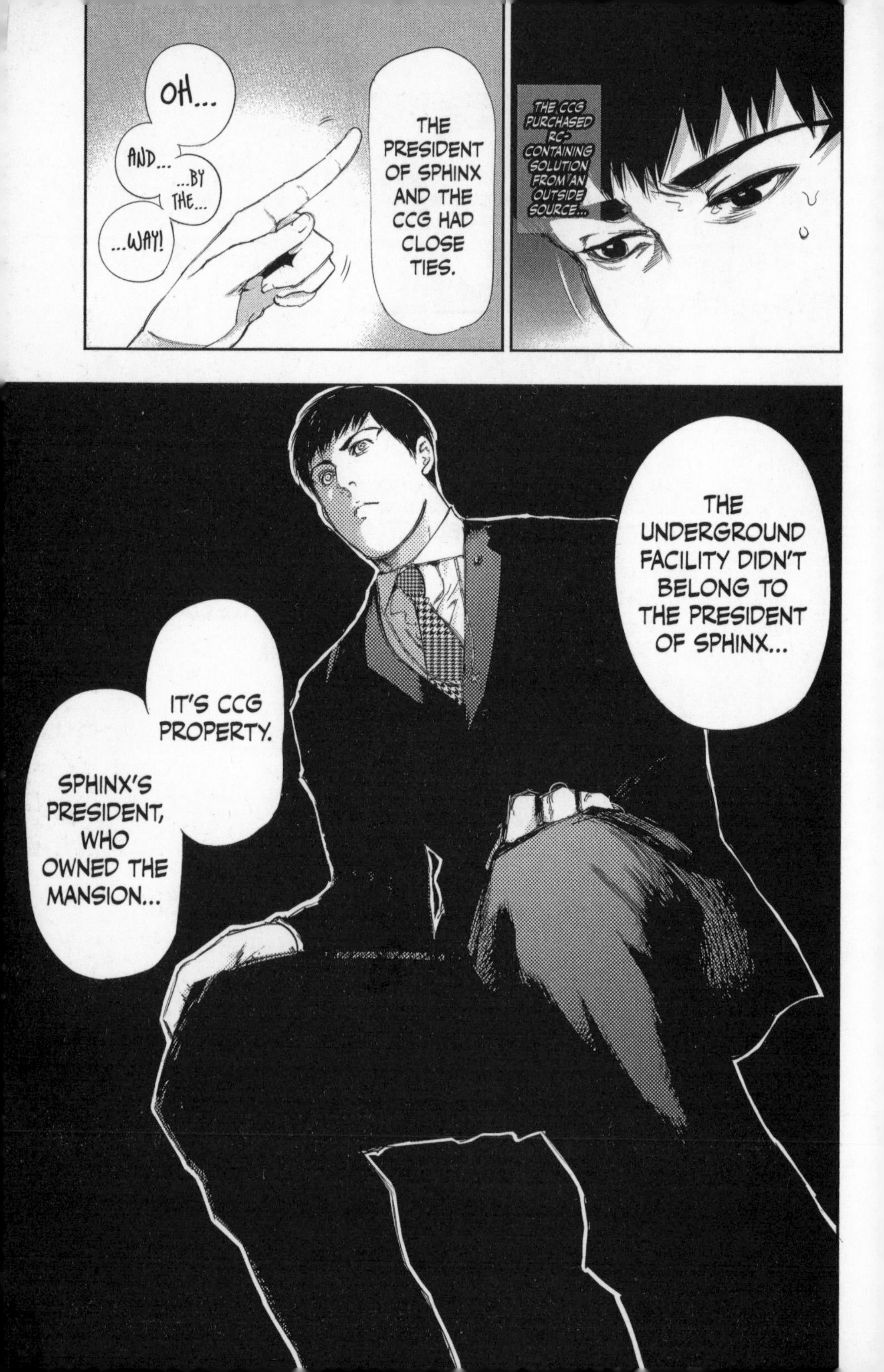
THE CCG PURCHASED RC-CONTAINING SOLUTION FROM AN OUTSIDE SOURCE...
THE PRESIDENT OF SPHINX AND THE CCG HAD CLOSE TIES.
OH...
AND... ...BY THE... ...WAY!
THE UNDERGROUND FACILITY DIDN'T BELONG TO THE PRESIDENT OF SPHINX...
IT'S CCG PROPERTY.
SPHINX'S PRESIDENT, WHO OWNED THE MANSION...

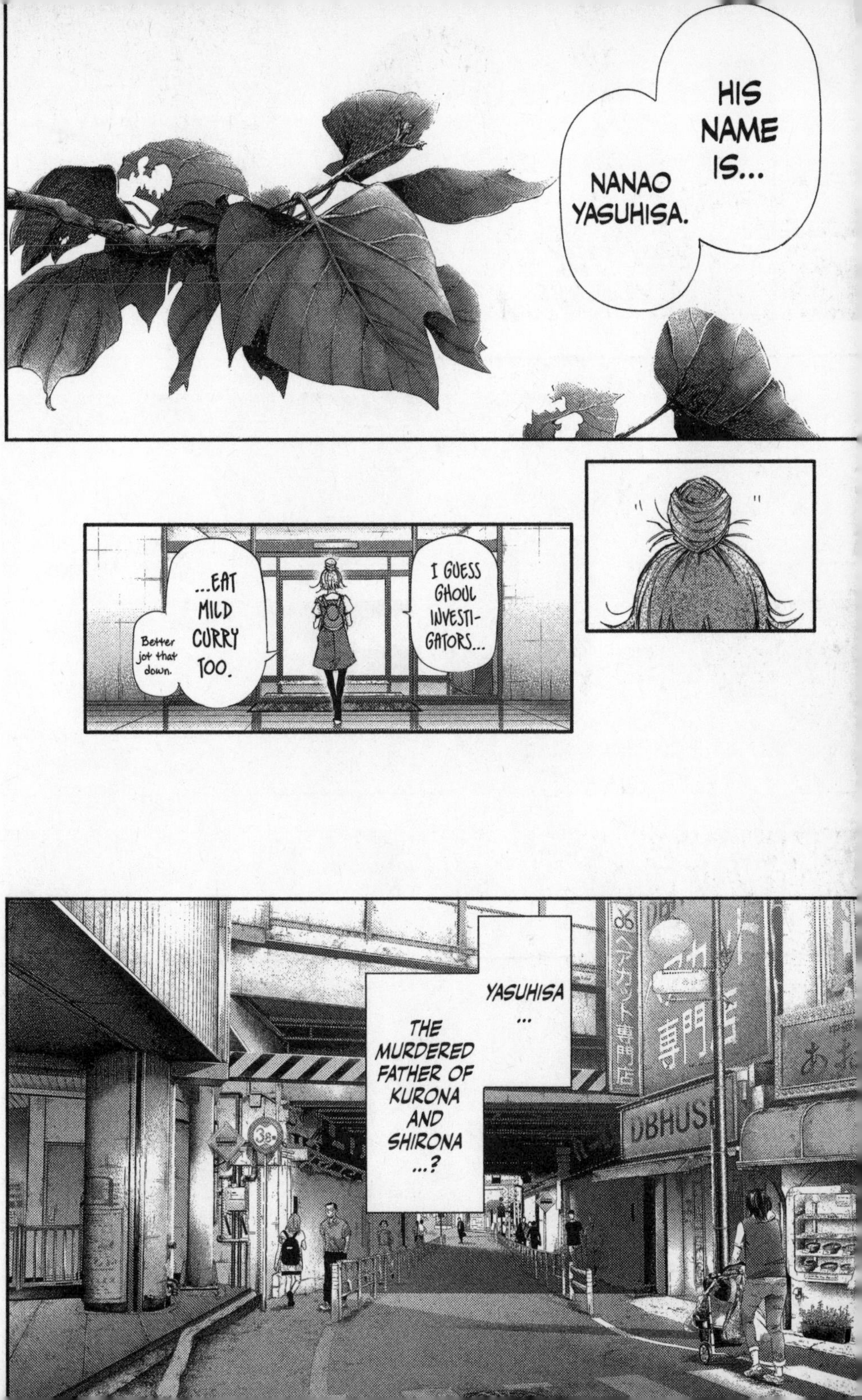
HIS NAME IS...
NANAO YASUHISA.
I GUESS GHOUL INVESTIGATORS...
...EAT MILD CURRY TOO.
Better jot that down.
YASUHISA...
THE MURDERED FATHER OF KURONA AND SHIRONA...?

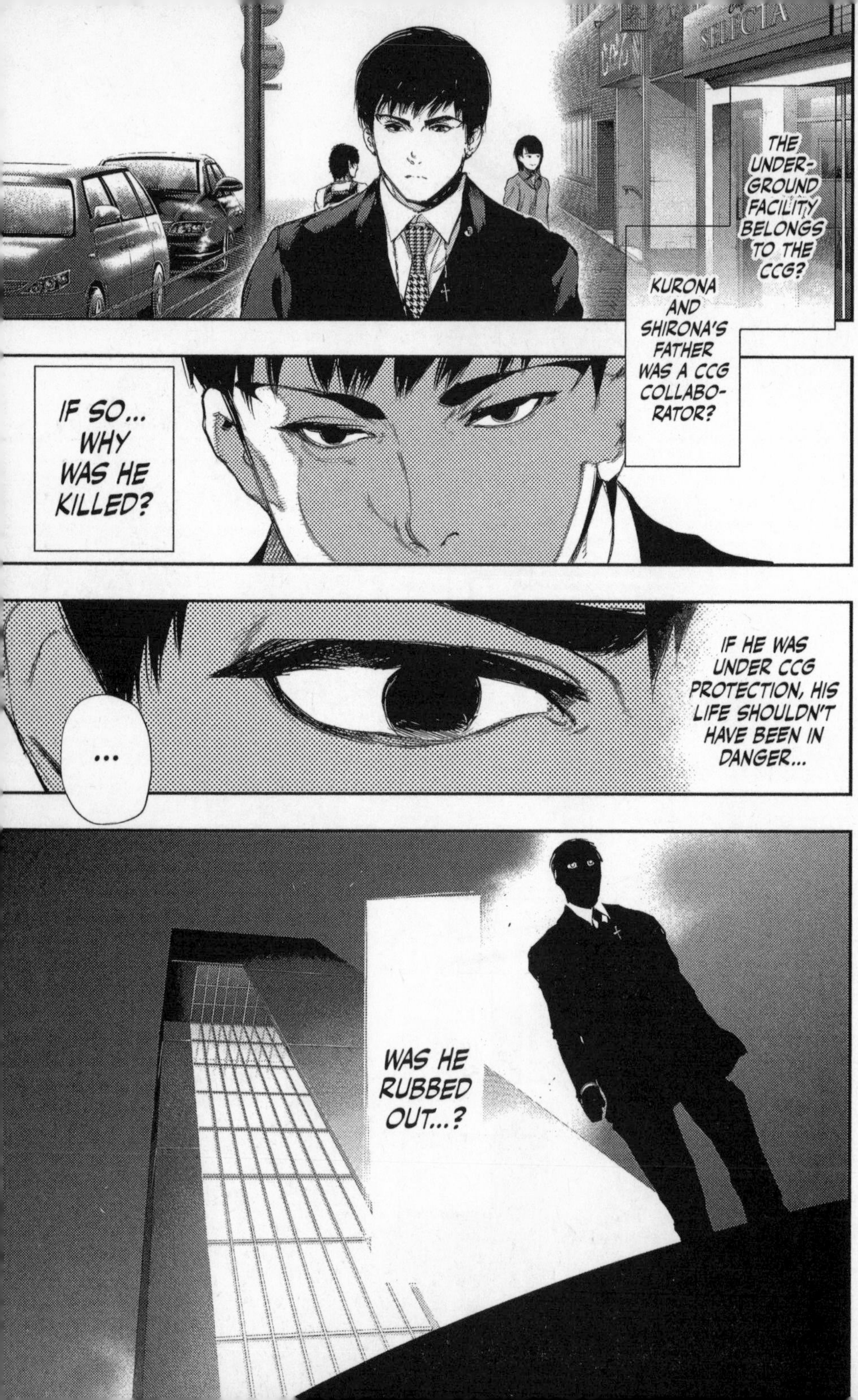
THE UNDER-GROUND FACILITY BELONGS TO THE CCG?
KURONA AND SHIRONA'S FATHER WAS A CCG COLLABO-RATOR?
IF SO... WHY WAS HE KILLED?
IF HE WAS UNDER CCG PROTECTION, HIS LIFE SHOULDN'T HAVE BEEN IN DANGER...
...
WAS HE RUBBED OUT...?

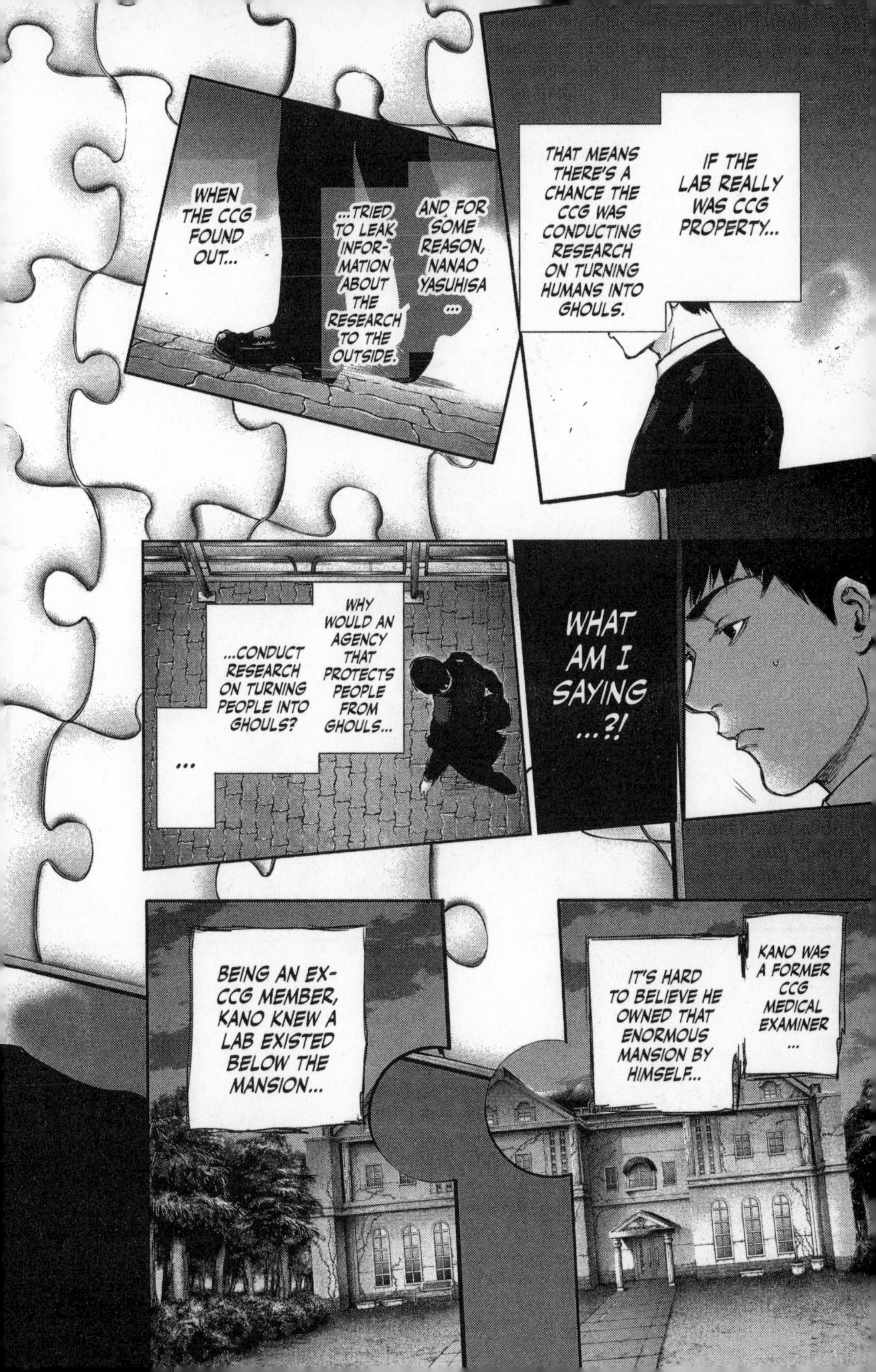
IF THE LAB REALLY WAS CCG PROPERTY...
THAT MEANS THERE'S A CHANCE THE CCG WAS CONDUCTING RESEARCH ON TURNING HUMANS INTO GHOULS.
AND FOR SOME REASON, NANAO YASUHISA...
...TRIED TO LEAK INFORMATION ABOUT THE RESEARCH TO THE OUTSIDE.
WHEN THE CCG FOUND OUT...
WHAT AM I SAYING...?!
WHY WOULD AN AGENCY THAT PROTECTS PEOPLE FROM GHOULS...
...CONDUCT RESEARCH ON TURNING PEOPLE INTO GHOULS?
...
KANO WAS A FORMER CCG MEDICAL EXAMINER...
IT'S HARD TO BELIEVE HE OWNED THAT ENORMOUS MANSION BY HIMSELF...
BEING AN EX-CCG MEMBER, KANO KNEW A LAB EXISTED BELOW THE MANSION...

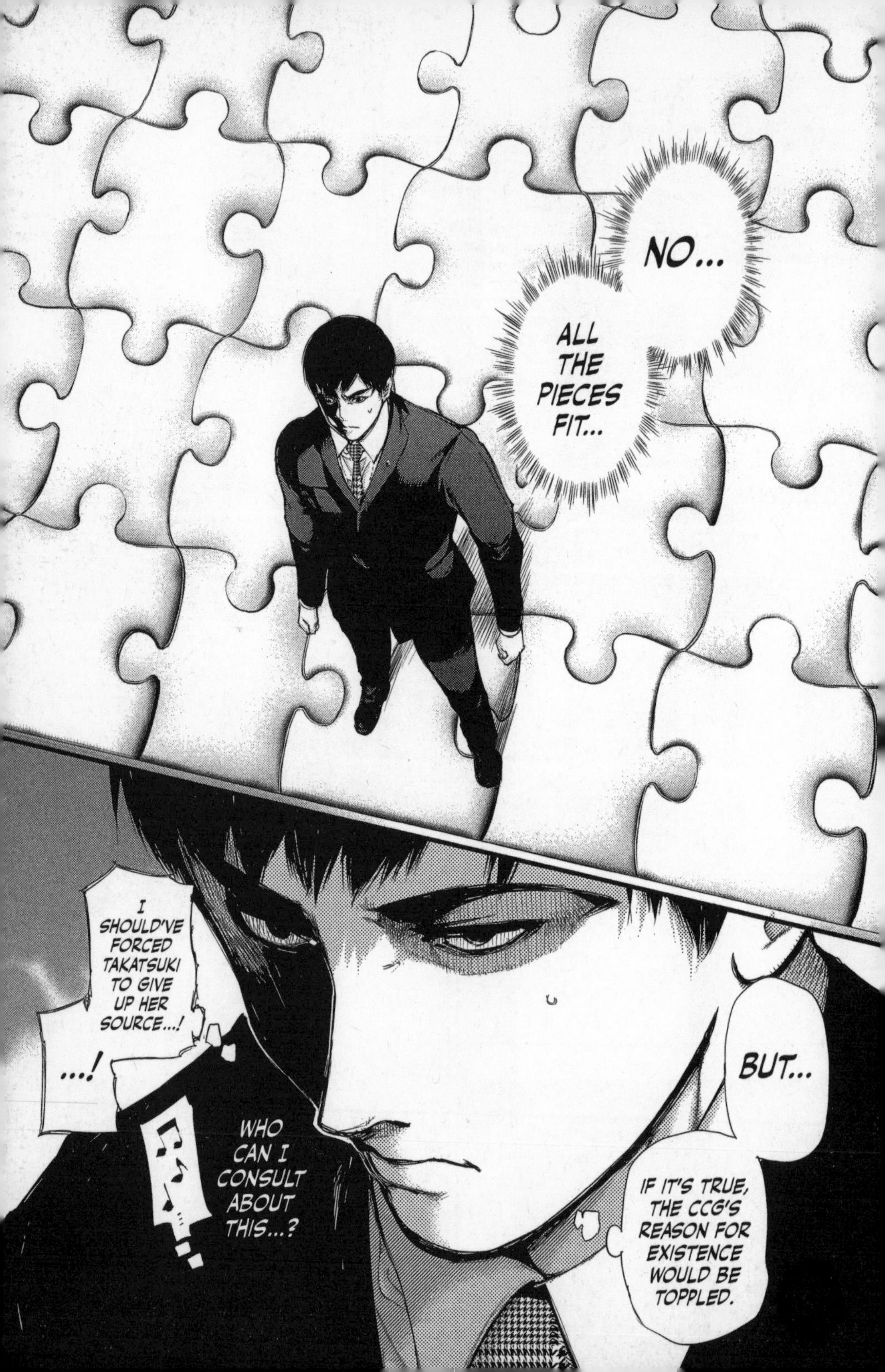
NO...
ALL THE PIECES FIT...
BUT...
IF IT'S TRUE, THE CCG'S REASON FOR EXISTENCE WOULD BE TOPPLED.
I SHOULD'VE FORCED TAKATSUKI TO GIVE UP HER SOURCE...!
...!
WHO CAN I CONSULT ABOUT THIS...?

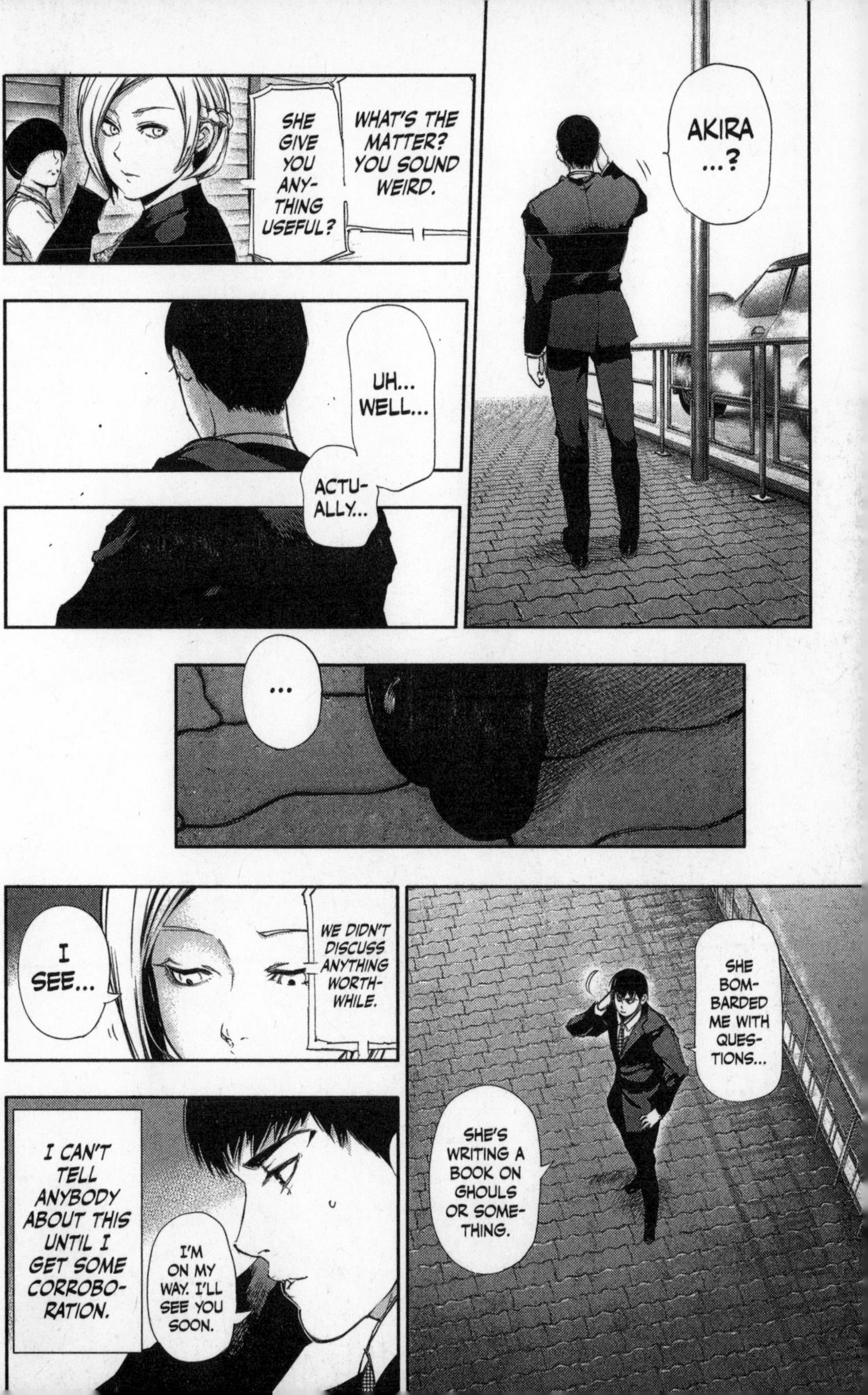
AKIRA ...?
WHAT'S THE MATTER? YOU SOUND WEIRD.
SHE GIVE YOU ANYTHING USEFUL?
UH... WELL...
ACTUALLY...
...
SHE BOMBARDED ME WITH QUESTIONS...
SHE'S WRITING A BOOK ON GHOULS OR SOMETHING.
WE DIDN'T DISCUSS ANYTHING WORTHWHILE.
I SEE...
I CAN'T TELL ANYBODY ABOUT THIS UNTIL I GET SOME CORROBORATION.
I'M ON MY WAY. I'LL SEE YOU SOON.

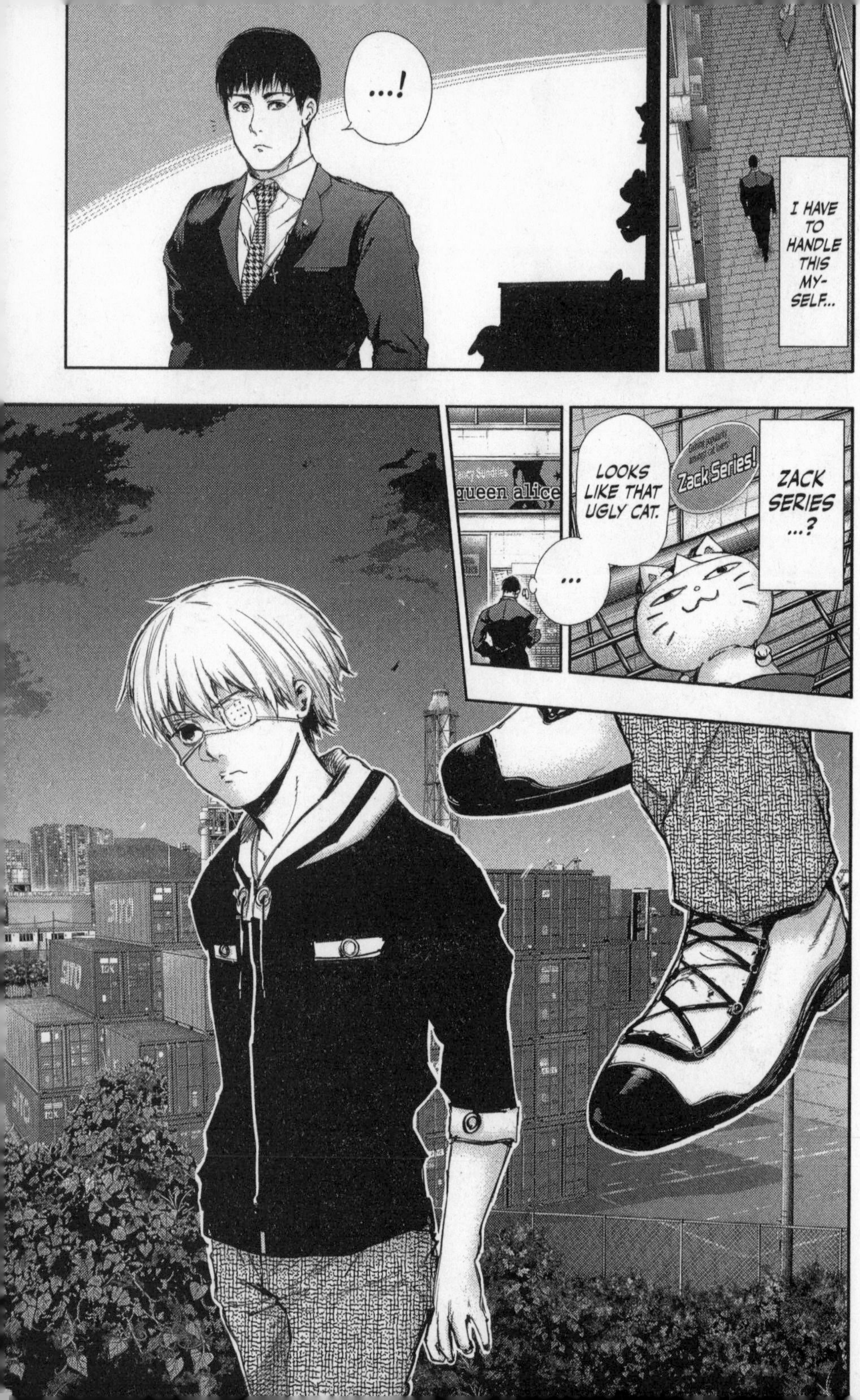
I HAVE TO HANDLE THIS MY-SELF...
...!
ZACK SERIES ...?
Zack Series!
LOOKS LIKE THAT UGLY CAT.
queen alice
...

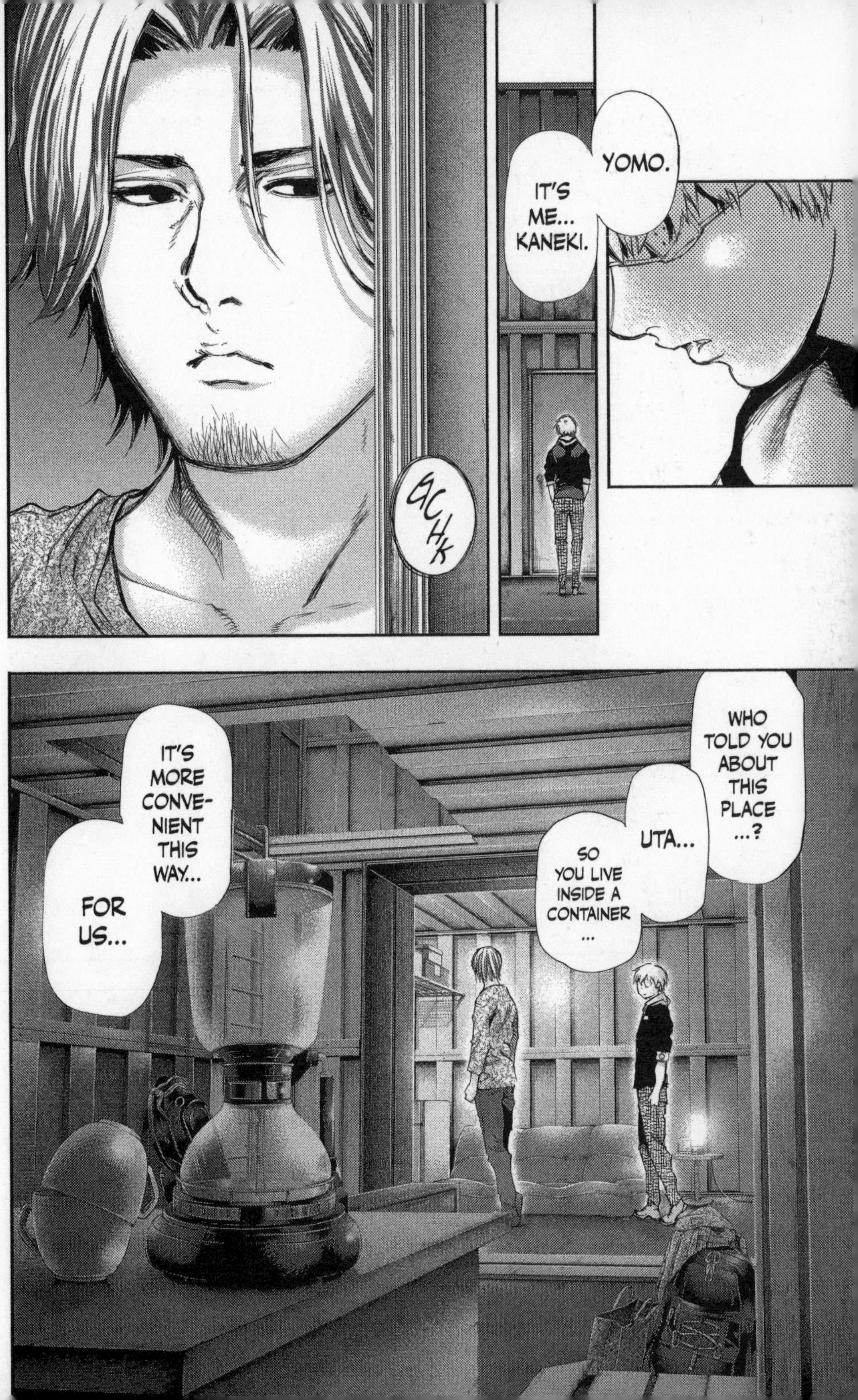
YOMO.
IT'S ME... KANEKI.
GCHK
WHO TOLD YOU ABOUT THIS PLACE ...?
UTA...
SO YOU LIVE INSIDE A CONTAINER ...
IT'S MORE CONVE-NIENT THIS WAY...
FOR US...

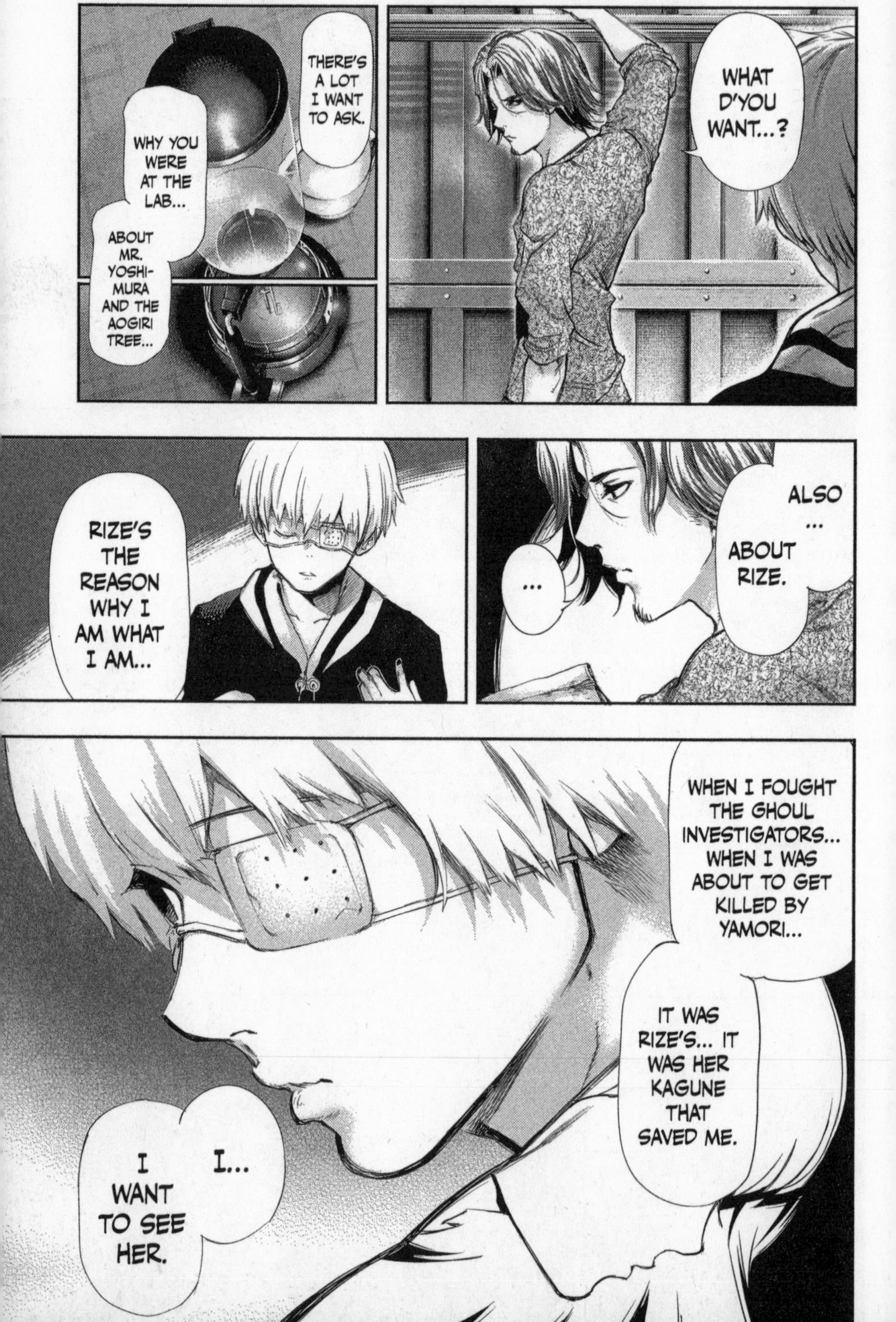
WHAT D'YOU WANT...?
THERE'S A LOT I WANT TO ASK.
WHY YOU WERE AT THE LAB...
ABOUT MR. YOSHI-MURA AND THE AOGIRI TREE...
ALSO ... ABOUT RIZE.
...
RIZE'S THE REASON WHY I AM WHAT I AM...
WHEN I FOUGHT THE GHOUL INVESTIGATORS... WHEN I WAS ABOUT TO GET KILLED BY YAMORI...
IT WAS RIZE'S... IT WAS HER KAGUNE THAT SAVED ME.
I...
I WANT TO SEE HER.

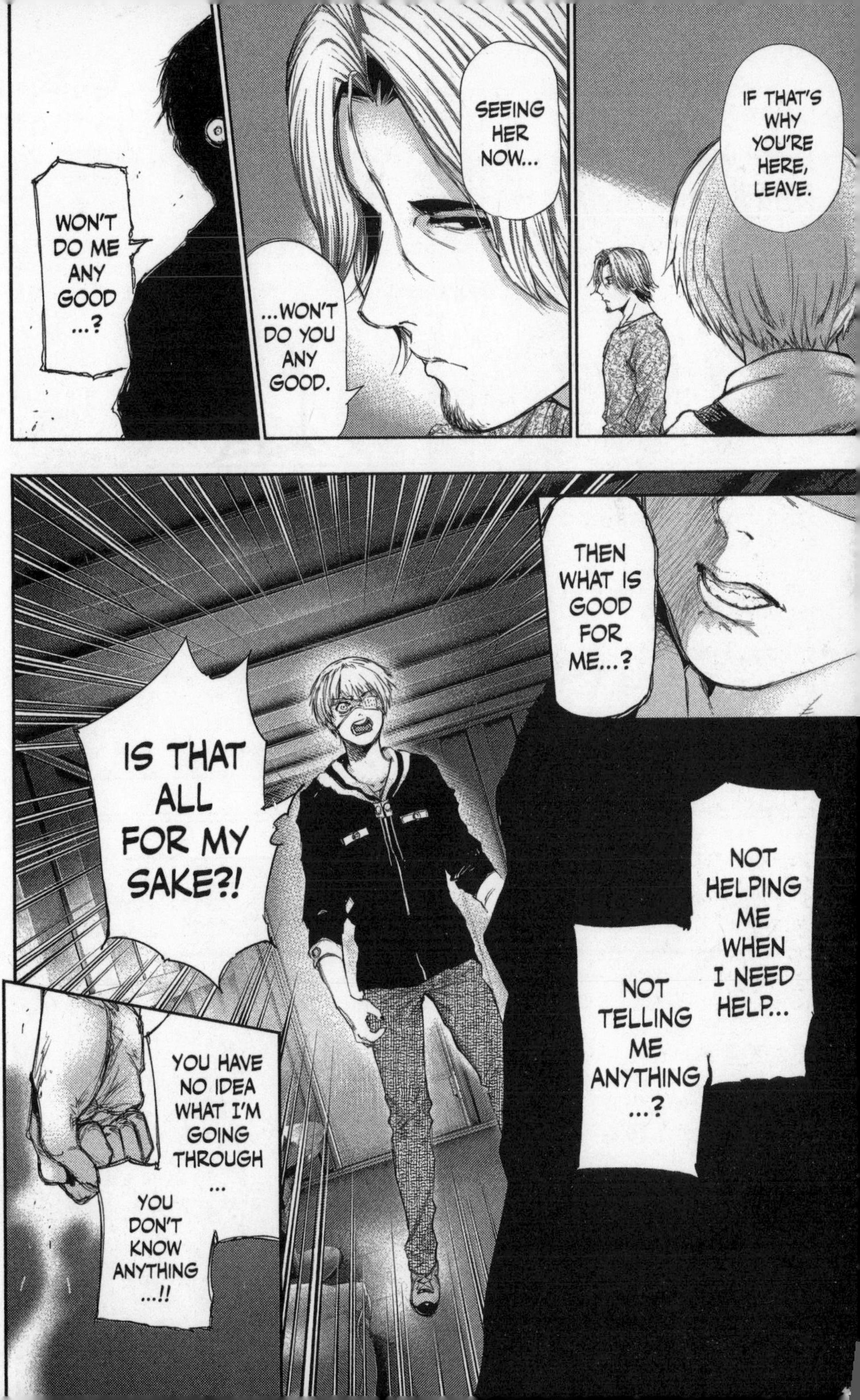
IF THAT'S WHY YOU'RE HERE, LEAVE.
SEEING HER NOW...
...WON'T DO YOU ANY GOOD.
WON'T DO ME ANY GOOD...?
THEN WHAT IS GOOD FOR ME...?
NOT HELPING ME WHEN I NEED HELP...
NOT TELLING ME ANYTHING...?
IS THAT ALL FOR MY SAKE?!
YOU HAVE NO IDEA WHAT I'M GOING THROUGH...
YOU DON'T KNOW ANYTHING...!!

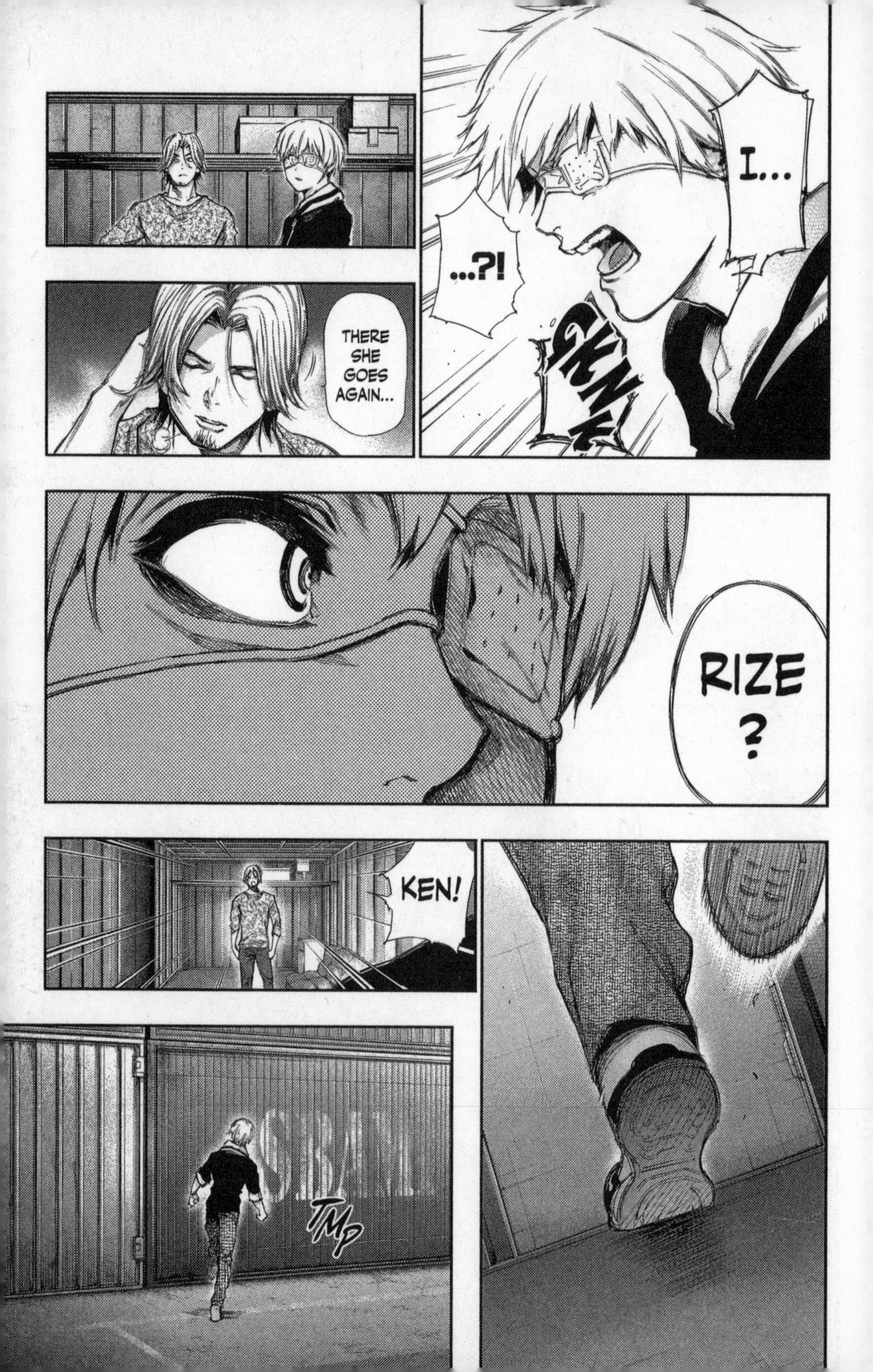
I...
...?!
GKNK
THERE SHE GOES AGAIN...
RIZE?
KEN!
TMP

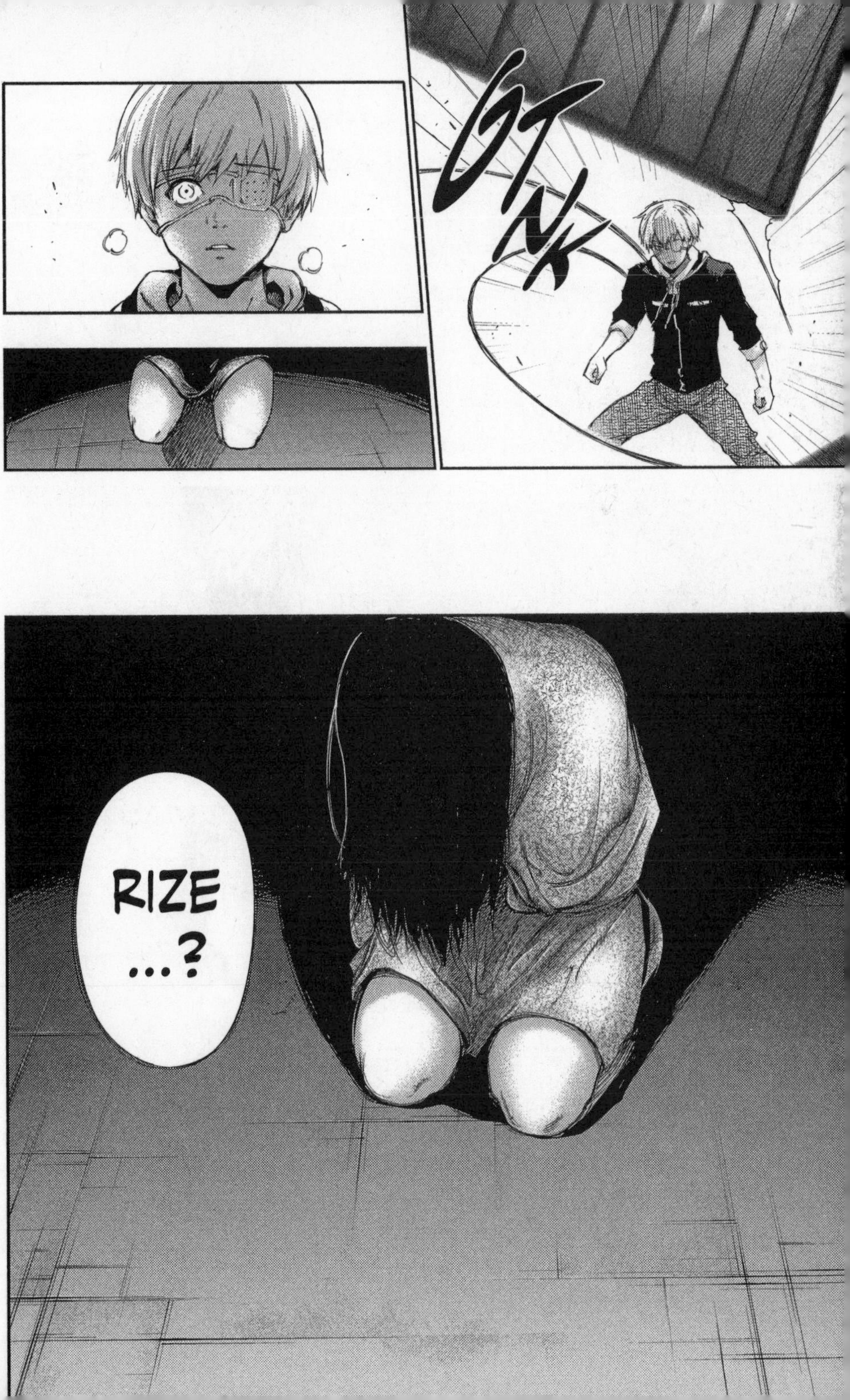
GINK
RIZE ...?

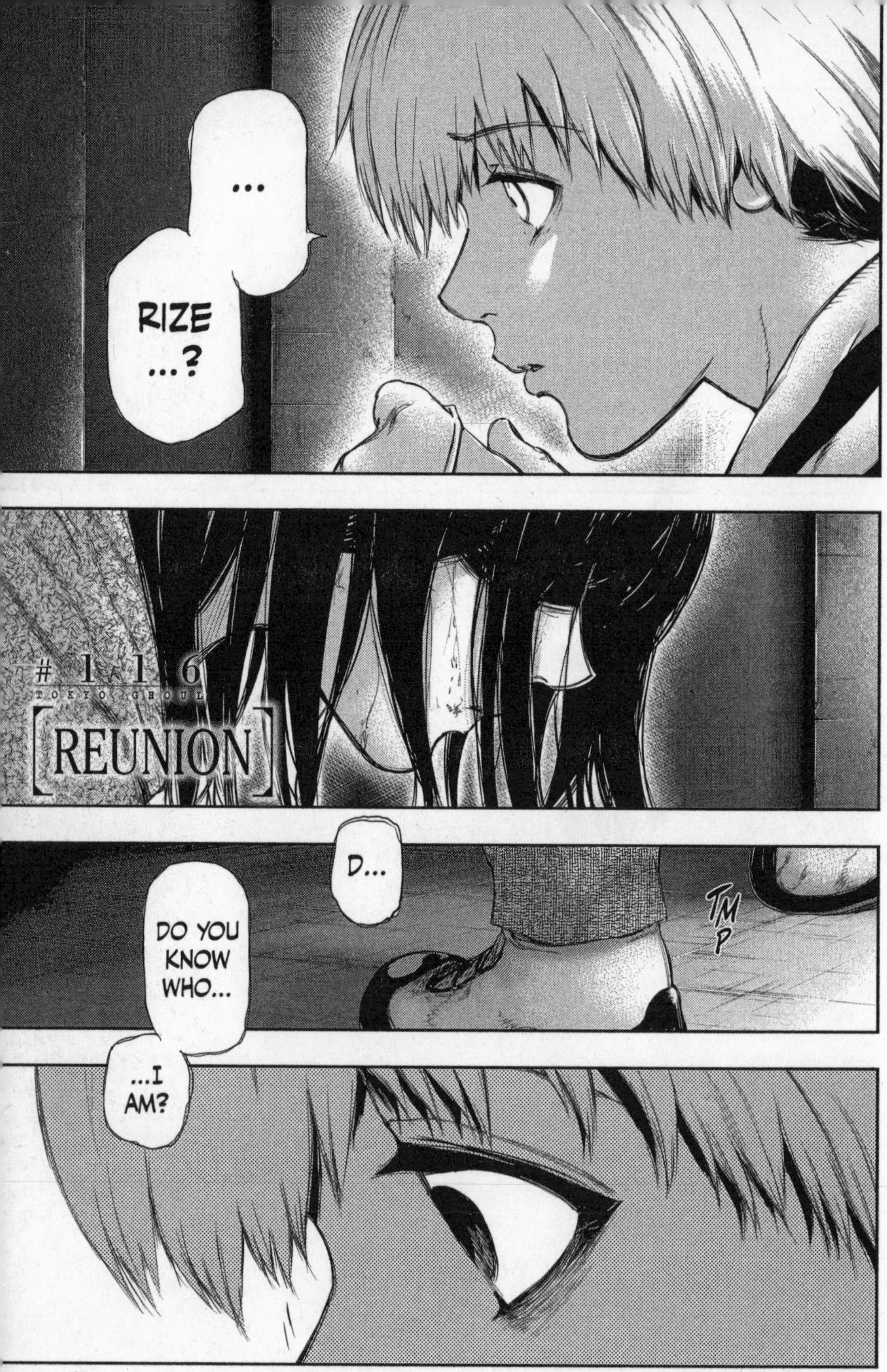
...
RIZE ...?
1 1 6
TOKYO GHOUL
[REUNION]
TMP
D...
DO YOU KNOW WHO...
...I AM?

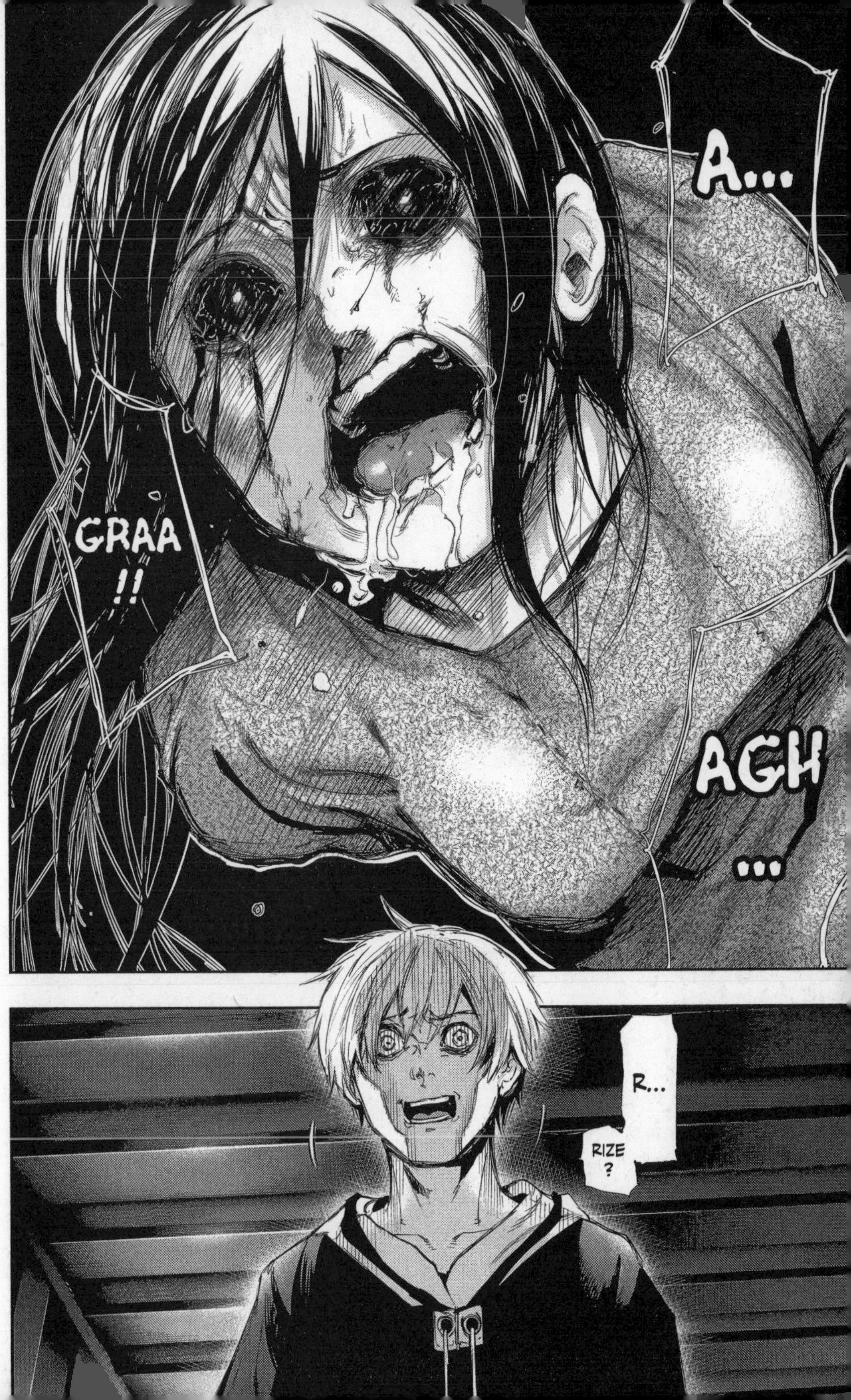
A...
AGH ...
GRAA !!
R...
RIZE ?

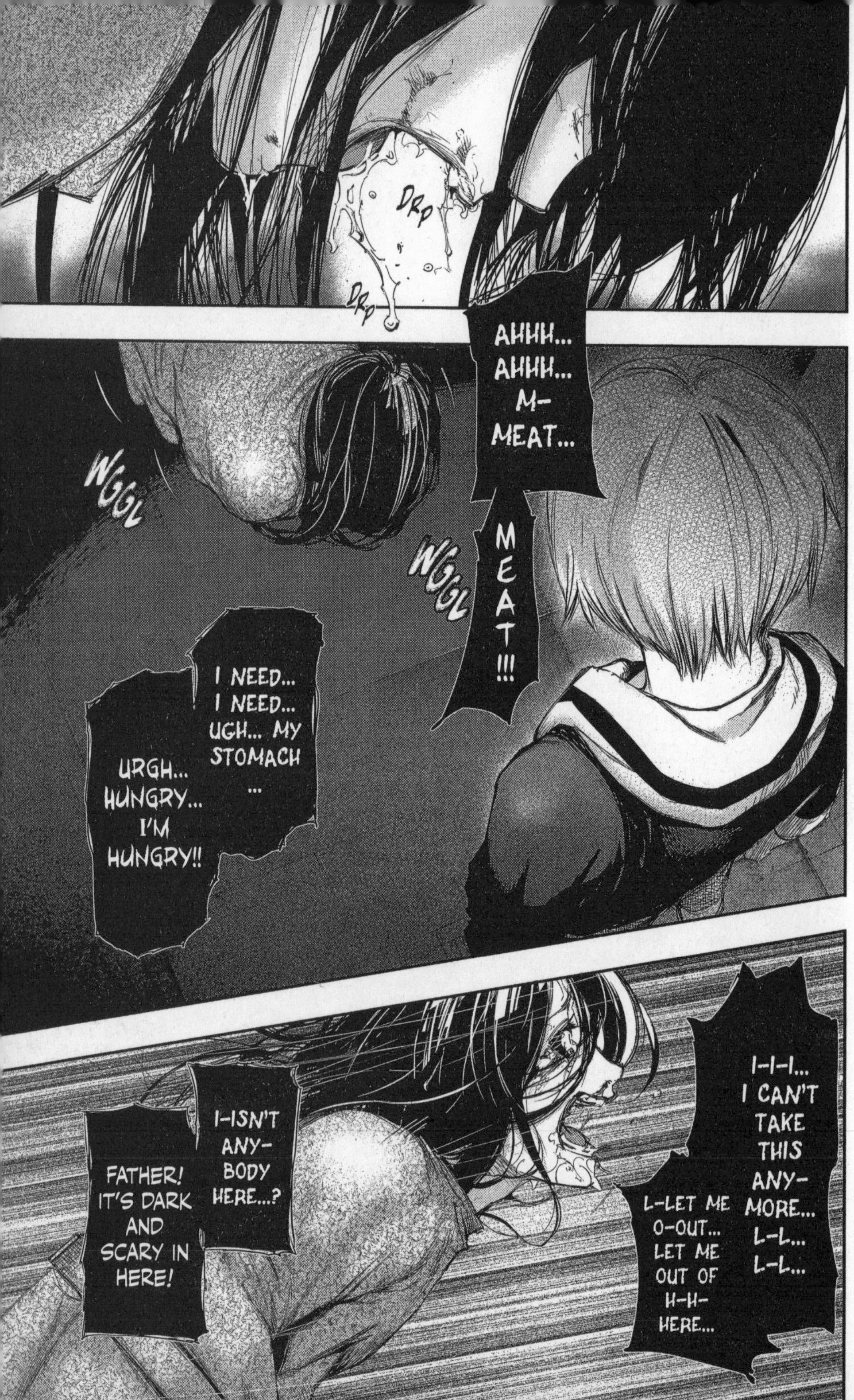
DRP
DRP
AHHH... AHHH... M-MEAT...
MEAT!!!
WGGL
WGGL
I NEED... I NEED... UGH... MY STOMACH ...
URGH... HUNGRY... I'M HUNGRY!!
I-I-I... I CAN'T TAKE THIS ANY-MORE... L-L... L-L...
L-LET ME O-OUT... LET ME OUT OF H-H-HERE...
I-ISN'T ANY-BODY HERE...?
FATHER! IT'S DARK AND SCARY IN HERE!

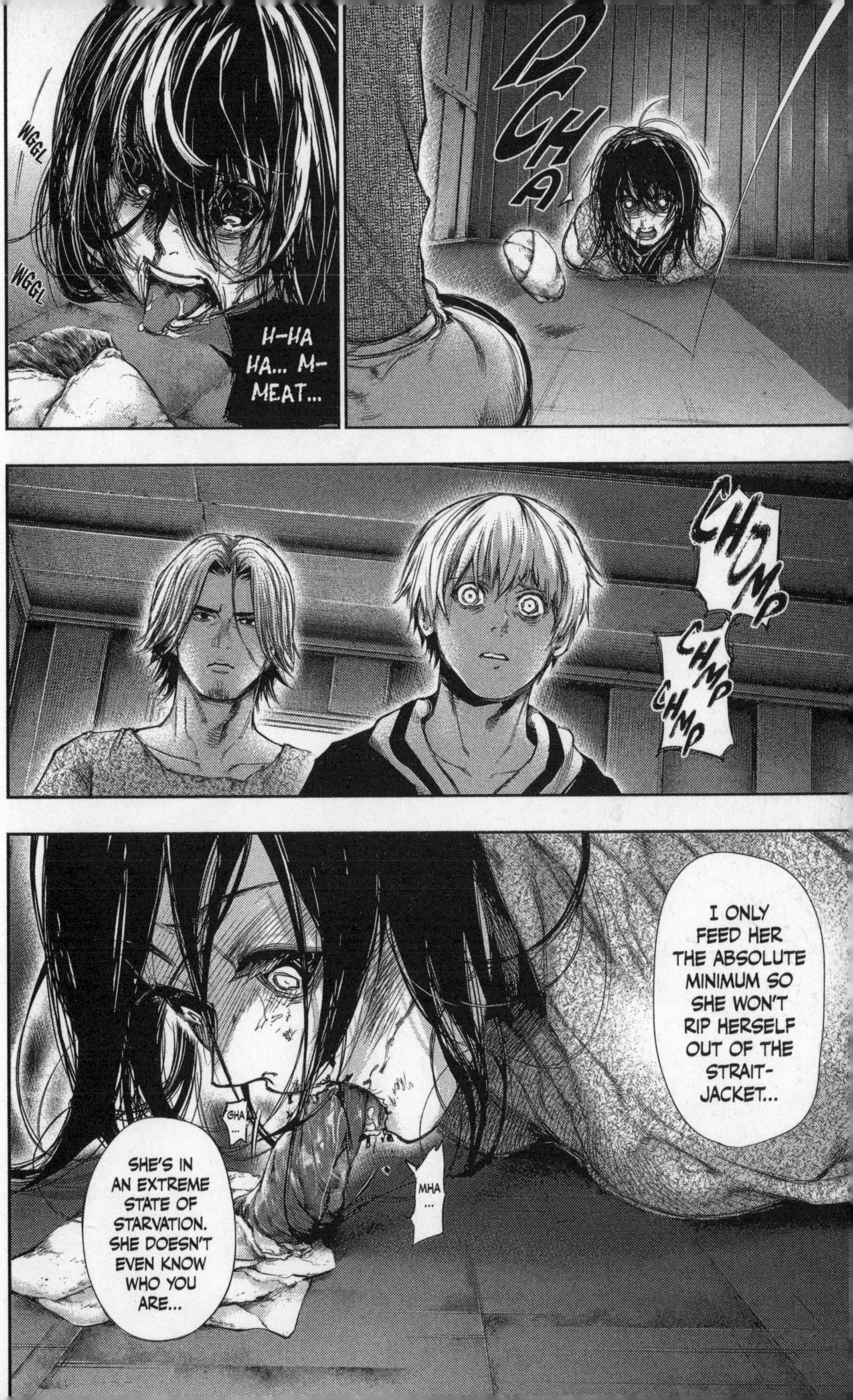
PICHA
WGGL
WGGL
H-HA HA... M-MEAT...
CHOMP
CHMP
CHMP
I ONLY FEED HER THE ABSOLUTE MINIMUM SO SHE WON'T RIP HERSELF OUT OF THE STRAIT-JACKET...
GHA...
MHA...
SHE'S IN AN EXTREME STATE OF STARVATION. SHE DOESN'T EVEN KNOW WHO YOU ARE...

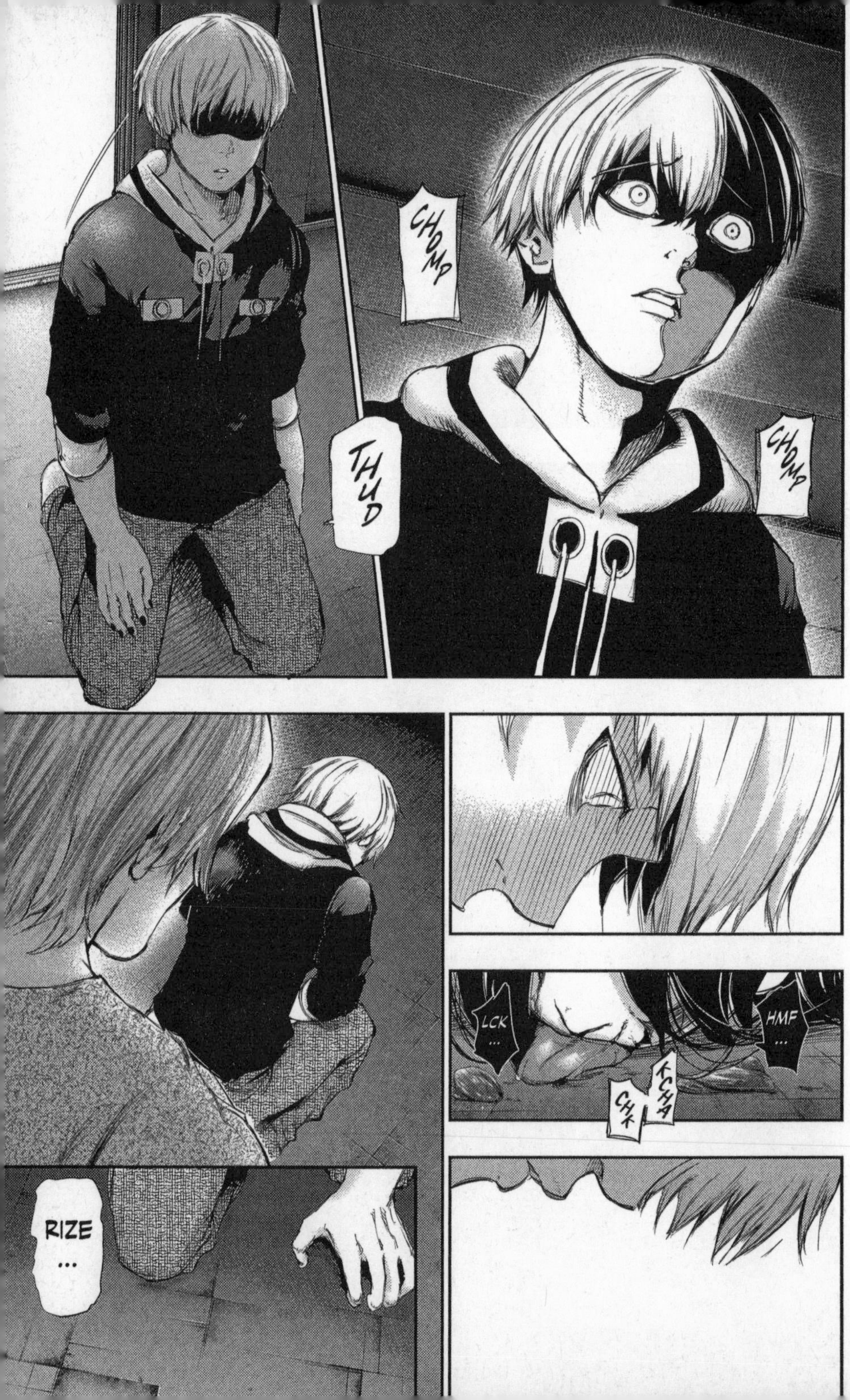
CHOMP
CHOMP
THUD
HMF ...
KCHA
CHK
LCK ...
RIZE ...

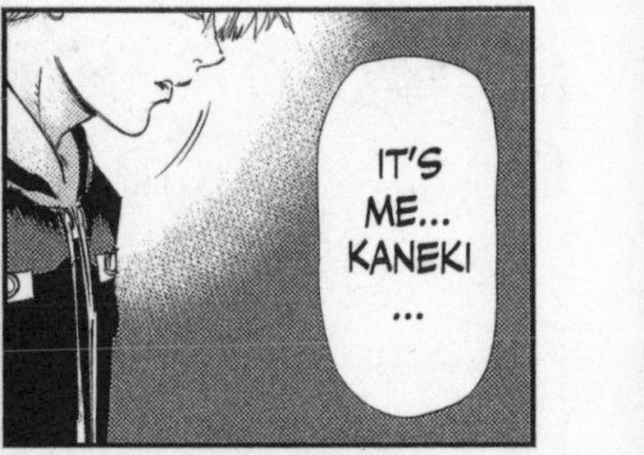
IT'S ME... KANEKI ...

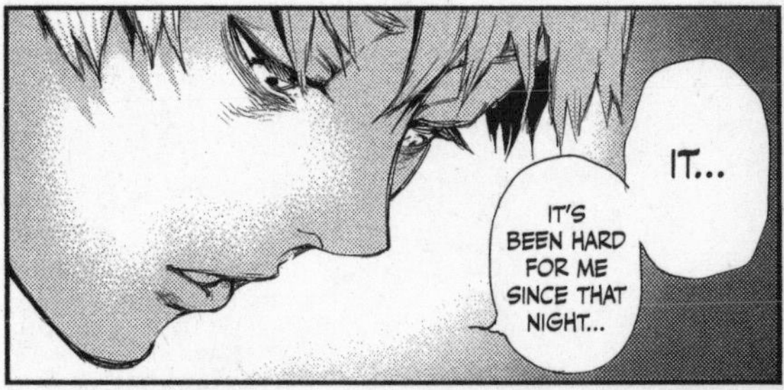
IT...
IT'S BEEN HARD FOR ME SINCE THAT NIGHT...

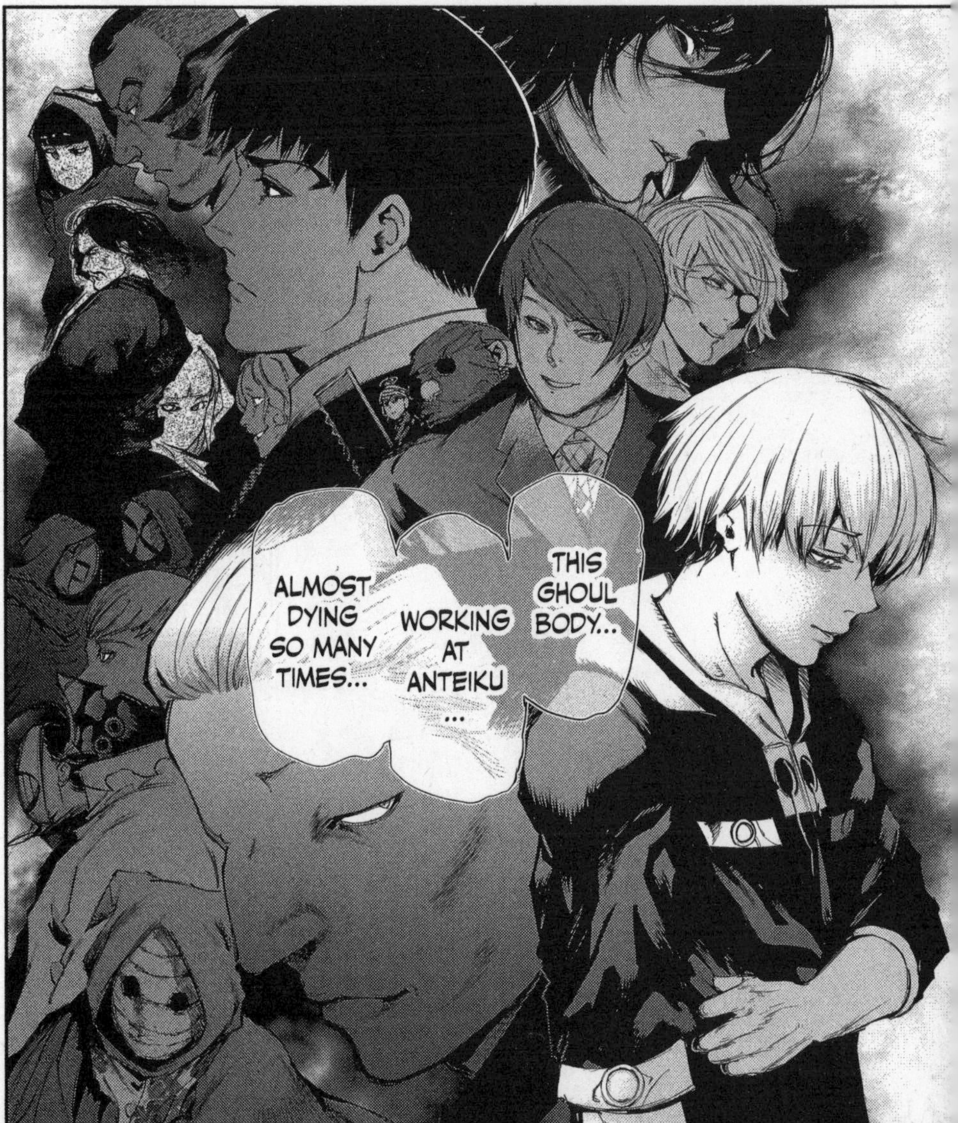
THIS GHOUL BODY...
WORKING AT ANTEIKU ...
ALMOST DYING SO MANY TIMES...

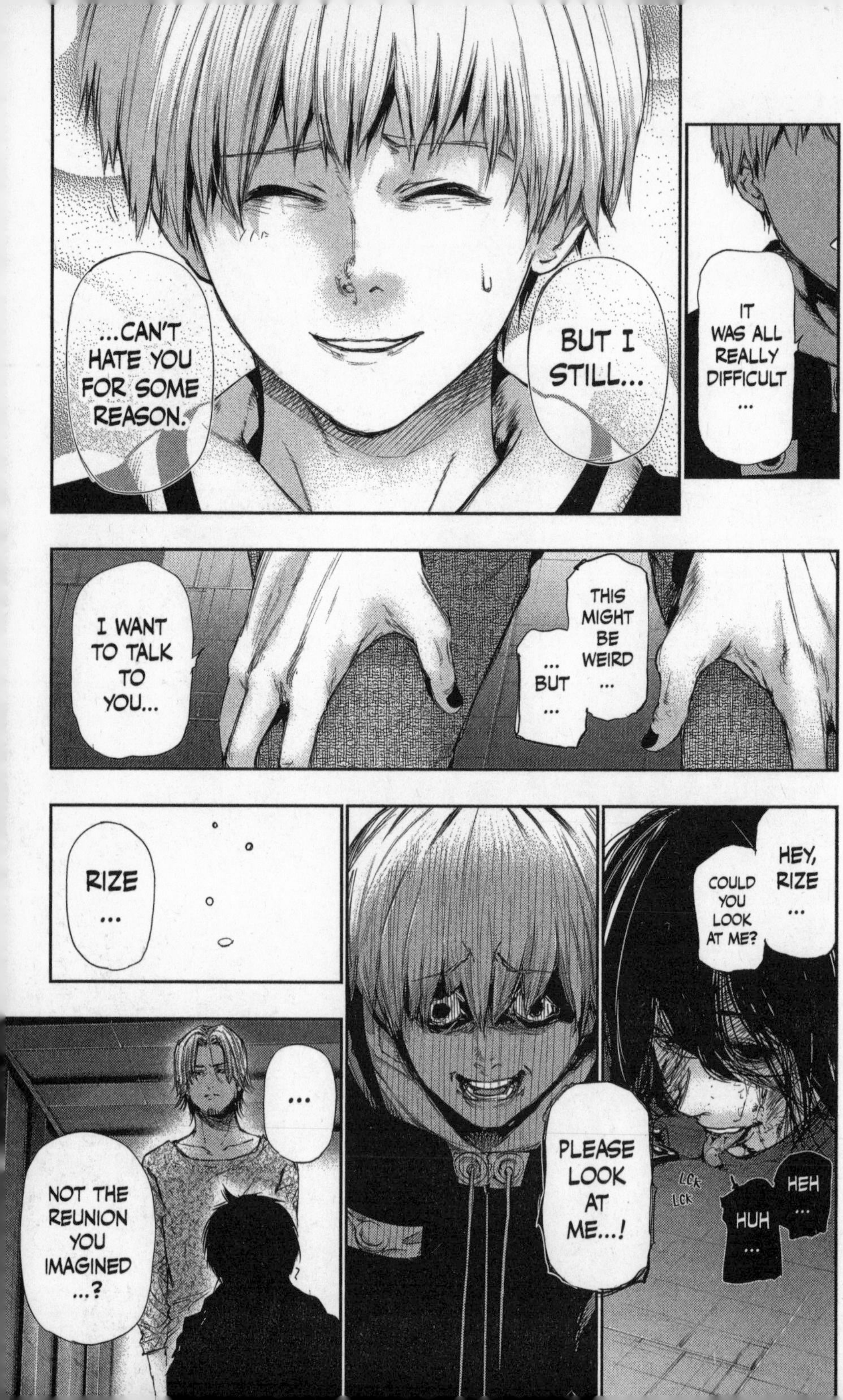
IT WAS ALL REALLY DIFFICULT ...
BUT I STILL...
...CAN'T HATE YOU FOR SOME REASON.
THIS MIGHT BE WEIRD ... BUT ...
I WANT TO TALK TO YOU...
HEY, RIZE ...
COULD YOU LOOK AT ME?
LCK LCK
HEH ...
HUH ...
PLEASE LOOK AT ME...!
RIZE ...
...
NOT THE REUNION YOU IMAGINED ...?

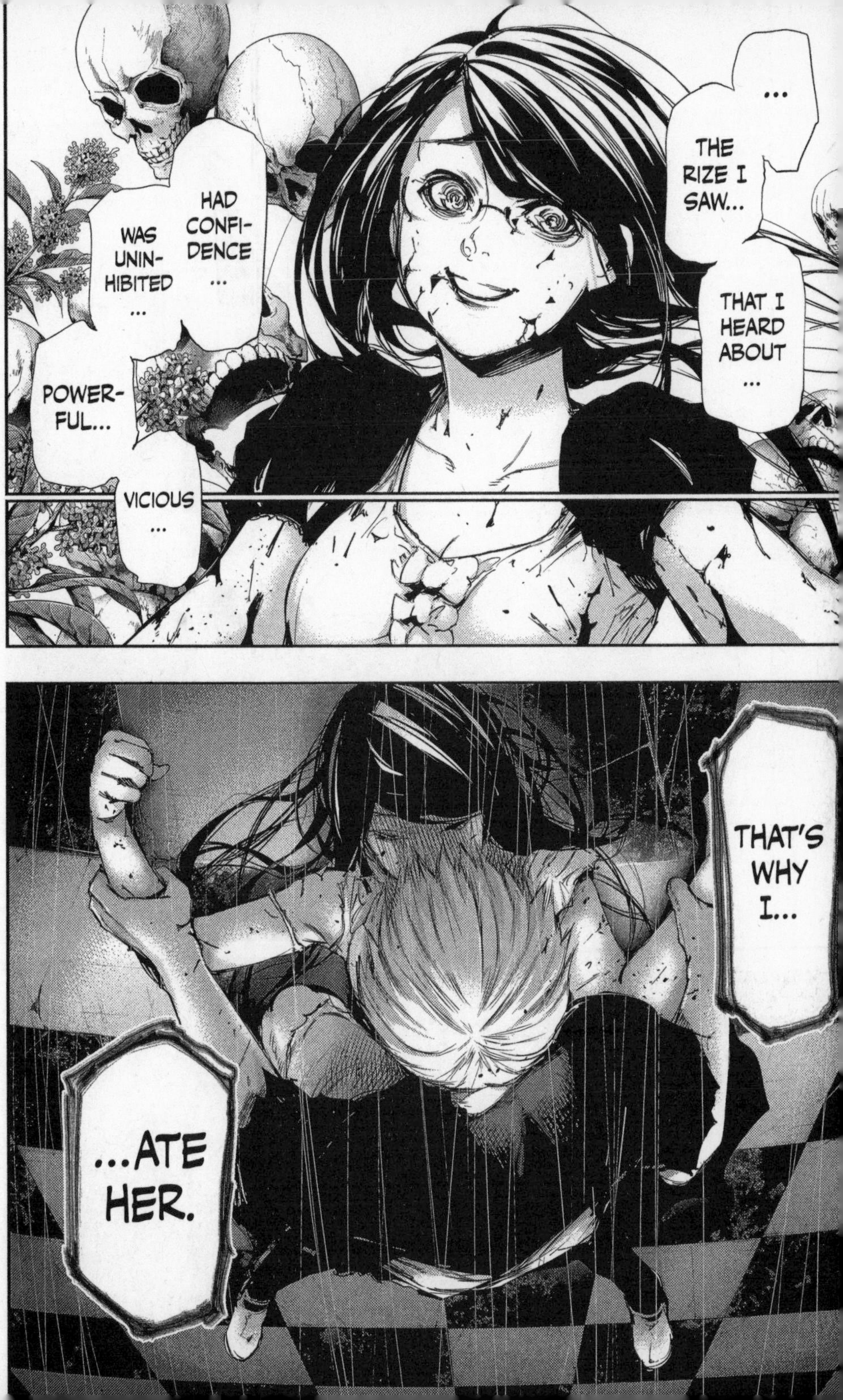
...
THE RIZE I SAW...
THAT I HEARD ABOUT ...
HAD CONFIDENCE ...
WAS UNINHIBITED ...
POWERFUL...
VICIOUS ...
THAT'S WHY I...
...ATE HER.

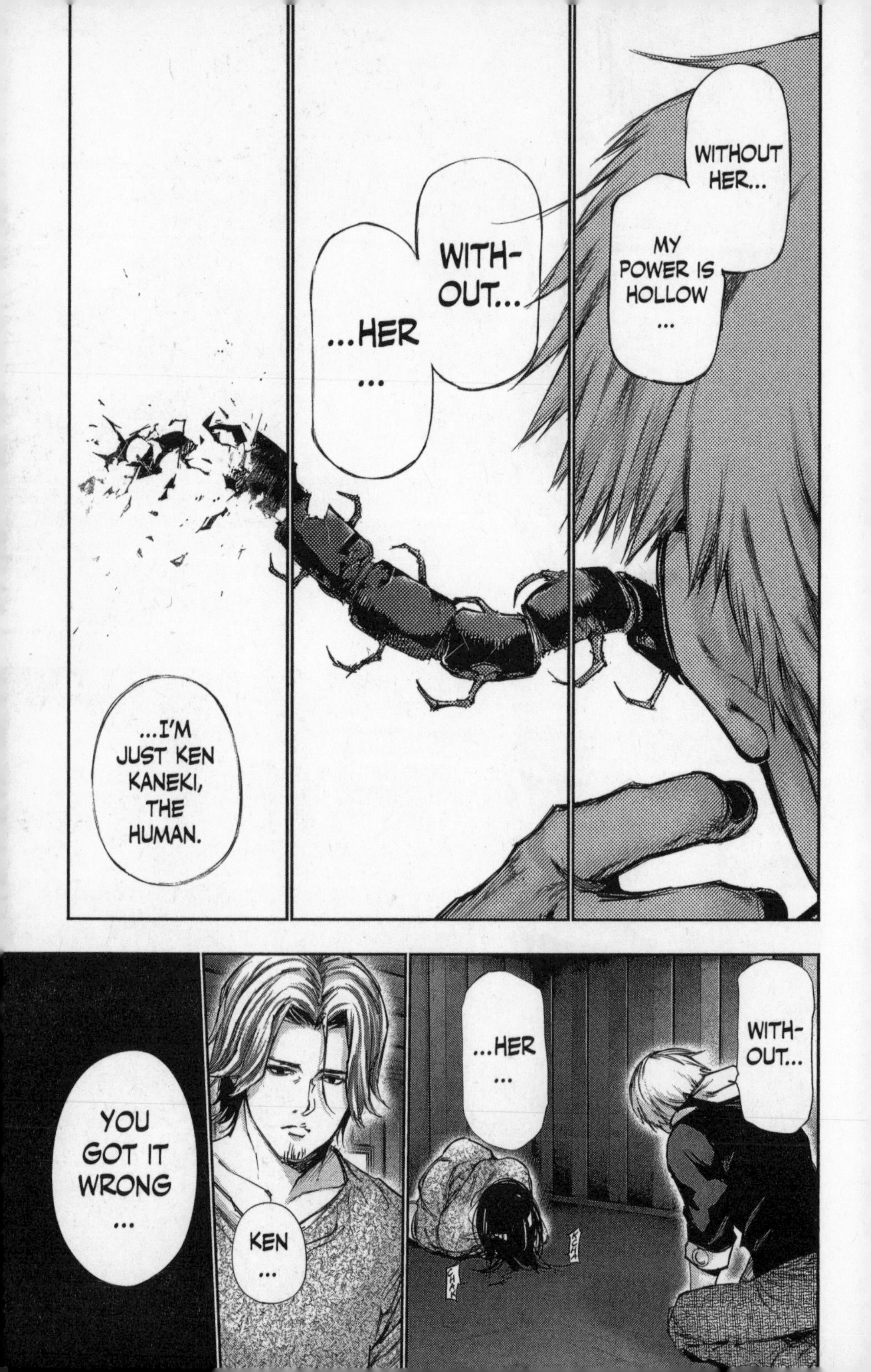
WITHOUT HER...
MY POWER IS HOLLOW ...
WITH-OUT...
...HER ...
...I'M JUST KEN KANEKI, THE HUMAN.
WITH-OUT...
...HER ...
KEN ...
YOU GOT IT WRONG ...

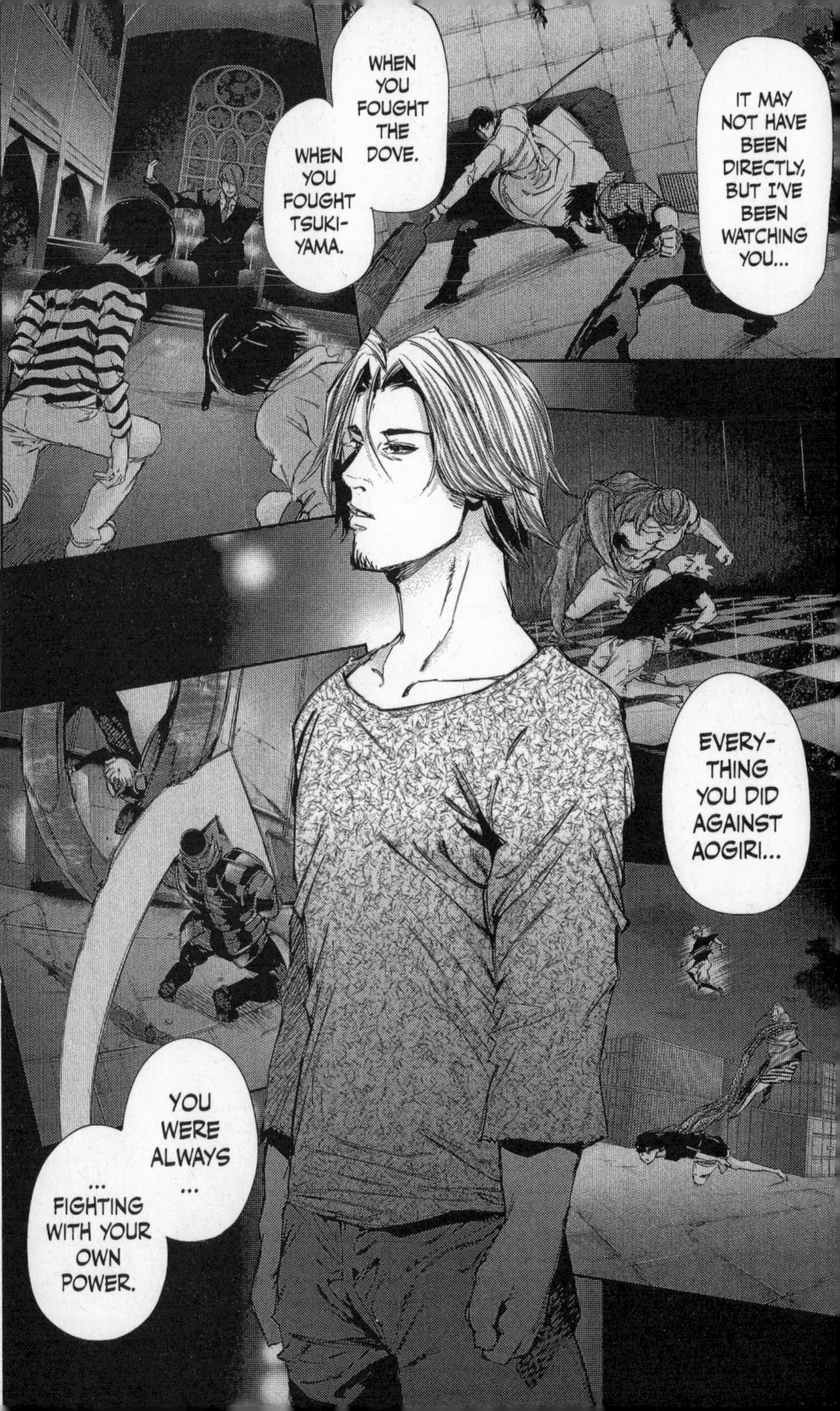
IT MAY NOT HAVE BEEN DIRECTLY, BUT I'VE BEEN WATCHING YOU...
WHEN YOU FOUGHT THE DOVE.
WHEN YOU FOUGHT TSUKI-YAMA.
EVERY-THING YOU DID AGAINST AOGIRI...
YOU WERE ALWAYS ...
... FIGHTING WITH YOUR OWN POWER.

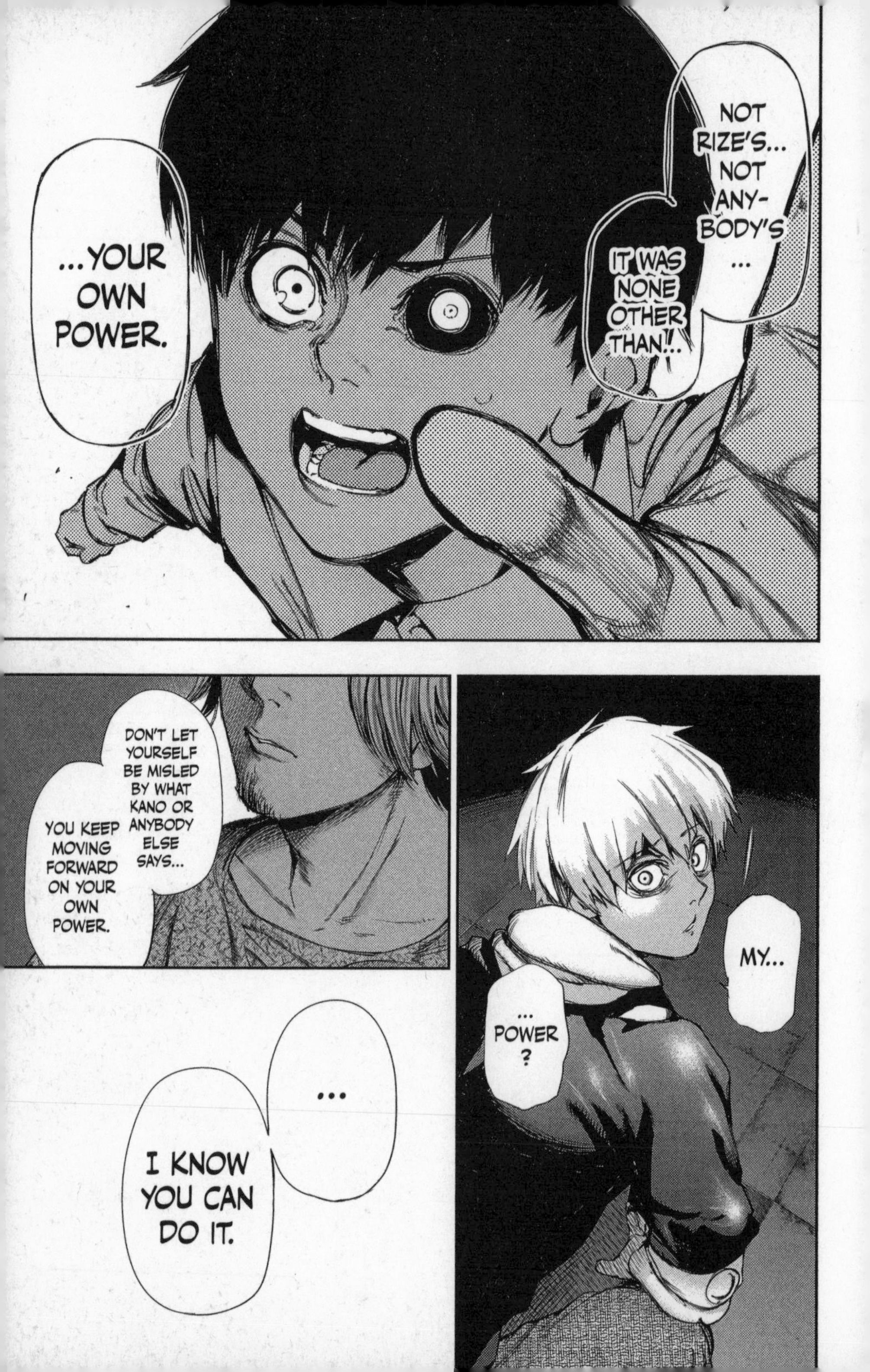
NOT RIZE'S... NOT ANY-BODY'S ...
IT WAS NONE OTHER THAN!!...
...YOUR OWN POWER.
MY...
...POWER?
DON'T LET YOURSELF BE MISLED BY WHAT KANO OR ANYBODY ELSE SAYS...
YOU KEEP MOVING FORWARD ON YOUR OWN POWER.
...
I KNOW YOU CAN DO IT.

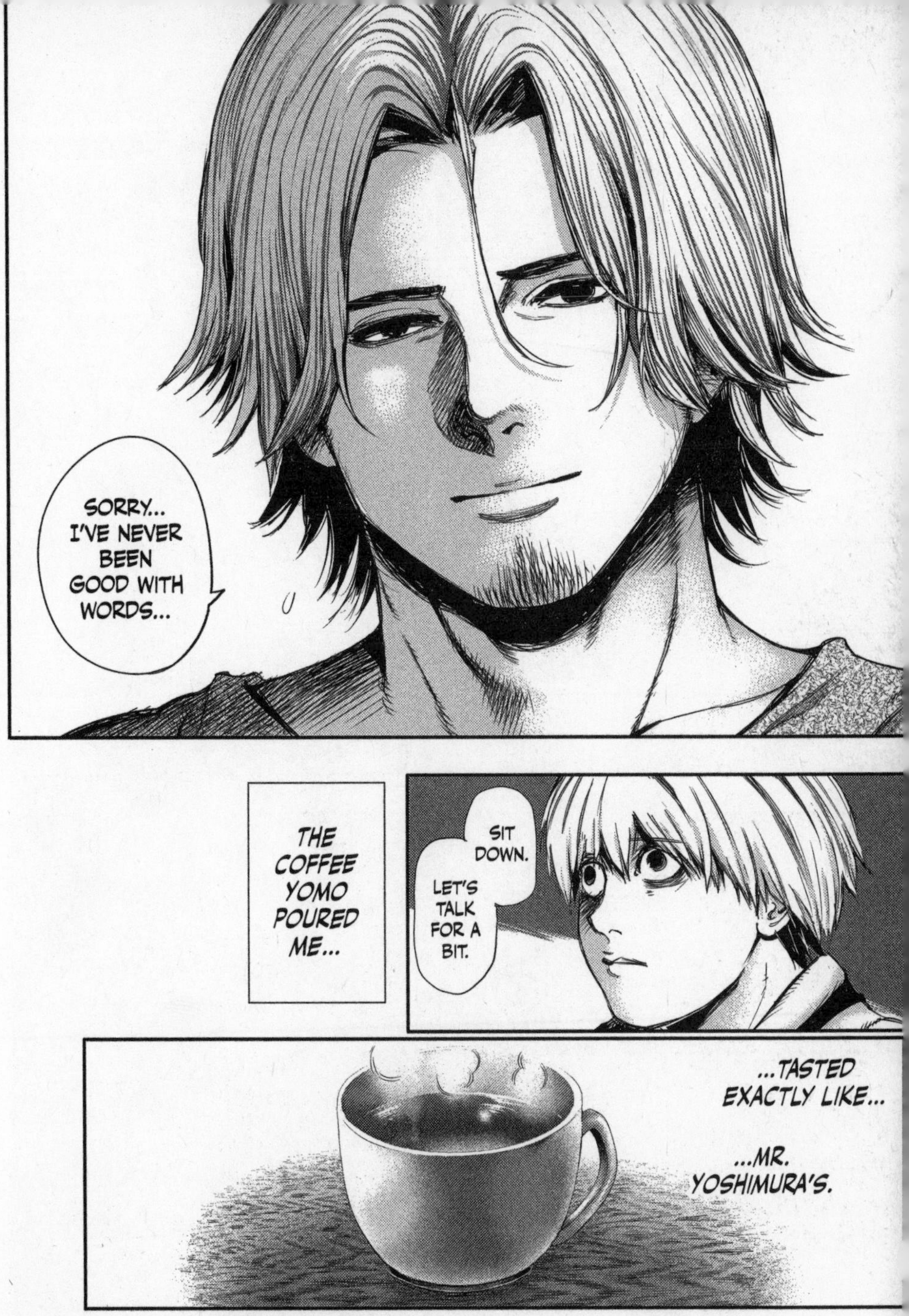
SORRY... I'VE NEVER BEEN GOOD WITH WORDS...
SIT DOWN.
LET'S TALK FOR A BIT.
THE COFFEE YOMO POURED ME...
...TASTED EXACTLY LIKE...
...MR. YOSHIMURA'S.

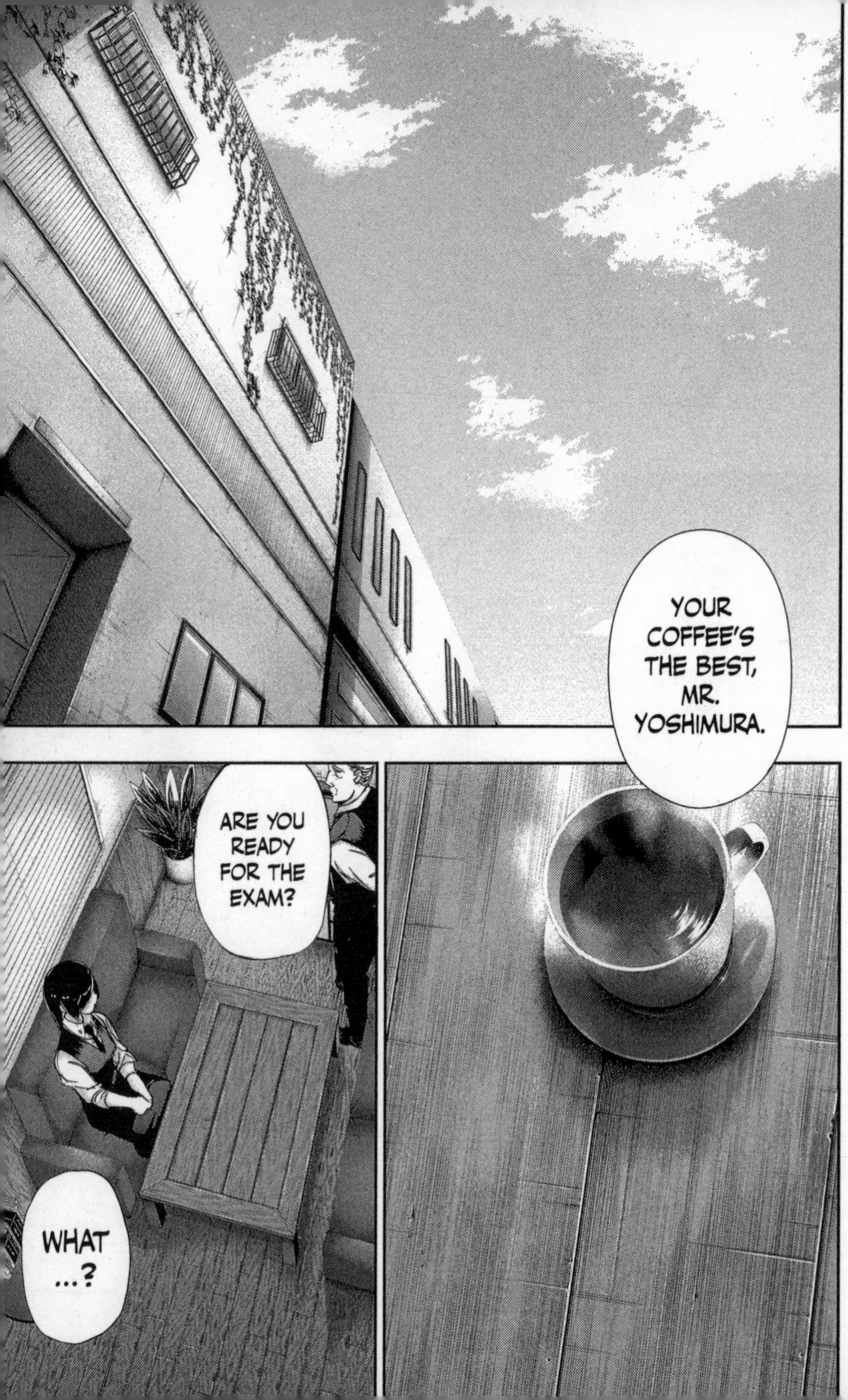
YOUR COFFEE'S THE BEST, MR. YOSHIMURA.
ARE YOU READY FOR THE EXAM?
WHAT ...?

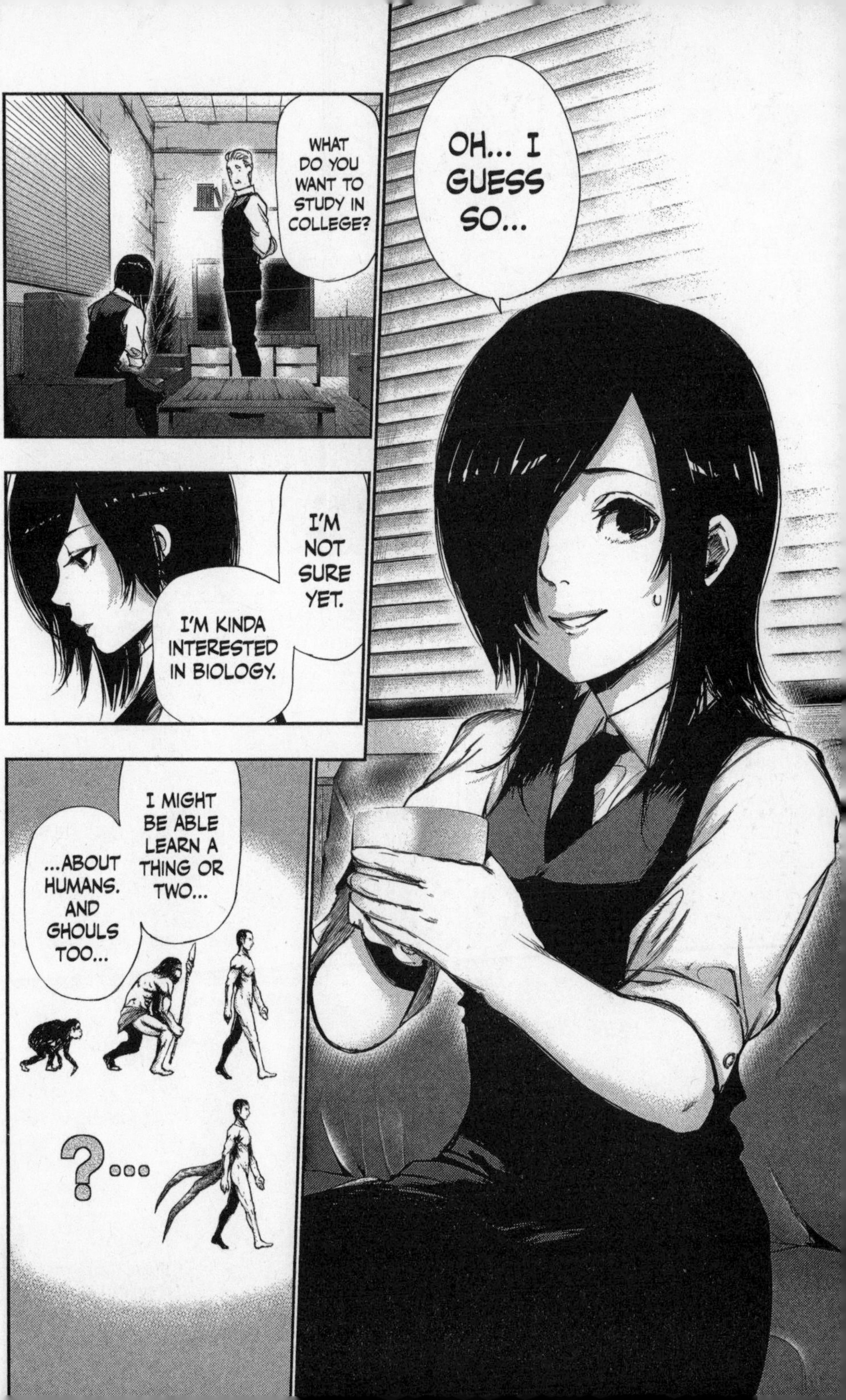
OH... I GUESS SO...
WHAT DO YOU WANT TO STUDY IN COLLEGE?
I'M NOT SURE YET.
I'M KINDA INTERESTED IN BIOLOGY.
I MIGHT BE ABLE LEARN A THING OR TWO...
...ABOUT HUMANS. AND GHOULS TOO...
?...

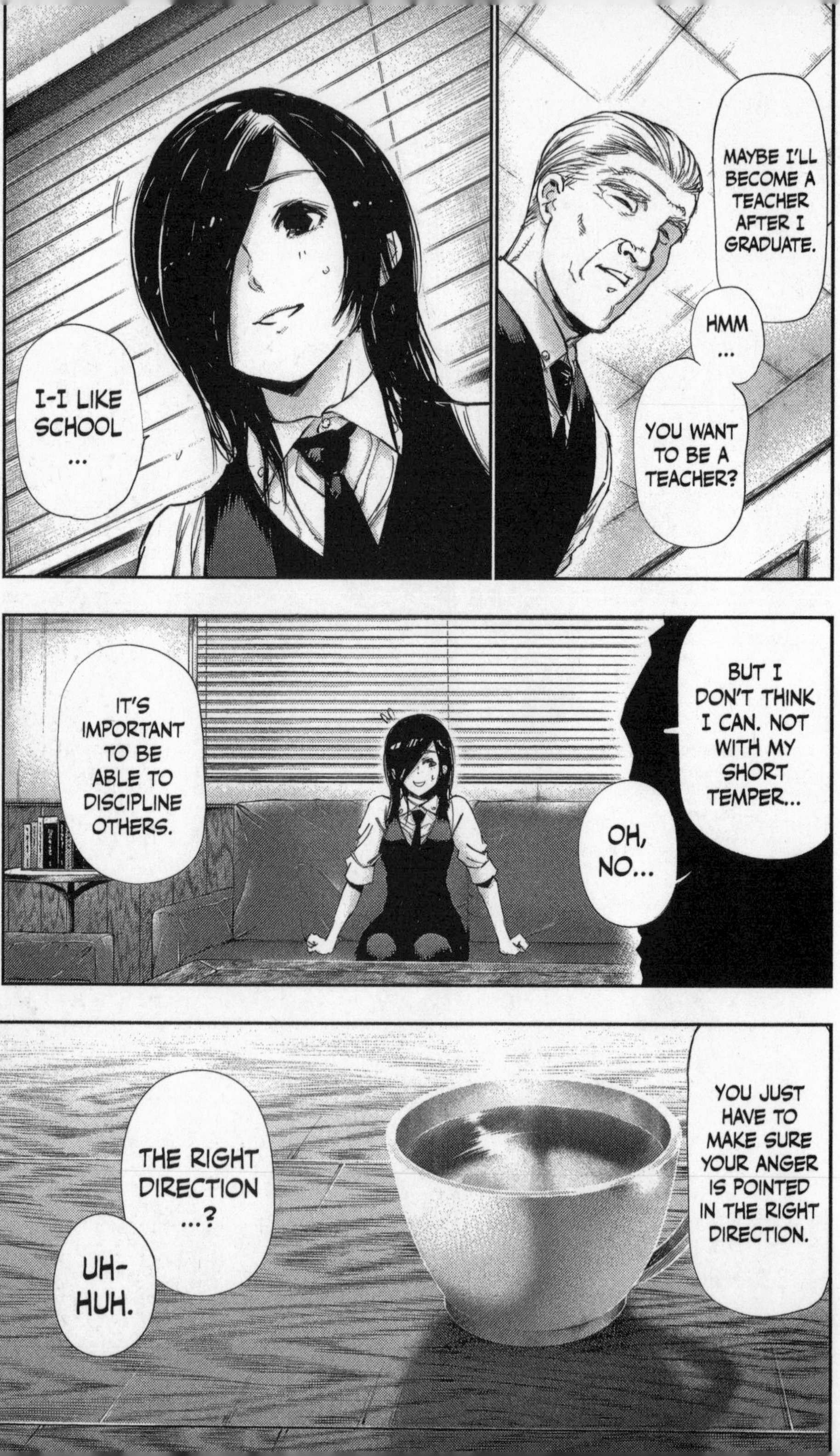
MAYBE I'LL BECOME A TEACHER AFTER I GRADUATE.
HMM...
YOU WANT TO BE A TEACHER?
I-I LIKE SCHOOL...
BUT I DON'T THINK I CAN. NOT WITH MY SHORT TEMPER...
OH, NO...
IT'S IMPORTANT TO BE ABLE TO DISCIPLINE OTHERS.
YOU JUST HAVE TO MAKE SURE YOUR ANGER IS POINTED IN THE RIGHT DIRECTION.
THE RIGHT DIRECTION...?
UH-HUH.

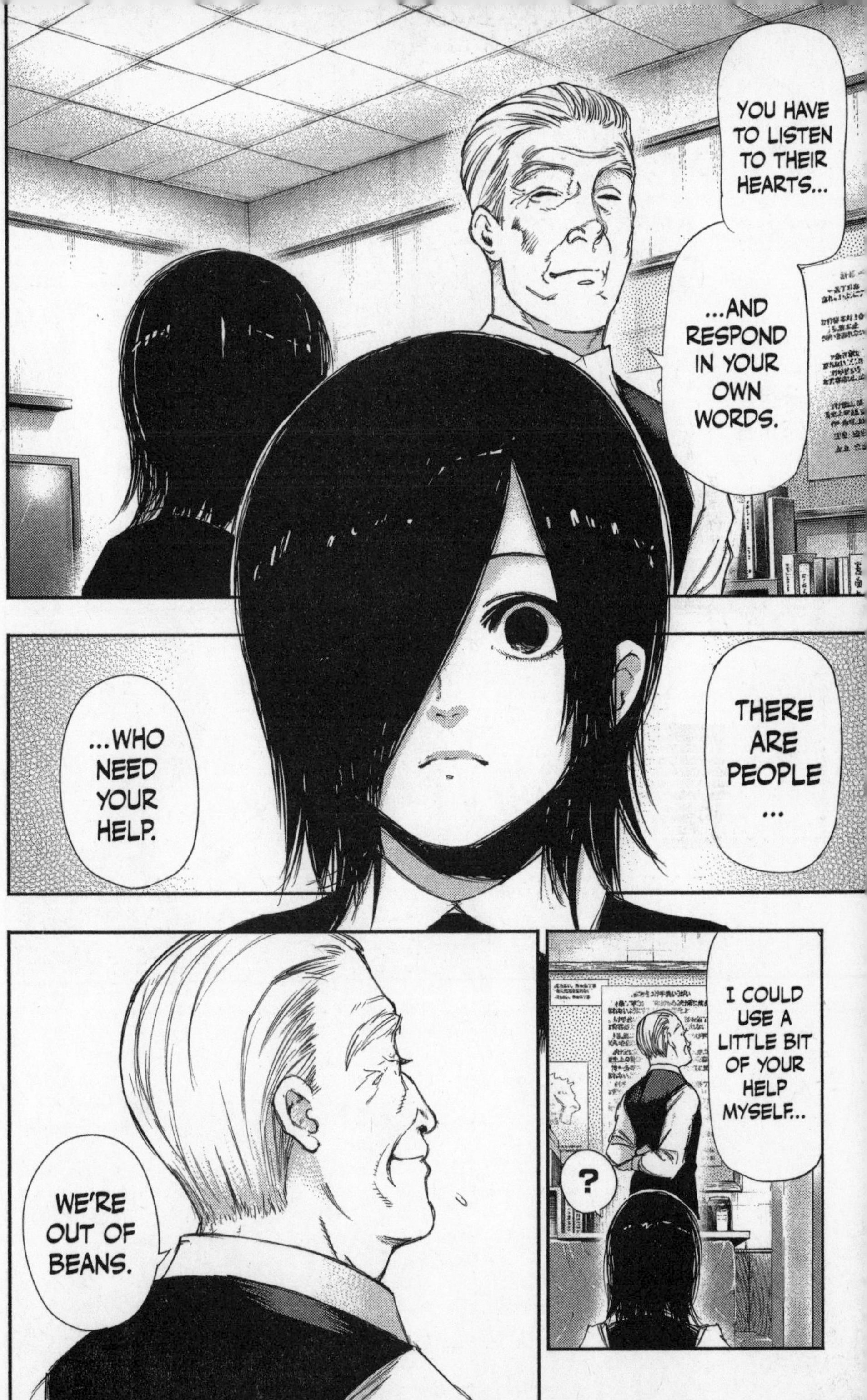
YOU HAVE TO LISTEN TO THEIR HEARTS...
...AND RESPOND IN YOUR OWN WORDS.
THERE ARE PEOPLE ...
...WHO NEED YOUR HELP.
I COULD USE A LITTLE BIT OF YOUR HELP MYSELF...
?
WE'RE OUT OF BEANS.

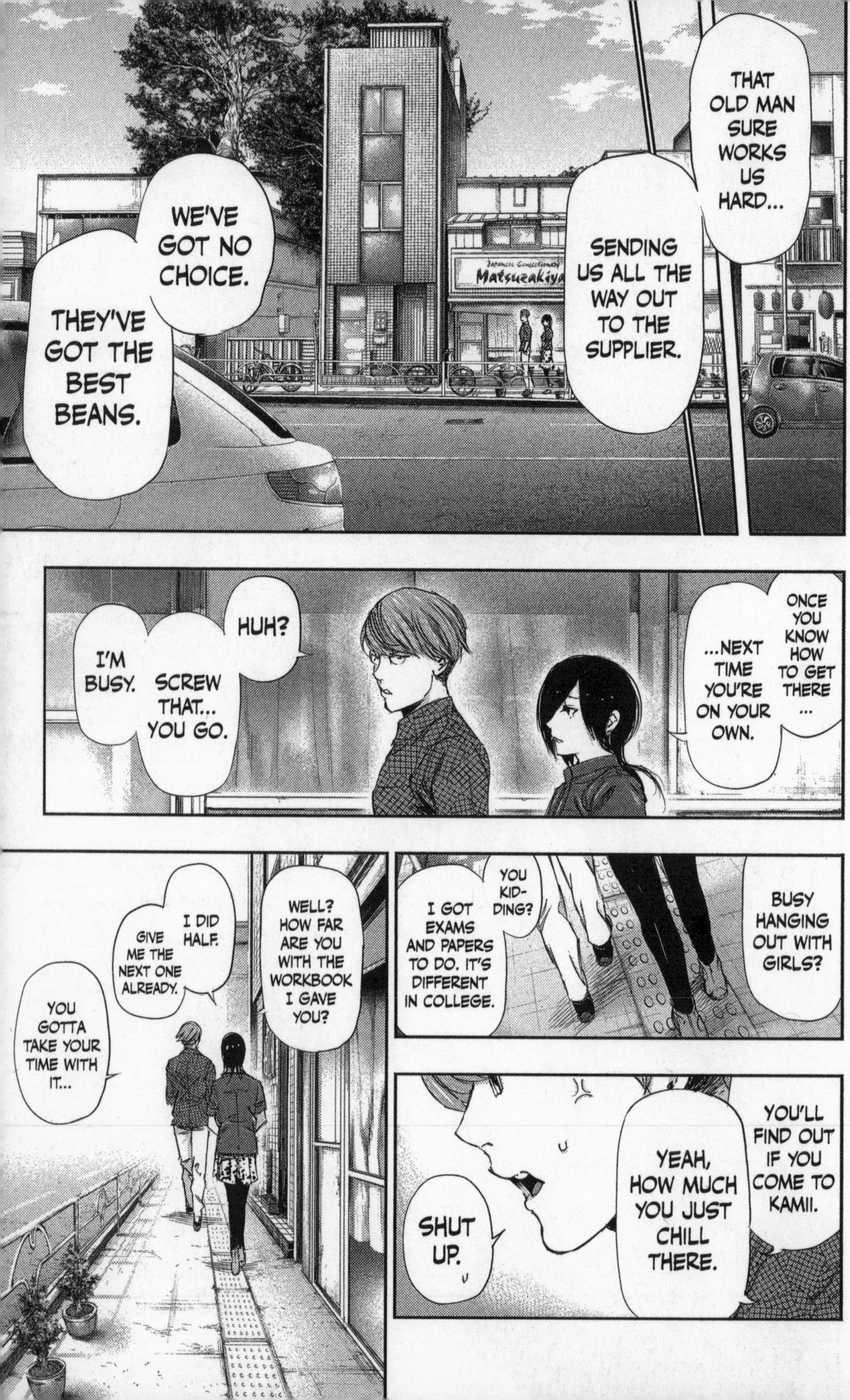
THAT OLD MAN SURE WORKS US HARD...
SENDING US ALL THE WAY OUT TO THE SUPPLIER.
WE'VE GOT NO CHOICE.
THEY'VE GOT THE BEST BEANS.
ONCE YOU KNOW HOW TO GET THERE ...
...NEXT TIME YOU'RE ON YOUR OWN.
HUH?
SCREW THAT... YOU GO.
I'M BUSY.
BUSY HANGING OUT WITH GIRLS?
YOU KID-DING?
I GOT EXAMS AND PAPERS TO DO. IT'S DIFFERENT IN COLLEGE.
YOU'LL FIND OUT IF YOU COME TO KAMII.
YEAH, HOW MUCH YOU JUST CHILL THERE.
SHUT UP.
WELL? HOW FAR ARE YOU WITH THE WORKBOOK I GAVE YOU?
I DID HALF.
GIVE ME THE NEXT ONE ALREADY.
YOU GOTTA TAKE YOUR TIME WITH IT...

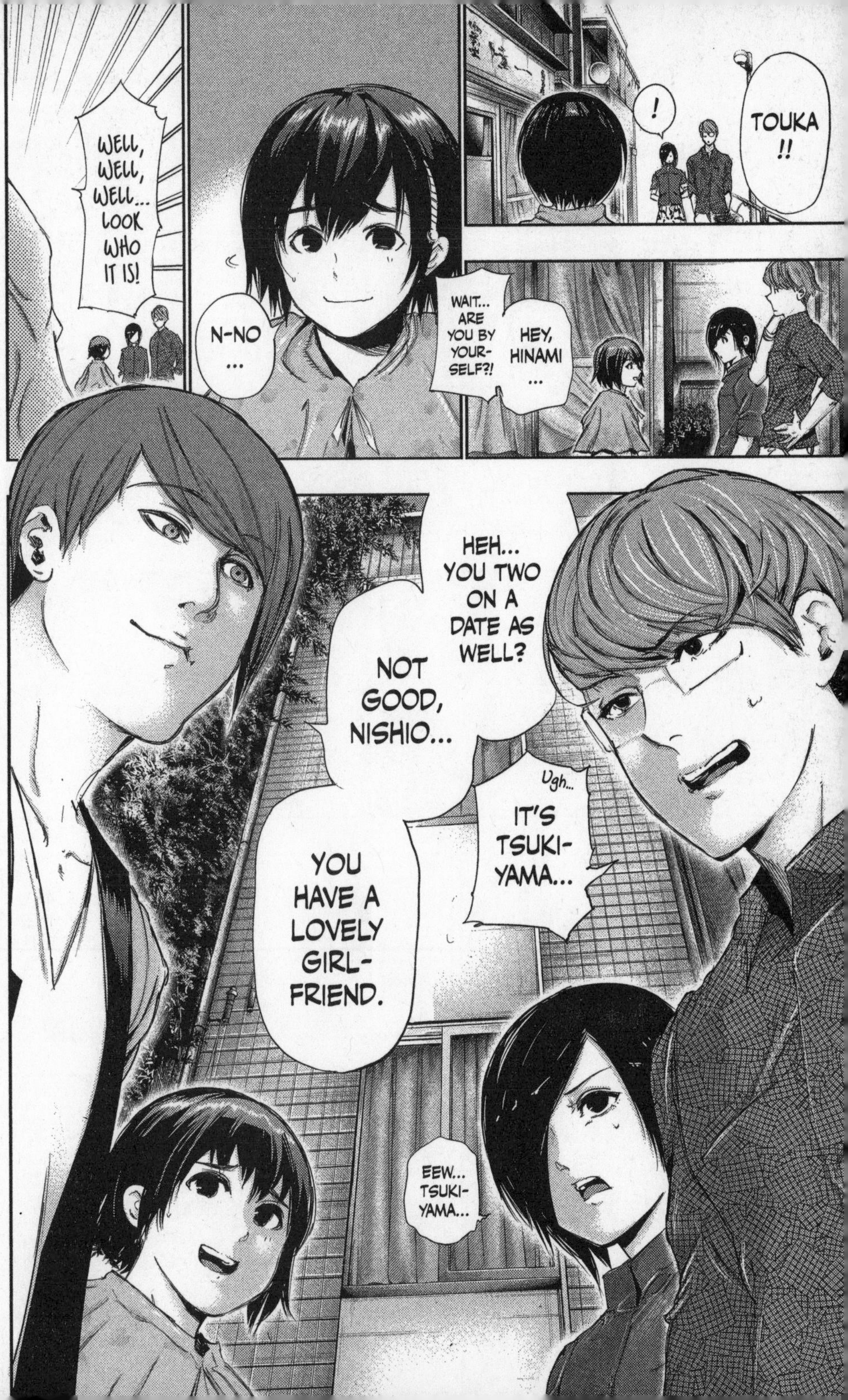
TOUKA !!
!
HEY, HINAMI ...
WAIT... ARE YOU BY YOURSELF?!
N-NO ...
WELL, WELL, WELL... LOOK WHO IT IS!
HEH... YOU TWO ON A DATE AS WELL?
NOT GOOD, NISHIO...
Ugh...
IT'S TSUKIYAMA...
YOU HAVE A LOVELY GIRLFRIEND.
EEW... TSUKIYAMA...

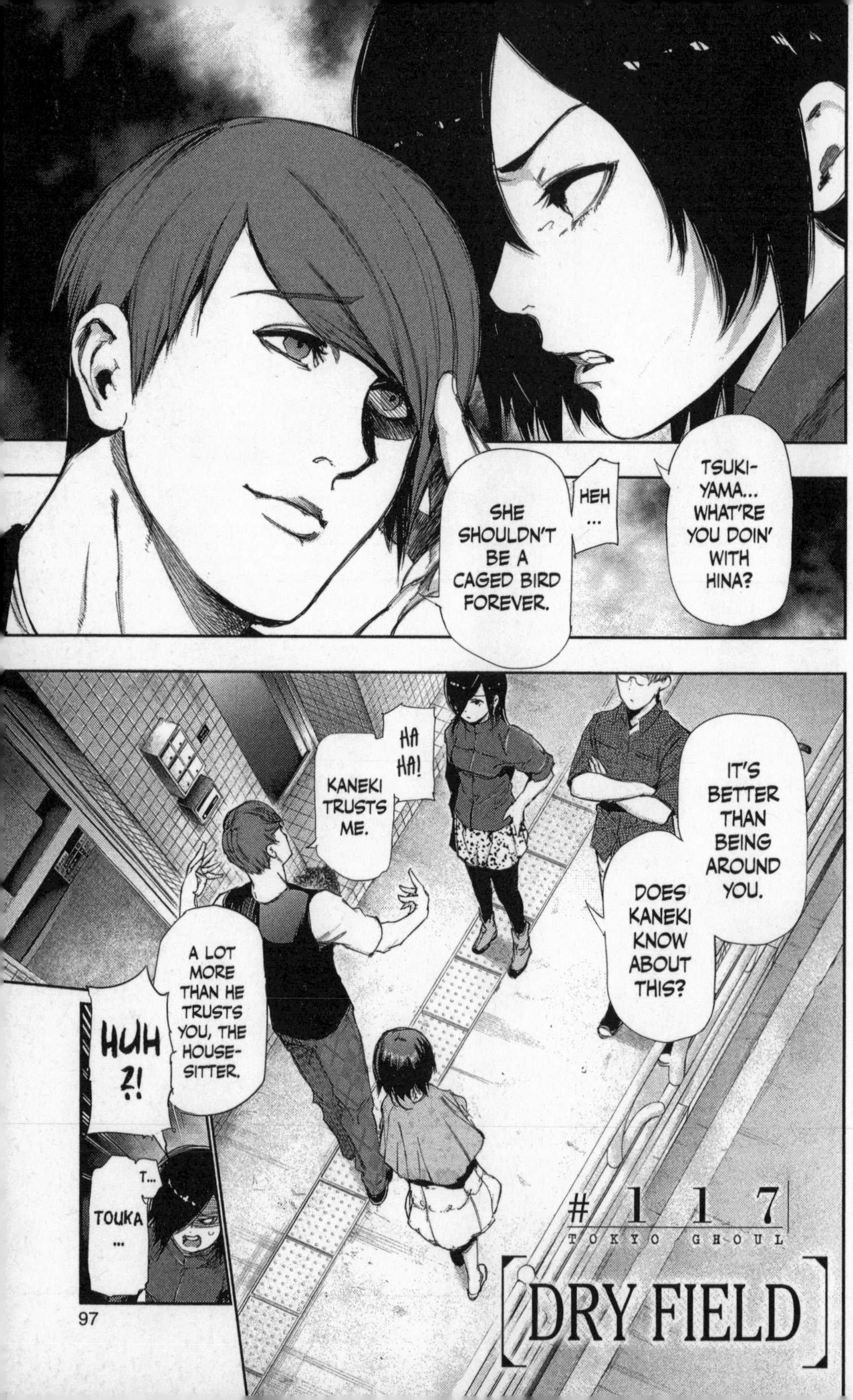
TSUKI-YAMA... WHAT'RE YOU DOIN' WITH HINA?
HEH...
SHE SHOULDN'T BE A CAGED BIRD FOREVER.
IT'S BETTER THAN BEING AROUND YOU.
DOES KANEKI KNOW ABOUT THIS?
HA HA!
KANEKI TRUSTS ME.
A LOT MORE THAN HE TRUSTS YOU, THE HOUSE-SITTER.
#117
TOKYO GHOUL
DRY FIELD
HUH?!
T...
TOUKA...

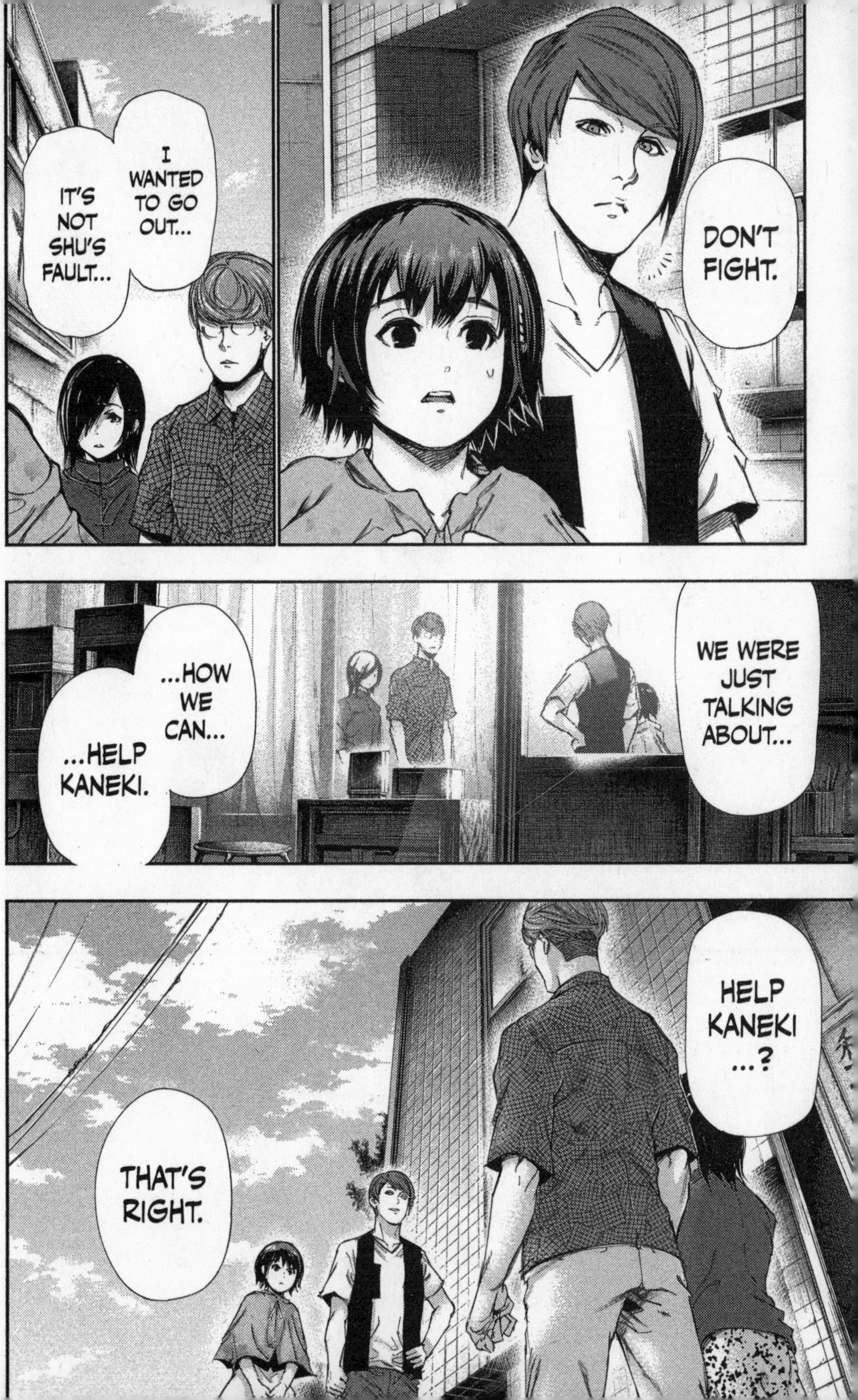
DON'T FIGHT.
I WANTED TO GO OUT...
IT'S NOT SHU'S FAULT...
WE WERE JUST TALKING ABOUT...
...HOW WE CAN...
...HELP KANEKI.
HELP KANEKI ...?
THAT'S RIGHT.

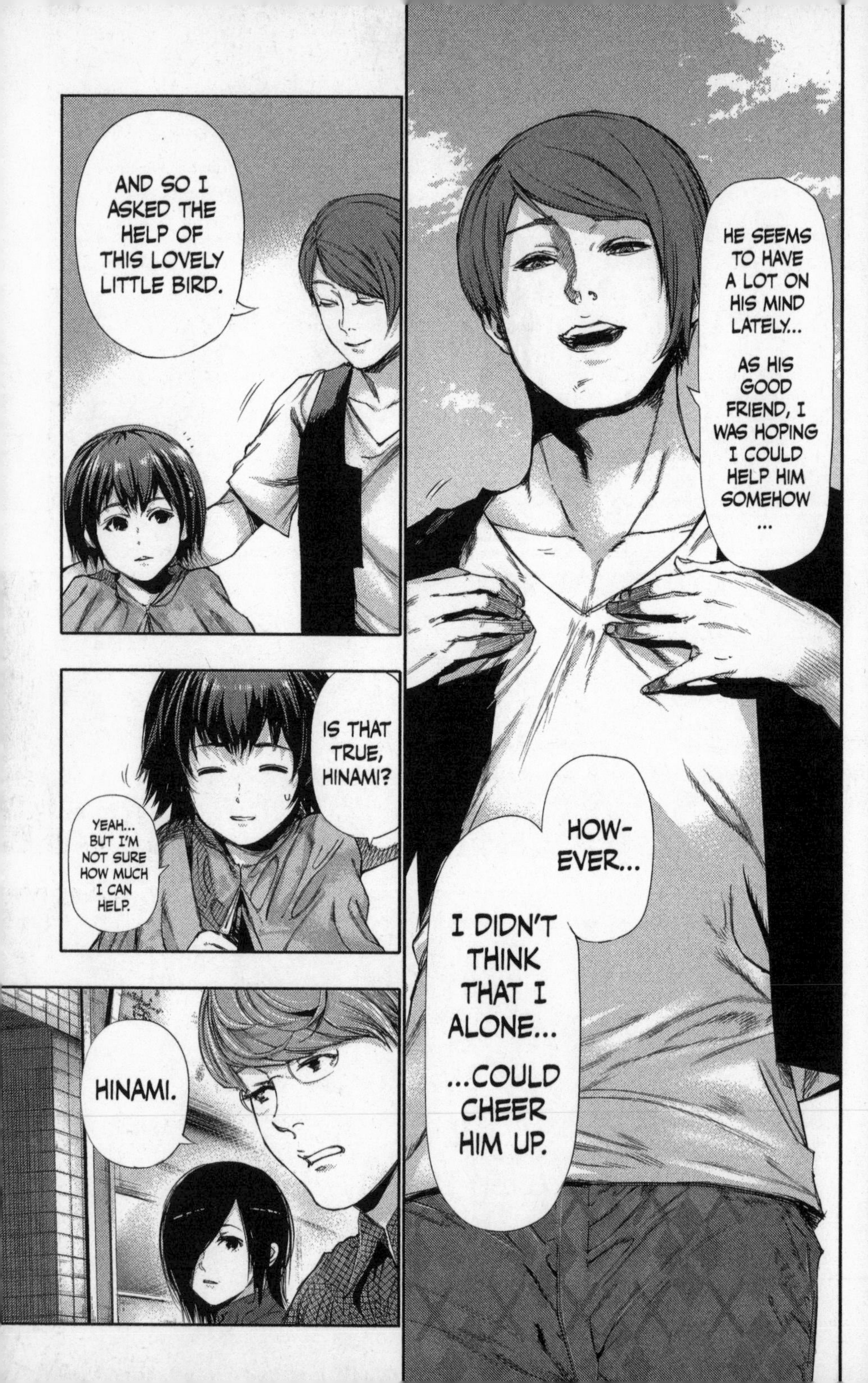
HE SEEMS TO HAVE A LOT ON HIS MIND LATELY... AS HIS GOOD FRIEND, I WAS HOPING I COULD HELP HIM SOMEHOW ...
HOW-EVER...
I DIDN'T THINK THAT I ALONE... ...COULD CHEER HIM UP.
AND SO I ASKED THE HELP OF THIS LOVELY LITTLE BIRD.
IS THAT TRUE, HINAMI?
YEAH... BUT I'M NOT SURE HOW MUCH I CAN HELP.
HINAMI.

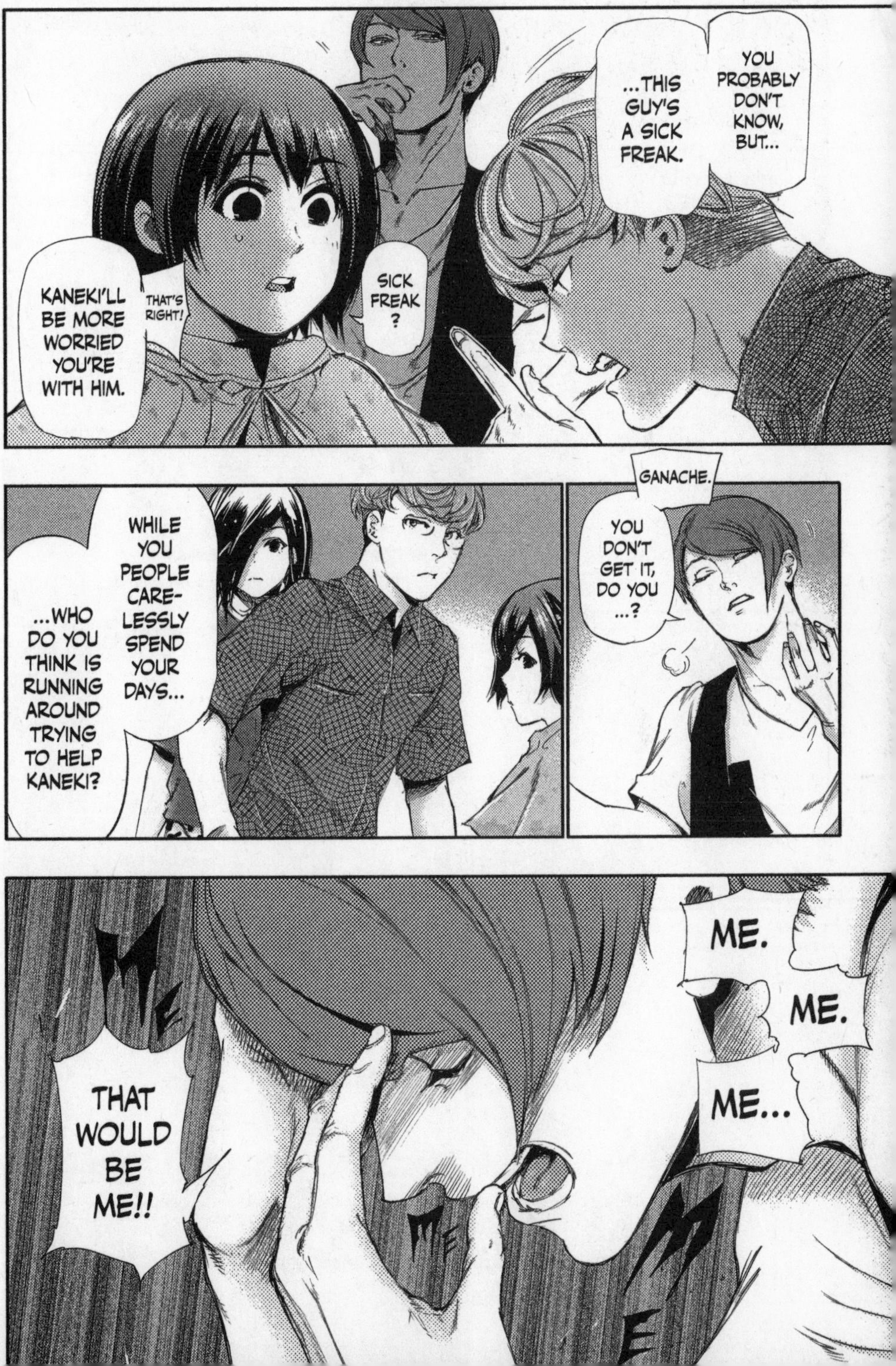
YOU PROBABLY DON'T KNOW, BUT...
...THIS GUY'S A SICK FREAK.
SICK FREAK?
THAT'S RIGHT!
KANEKI'LL BE MORE WORRIED YOU'RE WITH HIM.
GANACHE.
YOU DON'T GET IT, DO YOU ...?
WHILE YOU PEOPLE CARE-LESSLY SPEND YOUR DAYS...
...WHO DO YOU THINK IS RUNNING AROUND TRYING TO HELP KANEKI?
ME.
ME.
ME...
THAT WOULD BE ME!!

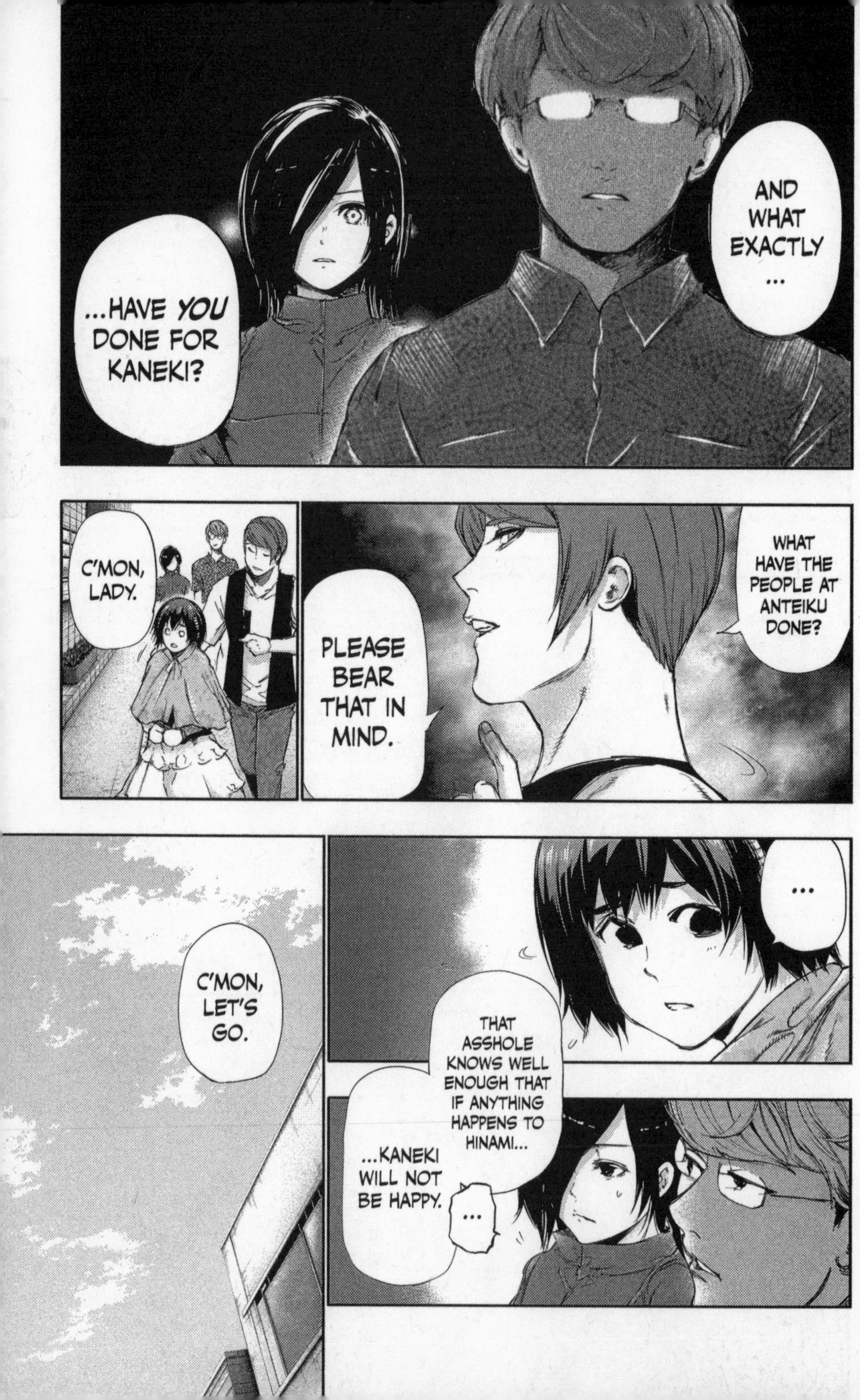
AND WHAT EXACTLY ...
...HAVE *YOU* DONE FOR KANEKI?
WHAT HAVE THE PEOPLE AT ANTEIKU DONE?
PLEASE BEAR THAT IN MIND.
C'MON, LADY.
...
THAT ASSHOLE KNOWS WELL ENOUGH THAT IF ANYTHING HAPPENS TO HINAMI...
...KANEKI WILL NOT BE HAPPY.
...
C'MON, LET'S GO.

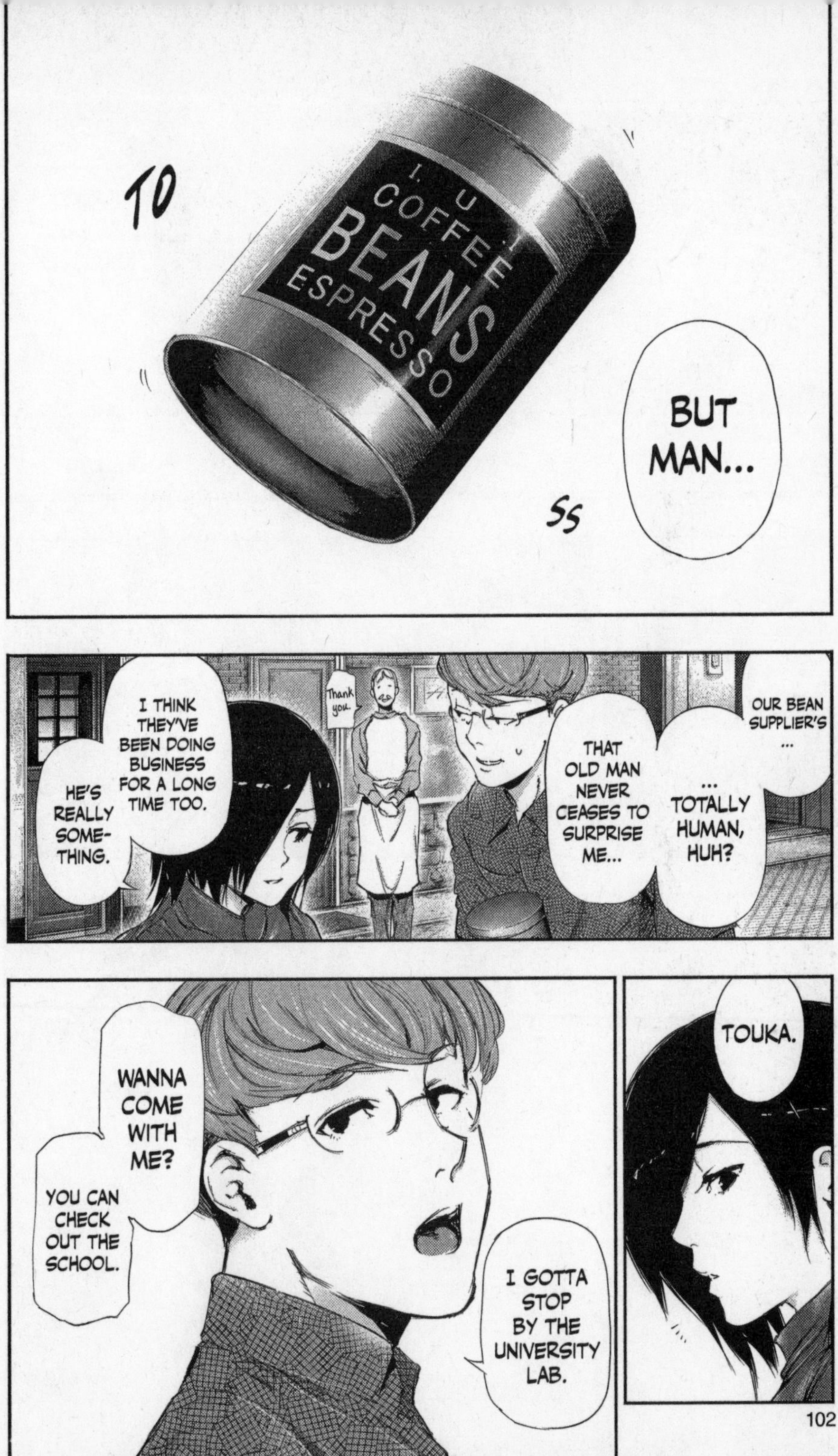
BUT MAN...
COFFEE
BEANS
ESPRESSO
TO
SS
OUR BEAN SUPPLIER'S ...
... TOTALLY HUMAN, HUH?
THAT OLD MAN NEVER CEASES TO SURPRISE ME...
Thank you.
I THINK THEY'VE BEEN DOING BUSINESS FOR A LONG TIME TOO.
HE'S REALLY SOME-THING.
TOUKA.
I GOTTA STOP BY THE UNIVERSITY LAB.
WANNA COME WITH ME?
YOU CAN CHECK OUT THE SCHOOL.

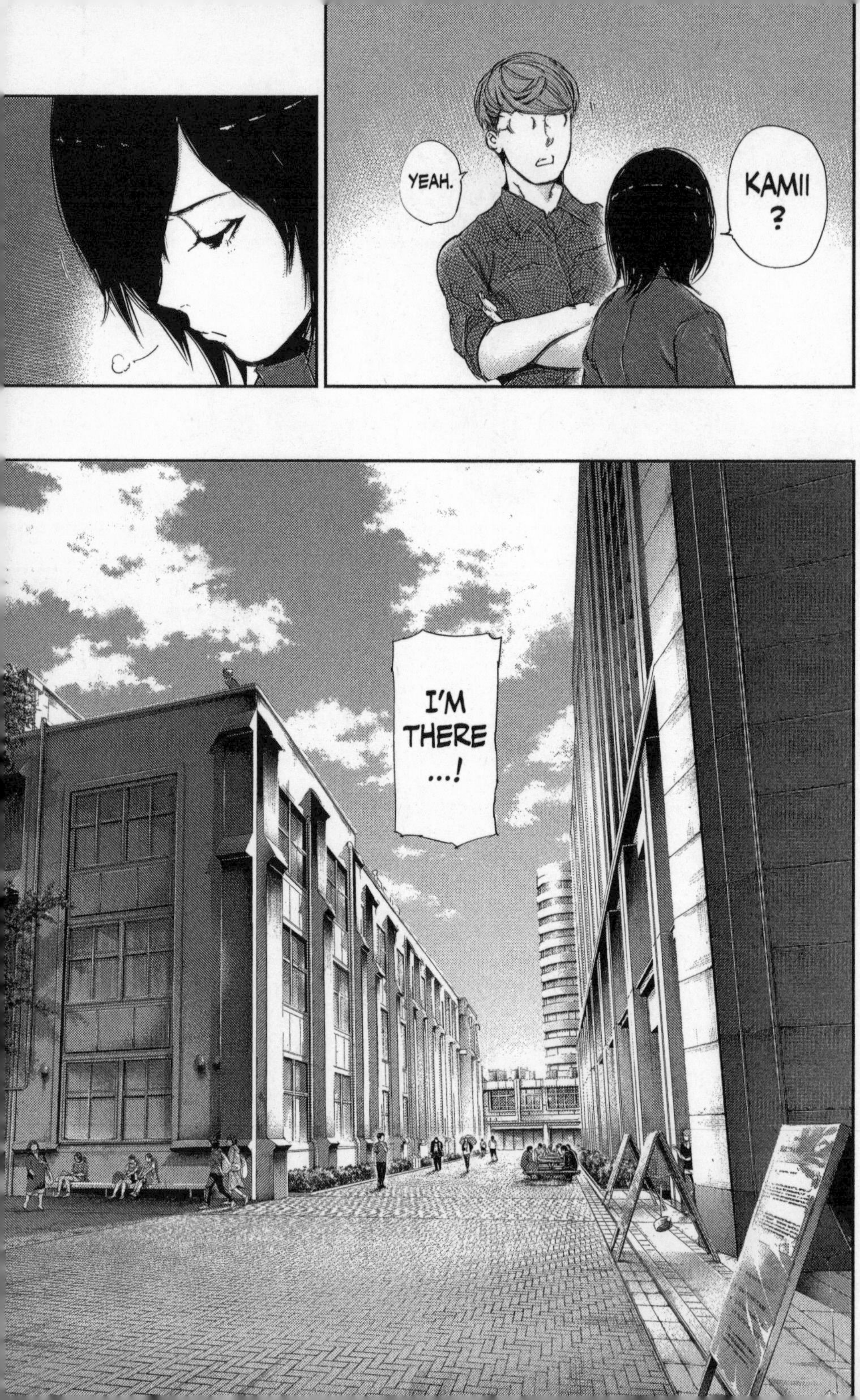
KAMII ?
YEAH.
I'M THERE ...!

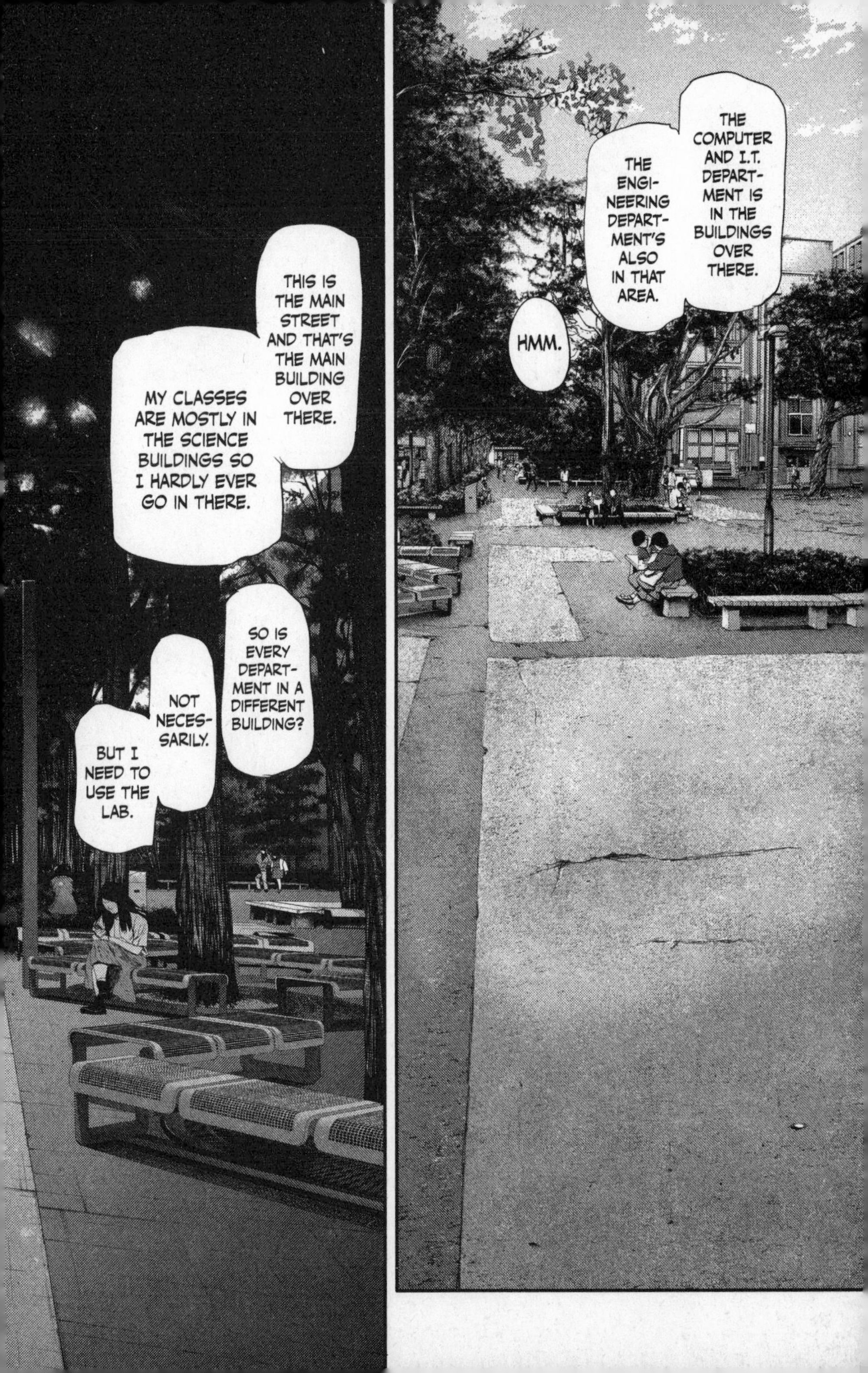
THE COMPUTER AND I.T. DEPARTMENT IS IN THE BUILDINGS OVER THERE.
THE ENGINEERING DEPARTMENT'S ALSO IN THAT AREA.
HMM.
THIS IS THE MAIN STREET AND THAT'S THE MAIN BUILDING OVER THERE.
MY CLASSES ARE MOSTLY IN THE SCIENCE BUILDINGS SO I HARDLY EVER GO IN THERE.
SO IS EVERY DEPARTMENT IN A DIFFERENT BUILDING?
NOT NECESSARILY.
BUT I NEED TO USE THE LAB.

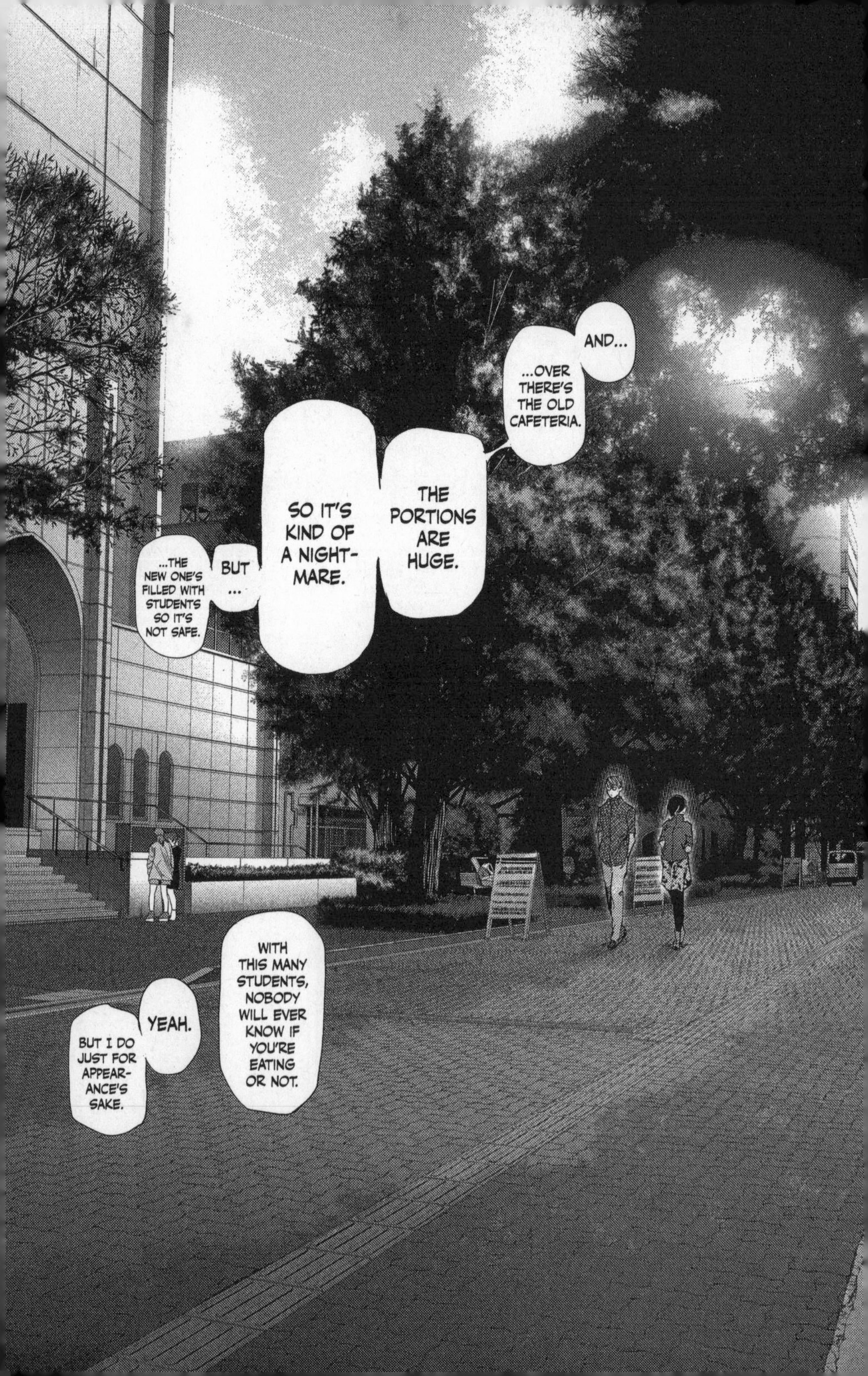
AND...
...OVER THERE'S THE OLD CAFETERIA.
THE PORTIONS ARE HUGE.
SO IT'S KIND OF A NIGHT-MARE.
BUT ...
...THE NEW ONE'S FILLED WITH STUDENTS SO IT'S NOT SAFE.
WITH THIS MANY STUDENTS, NOBODY WILL EVER KNOW IF YOU'RE EATING OR NOT.
YEAH.
BUT I DO JUST FOR APPEAR-ANCE'S SAKE.

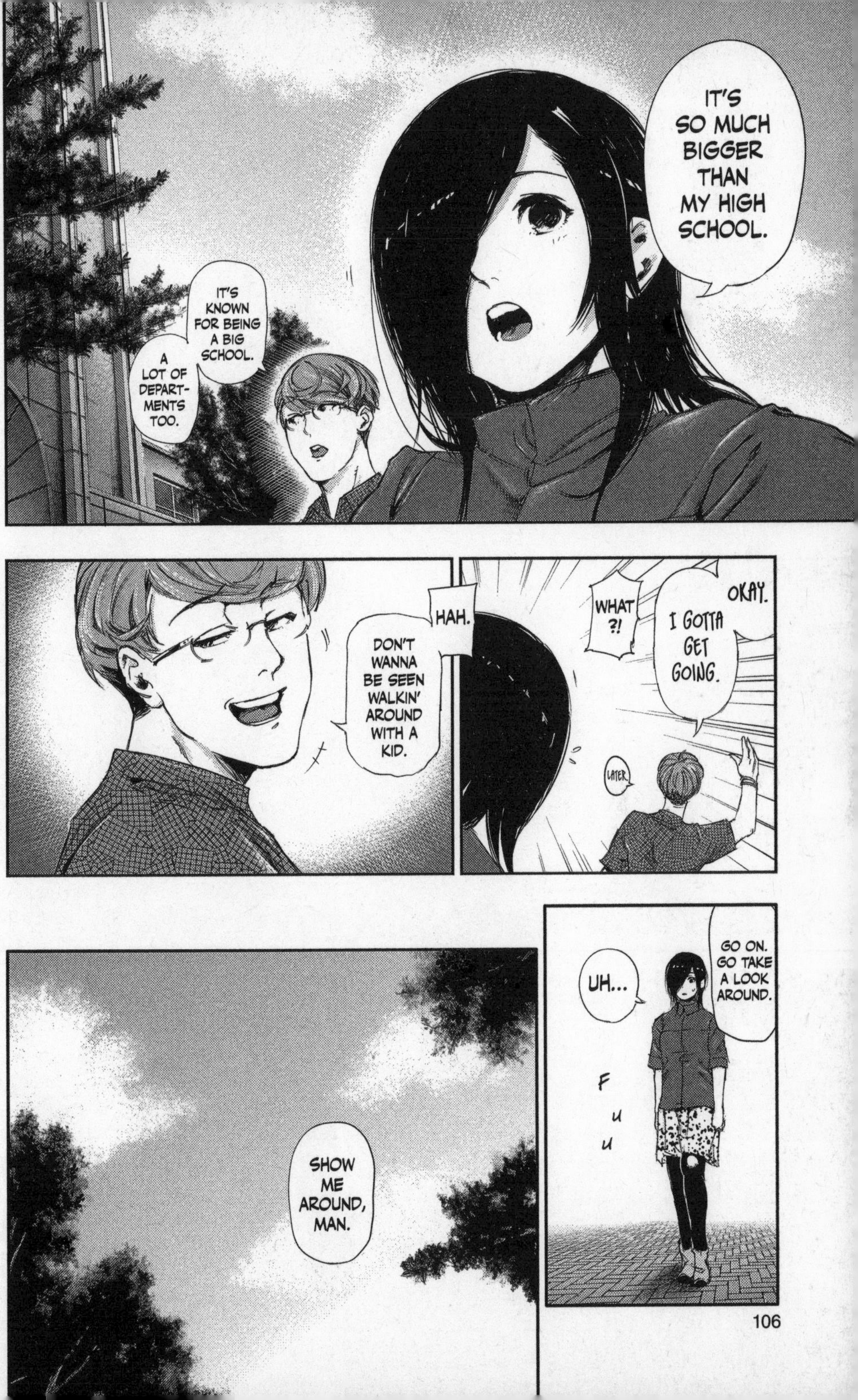

IT'S SO MUCH BIGGER THAN MY HIGH SCHOOL.
IT'S KNOWN FOR BEING A BIG SCHOOL.
A LOT OF DEPART-MENTS TOO.
OKAY. I GOTTA GET GOING.
WHAT ?!
LATER
HAH.
DON'T WANNA BE SEEN WALKIN' AROUND WITH A KID.
GO ON. GO TAKE A LOOK AROUND.
UH...
F u u
SHOW ME AROUND, MAN.

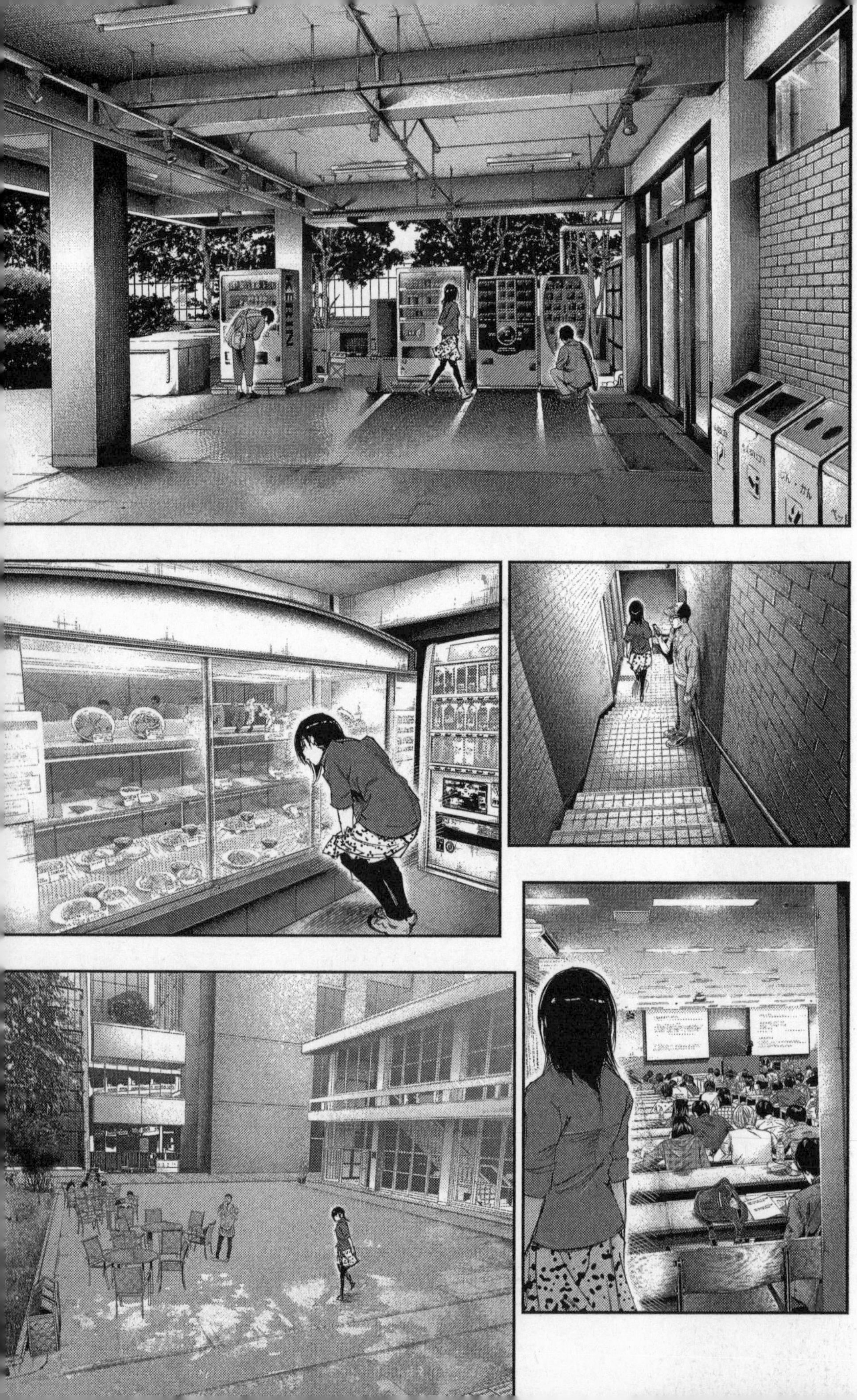

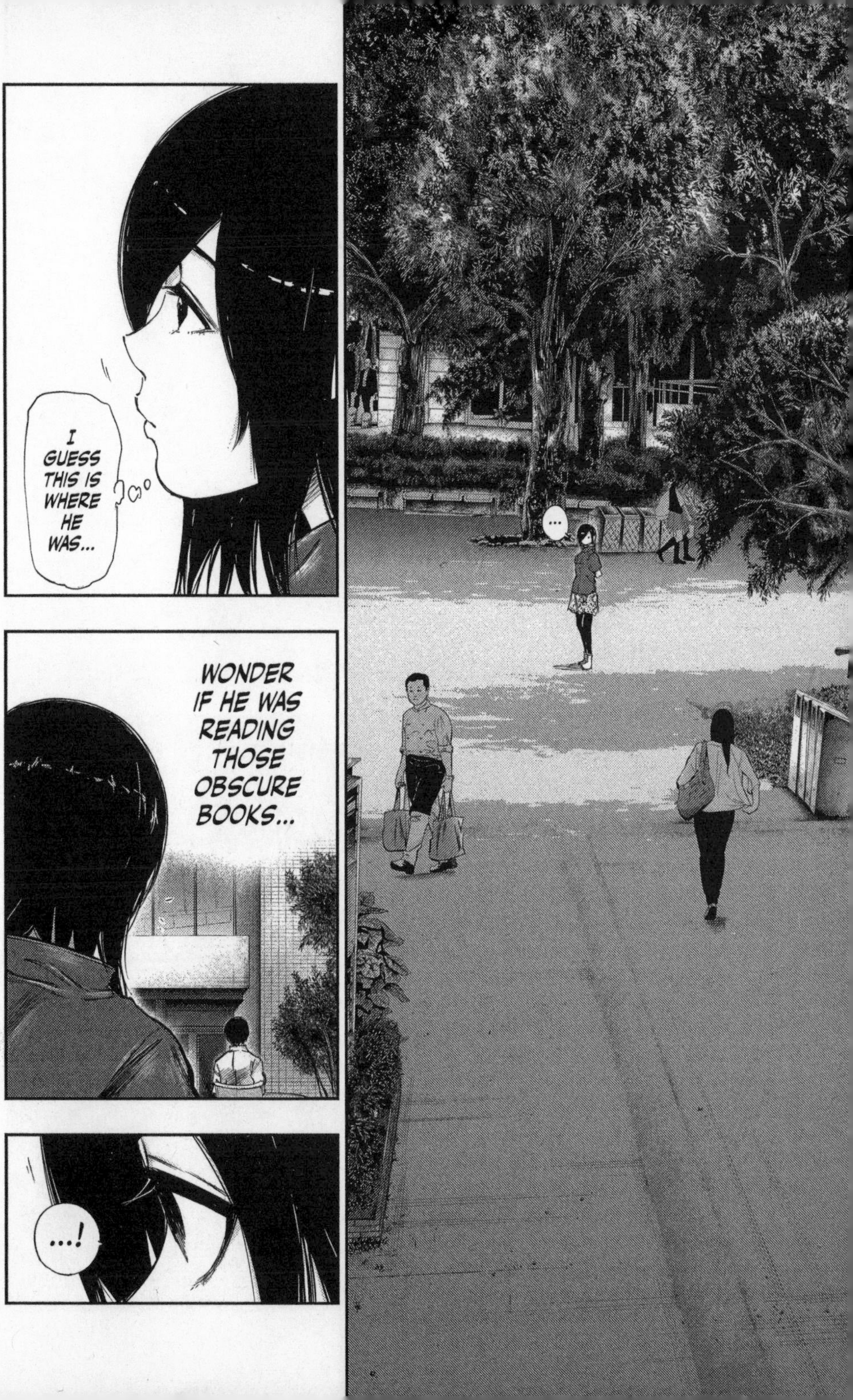
...
I GUESS THIS IS WHERE HE WAS...
WONDER IF HE WAS READING THOSE OBSCURE BOOKS...
...!

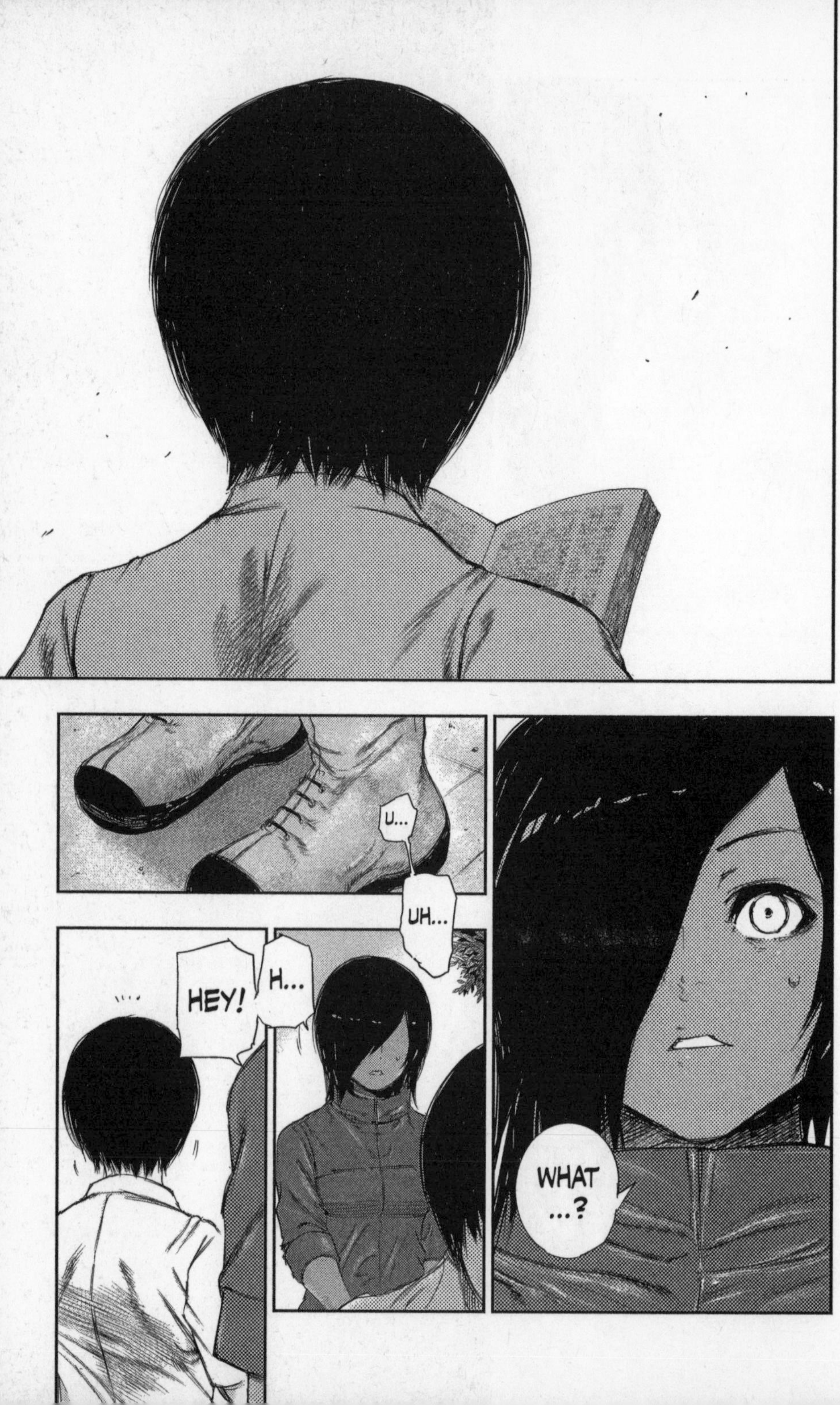
WHAT ...?
U...
UH...
H...
HEY!

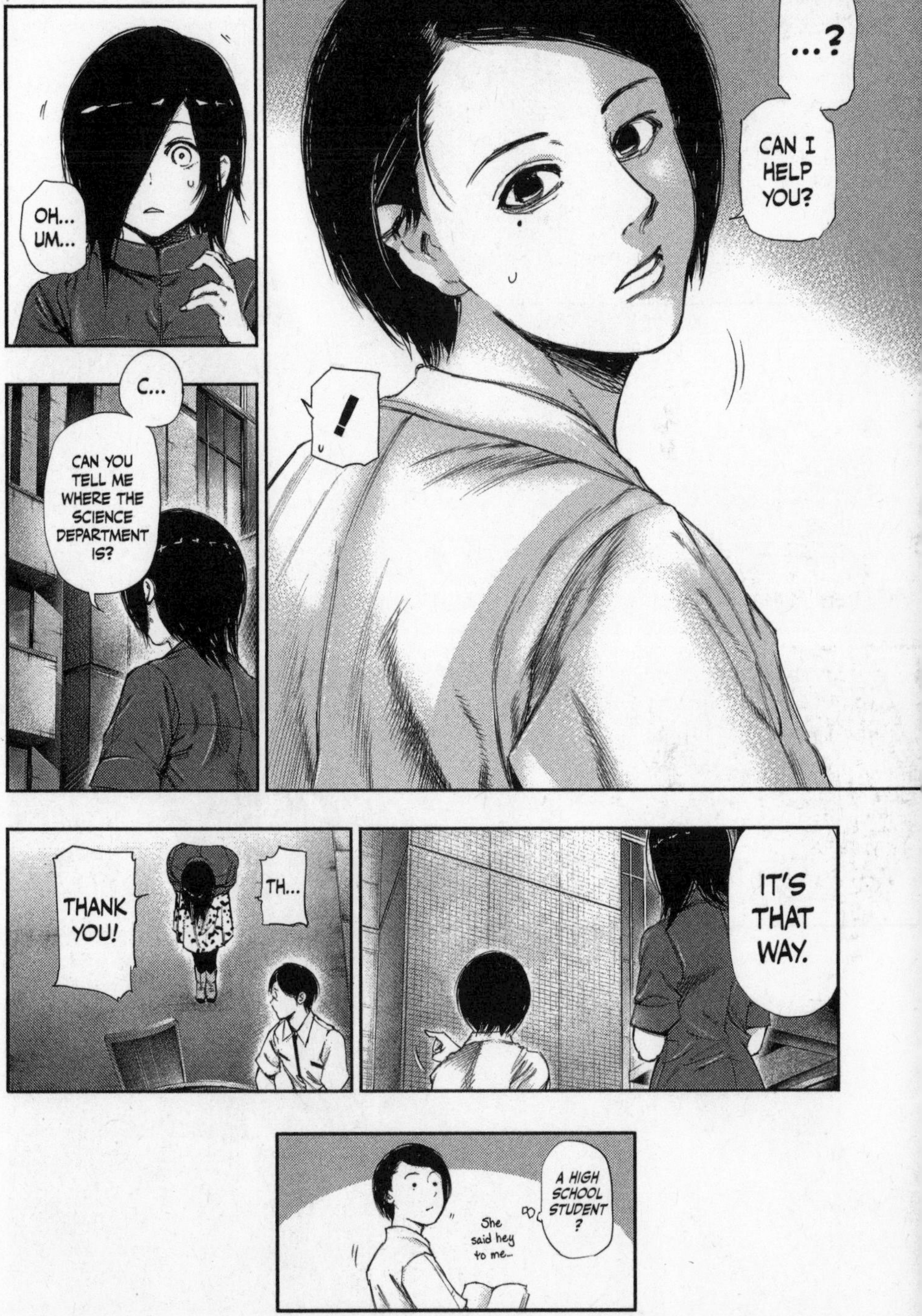
...?
CAN I HELP YOU?
!
OH... UM...
C...
CAN YOU TELL ME WHERE THE SCIENCE DEPARTMENT IS?
IT'S THAT WAY.
TH...
THANK YOU!
A HIGH SCHOOL STUDENT?
She said hey to me...

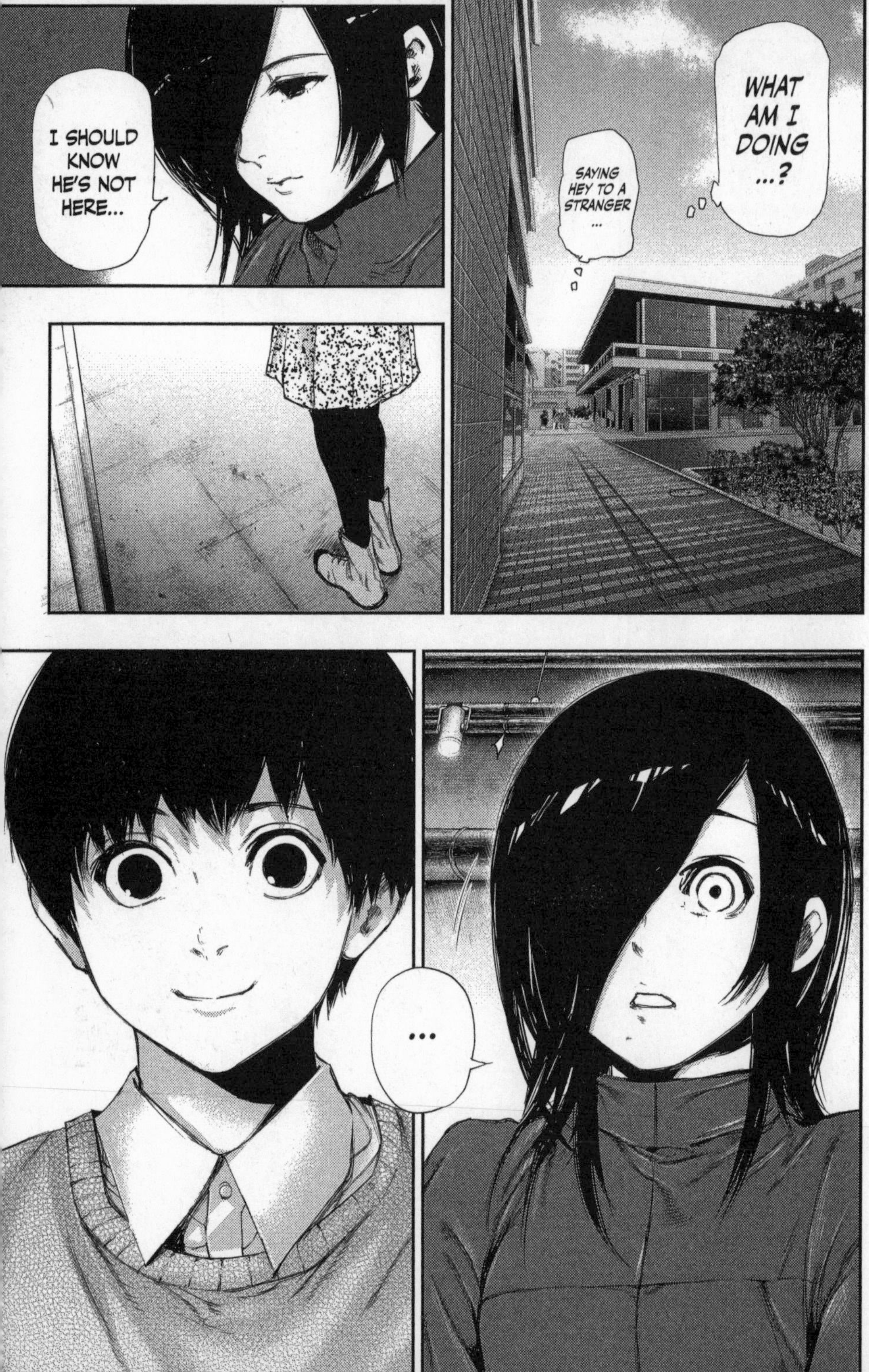
WHAT AM I DOING ...?
SAYING HEY TO A STRANGER ...
I SHOULD KNOW HE'S NOT HERE...
...

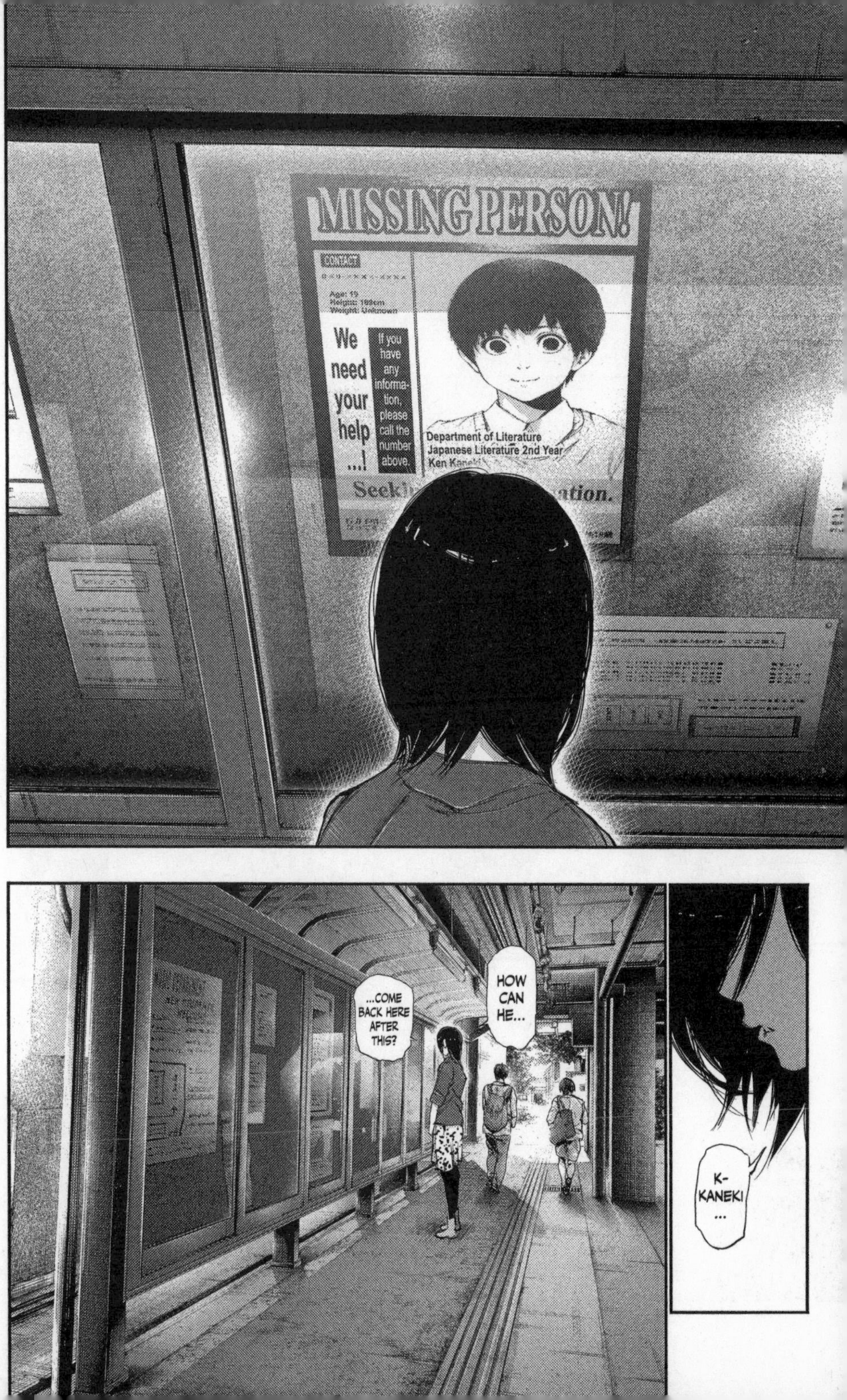
MISSING PERSON!
CONTACT
Weight: Unknown
We need your help ...!
If you have any information, please call the number above.
Department of Literature
Japanese Literature 2nd Year
Ken Kaneki
K-KANEKI...
HOW CAN HE...
...COME BACK HERE AFTER THIS?

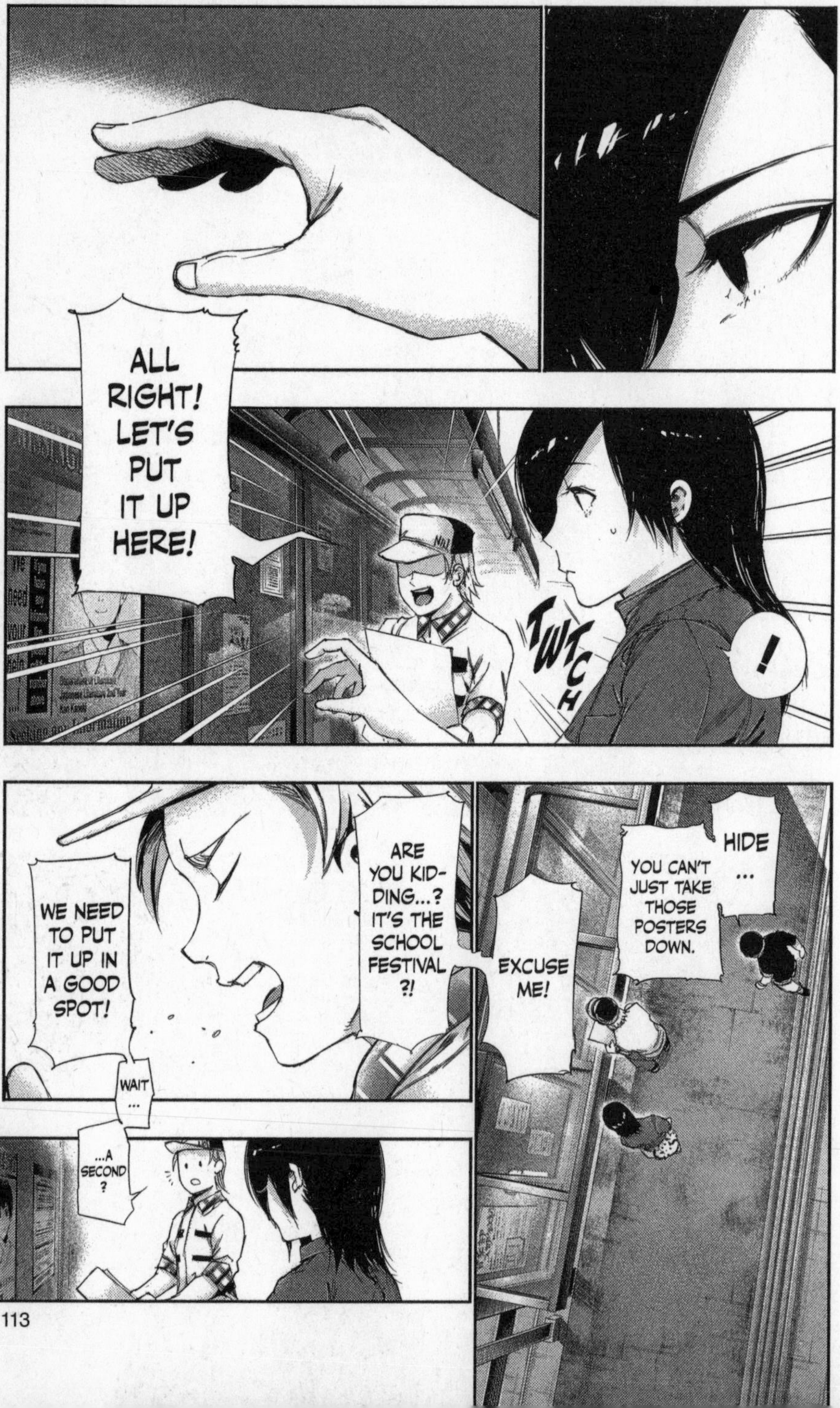
ALL RIGHT! LET'S PUT IT UP HERE!
!
TWITCH
HIDE...
YOU CAN'T JUST TAKE THOSE POSTERS DOWN.
EXCUSE ME!
ARE YOU KID-DING...? IT'S THE SCHOOL FESTIVAL?!
WE NEED TO PUT IT UP IN A GOOD SPOT!
WAIT...
...A SECOND?

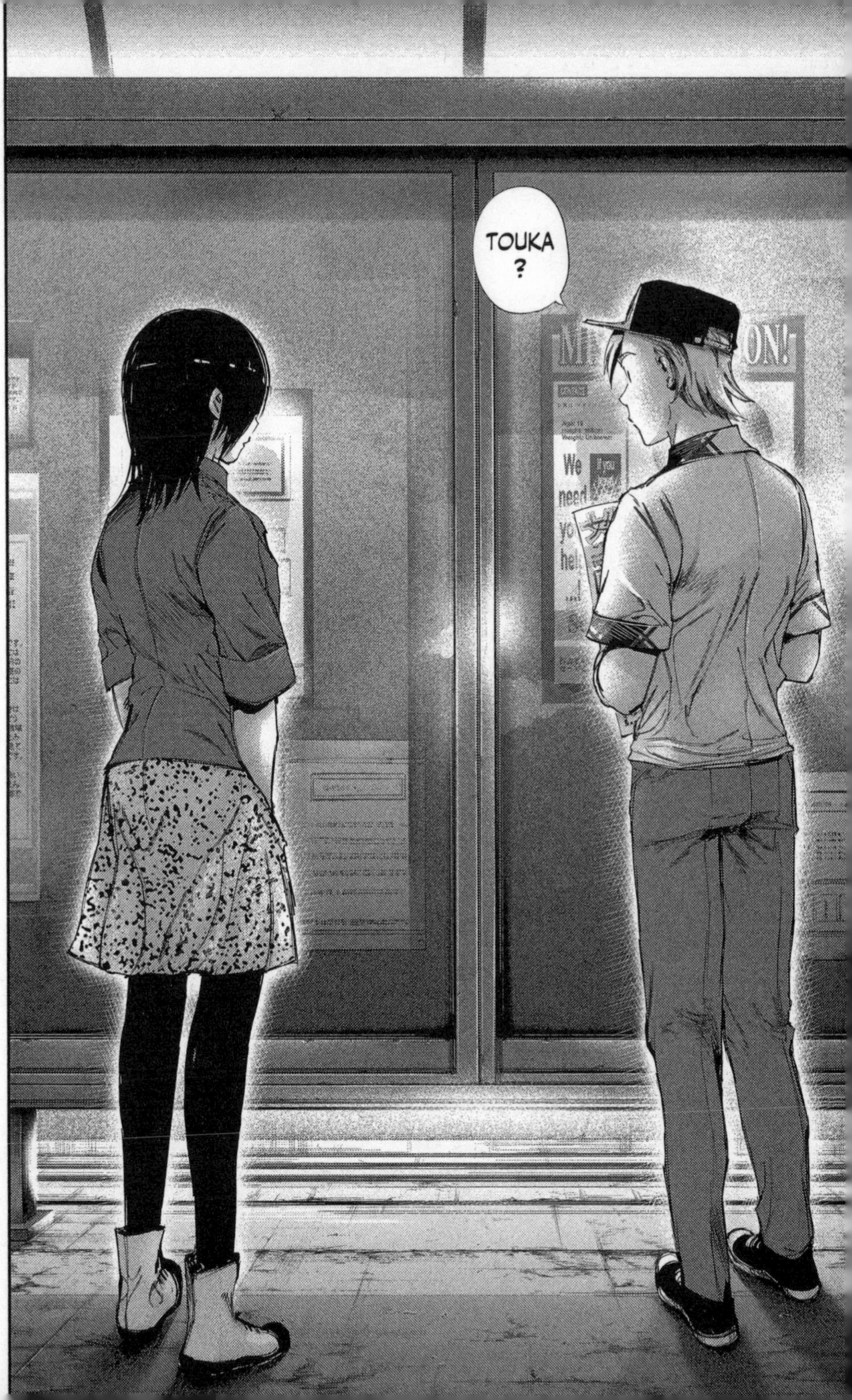
TOUKA ?

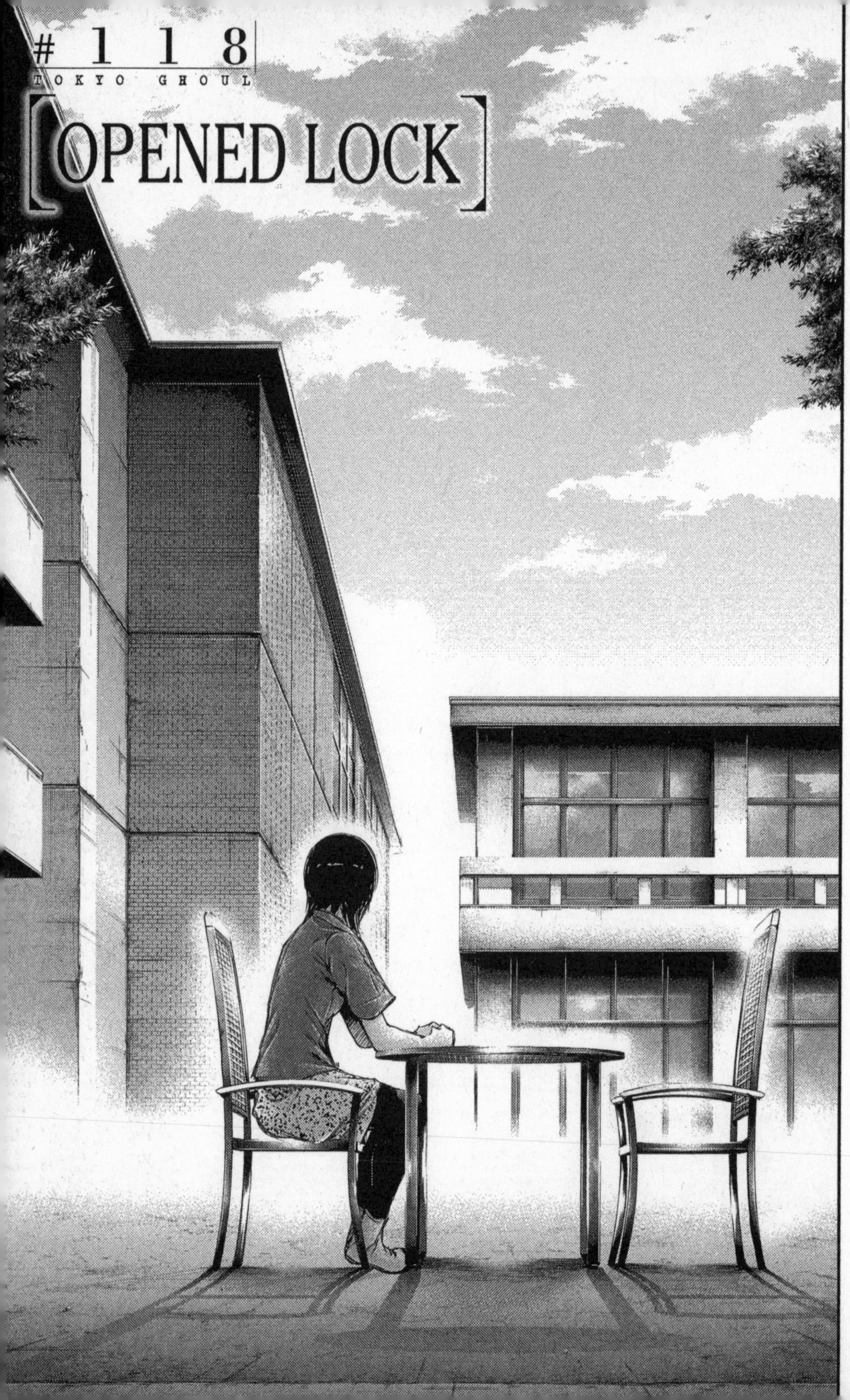
#118
TOKYO GHOUL
[OPENED LOCK]

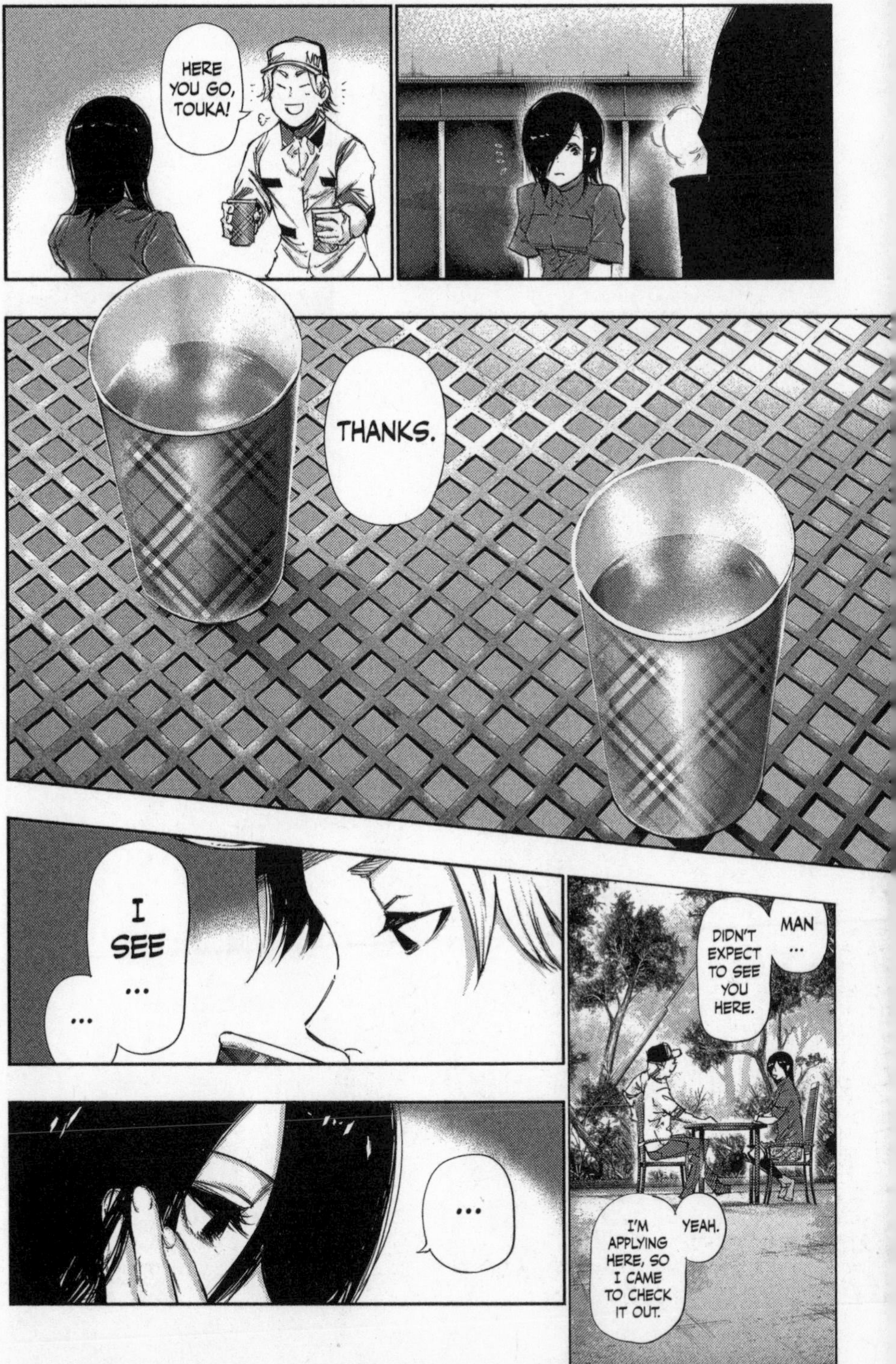
HERE YOU GO, TOUKA!
THANKS.
MAN ...
DIDN'T EXPECT TO SEE YOU HERE.
YEAH.
I'M APPLYING HERE, SO I CAME TO CHECK IT OUT.
I SEE ...
...
...

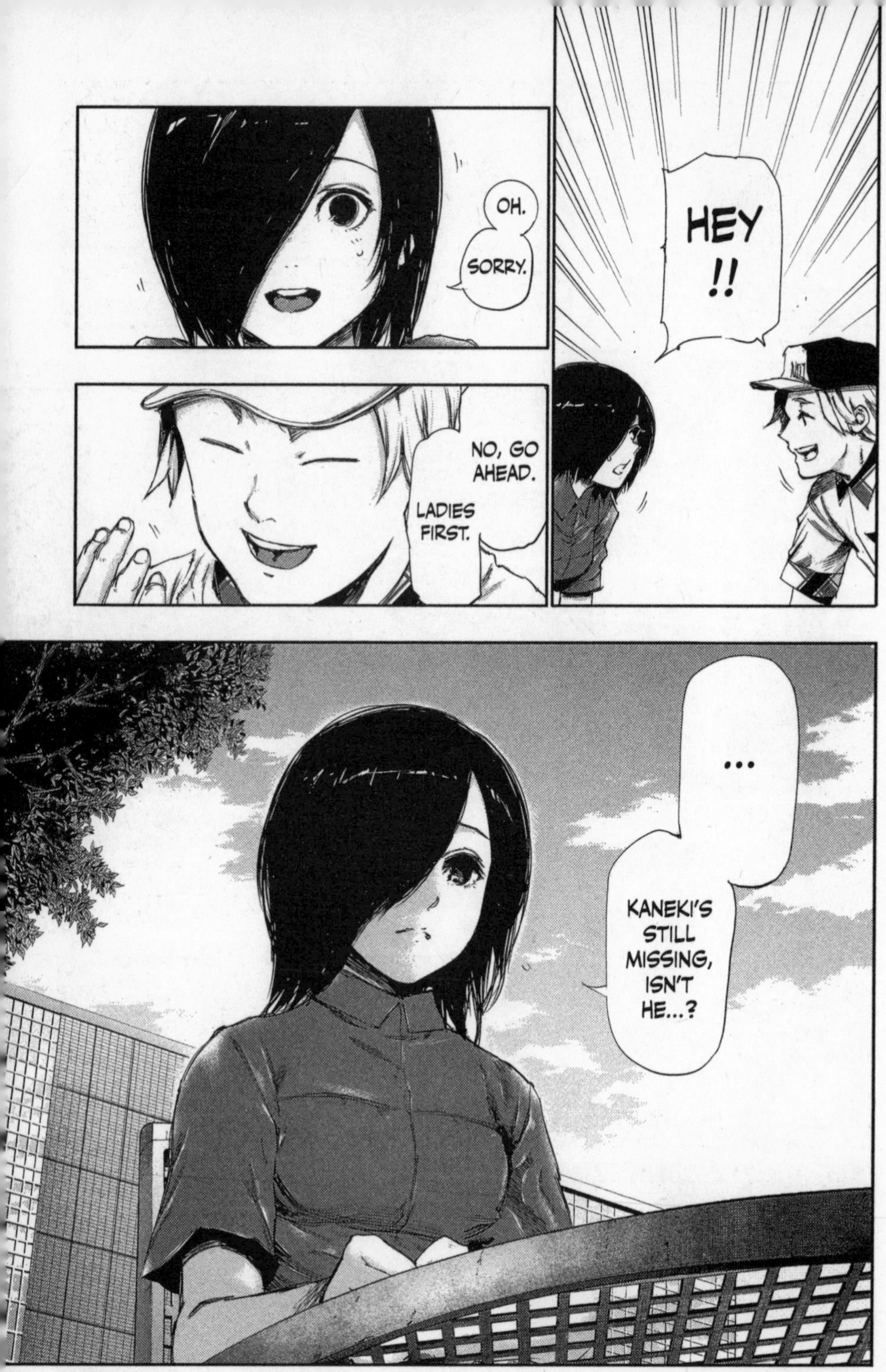
HEY !!
OH.
SORRY.
NO, GO AHEAD.
LADIES FIRST.
...
KANEKI'S STILL MISSING, ISN'T HE...?

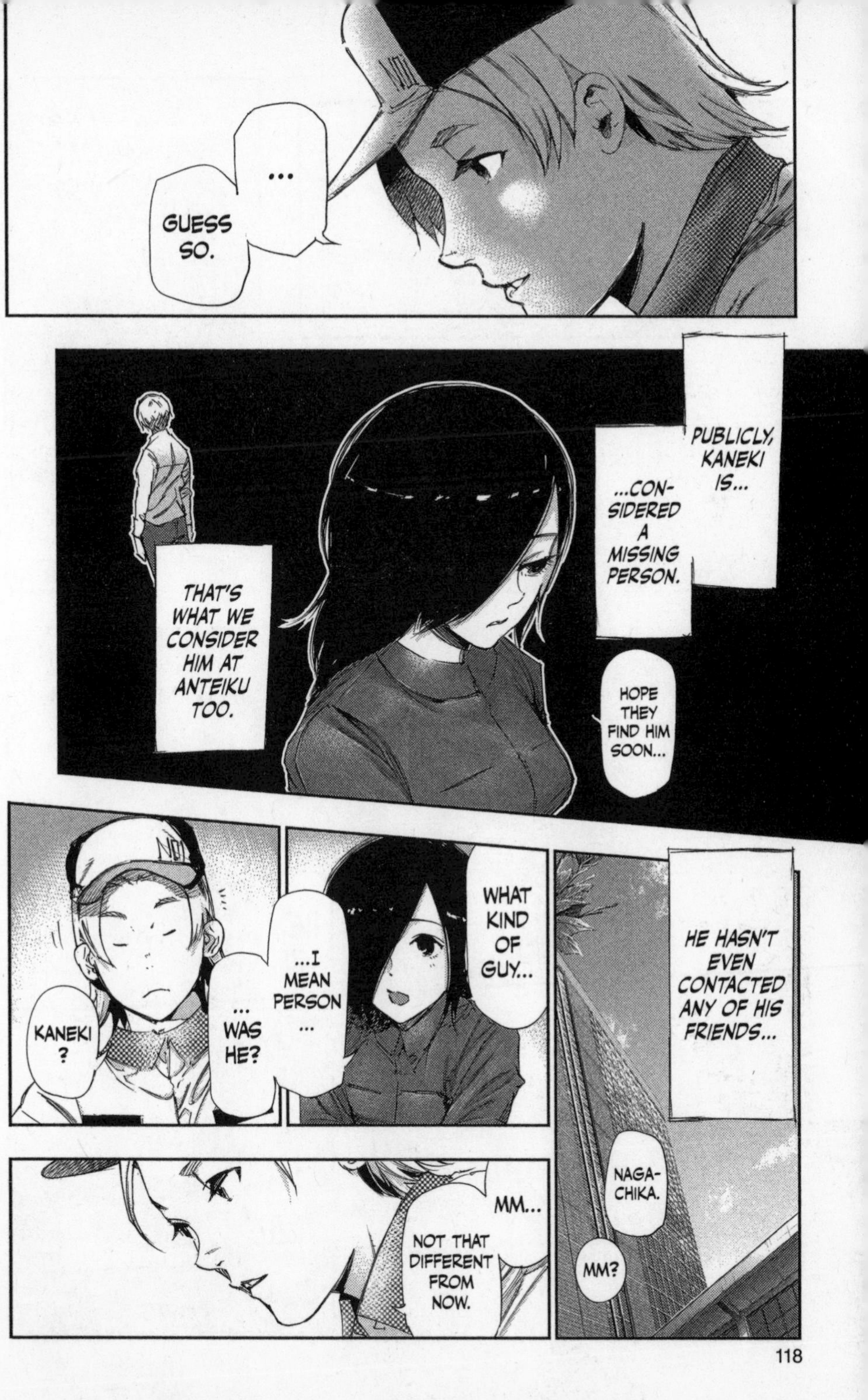
...
GUESS SO.
PUBLICLY, KANEKI IS...
...CON-SIDERED A MISSING PERSON.
HOPE THEY FIND HIM SOON...
THAT'S WHAT WE CONSIDER HIM AT ANTEIKU TOO.
HE HASN'T EVEN CONTACTED ANY OF HIS FRIENDS...
NAGA-CHIKA.
MM?
WHAT KIND OF GUY...
...I MEAN PERSON ...
... WAS HE?
KANEKI ?
MM...
NOT THAT DIFFERENT FROM NOW.

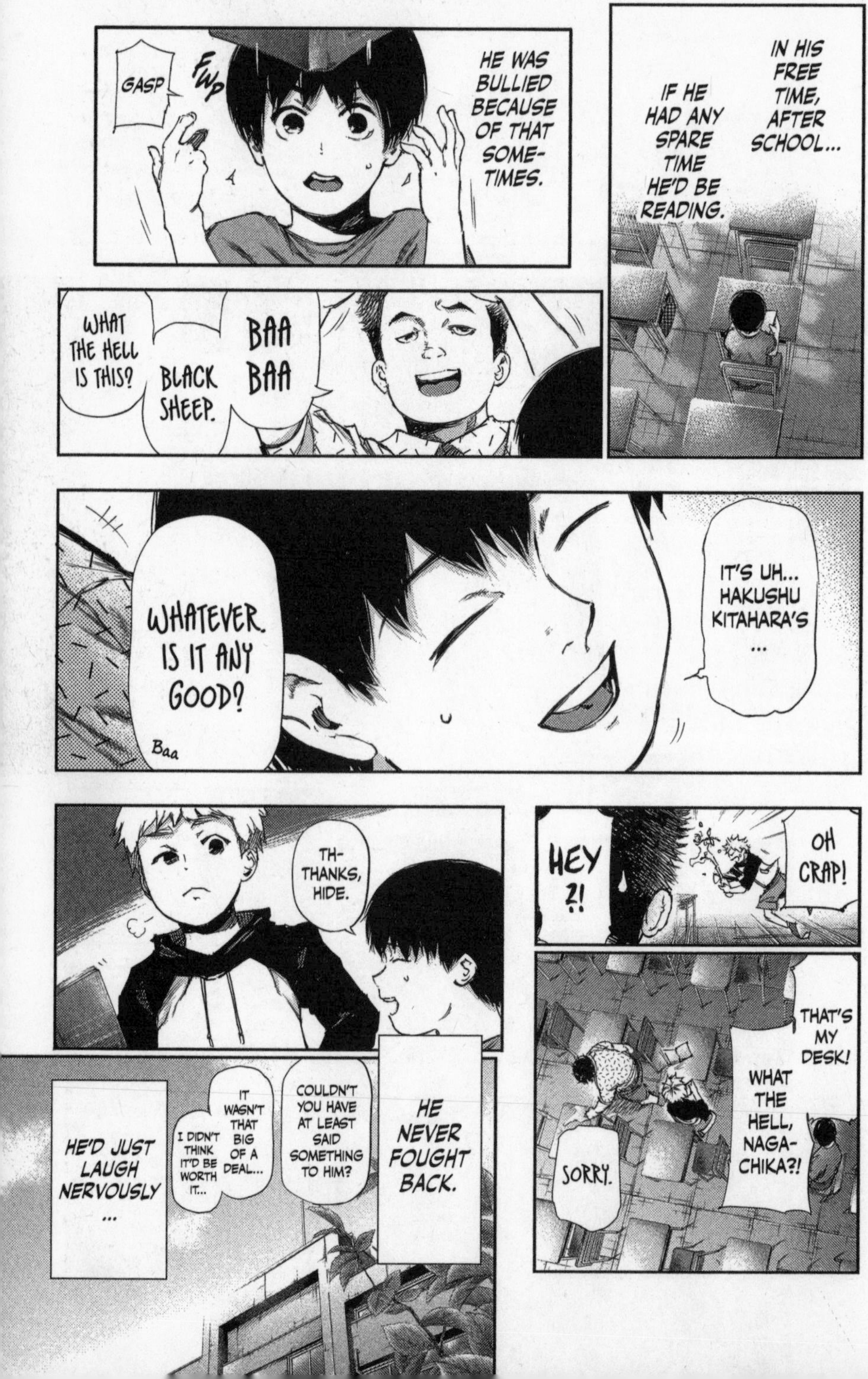
IN HIS FREE TIME, AFTER SCHOOL...
IF HE HAD ANY SPARE TIME HE'D BE READING.
HE WAS BULLIED BECAUSE OF THAT SOME-TIMES.
FWP
GASP
BAA BAA
BLACK SHEEP.
WHAT THE HELL IS THIS?
IT'S UH... HAKUSHU KITAHARA'S ...
WHATEVER. IS IT ANY GOOD?
Baa
OH CRAP!
HEY ?!
THAT'S MY DESK!
WHAT THE HELL, NAGA-CHIKA?!
SORRY.
TH-THANKS, HIDE.
HE NEVER FOUGHT BACK.
COULDN'T YOU HAVE AT LEAST SAID SOMETHING TO HIM?
IT WASN'T THAT BIG OF A DEAL...
I DIDN'T THINK IT'D BE WORTH IT...
HE'D JUST LAUGH NERVOUSLY ...

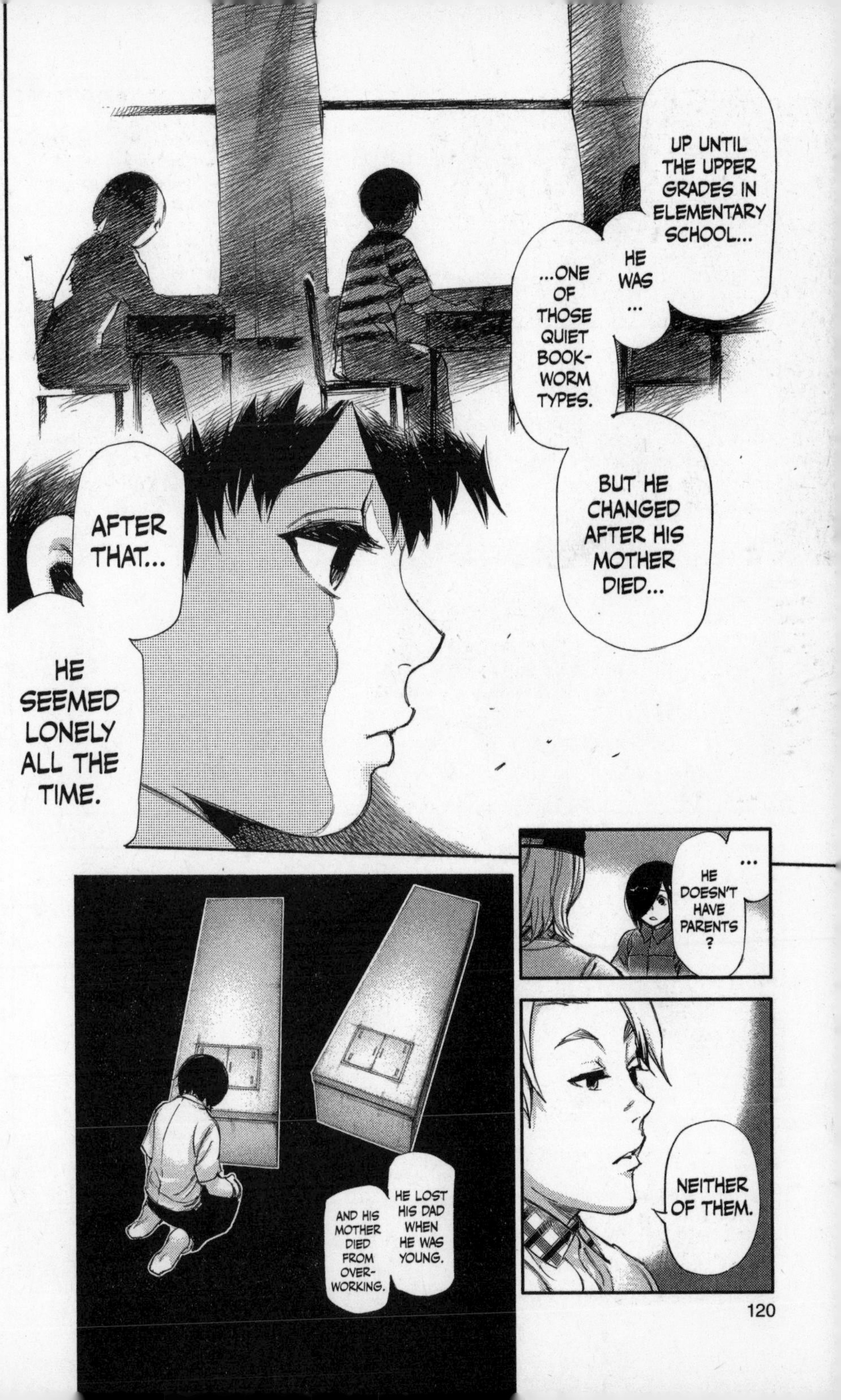
UP UNTIL THE UPPER GRADES IN ELEMENTARY SCHOOL...
HE WAS...
...ONE OF THOSE QUIET BOOK-WORM TYPES.
BUT HE CHANGED AFTER HIS MOTHER DIED...
AFTER THAT...
HE SEEMED LONELY ALL THE TIME.
...HE DOESN'T HAVE PARENTS?
NEITHER OF THEM.
HE LOST HIS DAD WHEN HE WAS YOUNG.
AND HIS MOTHER DIED FROM OVER-WORKING.

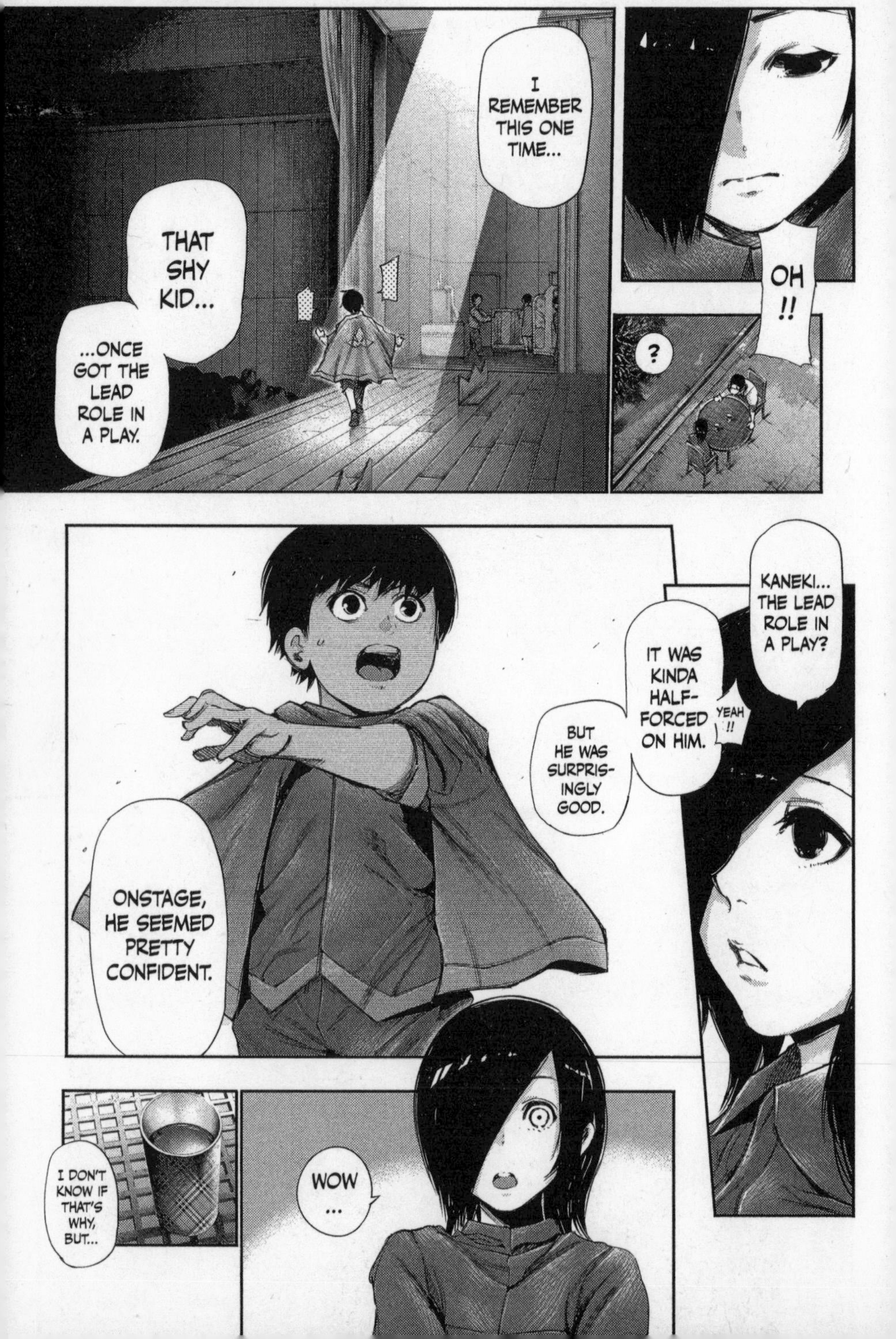
OH !!
?
I REMEMBER THIS ONE TIME...
THAT SHY KID...
...ONCE GOT THE LEAD ROLE IN A PLAY.
KANEKI... THE LEAD ROLE IN A PLAY?
YEAH !!
IT WAS KINDA HALF-FORCED ON HIM.
BUT HE WAS SURPRIS-INGLY GOOD.
ONSTAGE, HE SEEMED PRETTY CONFIDENT.
WOW ...
I DON'T KNOW IF THAT'S WHY, BUT...

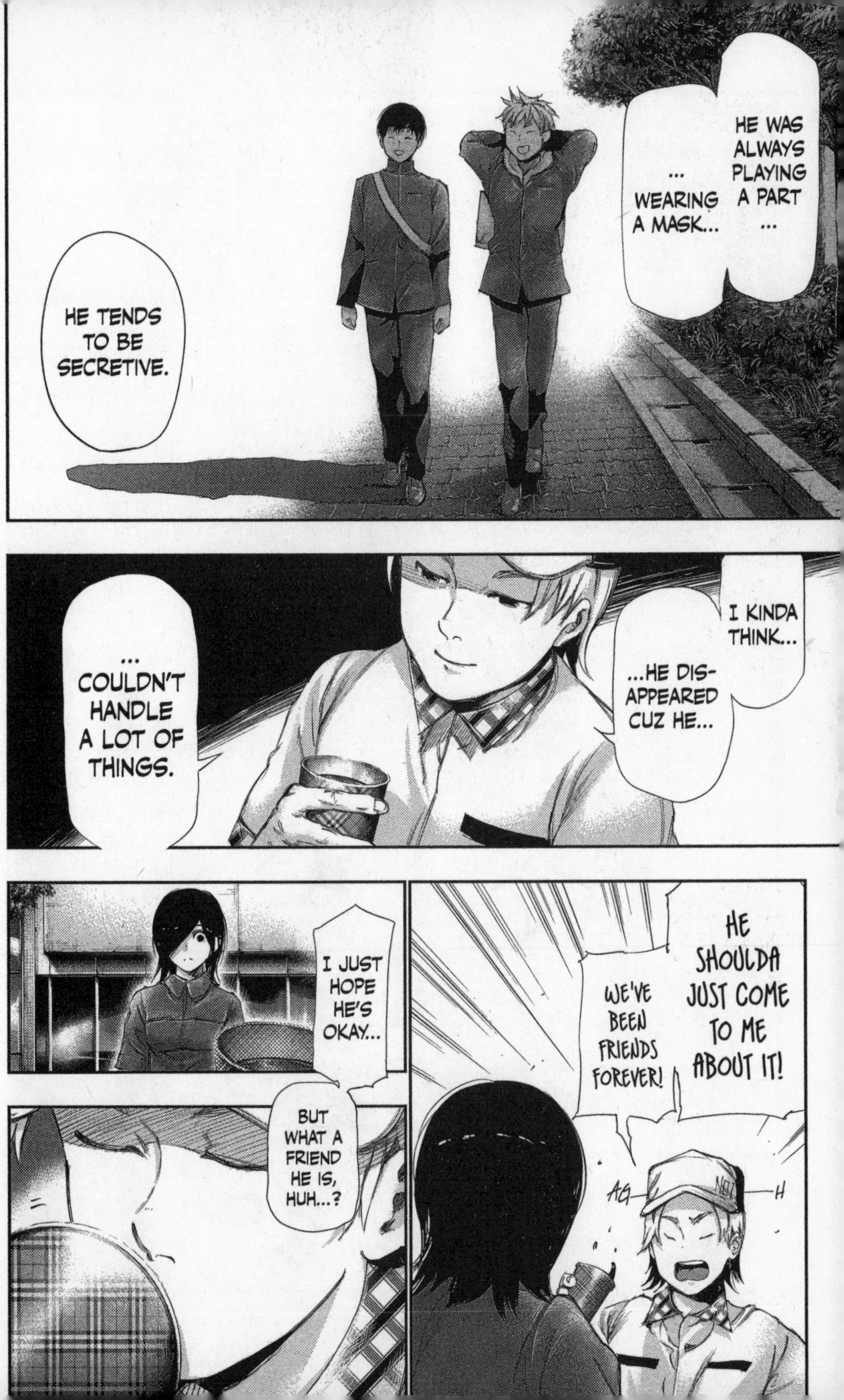
HE WAS ALWAYS PLAYING A PART ...
... WEARING A MASK...
HE TENDS TO BE SECRETIVE.
I KINDA THINK...
...HE DIS-APPEARED CUZ HE...
... COULDN'T HANDLE A LOT OF THINGS.
HE SHOULDA JUST COME TO ME ABOUT IT!
WE'VE BEEN FRIENDS FOREVER!
AGH
I JUST HOPE HE'S OKAY...
BUT WHAT A FRIEND HE IS, HUH...?

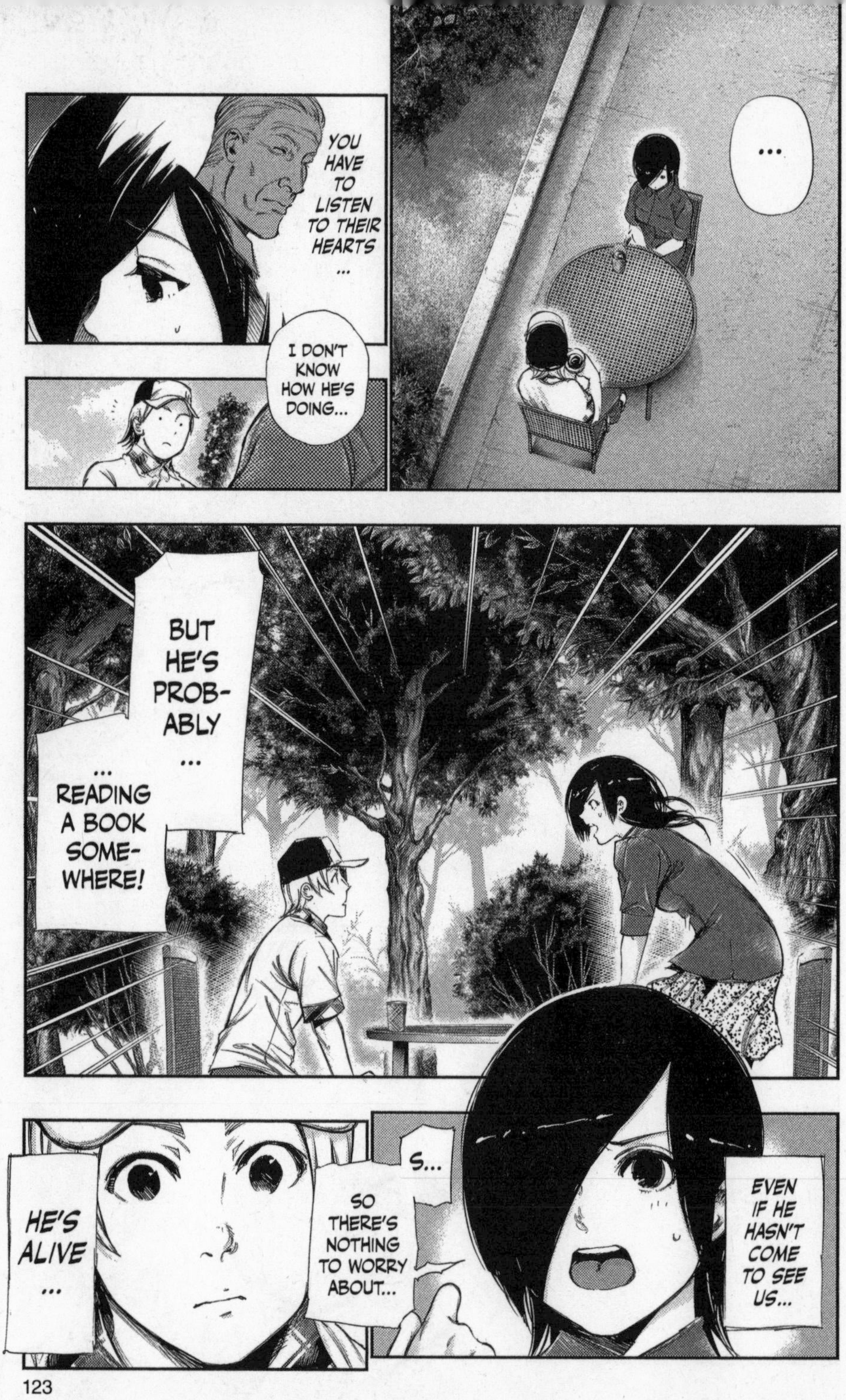
...
YOU HAVE TO LISTEN TO THEIR HEARTS ...
I DON'T KNOW HOW HE'S DOING...
BUT HE'S PROBABLY ...
... READING A BOOK SOMEWHERE!
EVEN IF HE HASN'T COME TO SEE US...
S...
SO THERE'S NOTHING TO WORRY ABOUT...
HE'S ALIVE ...

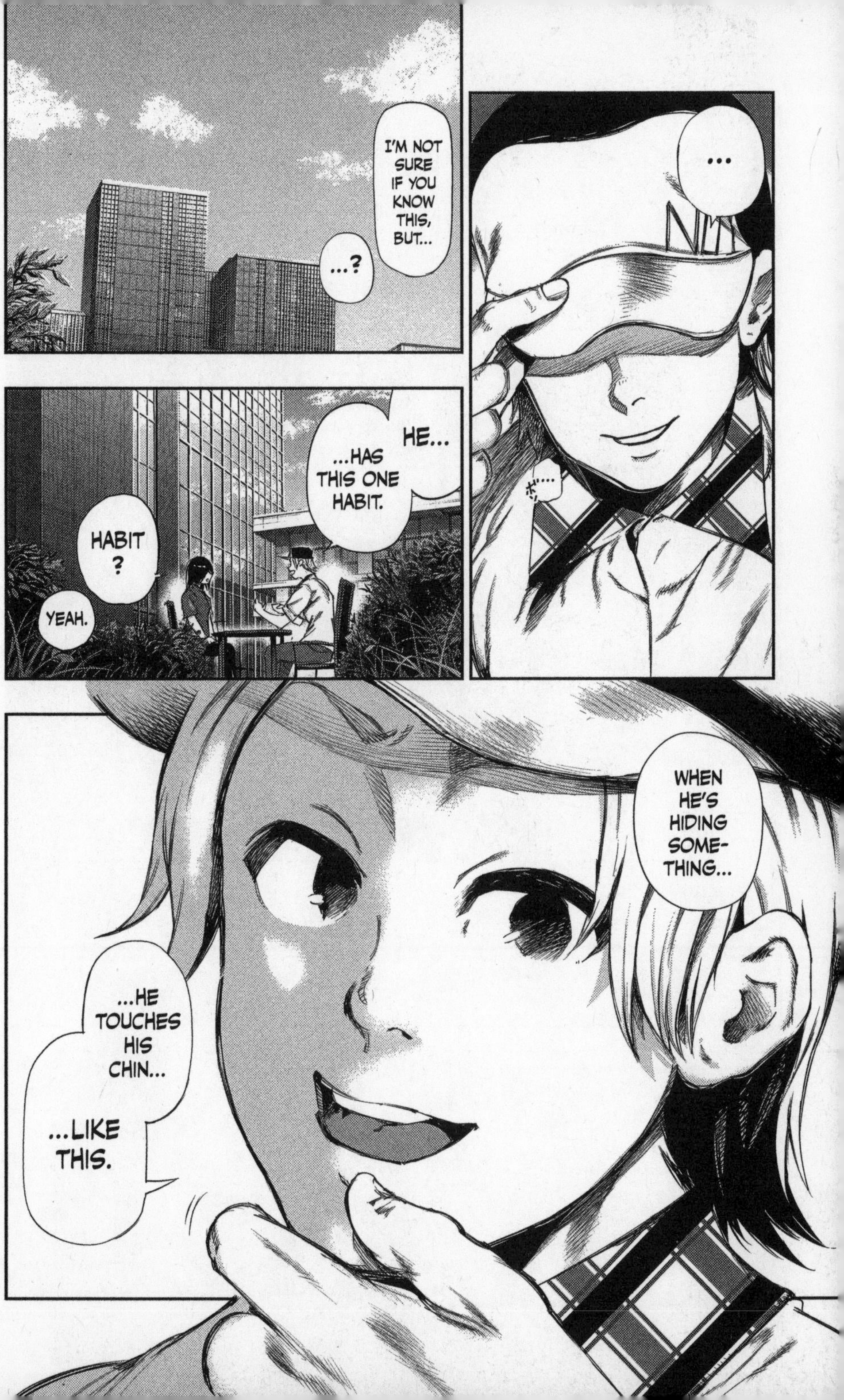
...
I'M NOT SURE IF YOU KNOW THIS, BUT...
...?
HE...
...HAS THIS ONE HABIT.
HABIT?
YEAH.
WHEN HE'S HIDING SOME-THING...
...HE TOUCHES HIS CHIN...
...LIKE THIS.

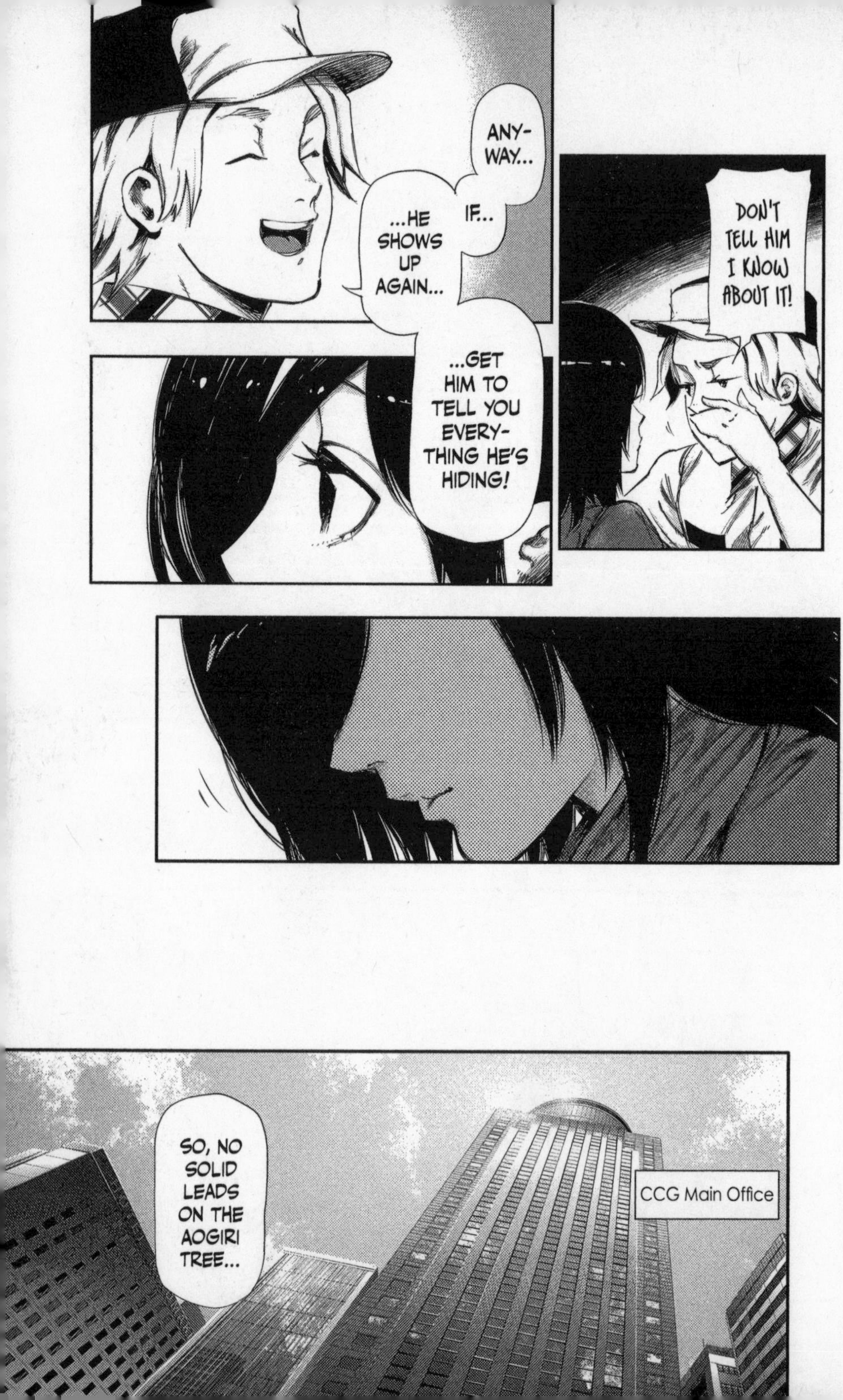
ANY-WAY...
IF...
...HE SHOWS UP AGAIN...
...GET HIM TO TELL YOU EVERY-THING HE'S HIDING!
DON'T TELL HIM I KNOW ABOUT IT!
CCG Main Office
SO, NO SOLID LEADS ON THE AOGIRI TREE...

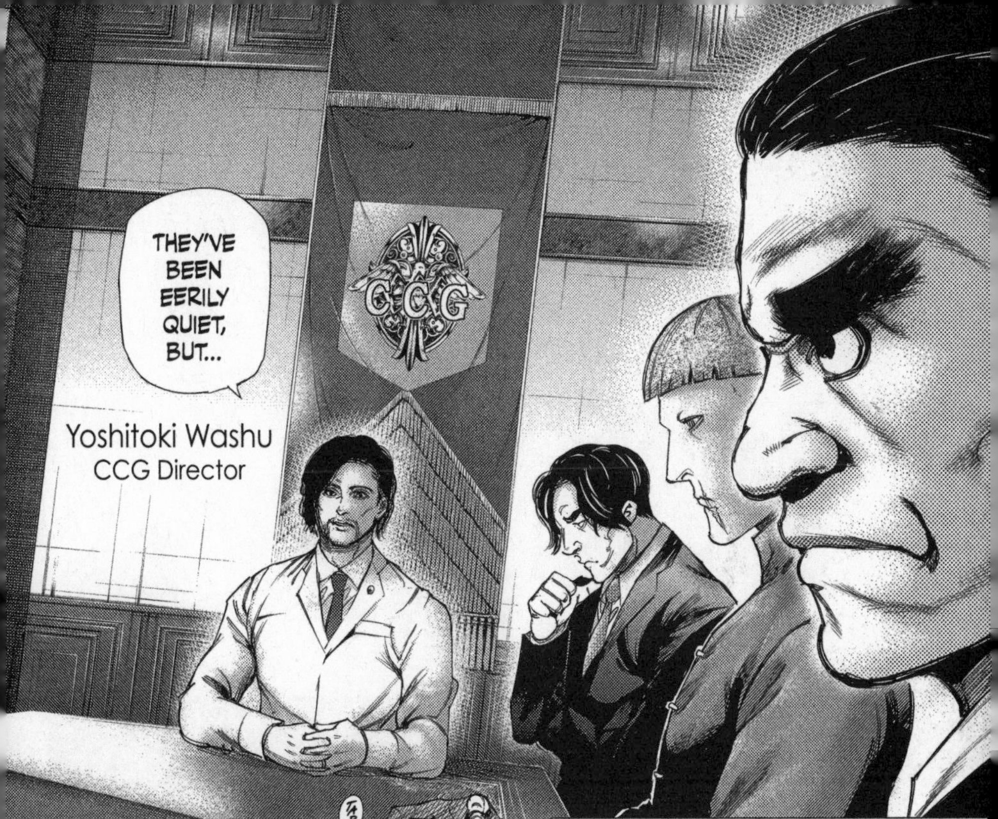
THEY'VE BEEN EERILY QUIET, BUT...
Yoshitoki Washu
CCG Director
TAP TAP
Special Investigators' Meeting

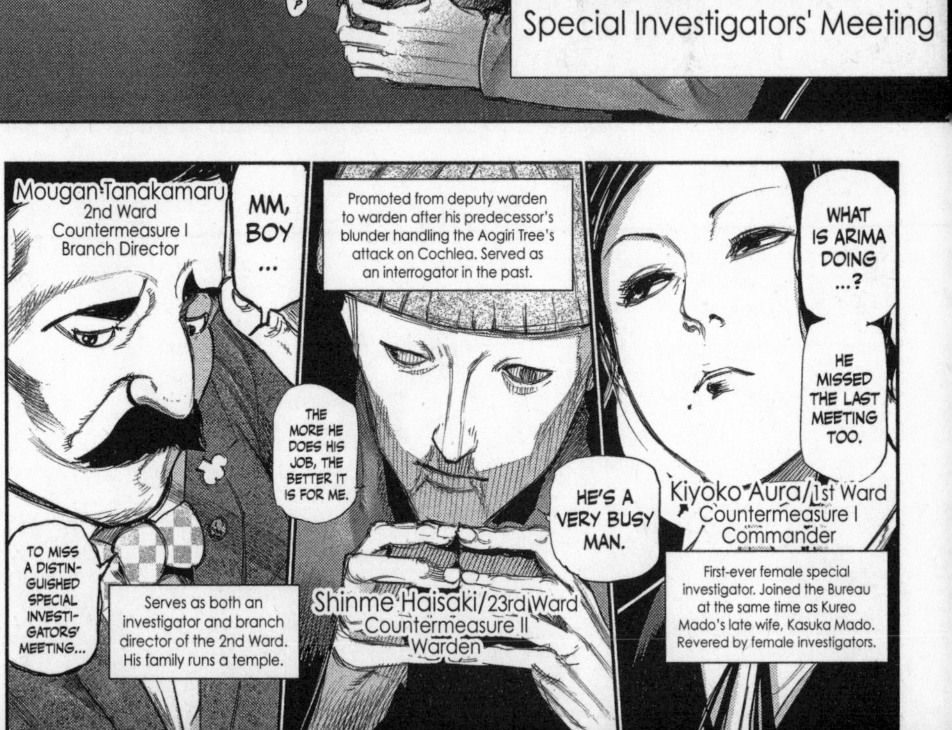
WHAT IS ARIMA DOING ...?
HE MISSED THE LAST MEETING TOO.
Kiyoko Aura/1st Ward Countermeasure I Commander
First-ever female special investigator. Joined the Bureau at the same time as Kureo Mado's late wife, Kasuka Mado. Revered by female investigators.
Promoted from deputy warden to warden after his predecessor's blunder handling the Aogiri Tree's attack on Cochlea. Served as an interrogator in the past.
HE'S A VERY BUSY MAN.
THE MORE HE DOES HIS JOB, THE BETTER IT IS FOR ME.
Shinme Haisaki/23rd Ward Countermeasure II Warden
MM, BOY ...
Mougan Tanakamaru
2nd Ward Countermeasure I Branch Director
TO MISS A DISTINGUISHED SPECIAL INVESTIGATORS' MEETING...
Serves as both an investigator and branch director of the 2nd Ward. His family runs a temple.

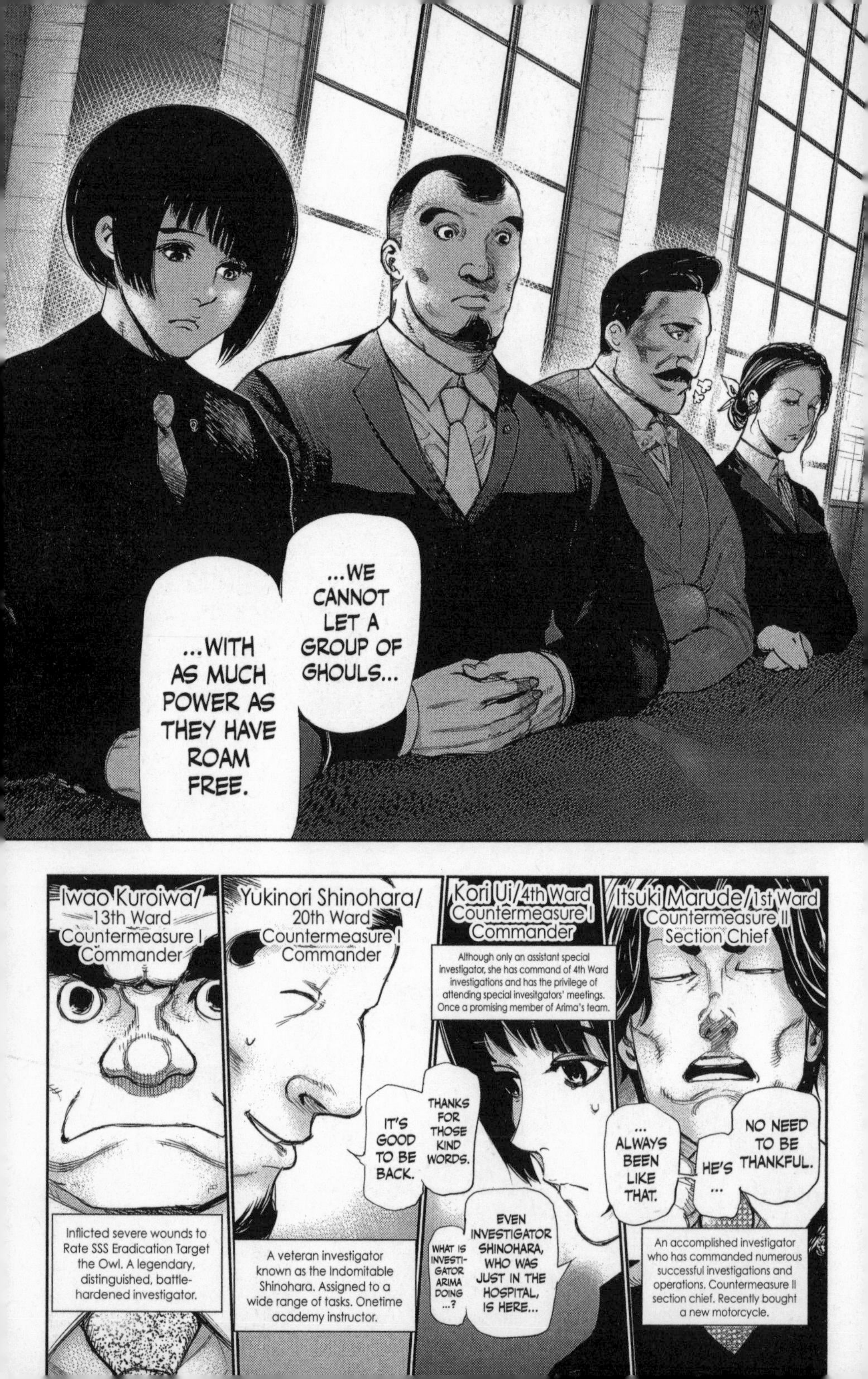
...WE CANNOT LET A GROUP OF GHOULS...
...WITH AS MUCH POWER AS THEY HAVE ROAM FREE.
Itsuki Marude/1st Ward Countermeasure II Section Chief
NO NEED TO BE THANKFUL.
HE'S ...
... ALWAYS BEEN LIKE THAT.
An accomplished investigator who has commanded numerous successful investigations and operations. Countermeasure II section chief. Recently bought a new motorcycle.
Kori Ui/4th Ward Countermeasure I Commander
Although only an assistant special investigator, she has command of 4th Ward investigations and has the privilege of attending special invesitgators' meetings. Once a promising member of Arima's team.
EVEN INVESTIGATOR SHINOHARA, WHO WAS JUST IN THE HOSPITAL, IS HERE...
WHAT IS INVESTI-GATOR ARIMA DOING ...?
Yukinori Shinohara/ 20th Ward Countermeasure I Commander
THANKS FOR THOSE KIND WORDS.
IT'S GOOD TO BE BACK.
A veteran investigator known as the Indomitable Shinohara. Assigned to a wide range of tasks. Onetime academy instructor.
Iwao Kuroiwa/ 13th Ward Countermeasure I Commander
Inflicted severe wounds to Rate SSS Eradication Target the Owl. A legendary, distinguished, battle-hardened investigator.

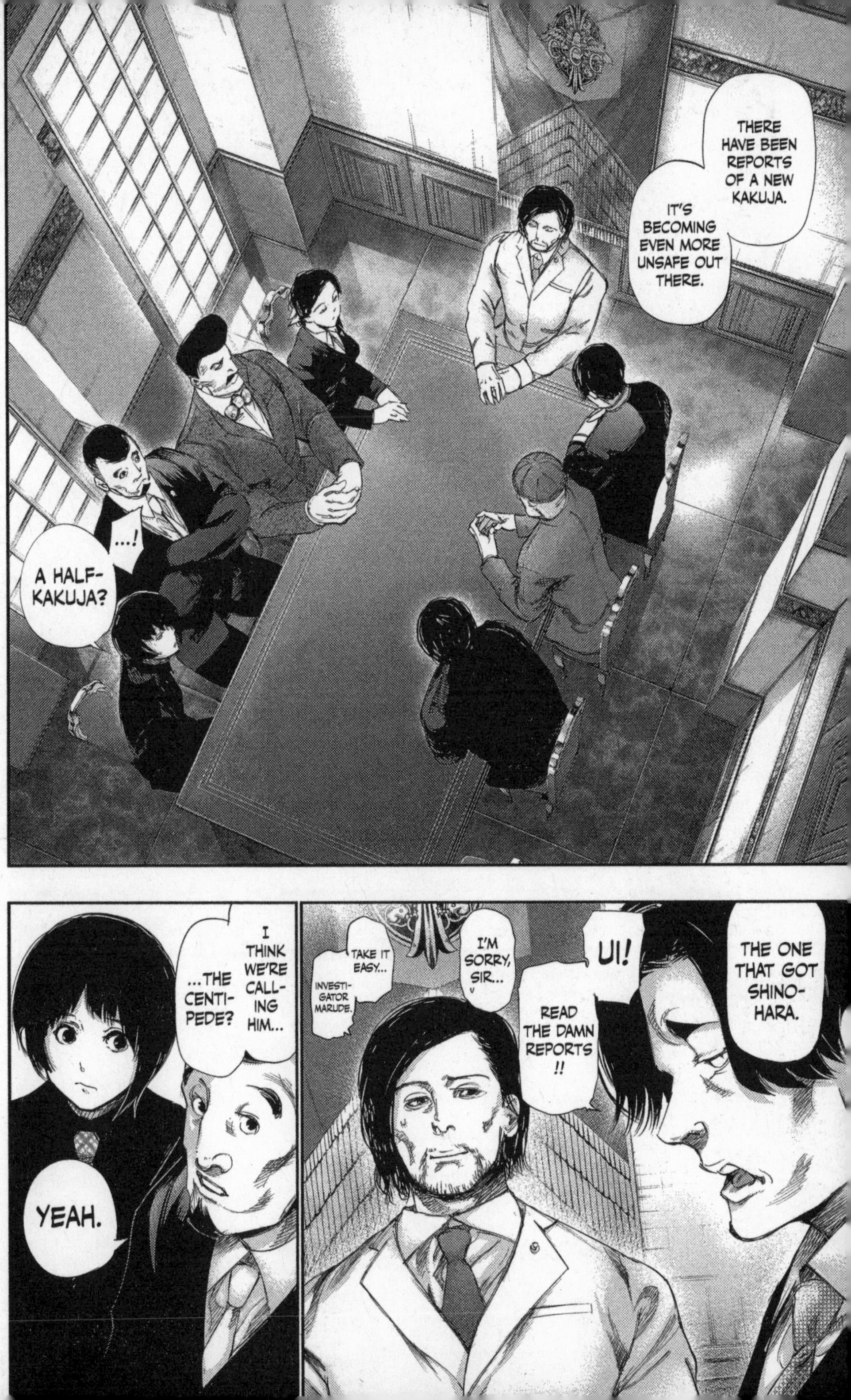
THERE HAVE BEEN REPORTS OF A NEW KAKUJA.
IT'S BECOMING EVEN MORE UNSAFE OUT THERE.
...!
A HALF-KAKUJA?
THE ONE THAT GOT SHINO-HARA.
UI!
READ THE DAMN REPORTS !!
I'M SORRY, SIR...
TAKE IT EASY...
INVESTI-GATOR MARUDE.
I THINK WE'RE CALL-ING HIM...
...THE CENTI-PEDE?
YEAH.

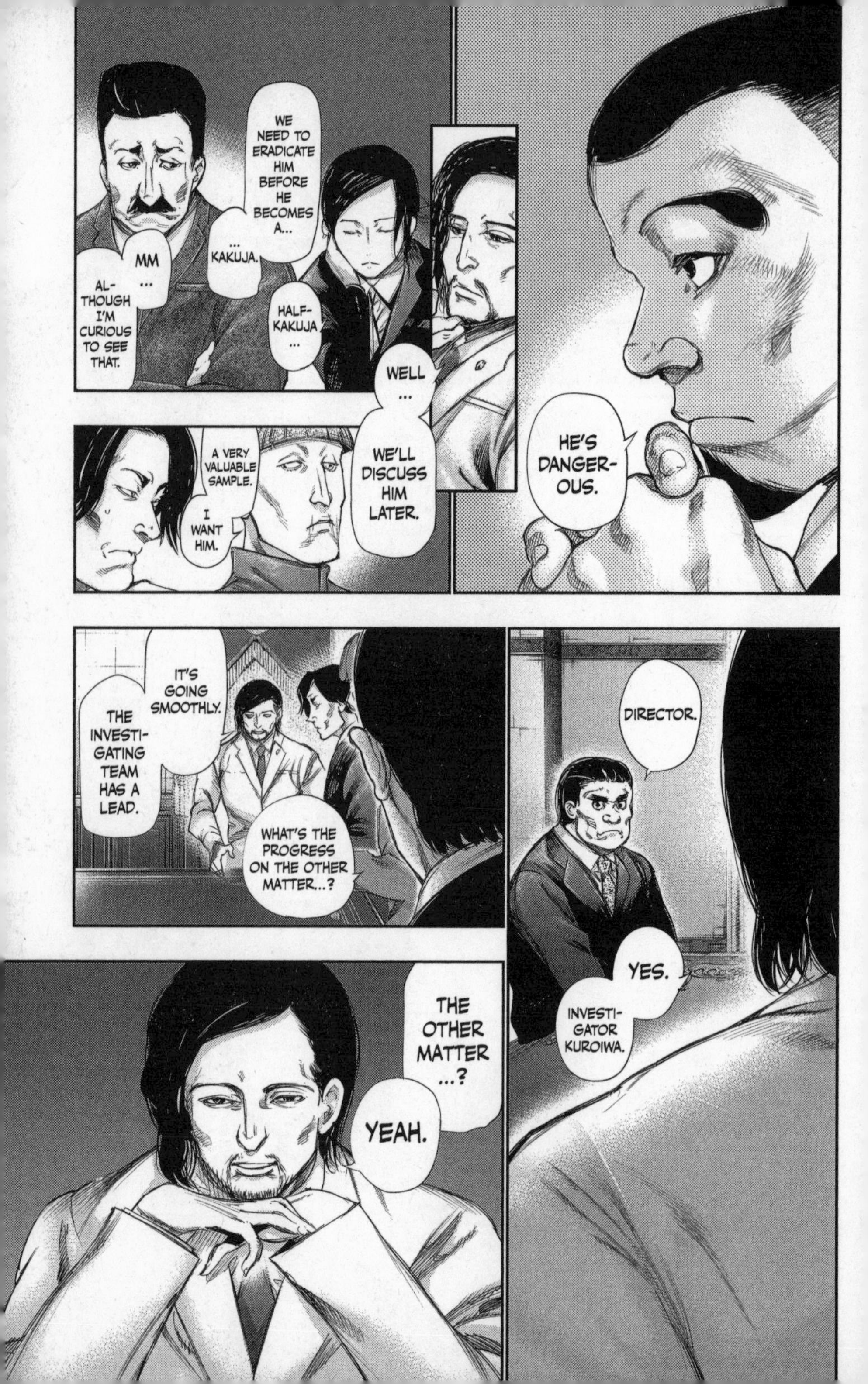
HE'S DANGER-OUS.
WE NEED TO ERADICATE HIM BEFORE HE BECOMES A...
...KAKUJA.
HALF-KAKUJA...
MM...
AL-THOUGH I'M CURIOUS TO SEE THAT.
WELL...
WE'LL DISCUSS HIM LATER.
A VERY VALUABLE SAMPLE.
I WANT HIM.
DIRECTOR.
YES.
INVESTI-GATOR KUROIWA.
IT'S GOING SMOOTHLY.
THE INVESTI-GATING TEAM HAS A LEAD.
WHAT'S THE PROGRESS ON THE OTHER MATTER...?
THE OTHER MATTER...?
YEAH.

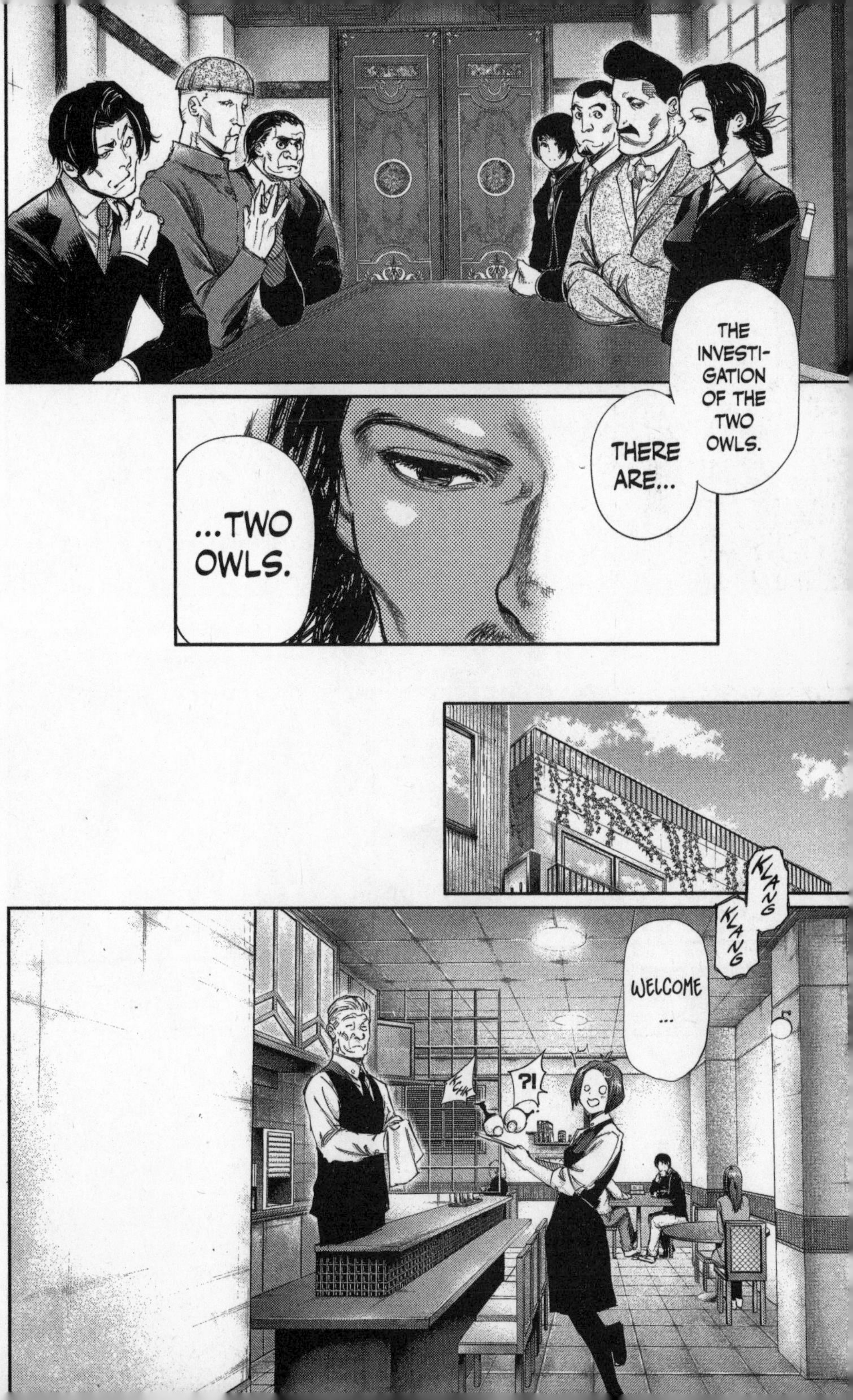
THE INVESTIGATION OF THE TWO OWLS.
THERE ARE...
...TWO OWLS.
KLANG
KLANG
WELCOME...
?!
KCHK

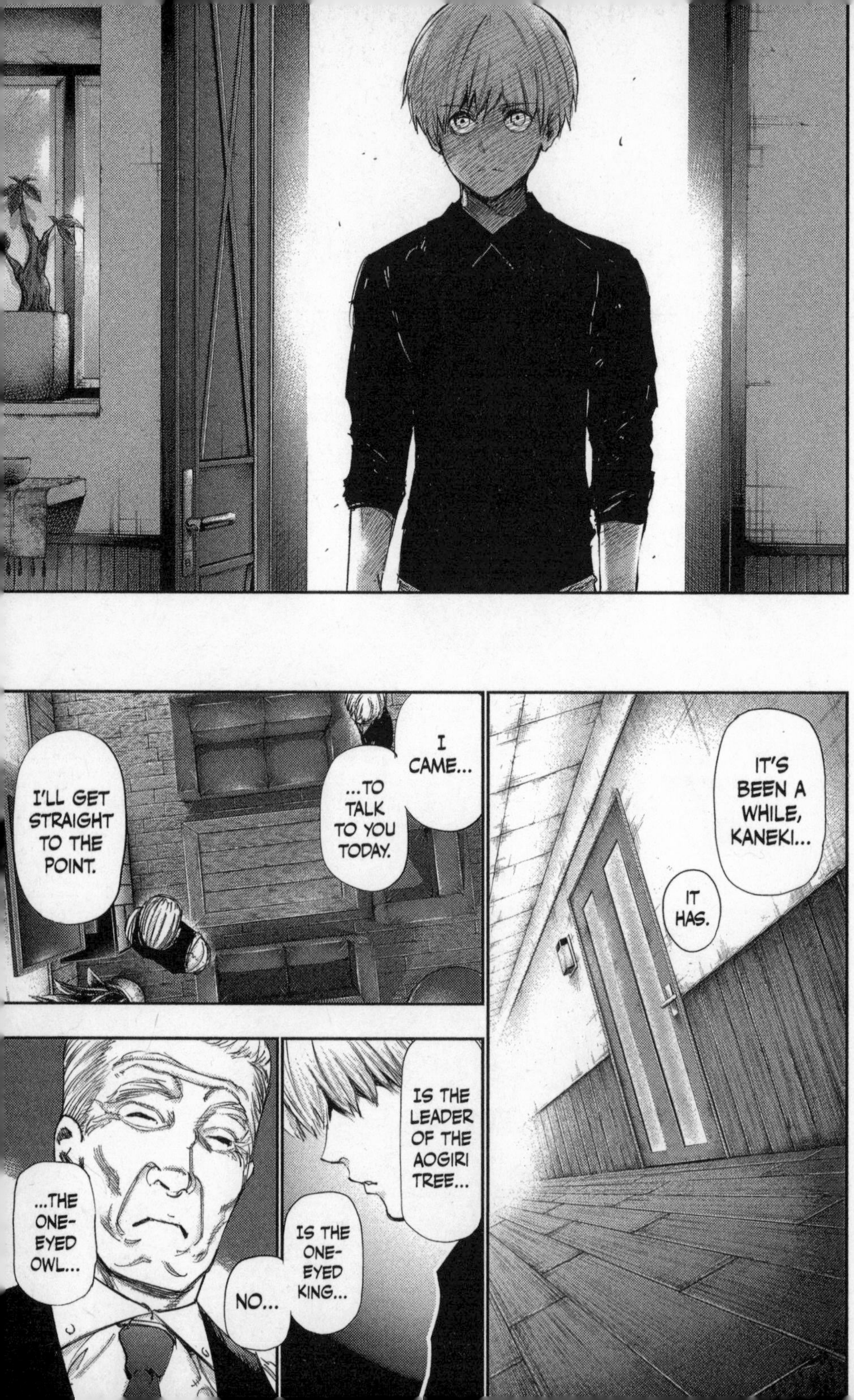
IT'S BEEN A WHILE, KANEKI...
IT HAS.
I CAME...
...TO TALK TO YOU TODAY.
I'LL GET STRAIGHT TO THE POINT.
IS THE LEADER OF THE AOGIRI TREE...
IS THE ONE-EYED KING...
NO...
...THE ONE-EYED OWL...

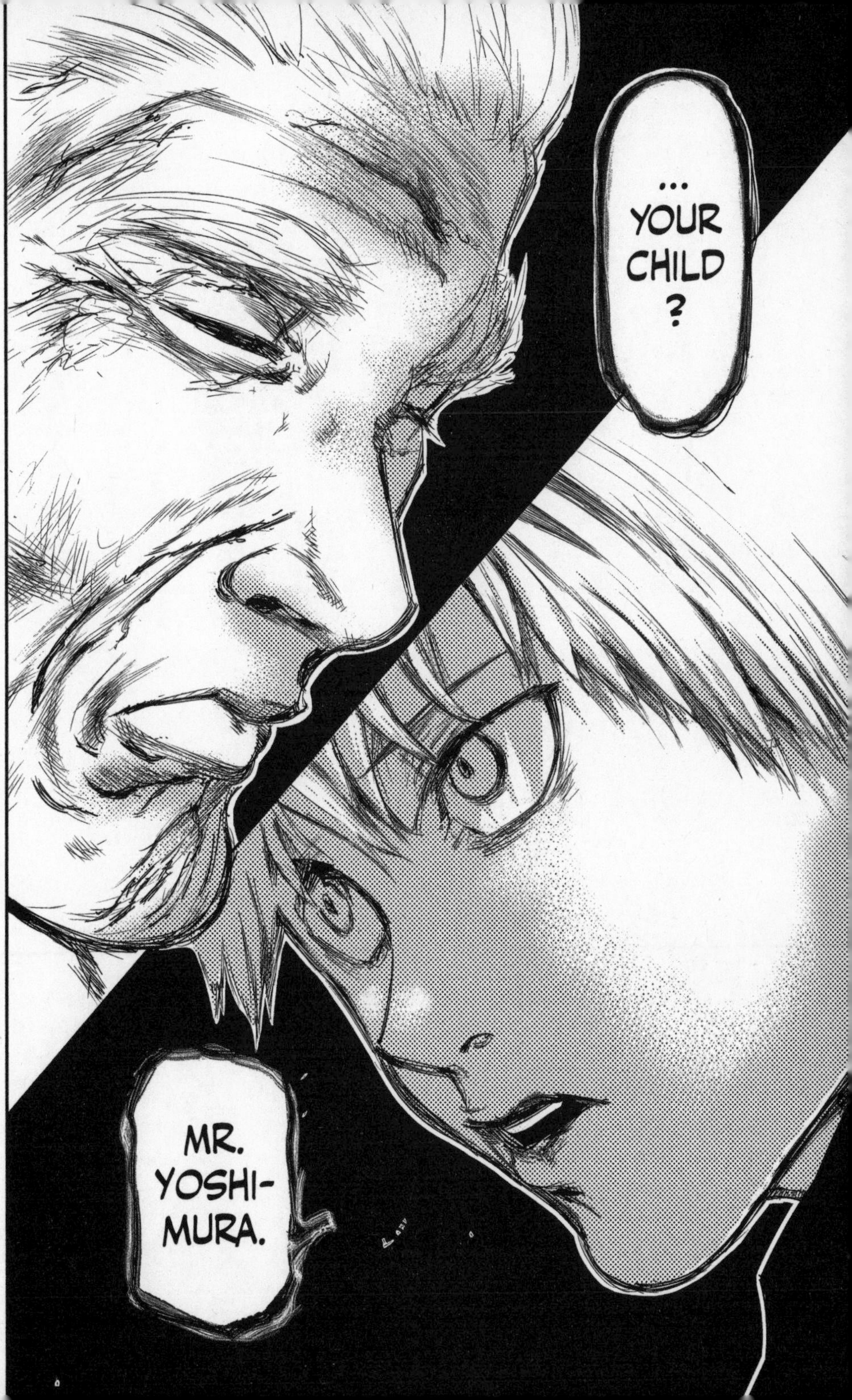
...YOUR CHILD?
MR. YOSHIMURA.

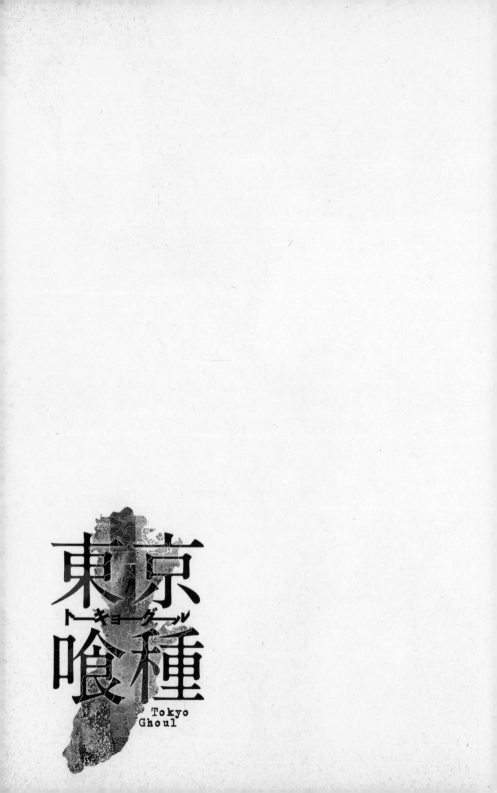

東京喰種
トーキョーグール
Tokyo
Ghoul

It's Poetry Time. (2)

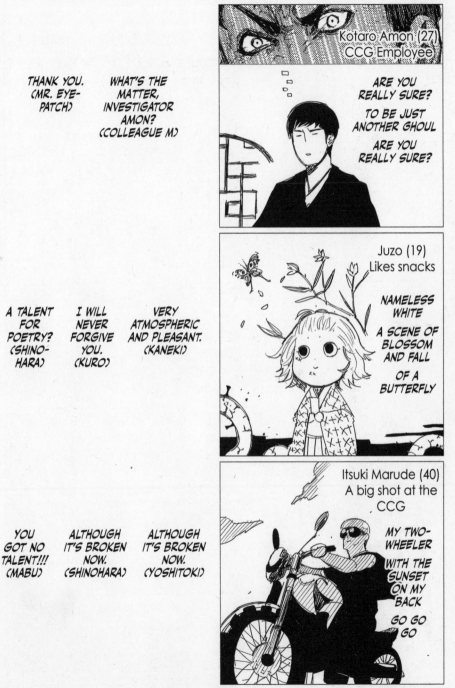

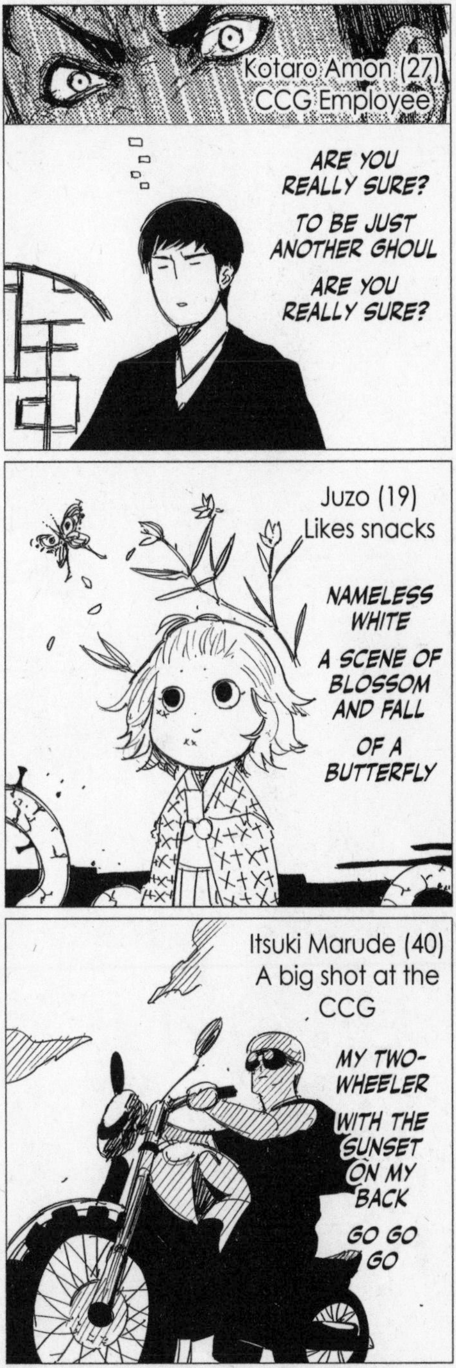
Kotaro Amon (27)
CCG Employee
ARE YOU REALLY SURE?
TO BE JUST ANOTHER GHOUL
ARE YOU REALLY SURE?
Juzo (19)
Likes snacks
NAMELESS WHITE
A SCENE OF BLOSSOM AND FALL
OF A BUTTERFLY
Itsuki Marude (40)
A big shot at the CCG
MY TWO-WHEELER
WITH THE SUNSET ON MY BACK
GO GO GO

WHAT'S THE MATTER, INVESTIGATOR AMON? (COLLEAGUE M)

THANK YOU. (MR. EYE-PATCH)

VERY ATMOSPHERIC AND PLEASANT. (KANEKI)

I WILL NEVER FORGIVE YOU. (KURO)

A TALENT FOR POETRY? (SHINO-HARA)

ALTHOUGH IT'S BROKEN NOW. (YOSHITOKI)

ALTHOUGH IT'S BROKEN NOW. (SHINOHARA)

YOU GOT NO TALENT!!! (MABU)

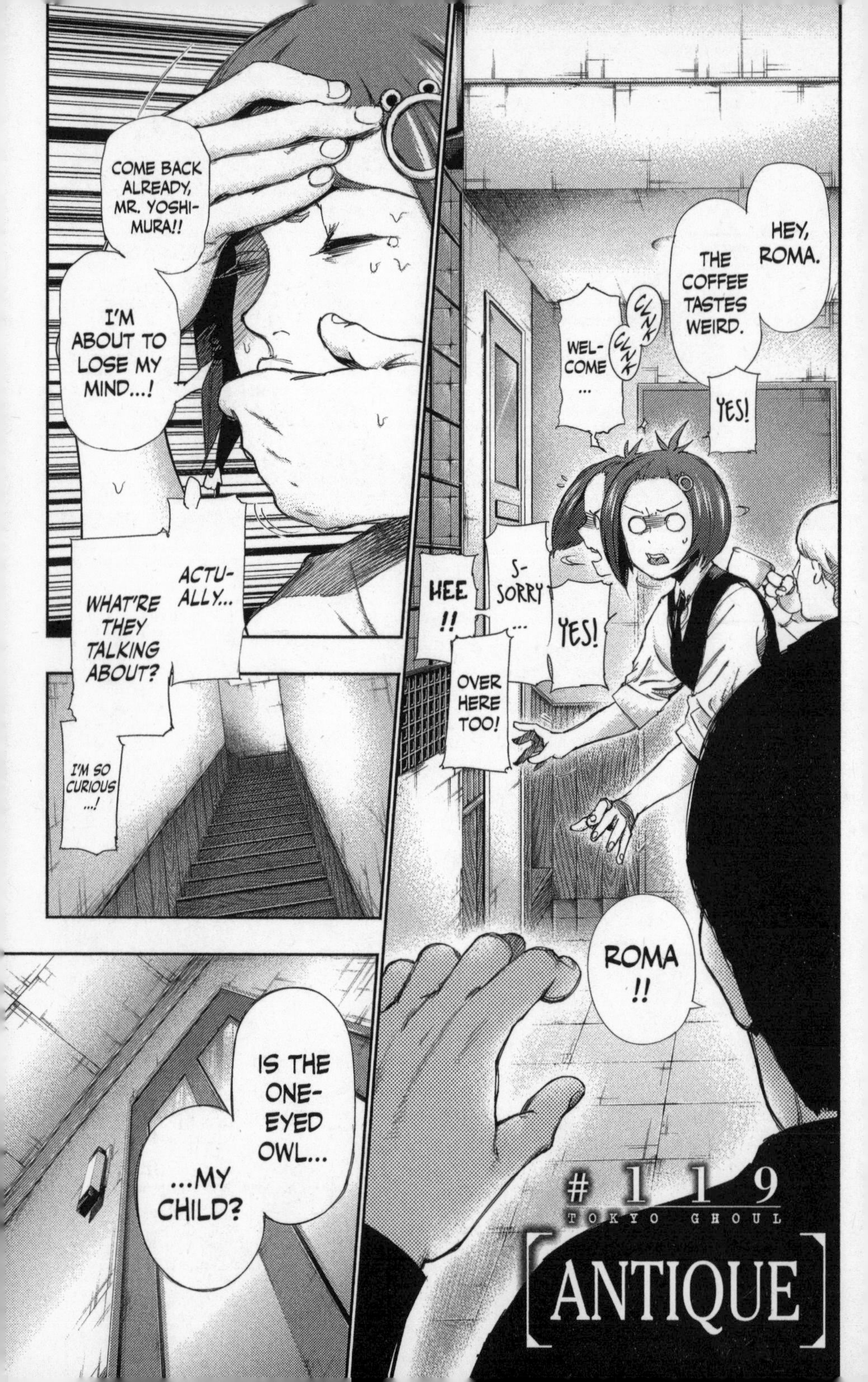
HEY, ROMA.
THE COFFEE TASTES WEIRD.
YES!
CLNK CLNK
WEL-COME ...
YES!
S-SORRY ...
HEE!!
OVER HERE TOO!
ROMA!!
COME BACK ALREADY, MR. YOSHI-MURA!!
I'M ABOUT TO LOSE MY MIND...!
ACTU-ALLY...
WHAT'RE THEY TALKING ABOUT?
I'M SO CURIOUS...!
IS THE ONE-EYED OWL...
...MY CHILD?
#119
TOKYO GHOUL
[ANTIQUE]

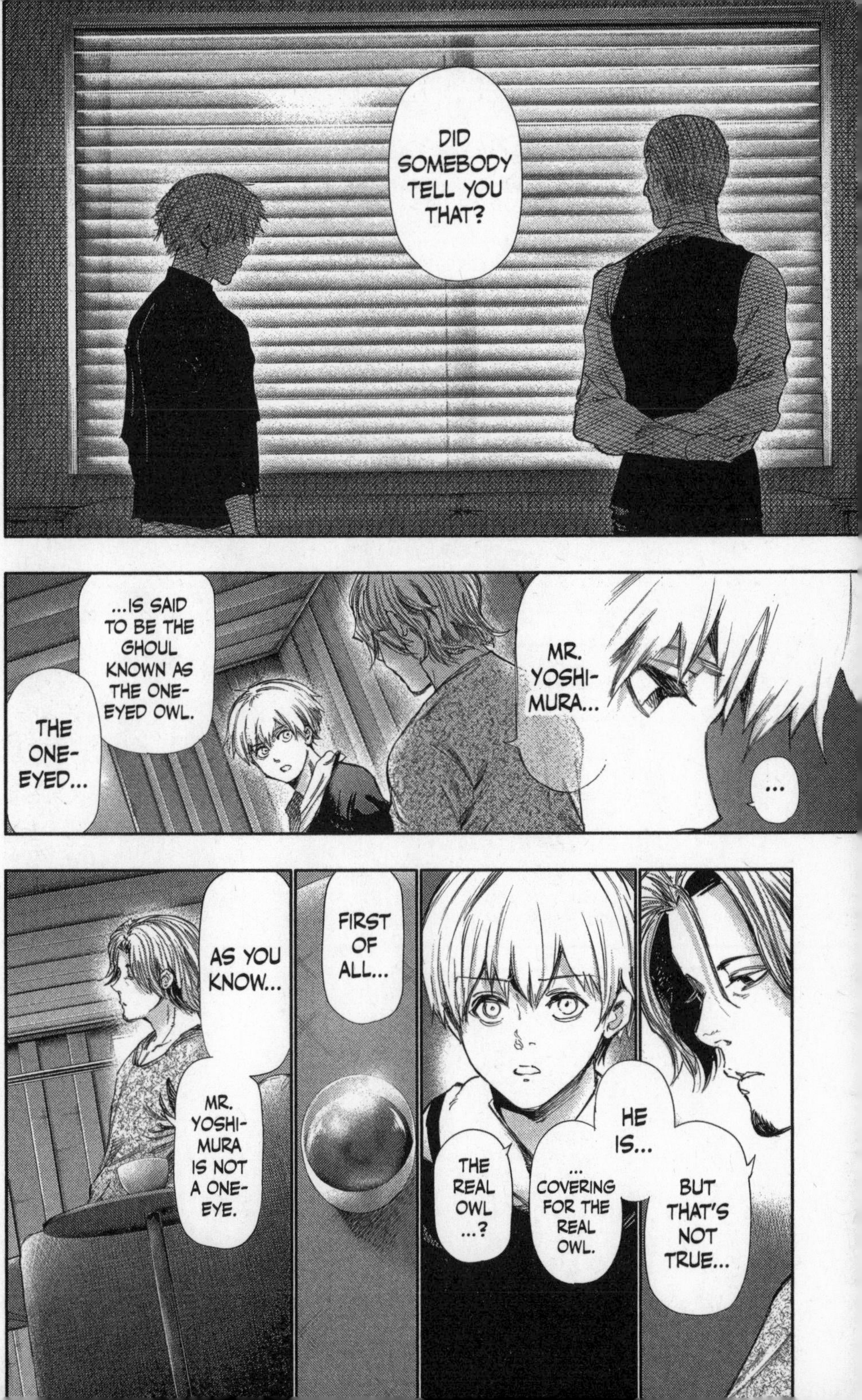
DID SOMEBODY TELL YOU THAT?
...
MR. YOSHIMURA...
...IS SAID TO BE THE GHOUL KNOWN AS THE ONE-EYED OWL.
THE ONE-EYED...
BUT THAT'S NOT TRUE...
HE IS...
...COVERING FOR THE REAL OWL.
THE REAL OWL...?
FIRST OF ALL...
AS YOU KNOW...
MR. YOSHIMURA IS NOT A ONE-EYE.

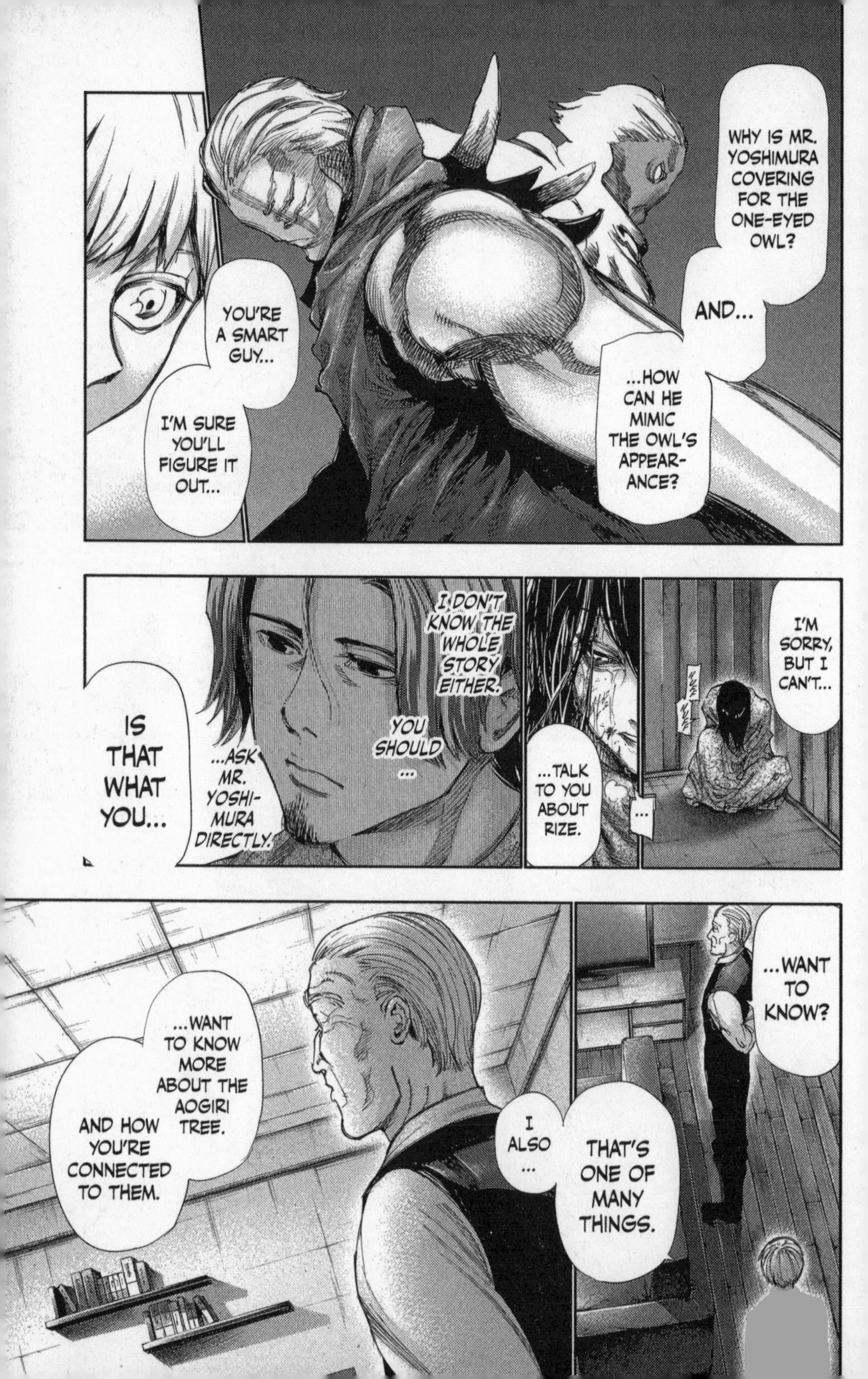
WHY IS MR. YOSHIMURA COVERING FOR THE ONE-EYED OWL?
AND...
...HOW CAN HE MIMIC THE OWL'S APPEARANCE?
YOU'RE A SMART GUY...
I'M SURE YOU'LL FIGURE IT OUT...
I'M SORRY, BUT I CAN'T...
...TALK TO YOU ABOUT RIZE.
...
I DON'T KNOW THE WHOLE STORY EITHER.
YOU SHOULD ...
...ASK MR. YOSHIMURA DIRECTLY.
IS THAT WHAT YOU...
...WANT TO KNOW?
THAT'S ONE OF MANY THINGS.
I ALSO ...
...WANT TO KNOW MORE ABOUT THE AOGIRI TREE.
AND HOW YOU'RE CONNECTED TO THEM.

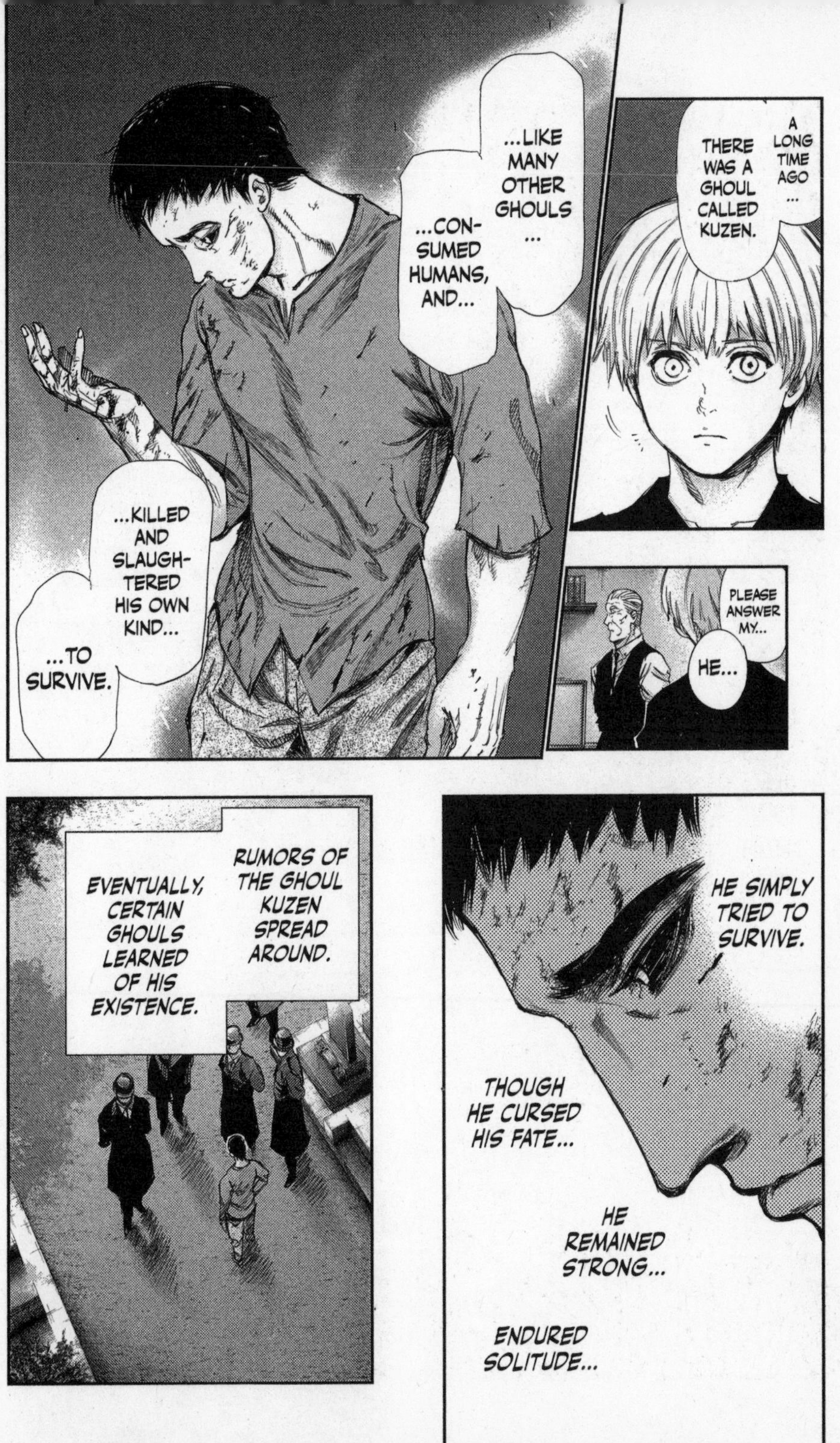
A LONG TIME AGO...
THERE WAS A GHOUL CALLED KUZEN.
PLEASE ANSWER MY...
HE...
...LIKE MANY OTHER GHOULS...
...CON-SUMED HUMANS, AND...
...KILLED AND SLAUGH-TERED HIS OWN KIND...
...TO SURVIVE.
HE SIMPLY TRIED TO SURVIVE.
THOUGH HE CURSED HIS FATE...
HE REMAINED STRONG...
ENDURED SOLITUDE...
RUMORS OF THE GHOUL KUZEN SPREAD AROUND.
EVENTUALLY, CERTAIN GHOULS LEARNED OF HIS EXISTENCE.

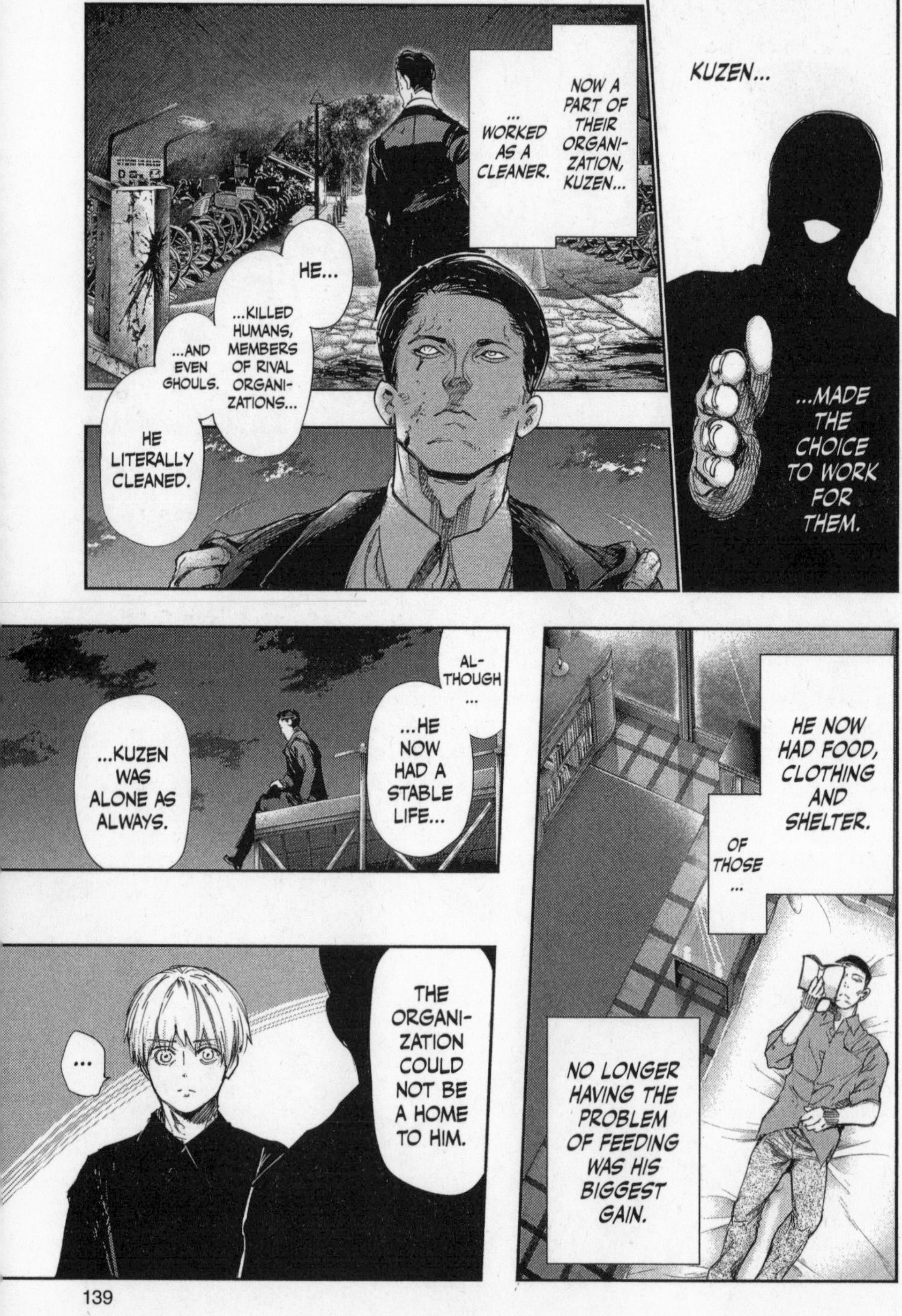
KUZEN...
...MADE THE CHOICE TO WORK FOR THEM.
NOW A PART OF THEIR ORGANIZATION, KUZEN...
...WORKED AS A CLEANER.
HE...
...KILLED HUMANS, MEMBERS OF RIVAL ORGANIZATIONS...
...AND EVEN GHOULS.
HE LITERALLY CLEANED.
HE NOW HAD FOOD, CLOTHING AND SHELTER.
OF THOSE...
NO LONGER HAVING THE PROBLEM OF FEEDING WAS HIS BIGGEST GAIN.
ALTHOUGH...
...HE NOW HAD A STABLE LIFE...
...KUZEN WAS ALONE AS ALWAYS.
THE ORGANIZATION COULD NOT BE A HOME TO HIM.
...

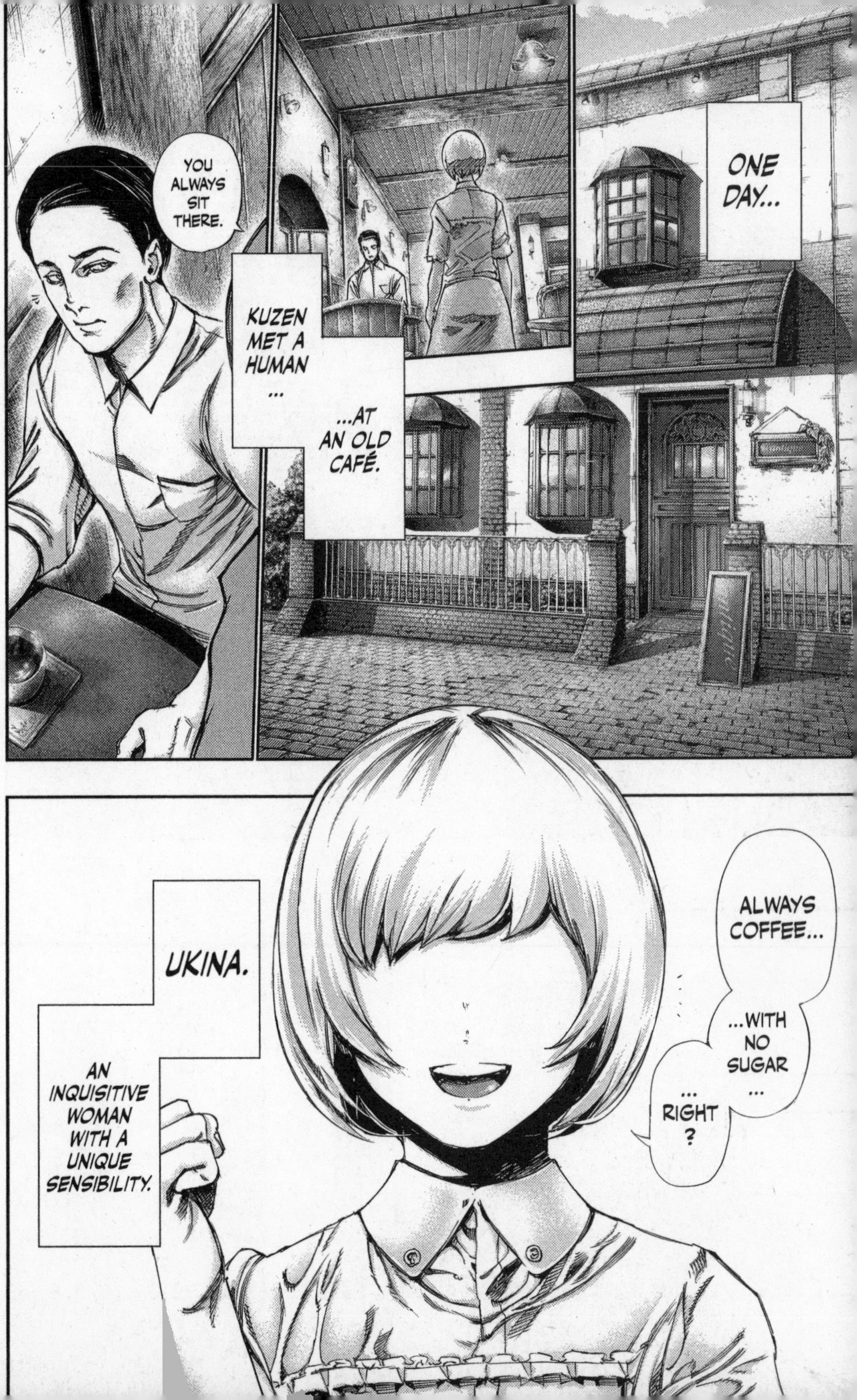
ONE DAY...
KUZEN MET A HUMAN ...
...AT AN OLD CAFÉ.
YOU ALWAYS SIT THERE.
ALWAYS COFFEE...
...WITH NO SUGAR ...
... RIGHT ?
UKINA.
AN INQUISITIVE WOMAN WITH A UNIQUE SENSIBILITY.

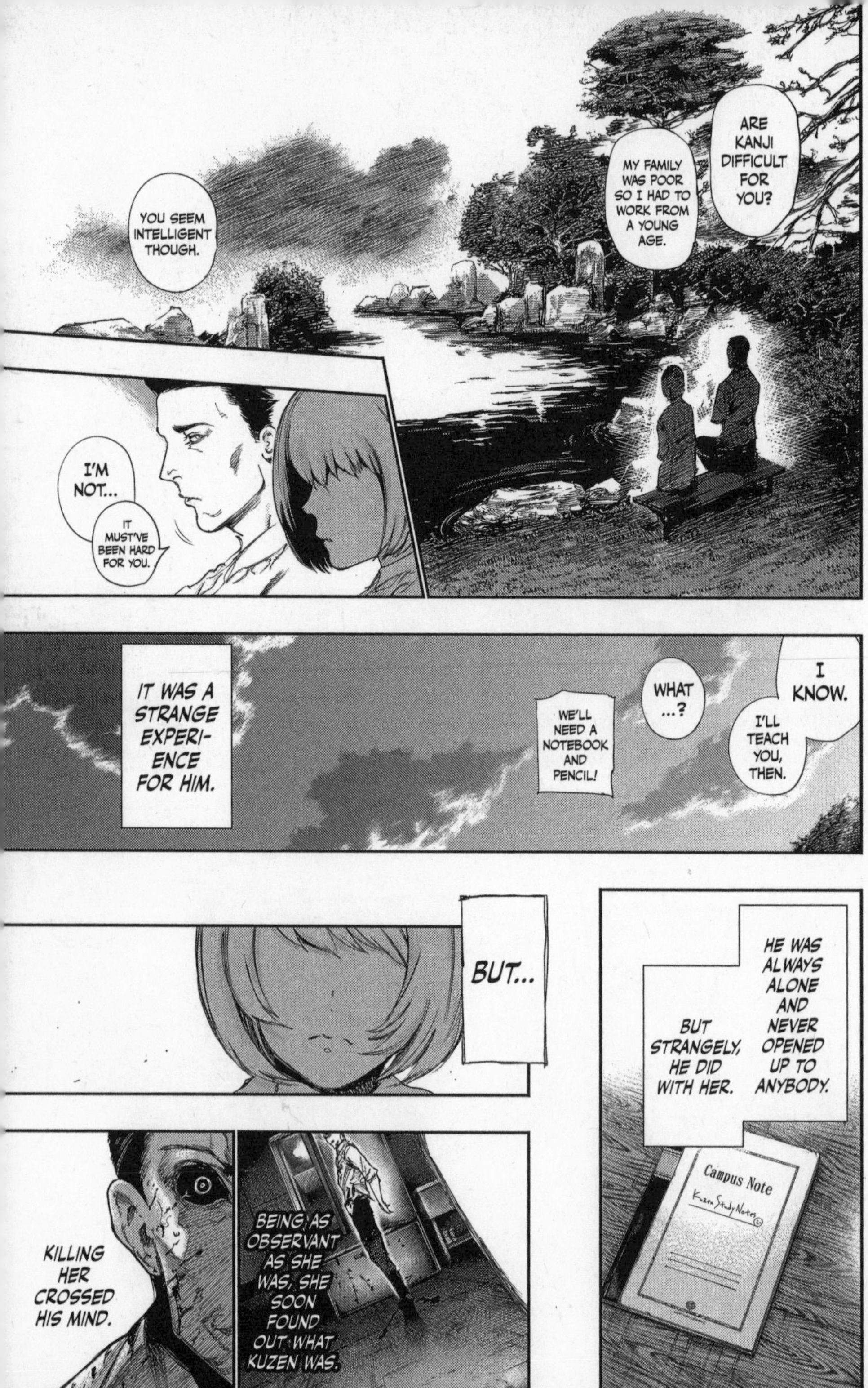
ARE KANJI DIFFICULT FOR YOU?
MY FAMILY WAS POOR SO I HAD TO WORK FROM A YOUNG AGE.
YOU SEEM INTELLIGENT THOUGH.
I'M NOT...
IT MUST'VE BEEN HARD FOR YOU.
I KNOW.
I'LL TEACH YOU, THEN.
WHAT ...?
WE'LL NEED A NOTEBOOK AND PENCIL!
IT WAS A STRANGE EXPERIENCE FOR HIM.
HE WAS ALWAYS ALONE AND NEVER OPENED UP TO ANYBODY.
BUT STRANGELY, HE DID WITH HER.
Campus Note
Kuzen Study Notes
BUT...
BEING AS OBSERVANT AS SHE WAS, SHE SOON FOUND OUT WHAT KUZEN WAS.
KILLING HER CROSSED HIS MIND.

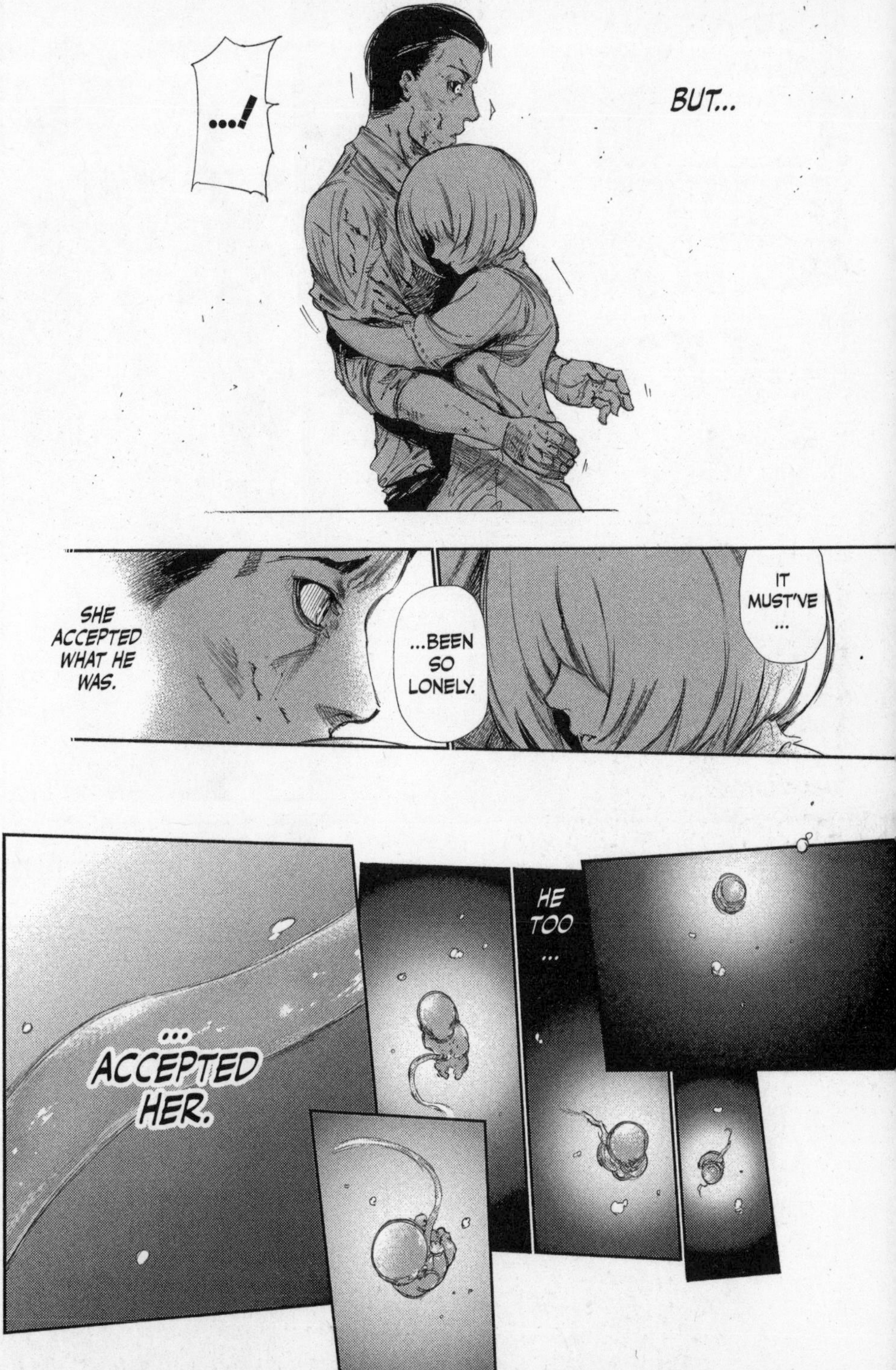
BUT...
...!
IT MUST'VE ...
...BEEN SO LONELY.
SHE ACCEPTED WHAT HE WAS.
HE TOO ...
... ACCEPTED HER.

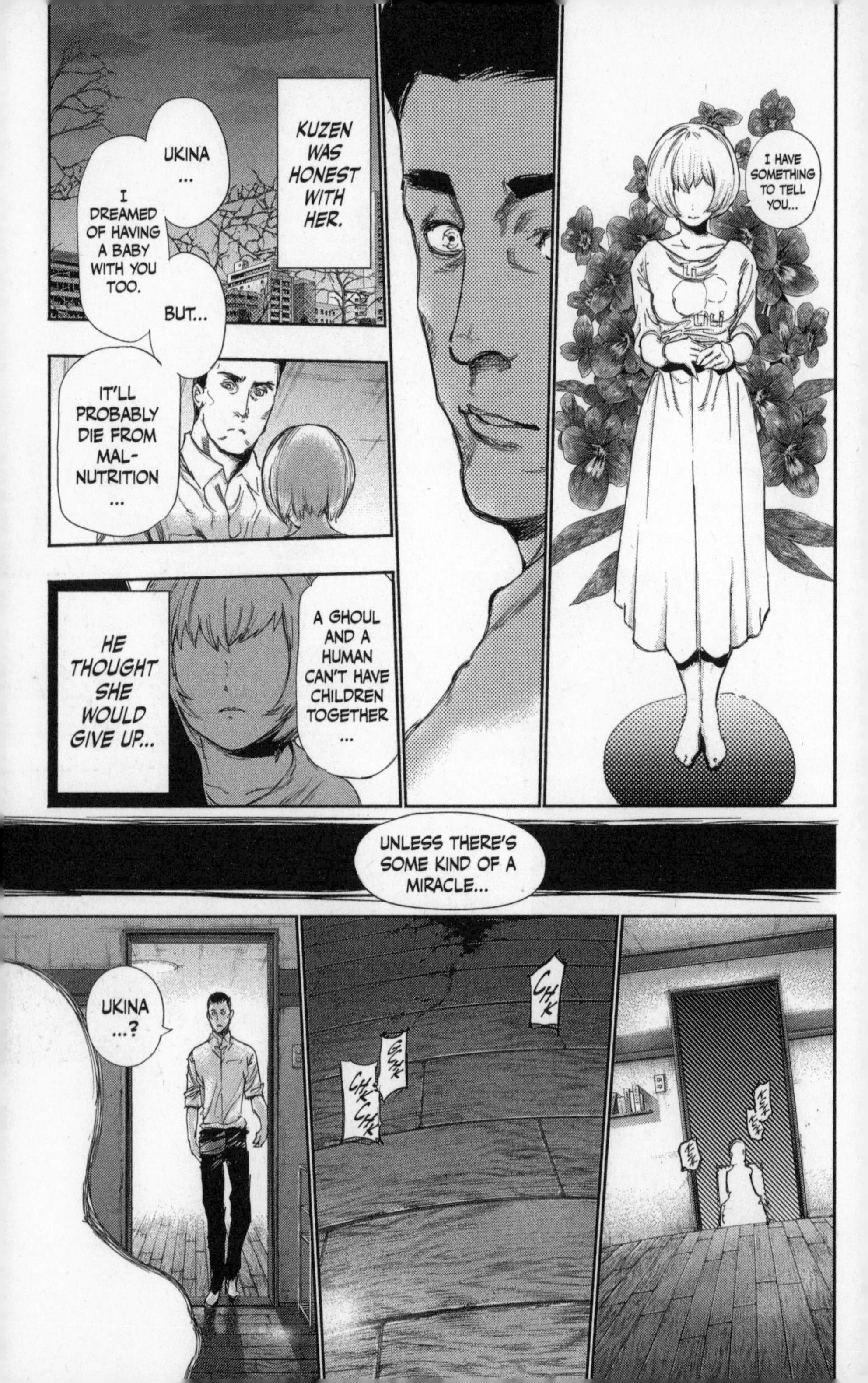
I HAVE SOMETHING TO TELL YOU...
KUZEN WAS HONEST WITH HER.
UKINA...
I DREAMED OF HAVING A BABY WITH YOU TOO.
BUT...
IT'LL PROBABLY DIE FROM MAL-NUTRITION...
A GHOUL AND A HUMAN CAN'T HAVE CHILDREN TOGETHER...
HE THOUGHT SHE WOULD GIVE UP...
UNLESS THERE'S SOME KIND OF A MIRACLE...
KLNK
KLNK
KLNK
CHK
GCHK
CHK CHK
UKINA...?

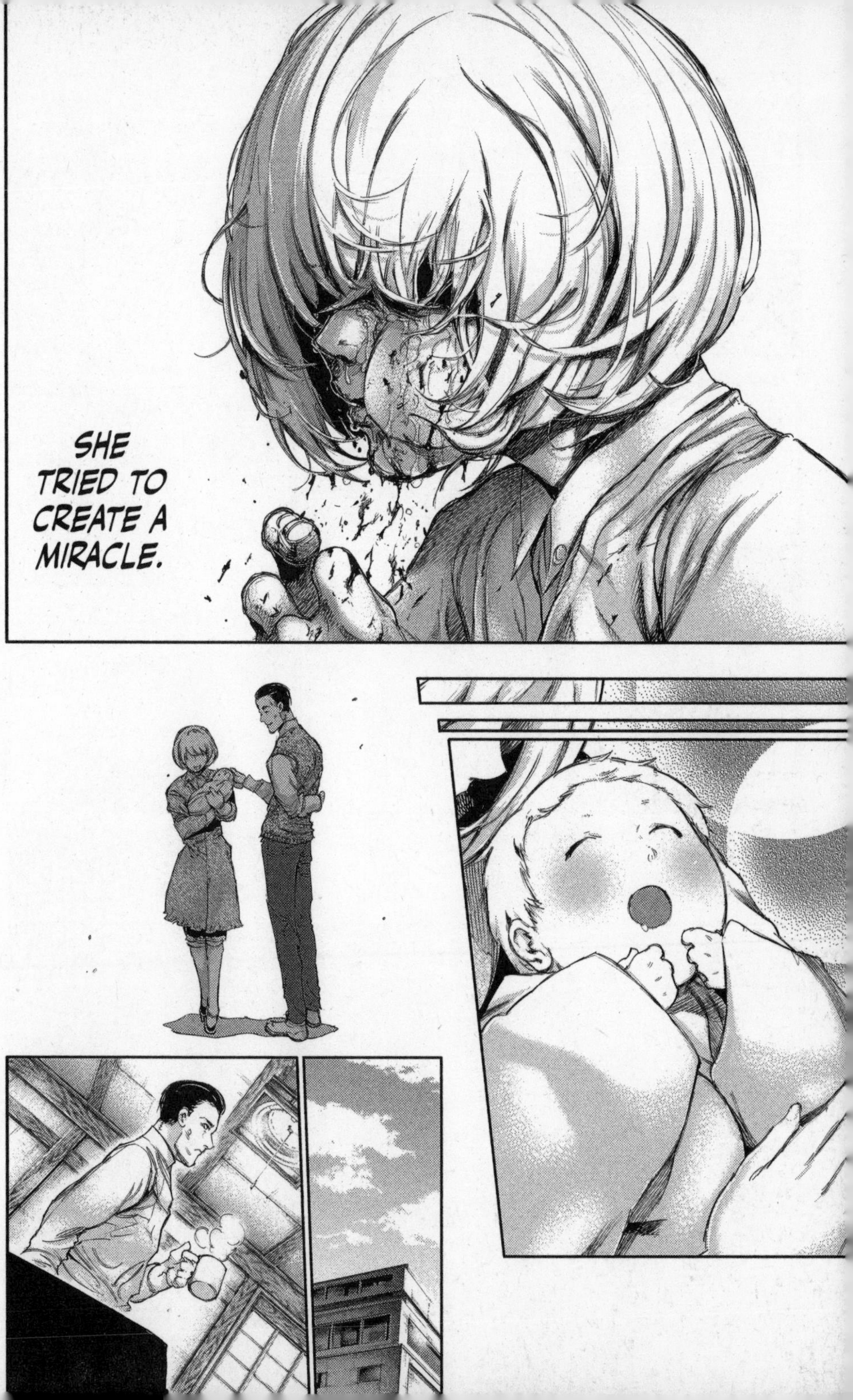
SHE TRIED TO CREATE A MIRACLE.

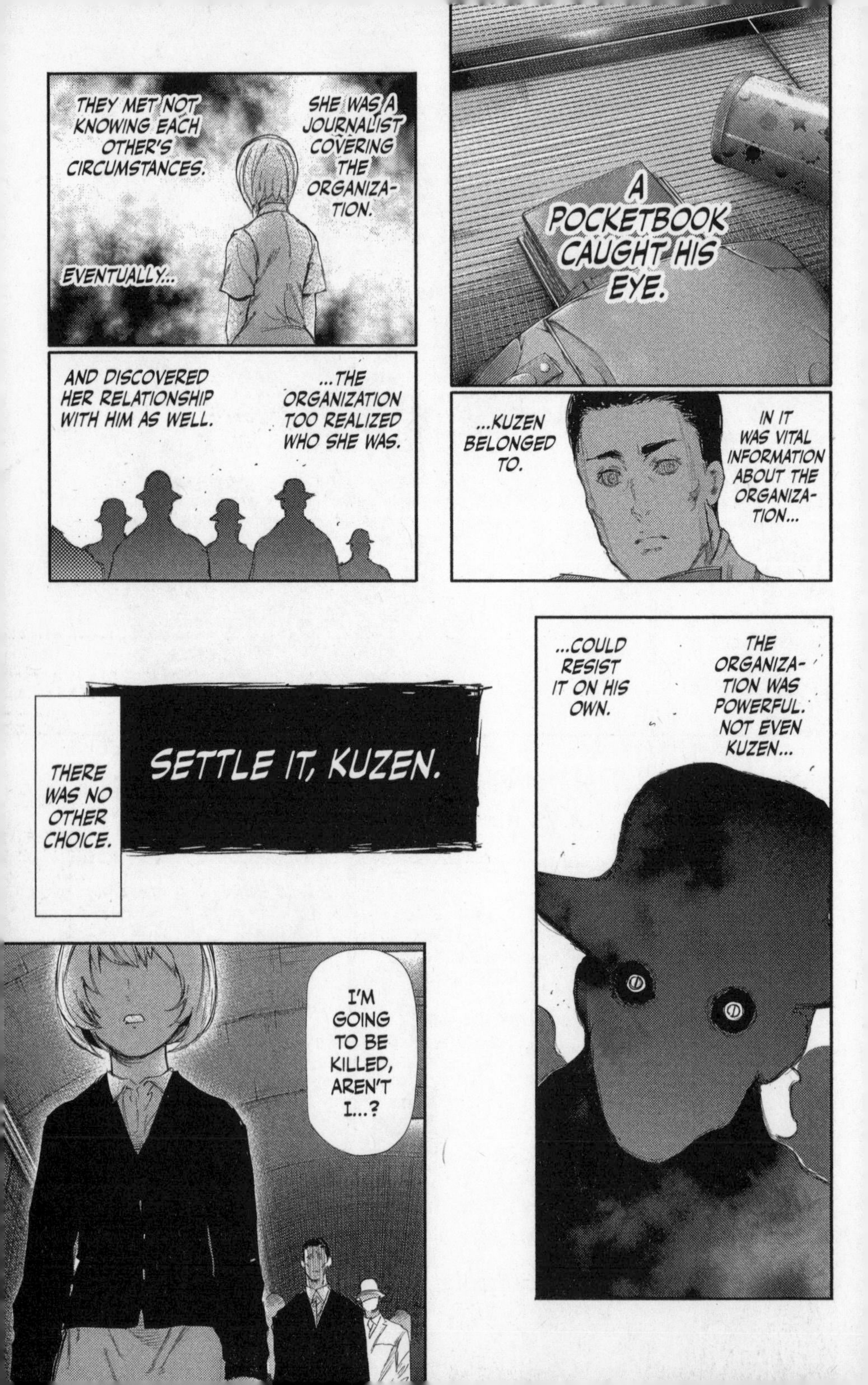

A POCKETBOOK CAUGHT HIS EYE.
IN IT WAS VITAL INFORMATION ABOUT THE ORGANIZATION...
...KUZEN BELONGED TO.
SHE WAS A JOURNALIST COVERING THE ORGANIZATION.
THEY MET NOT KNOWING EACH OTHER'S CIRCUMSTANCES.
EVENTUALLY...
...THE ORGANIZATION TOO REALIZED WHO SHE WAS.
AND DISCOVERED HER RELATIONSHIP WITH HIM AS WELL.
THE ORGANIZATION WAS POWERFUL. NOT EVEN KUZEN...
...COULD RESIST IT ON HIS OWN.
SETTLE IT, KUZEN.
THERE WAS NO OTHER CHOICE.
I'M GOING TO BE KILLED, AREN'T I...?

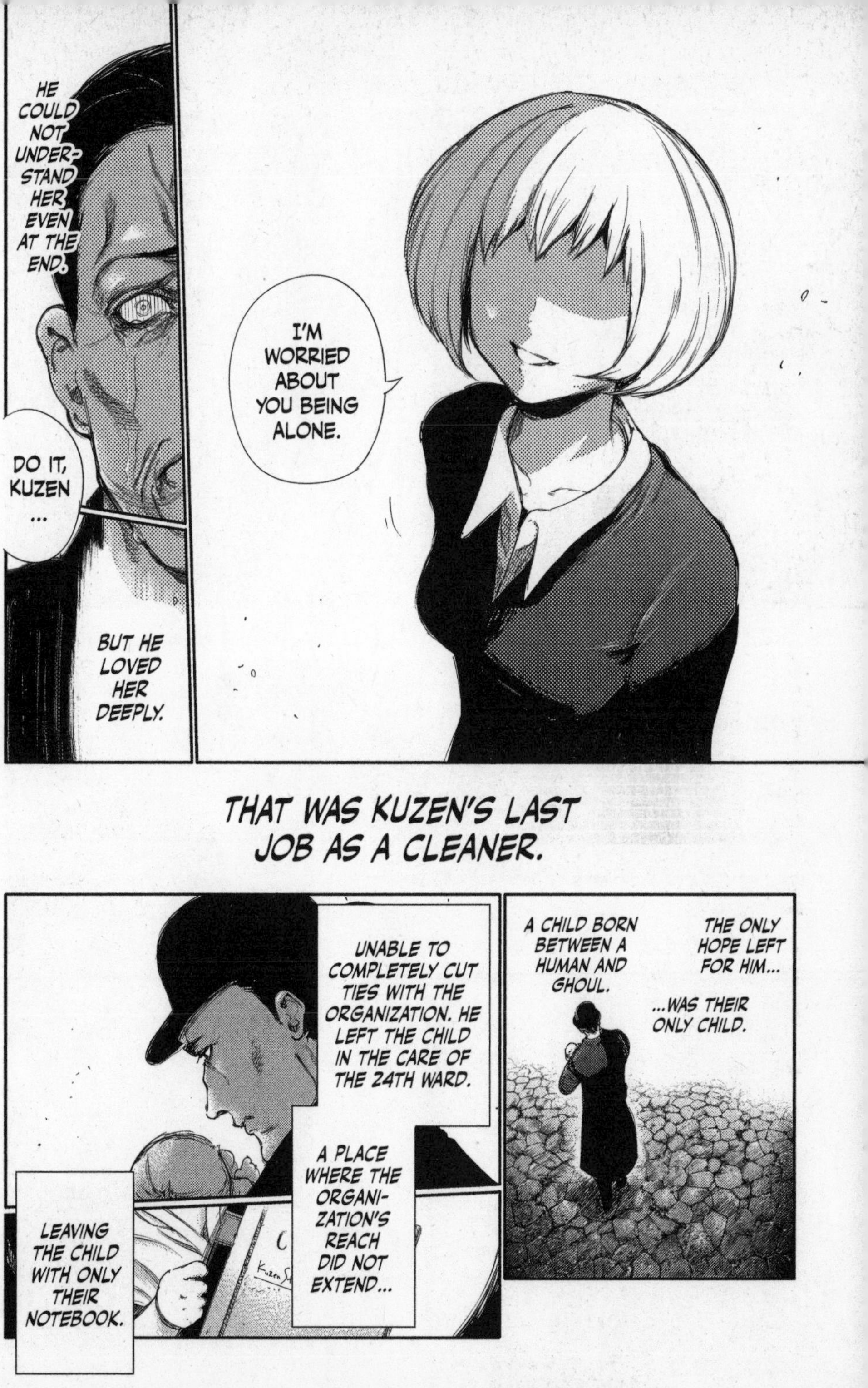
I'M WORRIED ABOUT YOU BEING ALONE.
HE COULD NOT UNDERSTAND HER EVEN AT THE END.
DO IT, KUZEN...
BUT HE LOVED HER DEEPLY.
THAT WAS KUZEN'S LAST JOB AS A CLEANER.
THE ONLY HOPE LEFT FOR HIM...
A CHILD BORN BETWEEN A HUMAN AND GHOUL.
...WAS THEIR ONLY CHILD.
UNABLE TO COMPLETELY CUT TIES WITH THE ORGANIZATION. HE LEFT THE CHILD IN THE CARE OF THE 24TH WARD.
A PLACE WHERE THE ORGANIZATION'S REACH DID NOT EXTEND...
LEAVING THE CHILD WITH ONLY THEIR NOTEBOOK.

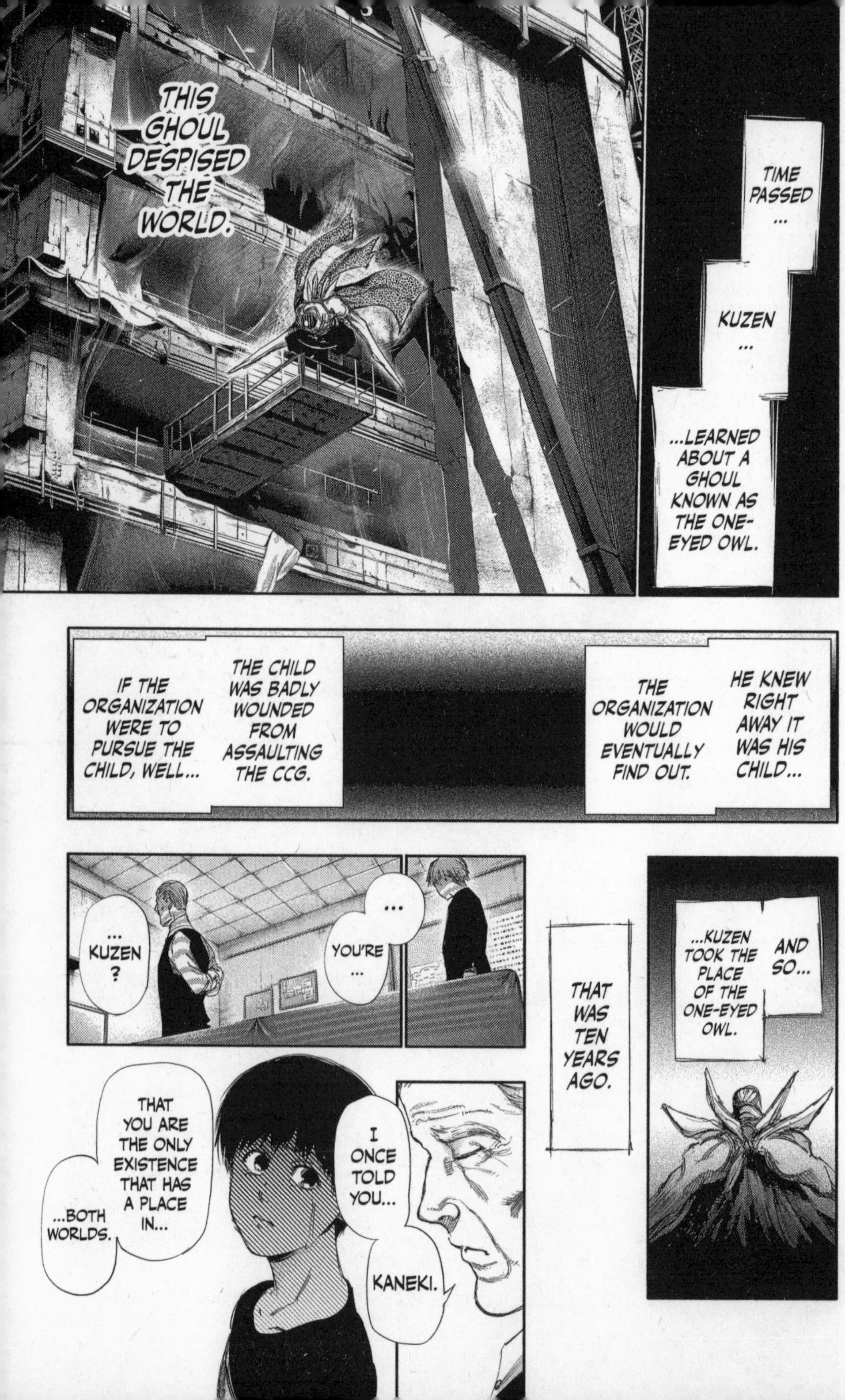
TIME PASSED ...
KUZEN ...
...LEARNED ABOUT A GHOUL KNOWN AS THE ONE-EYED OWL.
THIS GHOUL DESPISED THE WORLD.
HE KNEW RIGHT AWAY IT WAS HIS CHILD...
THE ORGANIZATION WOULD EVENTUALLY FIND OUT.
THE CHILD WAS BADLY WOUNDED FROM ASSAULTING THE CCG.
IF THE ORGANIZATION WERE TO PURSUE THE CHILD, WELL...
AND SO...
...KUZEN TOOK THE PLACE OF THE ONE-EYED OWL.
THAT WAS TEN YEARS AGO.
... YOU'RE ...
... KUZEN ?
I ONCE TOLD YOU...
KANEKI.
THAT YOU ARE THE ONLY EXISTENCE THAT HAS A PLACE IN...
...BOTH WORLDS.

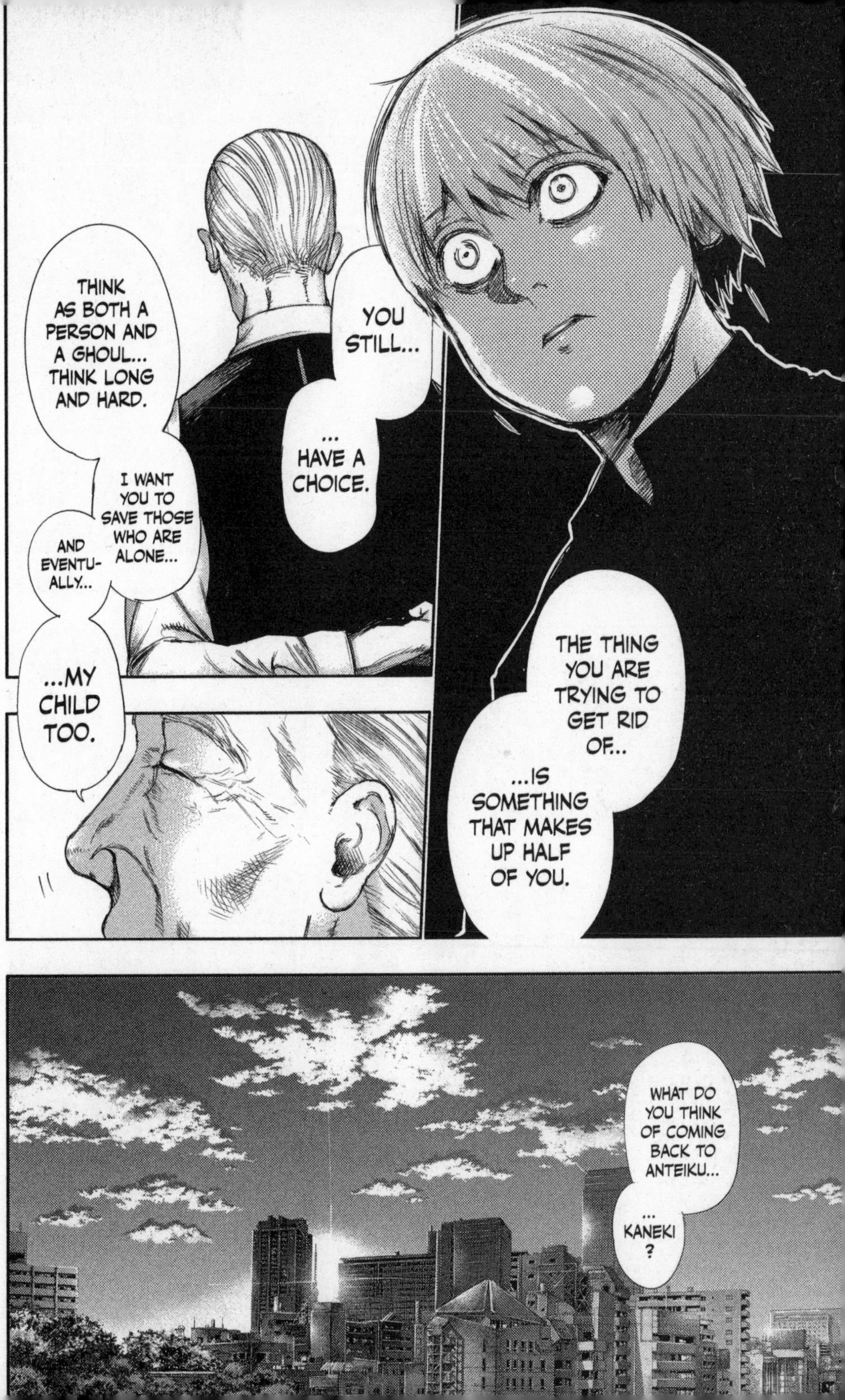
THE THING YOU ARE TRYING TO GET RID OF...
...IS SOMETHING THAT MAKES UP HALF OF YOU.
YOU STILL...
...HAVE A CHOICE.
THINK AS BOTH A PERSON AND A GHOUL... THINK LONG AND HARD.
I WANT YOU TO SAVE THOSE WHO ARE ALONE...
AND EVENTU-ALLY...
...MY CHILD TOO.
WHAT DO YOU THINK OF COMING BACK TO ANTEIKU...
...KANEKI?

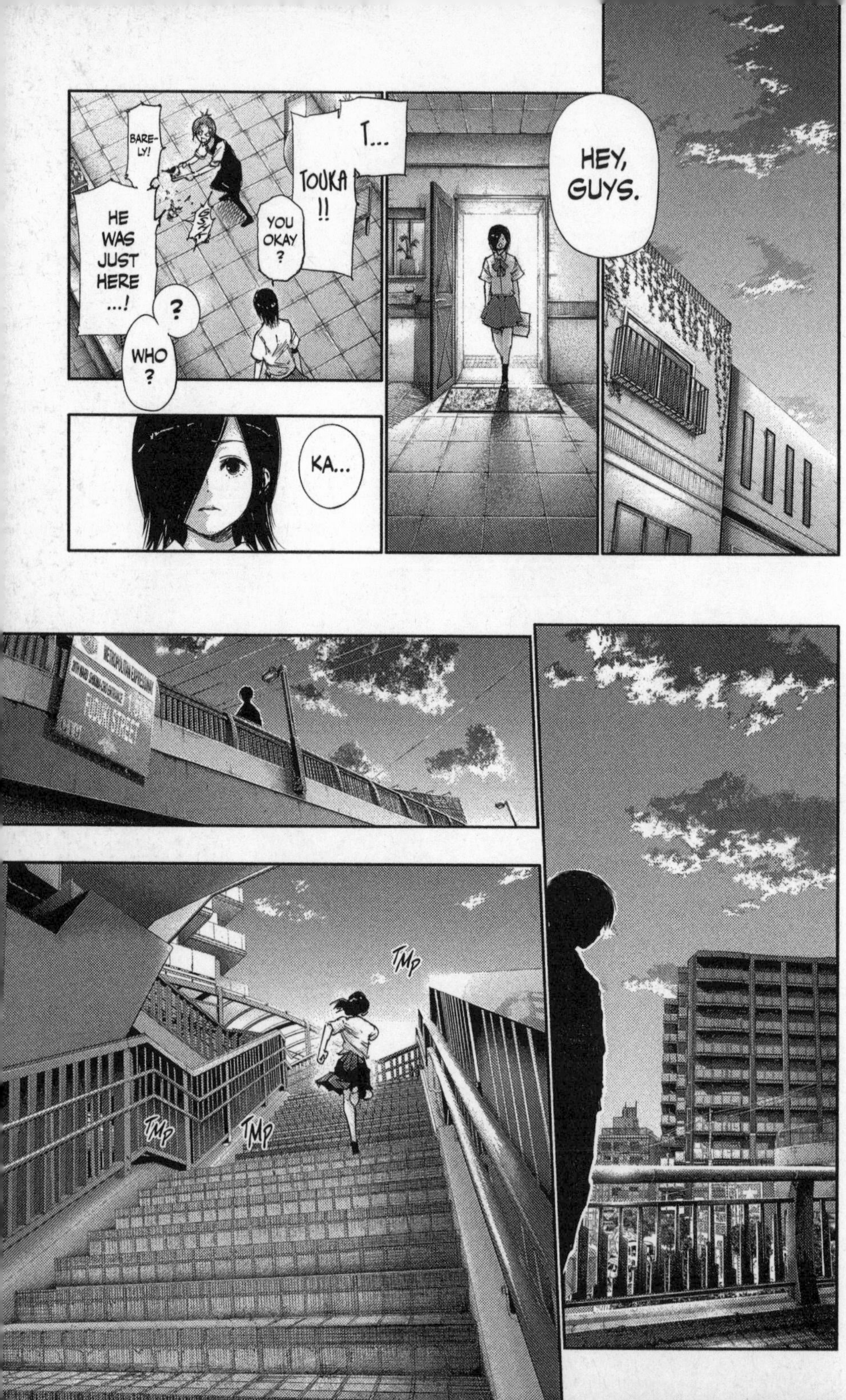
HEY, GUYS.
T...
TOUKA!!
YOU OKAY?
BARE-LY!
HE WAS JUST HERE...!
?
WHO?
KA...
TMP
TMP
TMP

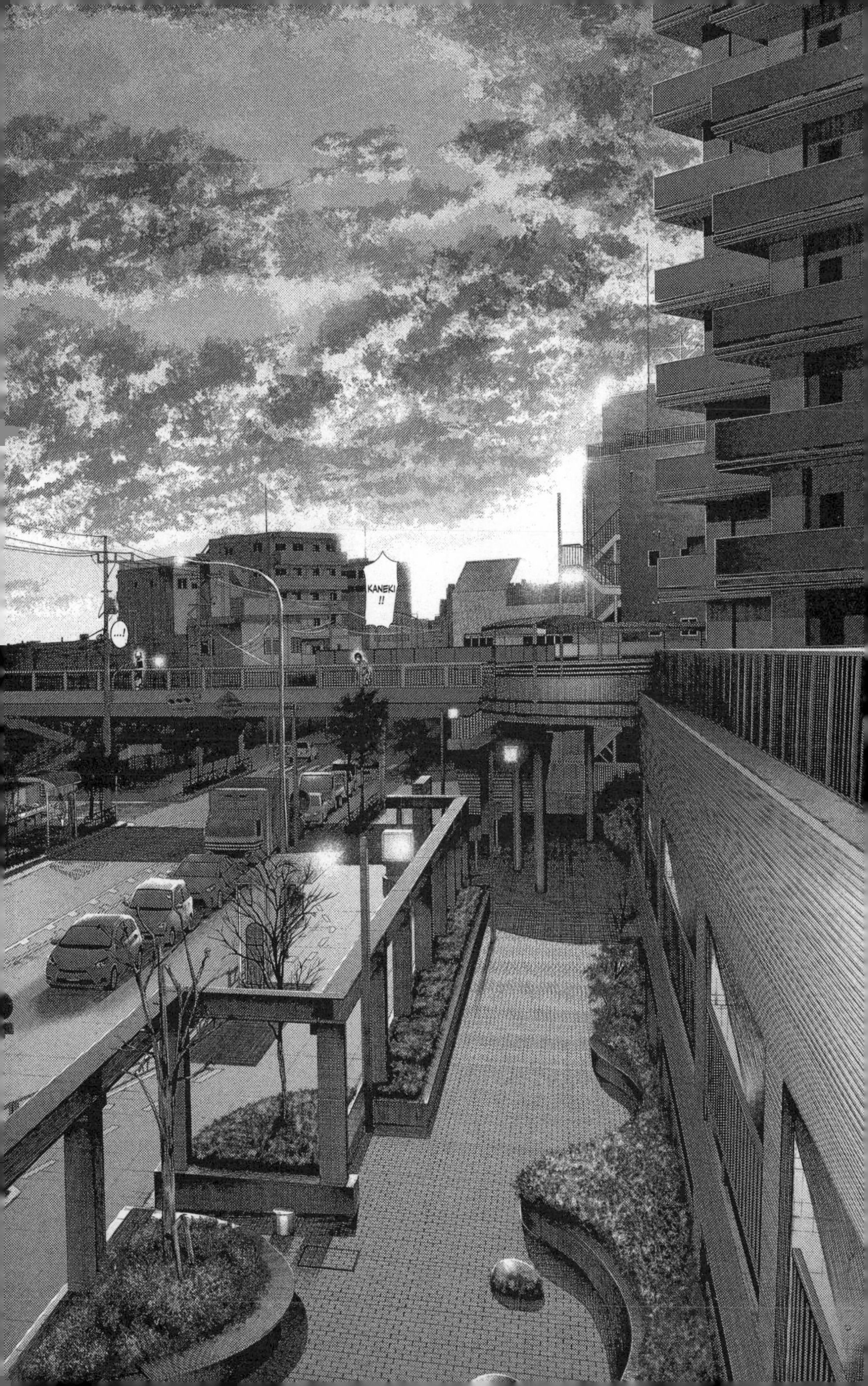
KANEKI !!
...!

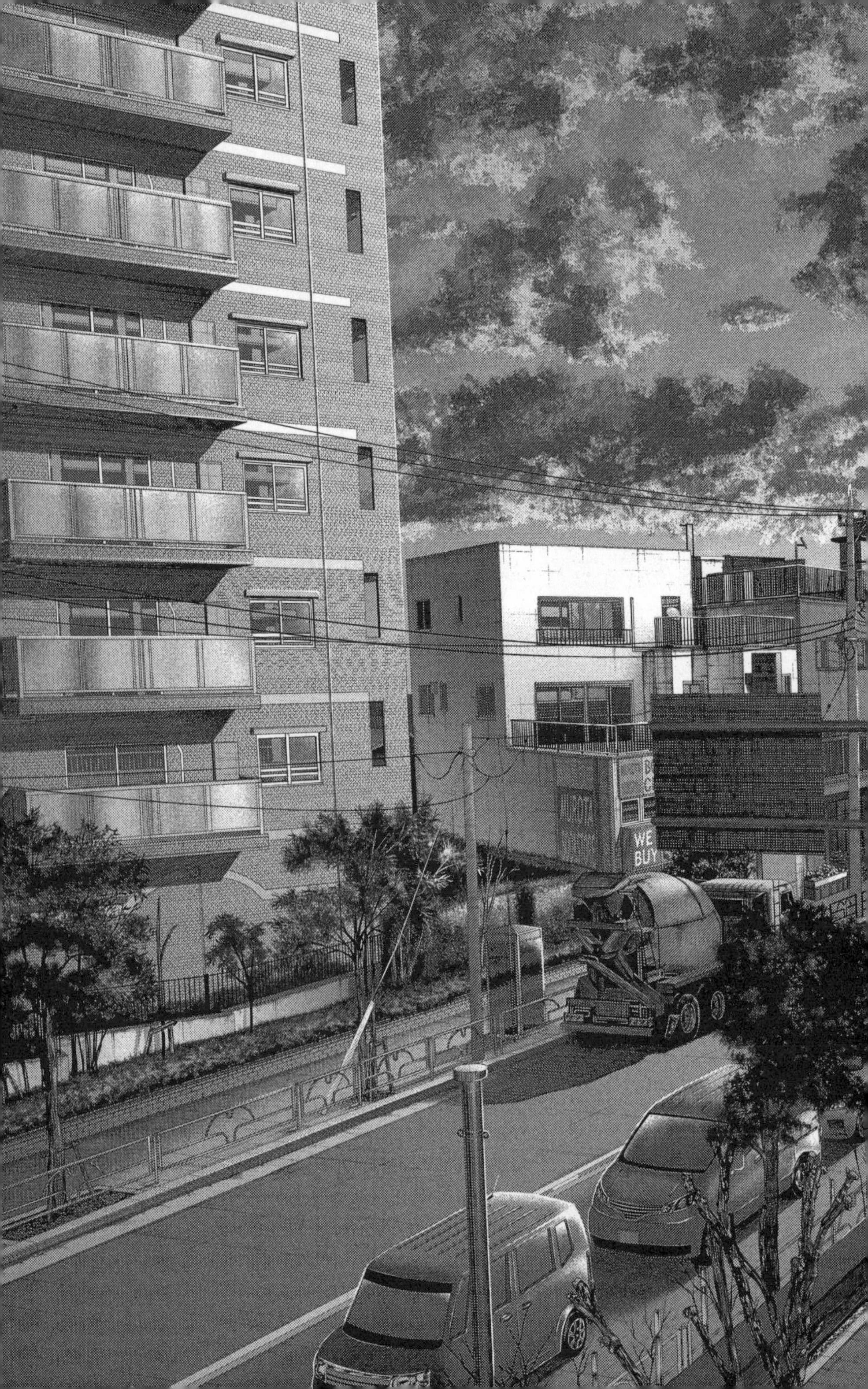
WE
BUY

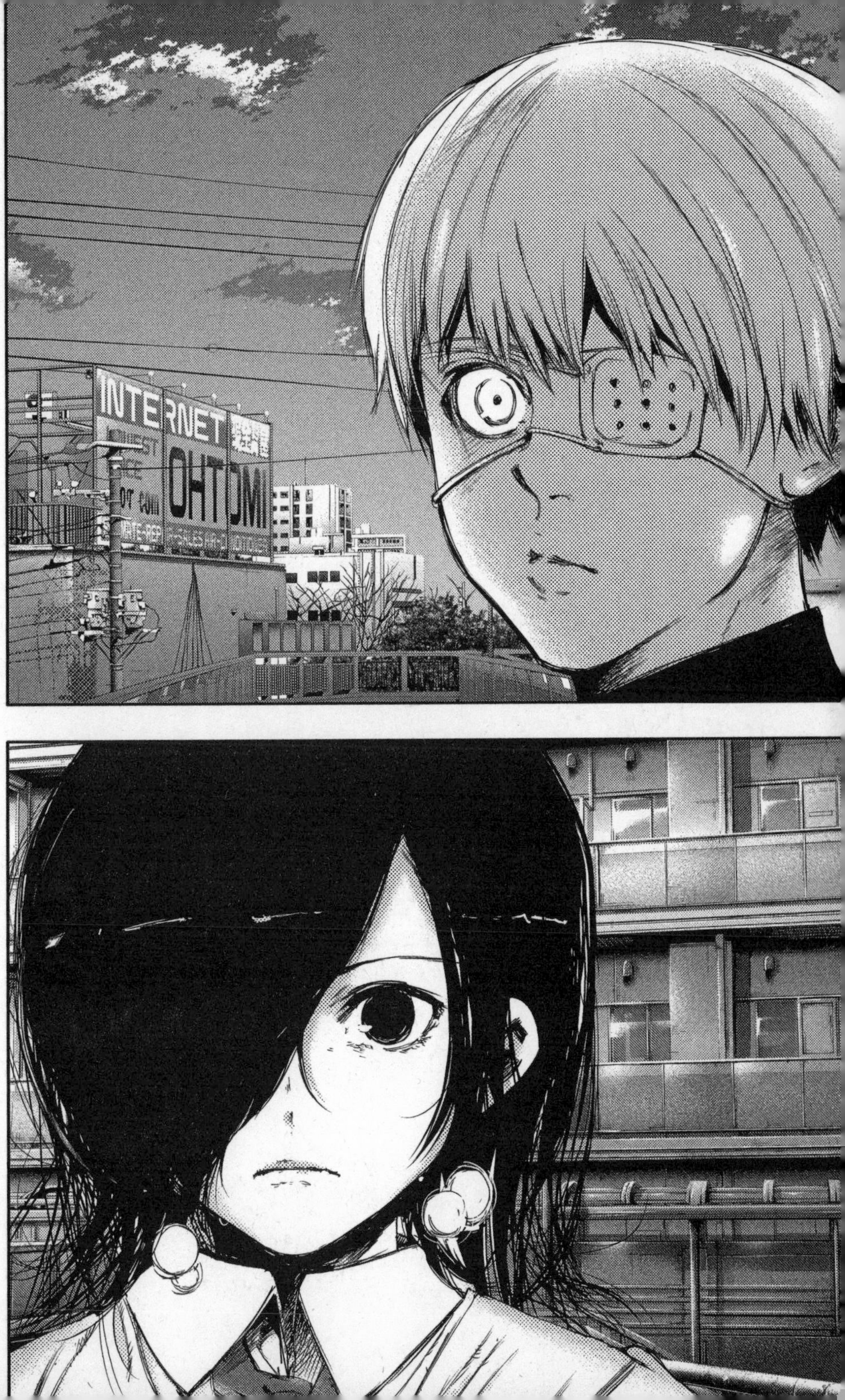
INTERNET
OHTOMI

#120 [TOUKA]

TOKYO GHOUL

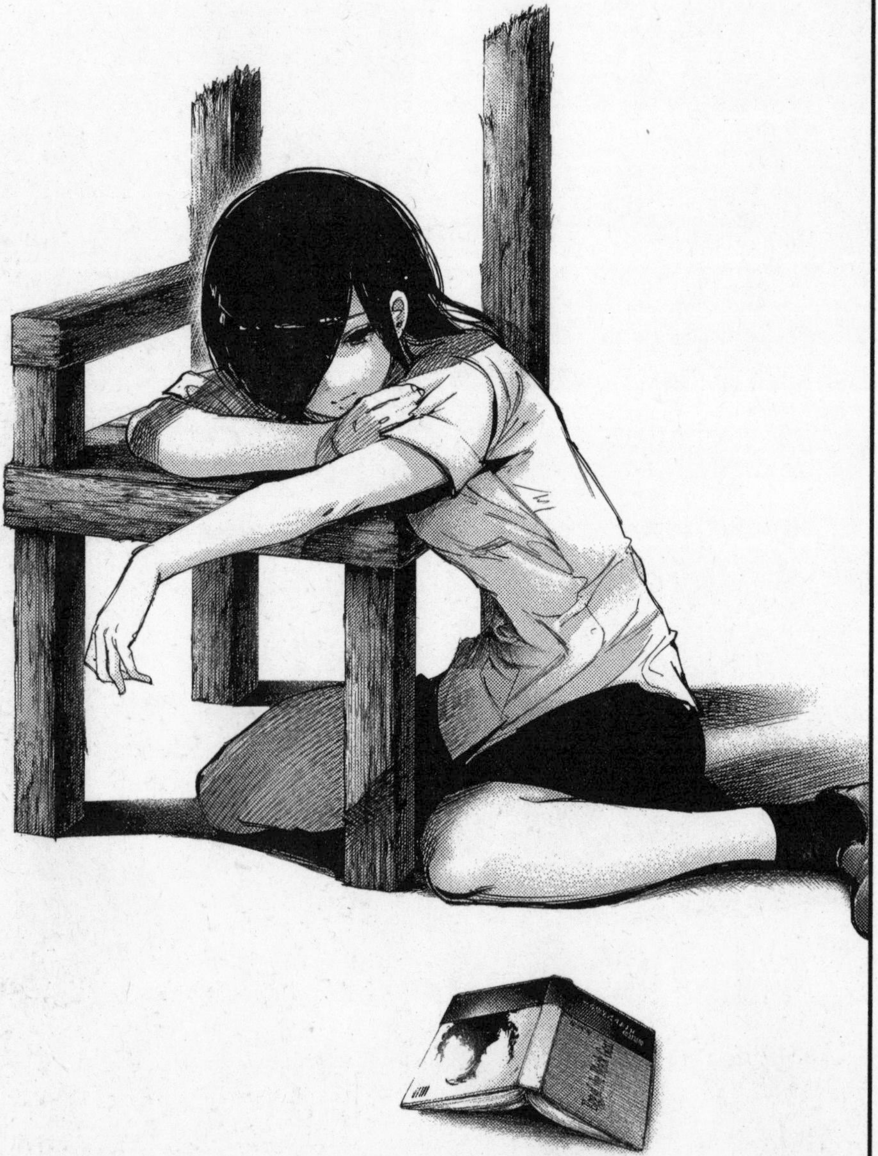

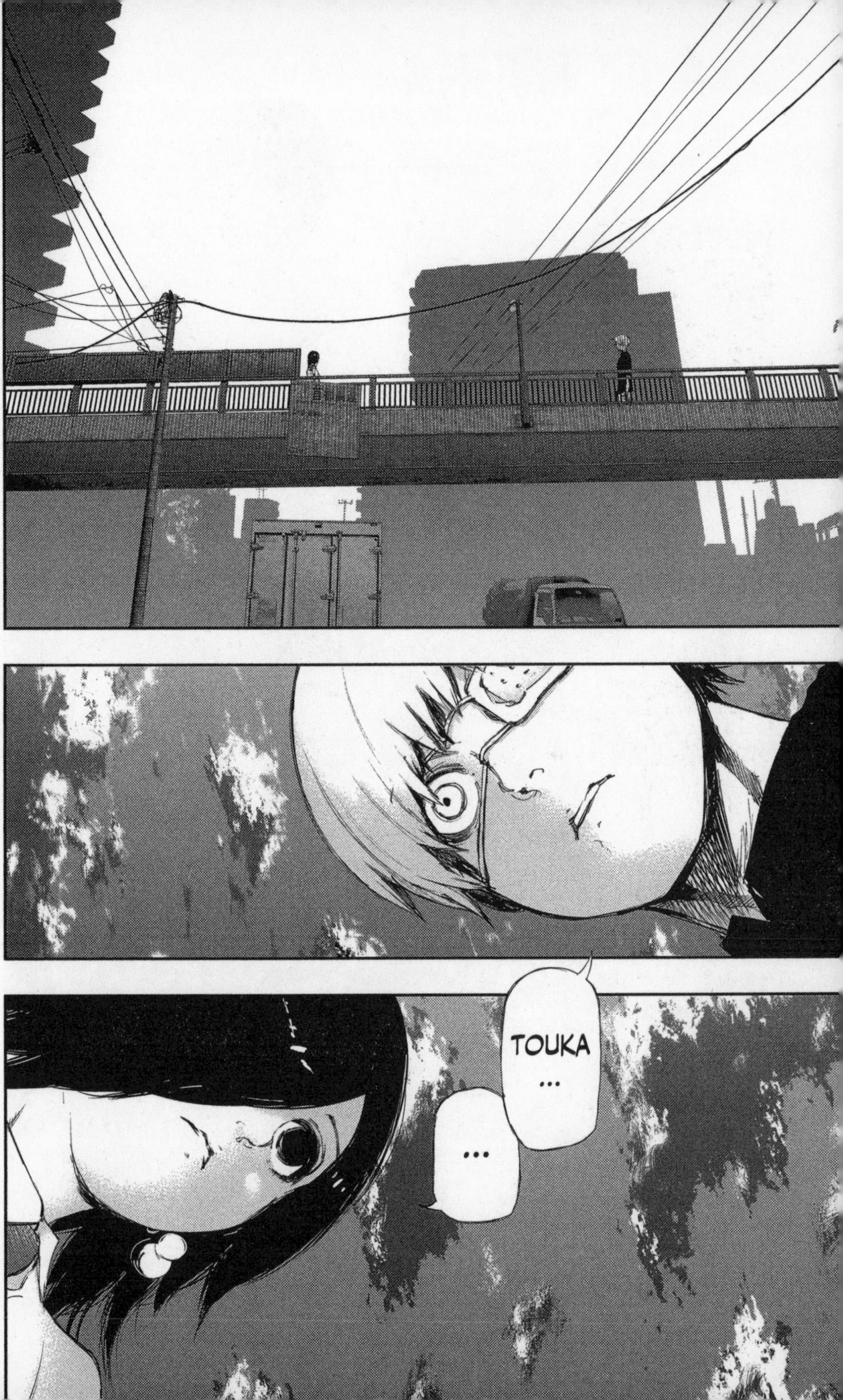
TOUKA
...
...

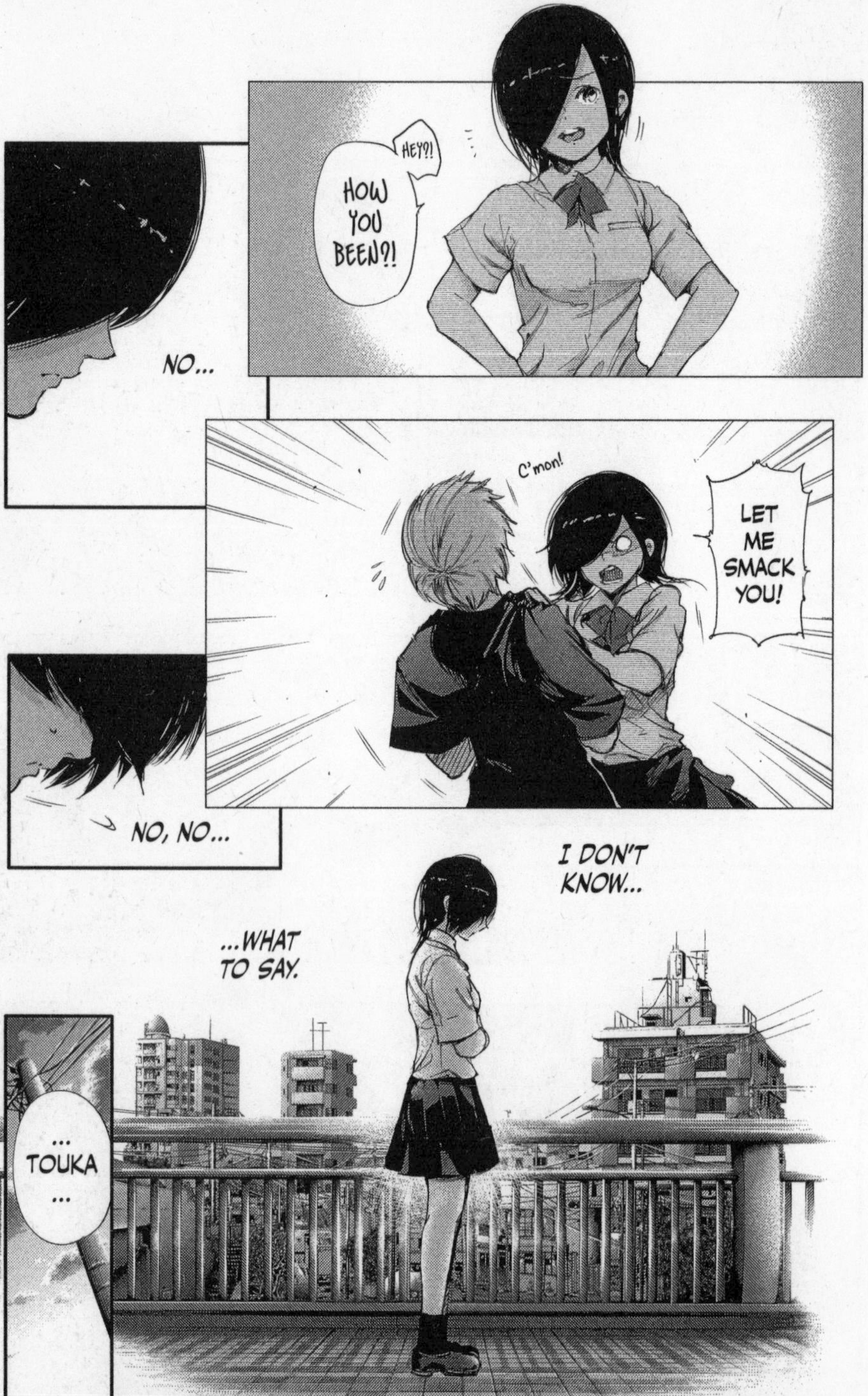
HEY?!
HOW YOU BEEN?!
NO...
LET ME SMACK YOU!
C'mon!
NO, NO...
I DON'T KNOW...
...WHAT TO SAY.
... TOUKA ...

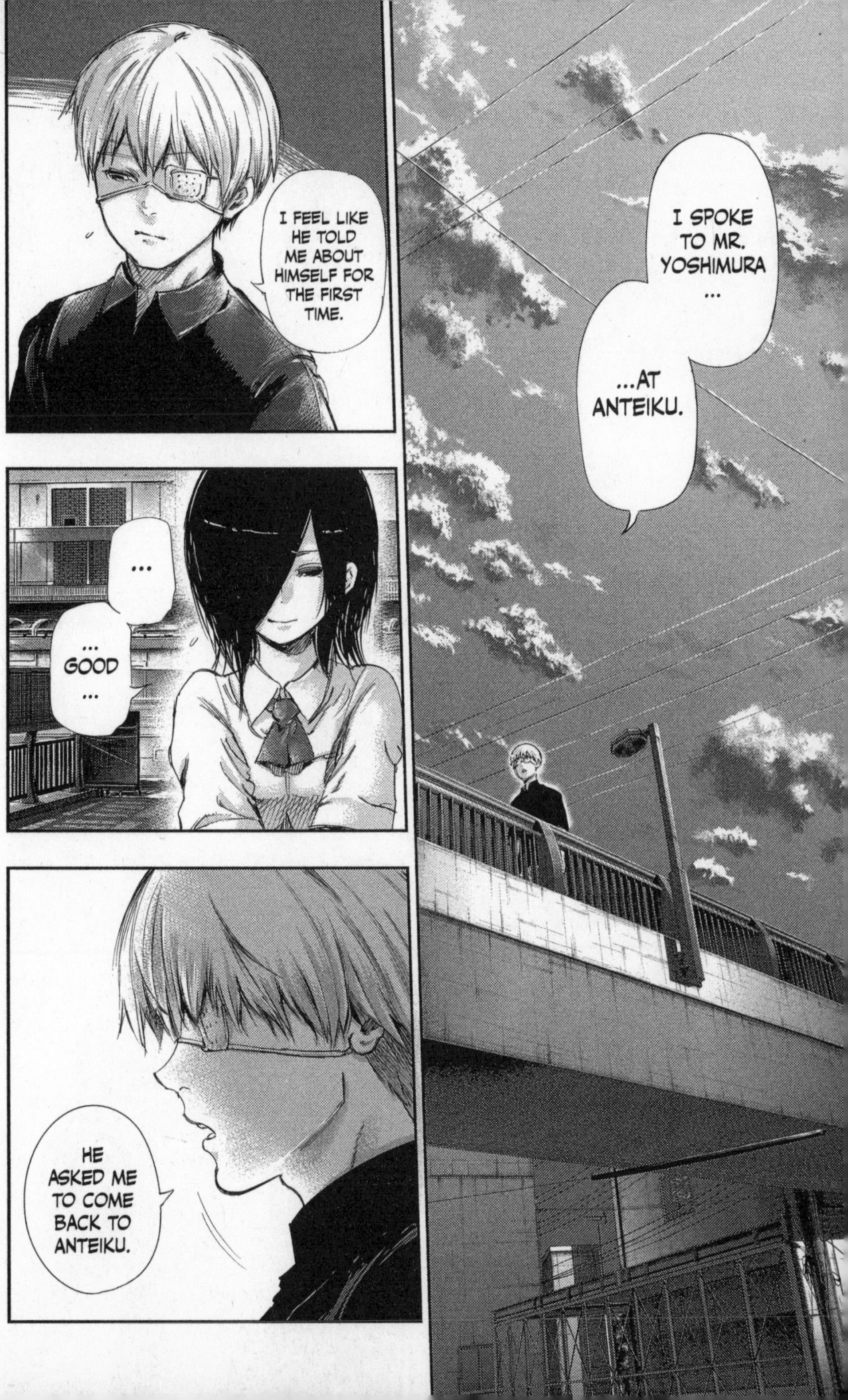
I SPOKE TO MR. YOSHIMURA ...
...AT ANTEIKU.
I FEEL LIKE HE TOLD ME ABOUT HIMSELF FOR THE FIRST TIME.
...
... GOOD ...
HE ASKED ME TO COME BACK TO ANTEIKU.

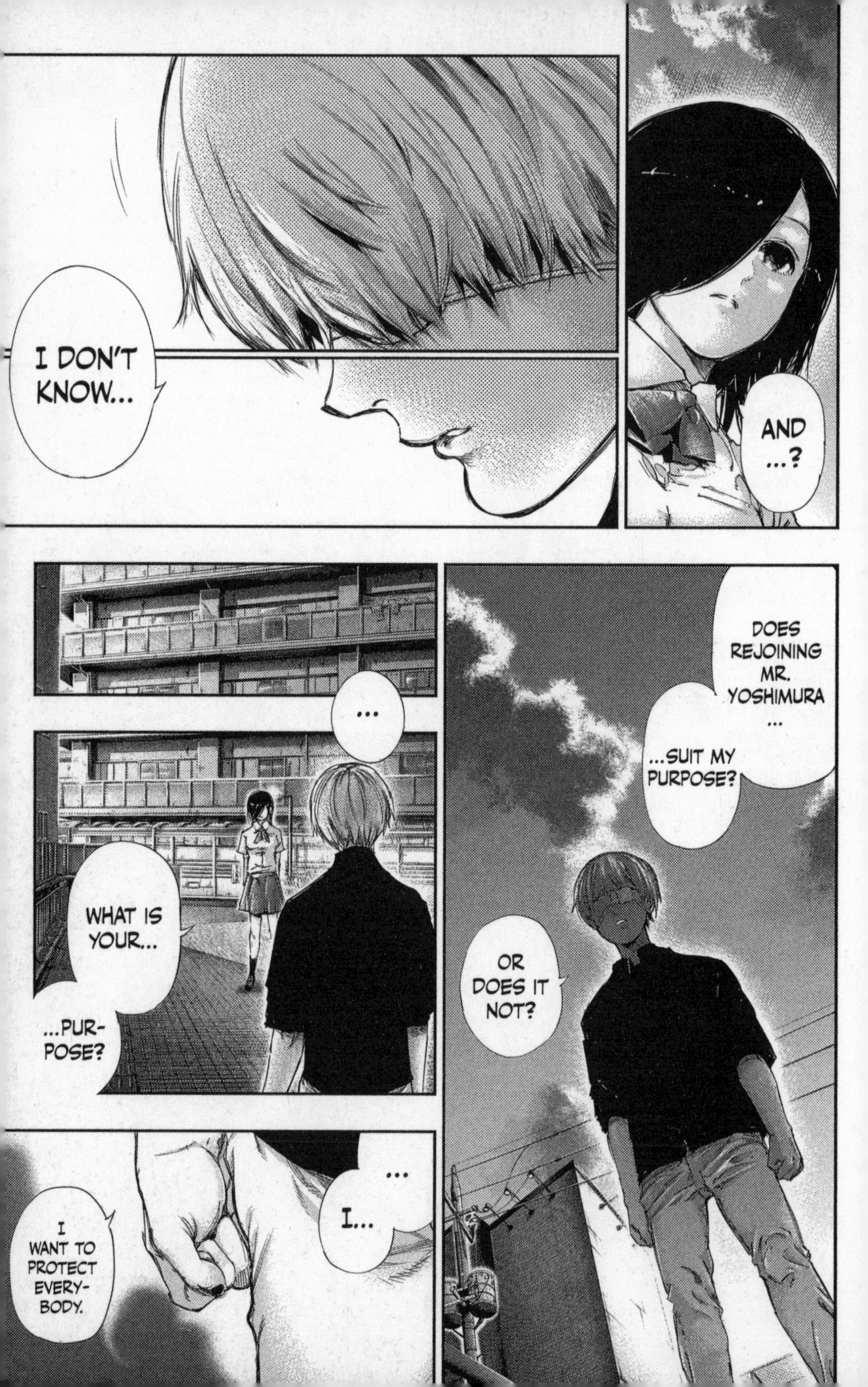
AND ...?
I DON'T KNOW...
DOES REJOINING MR. YOSHIMURA ...
...SUIT MY PURPOSE?
OR DOES IT NOT?
...
WHAT IS YOUR...
...PUR-POSE?
... I...
I WANT TO PROTECT EVERY-BODY.

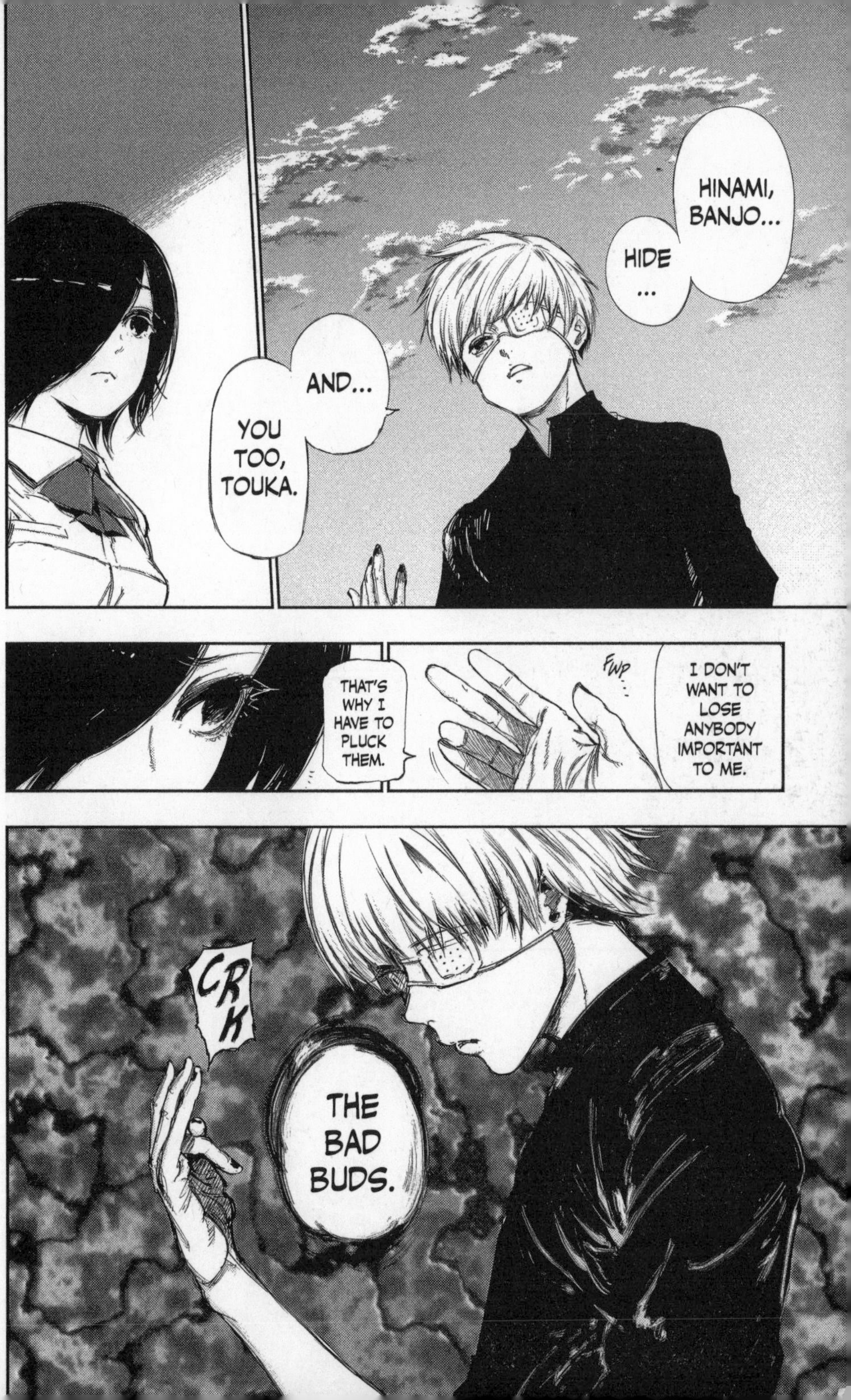
HINAMI, BANJO...
HIDE ...
AND...
YOU TOO, TOUKA.
FWP...
I DON'T WANT TO LOSE ANYBODY IMPORTANT TO ME.
THAT'S WHY I HAVE TO PLUCK THEM.
CRK
THE BAD BUDS.

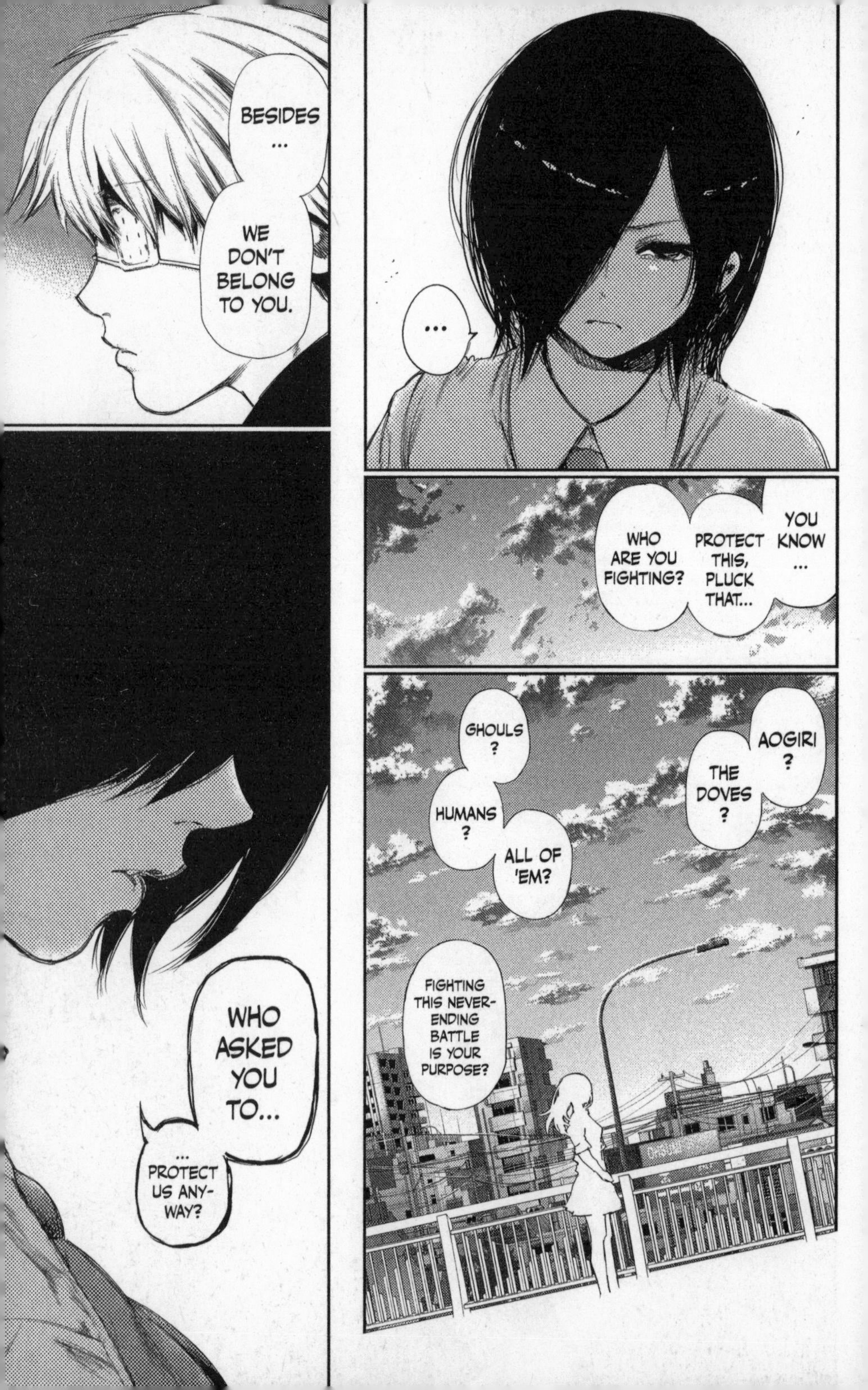
...
BESIDES ...
WE DON'T BELONG TO YOU.
YOU KNOW ...
PROTECT THIS, PLUCK THAT...
WHO ARE YOU FIGHTING?
AOGIRI ?
THE DOVES ?
GHOULS ?
HUMANS ?
ALL OF 'EM?
FIGHTING THIS NEVER-ENDING BATTLE IS YOUR PURPOSE?
WHO ASKED YOU TO...
... PROTECT US ANY-WAY?

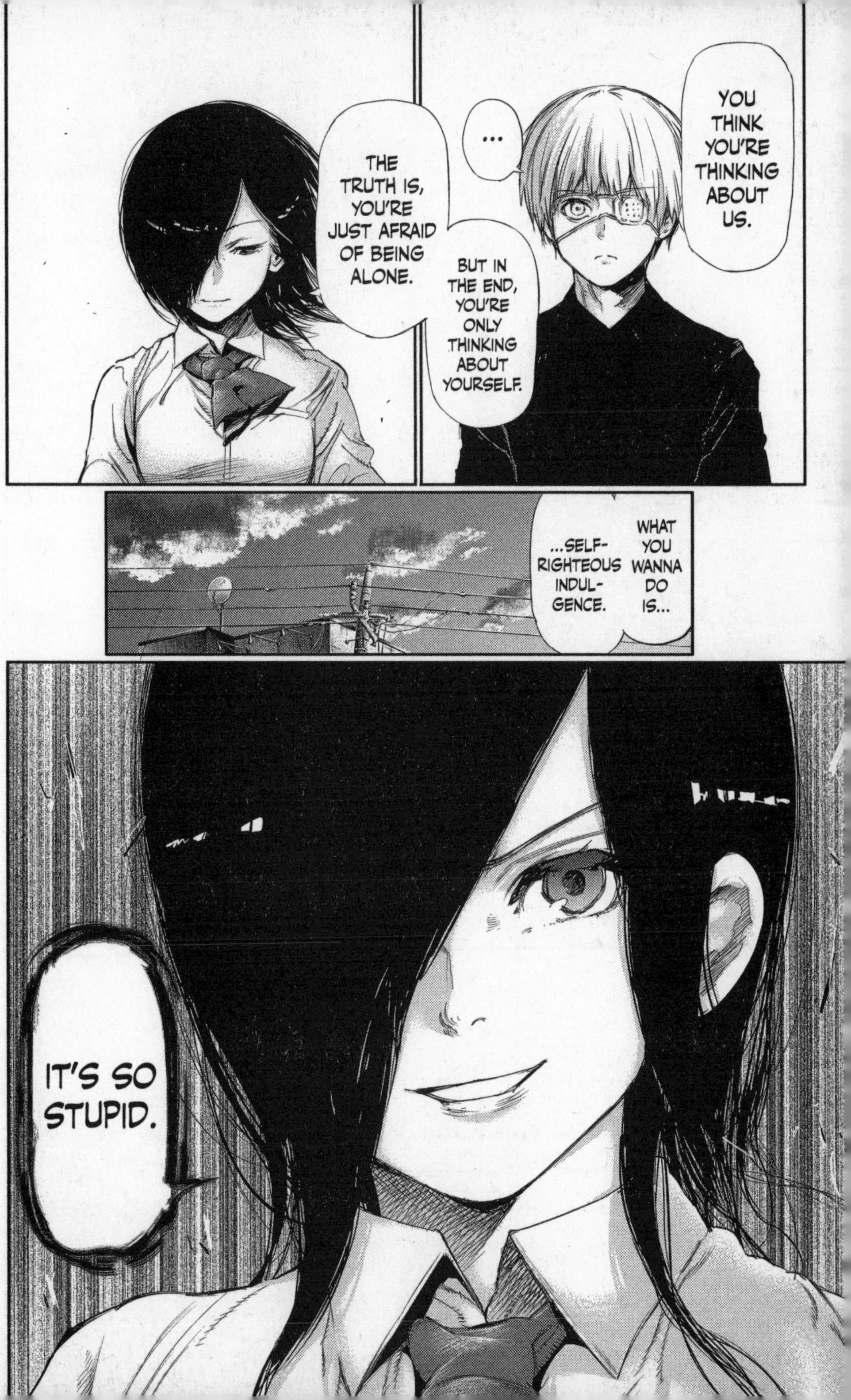
YOU THINK YOU'RE THINKING ABOUT US.
...
BUT IN THE END, YOU'RE ONLY THINKING ABOUT YOURSELF.
THE TRUTH IS, YOU'RE JUST AFRAID OF BEING ALONE.
WHAT YOU WANNA DO IS...
...SELF-RIGHTEOUS INDULGENCE.
IT'S SO STUPID.

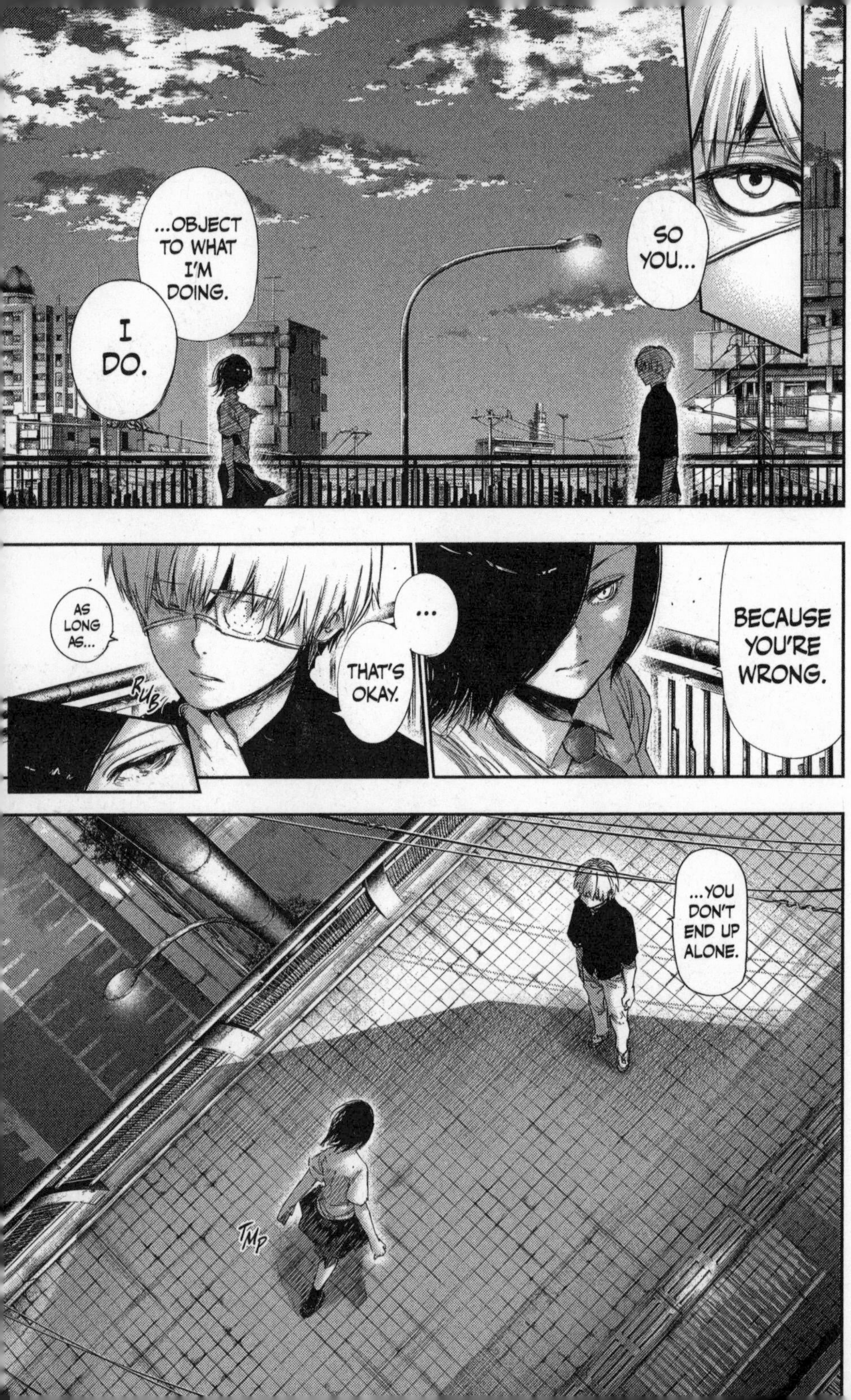
SO YOU...
...OBJECT TO WHAT I'M DOING.
I DO.
BECAUSE YOU'RE WRONG.
...
THAT'S OKAY.
AS LONG AS...
RUB
...YOU DON'T END UP ALONE.
TMP

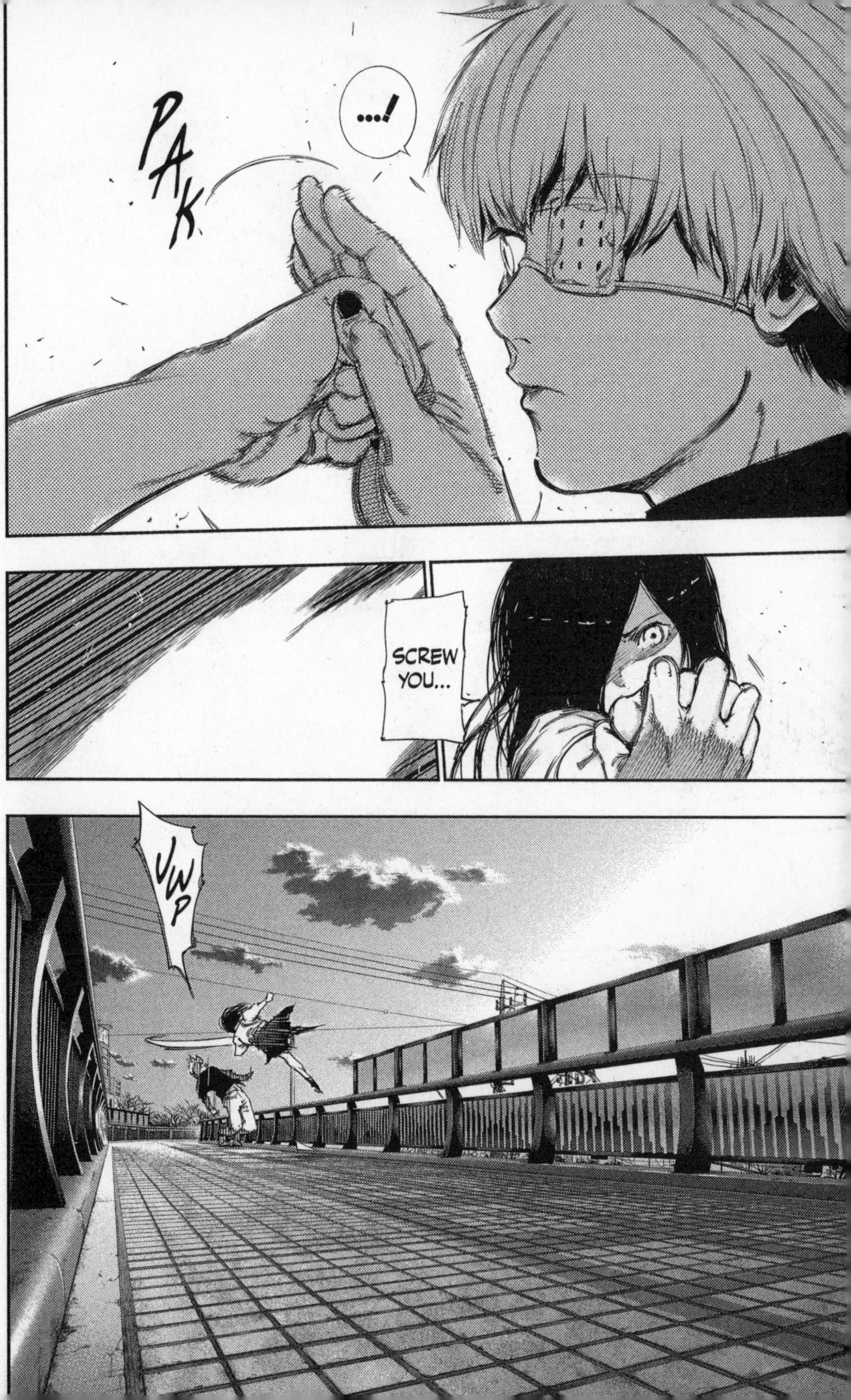
...!
PAK
SCREW YOU...
JWP

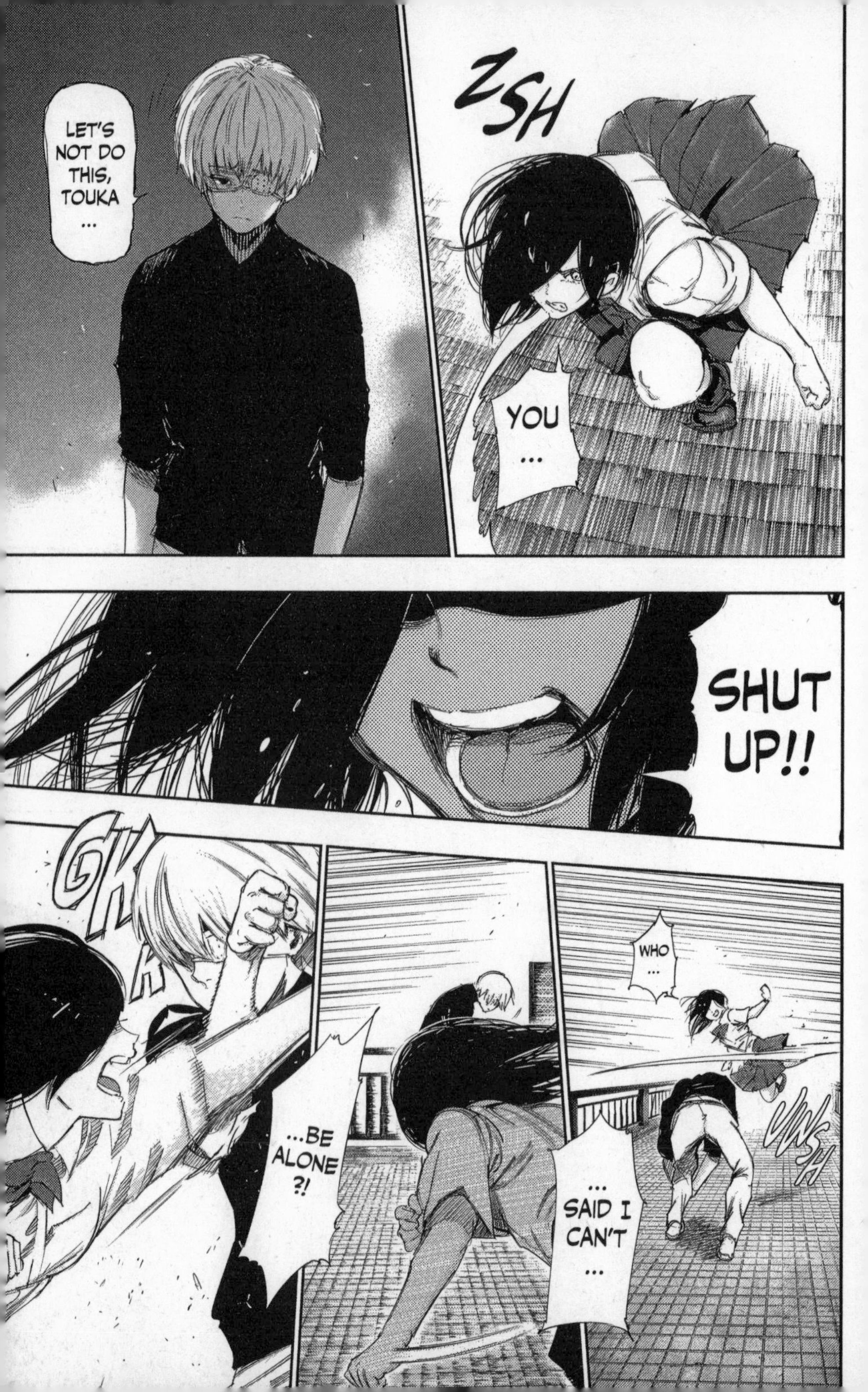
ZSH
YOU ...
LET'S NOT DO THIS, TOUKA ...
SHUT UP!!
WHO ...
VWSH
... SAID I CAN'T ...
...BE ALONE?!
GK

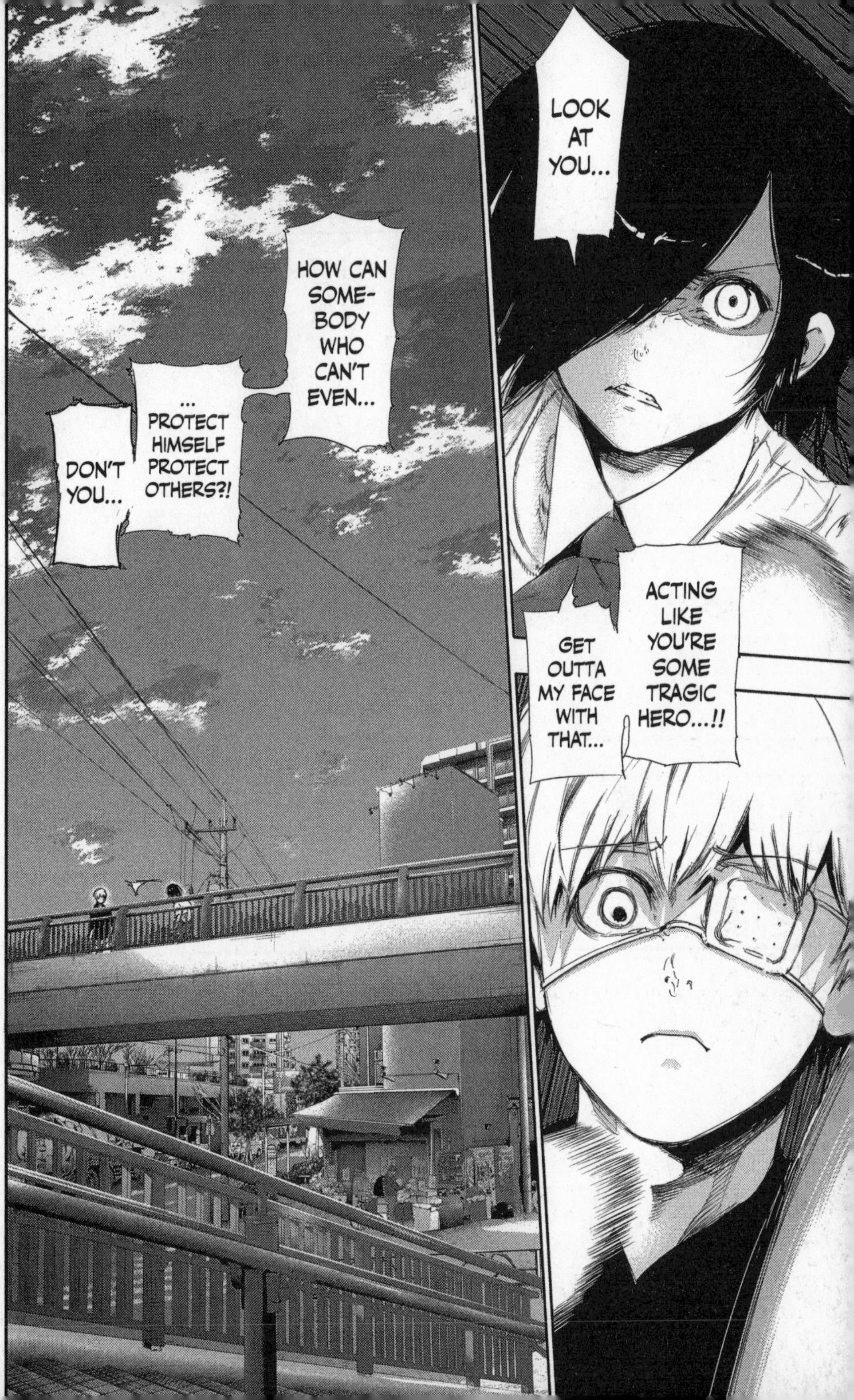
LOOK AT YOU...
ACTING LIKE YOU'RE SOME TRAGIC HERO...!!
GET OUTTA MY FACE WITH THAT...
HOW CAN SOME-BODY WHO CAN'T EVEN...
...PROTECT HIMSELF PROTECT OTHERS?!
DON'T YOU...

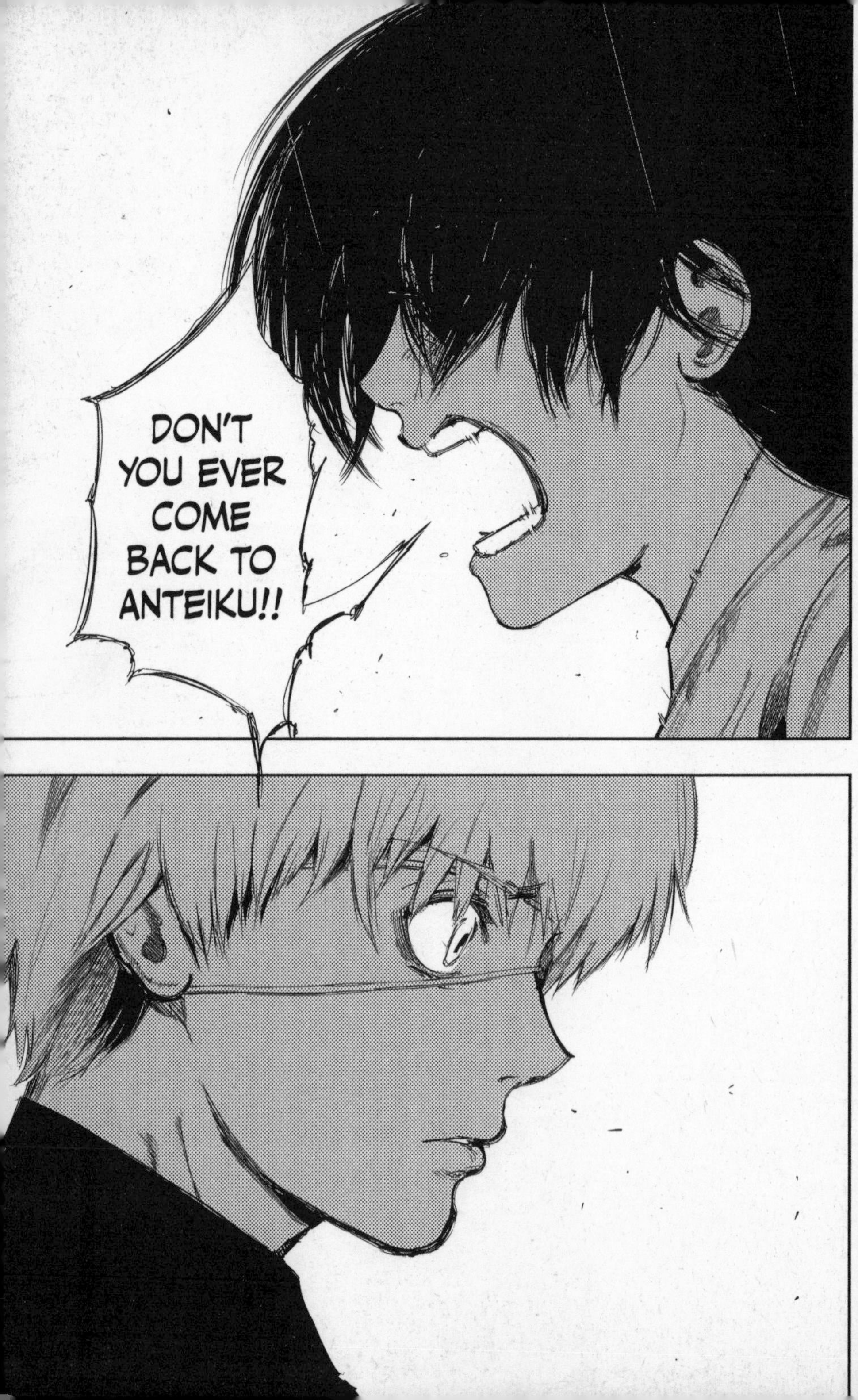
DON'T YOU EVER COME BACK TO ANTEIKU!!

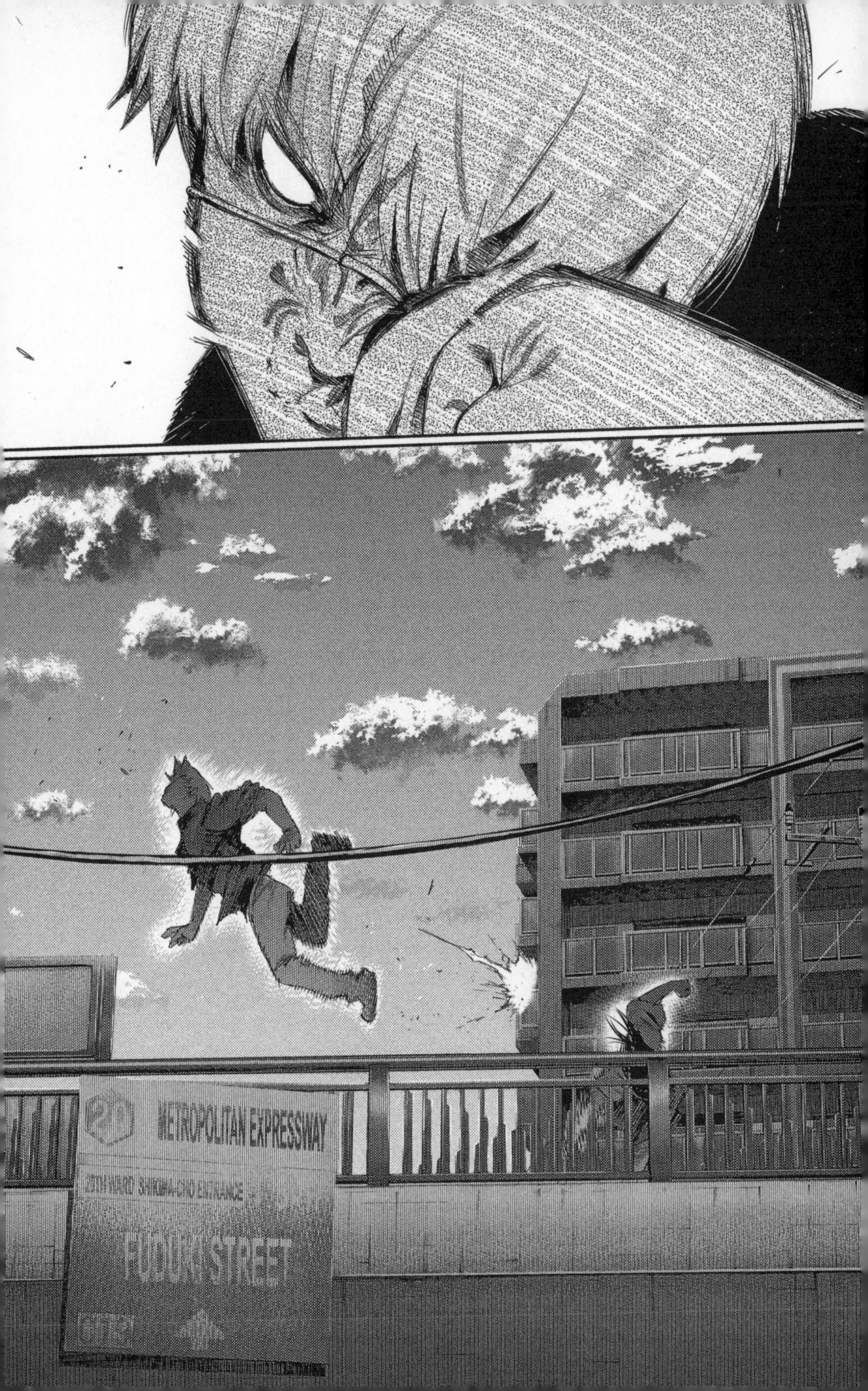
METROPOLITAN EXPRESSWAY

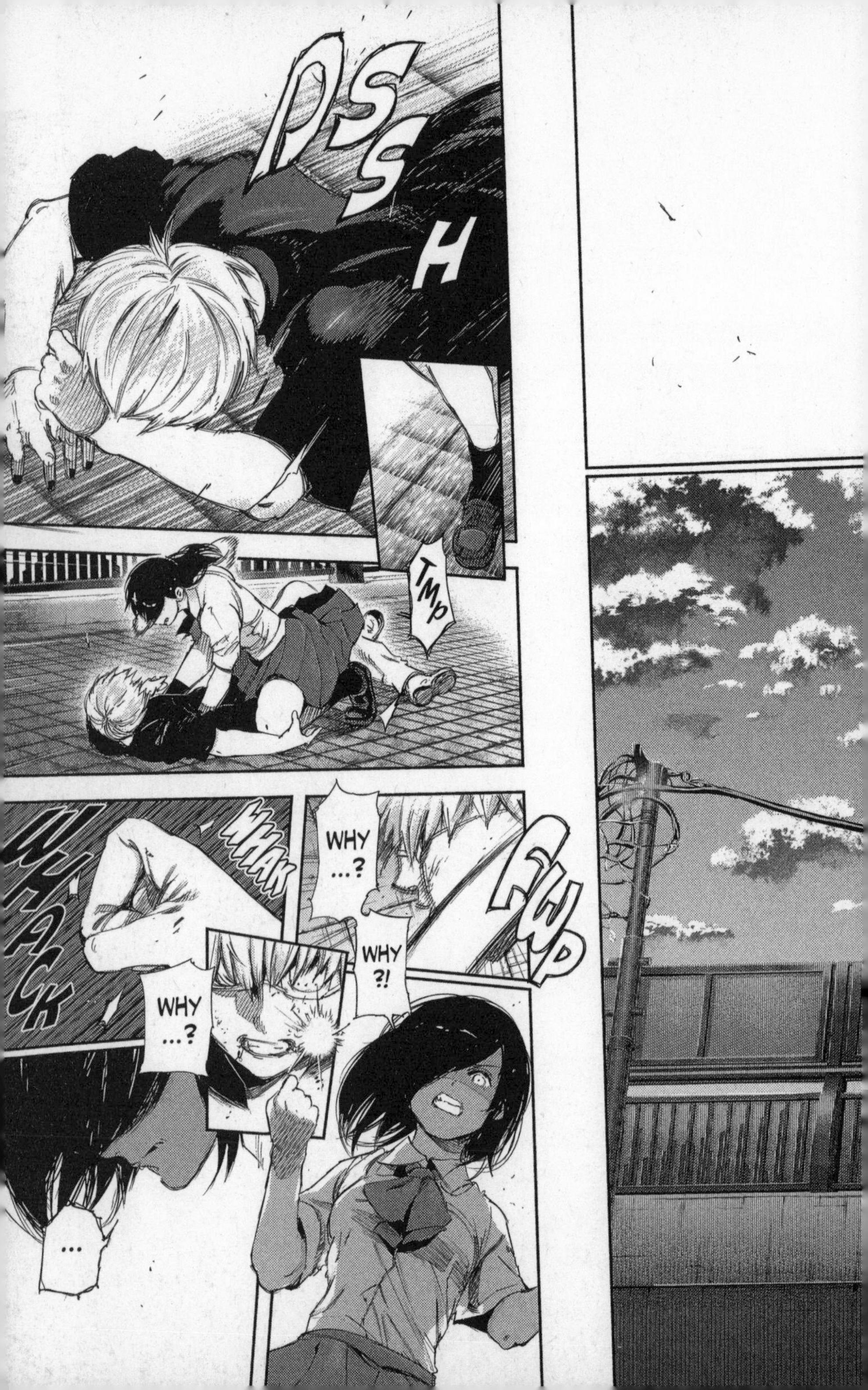
DSSH
TMP
GWP
WHY ...?
WHAK
WHACK
WHY ?!
WHY ...?
...

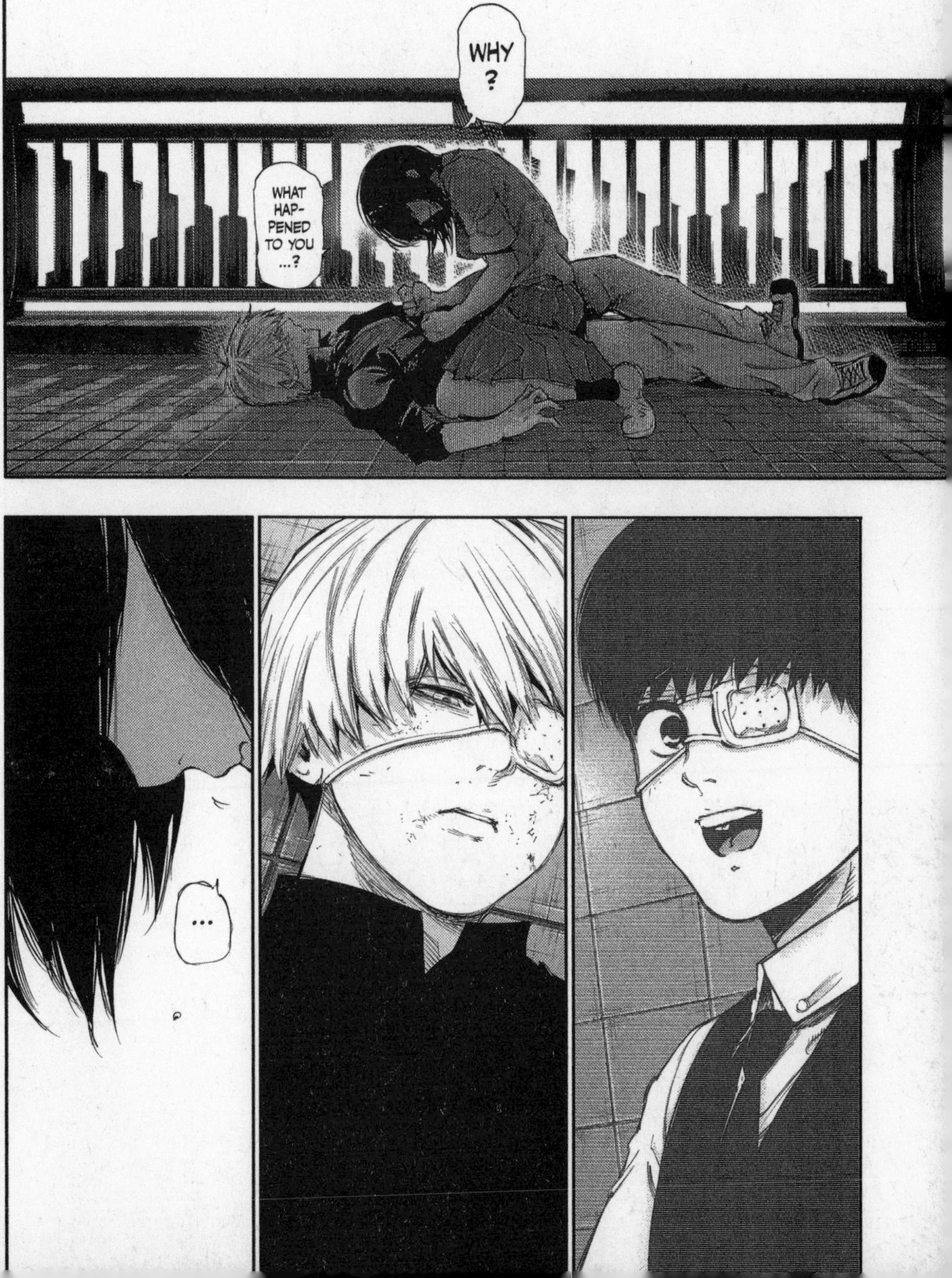
WHY ?
WHAT HAP-PENED TO YOU ...?
...

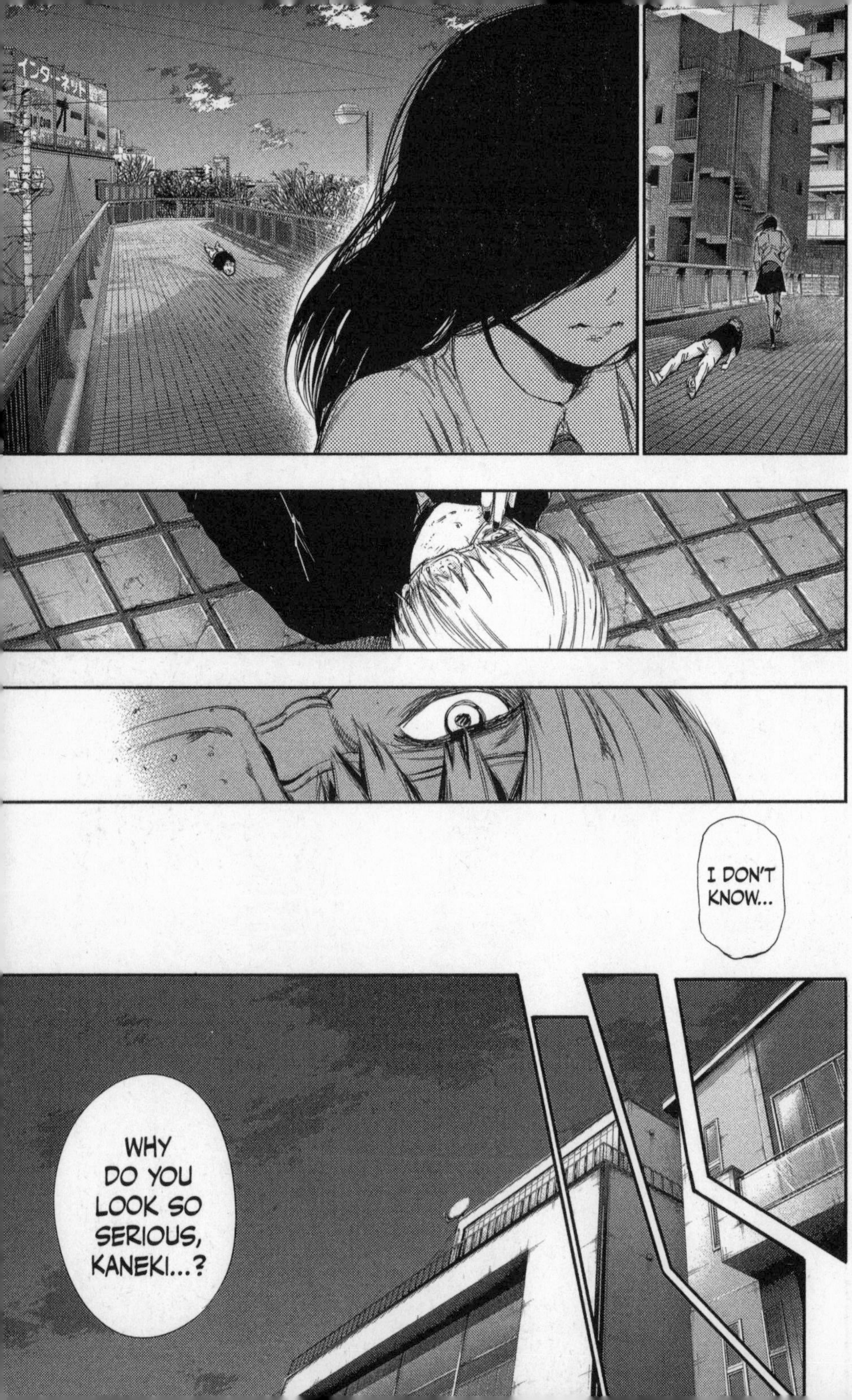
インターネット
I DON'T KNOW...
WHY DO YOU LOOK SO SERIOUS, KANEKI...?

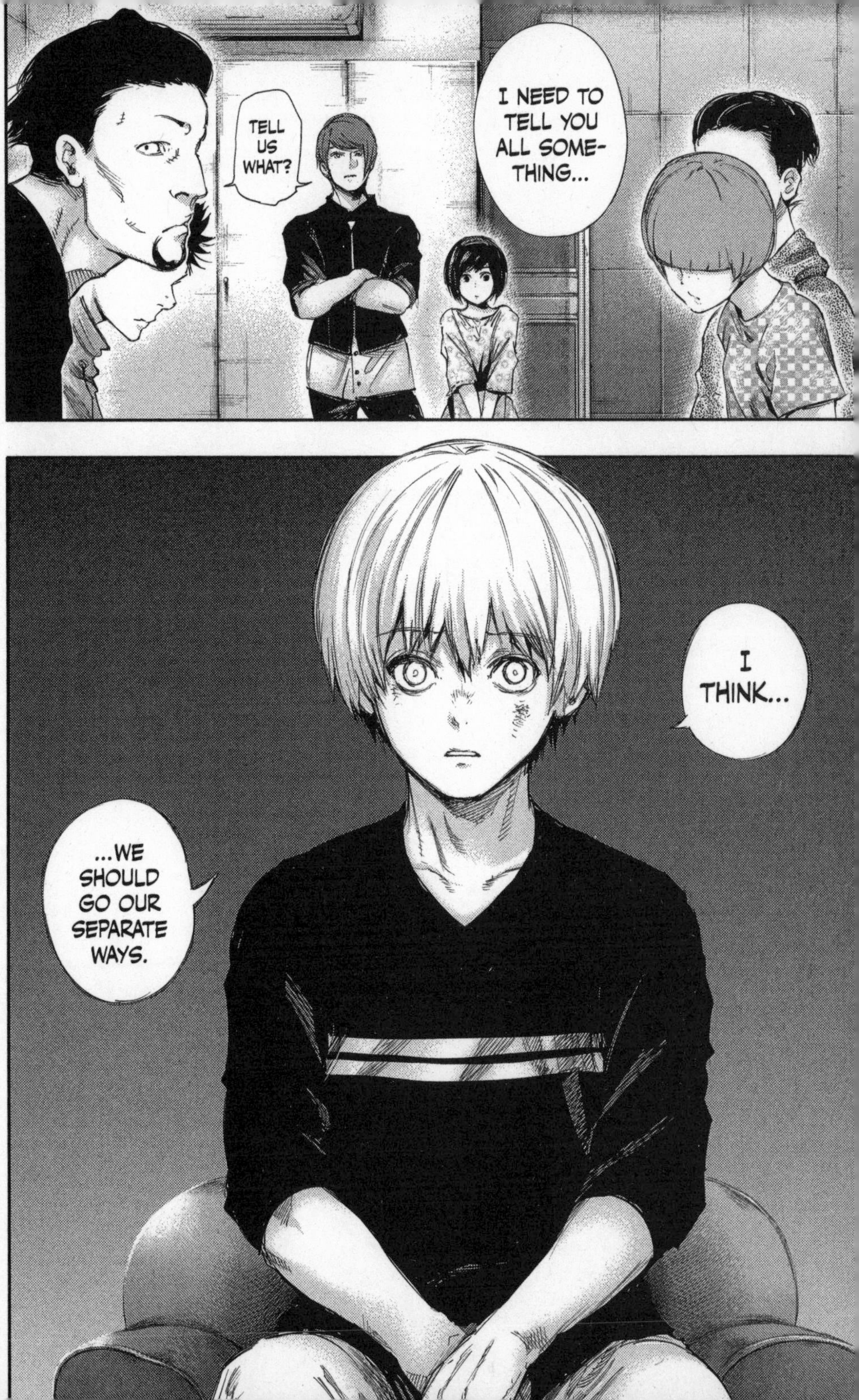
I NEED TO TELL YOU ALL SOME-THING...
TELL US WHAT?
I THINK...
...WE SHOULD GO OUR SEPARATE WAYS.

東京
トーキョーグール
喰種
Tokyo
Ghoul

It's Poetry Time. (3)

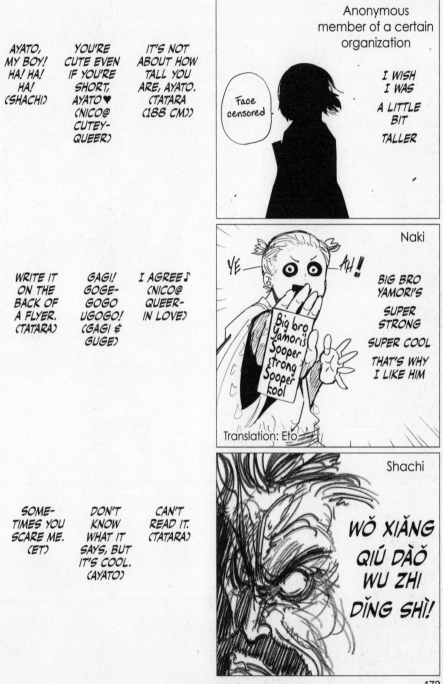

Anonymous member of a certain organization
I WISH I WAS A LITTLE BIT TALLER
Face censored

IT'S NOT ABOUT HOW TALL YOU ARE, AYATO. (TATARA (188 CM))

YOU'RE CUTE EVEN IF YOU'RE SHORT, AYATO♥ (NICO@CUTEY-QUEER)

AYATO, MY BOY! HA! HA! HA! (SHACHI)

Naki
BIG BRO YAMORI'S SUPER STRONG SUPER COOL THAT'S WHY I LIKE HIM
YE-AH!!
Big bro Yamori's Sooper strong Sooper kool
Translation: Eto

I AGREE♪ (NICO@QUEER-IN LOVE)

GAGI! GOGE-GOGO UGOGO! (GAGI & GUGE)

WRITE IT ON THE BACK OF A FLYER. (TATARA)

Shachi
WǑ XIǍNG QIÚ DÀǑ WU ZHI DǏNG SHÌ!

CAN'T READ IT. (TATARA)

DON'T KNOW WHAT IT SAYS, BUT IT'S COOL. (AYATO)

SOME-TIMES YOU SCARE ME. (ET)

#121 TOKYO GHOUL [BULL'S EYE]

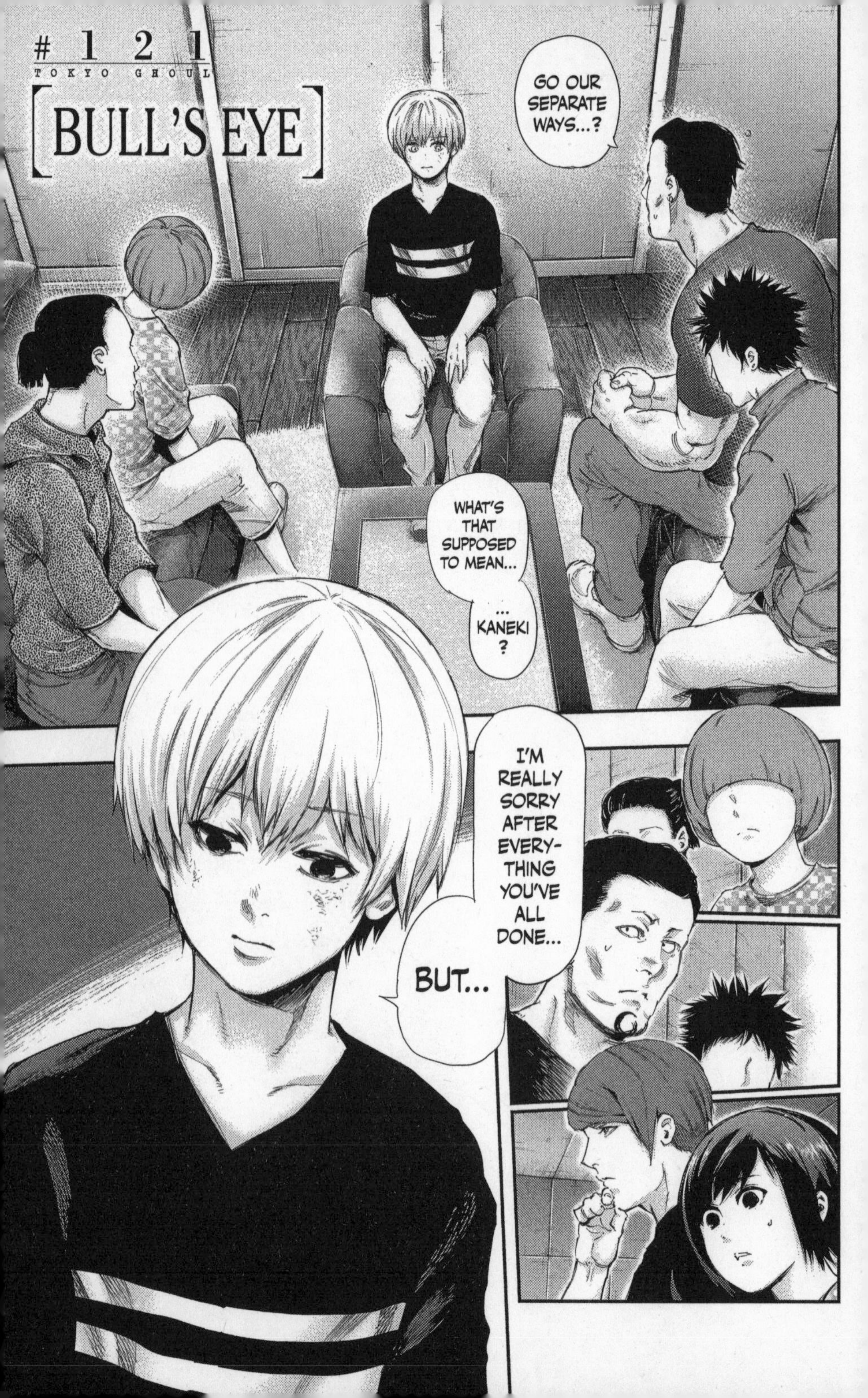
GO OUR SEPARATE WAYS...?
WHAT'S THAT SUPPOSED TO MEAN...
... KANEKI?
I'M REALLY SORRY AFTER EVERY-THING YOU'VE ALL DONE...
BUT...

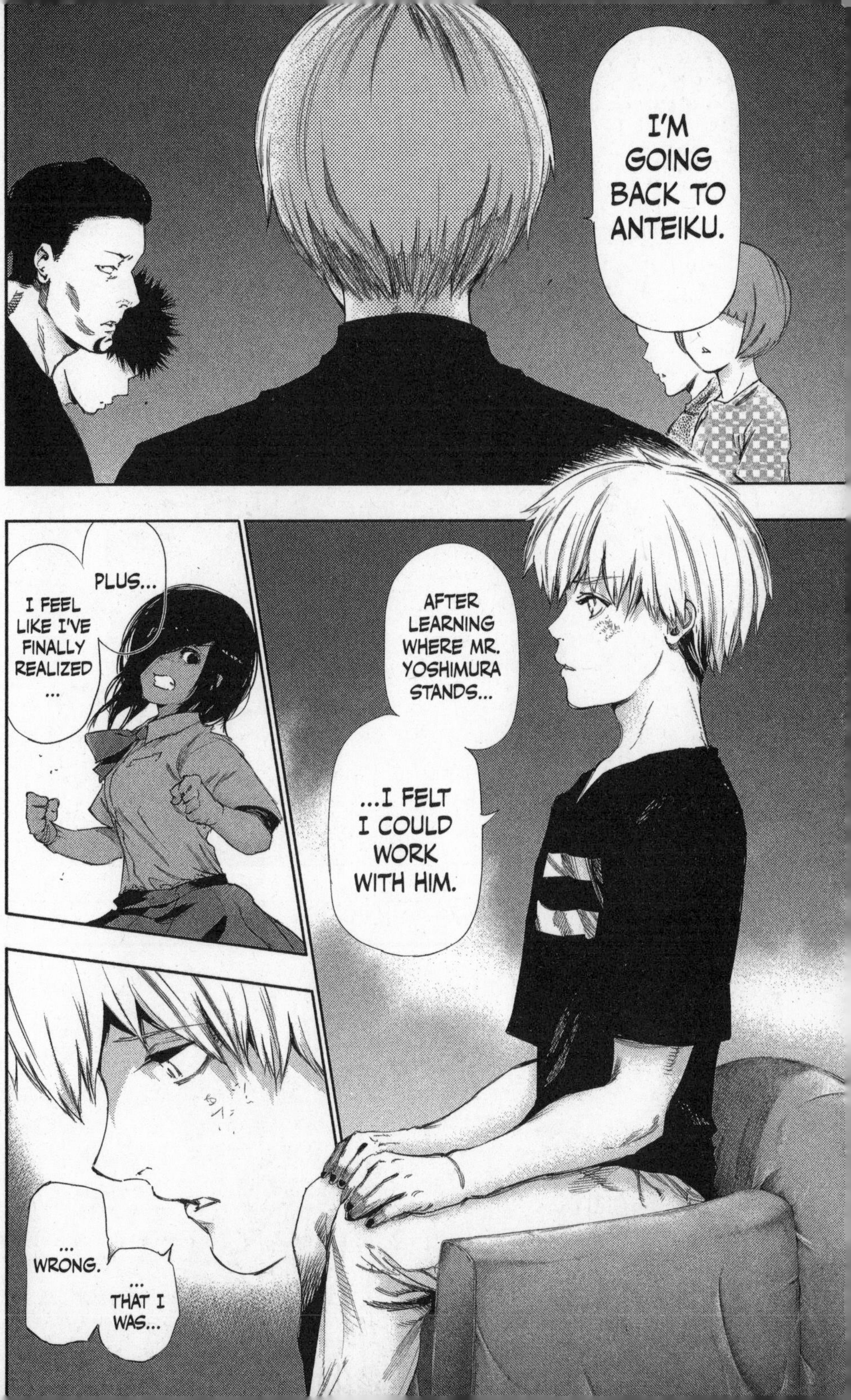
I'M GOING BACK TO ANTEIKU.
AFTER LEARNING WHERE MR. YOSHIMURA STANDS...
...I FELT I COULD WORK WITH HIM.
PLUS... I FEEL LIKE I'VE FINALLY REALIZED ...
... THAT I WAS...
... WRONG.

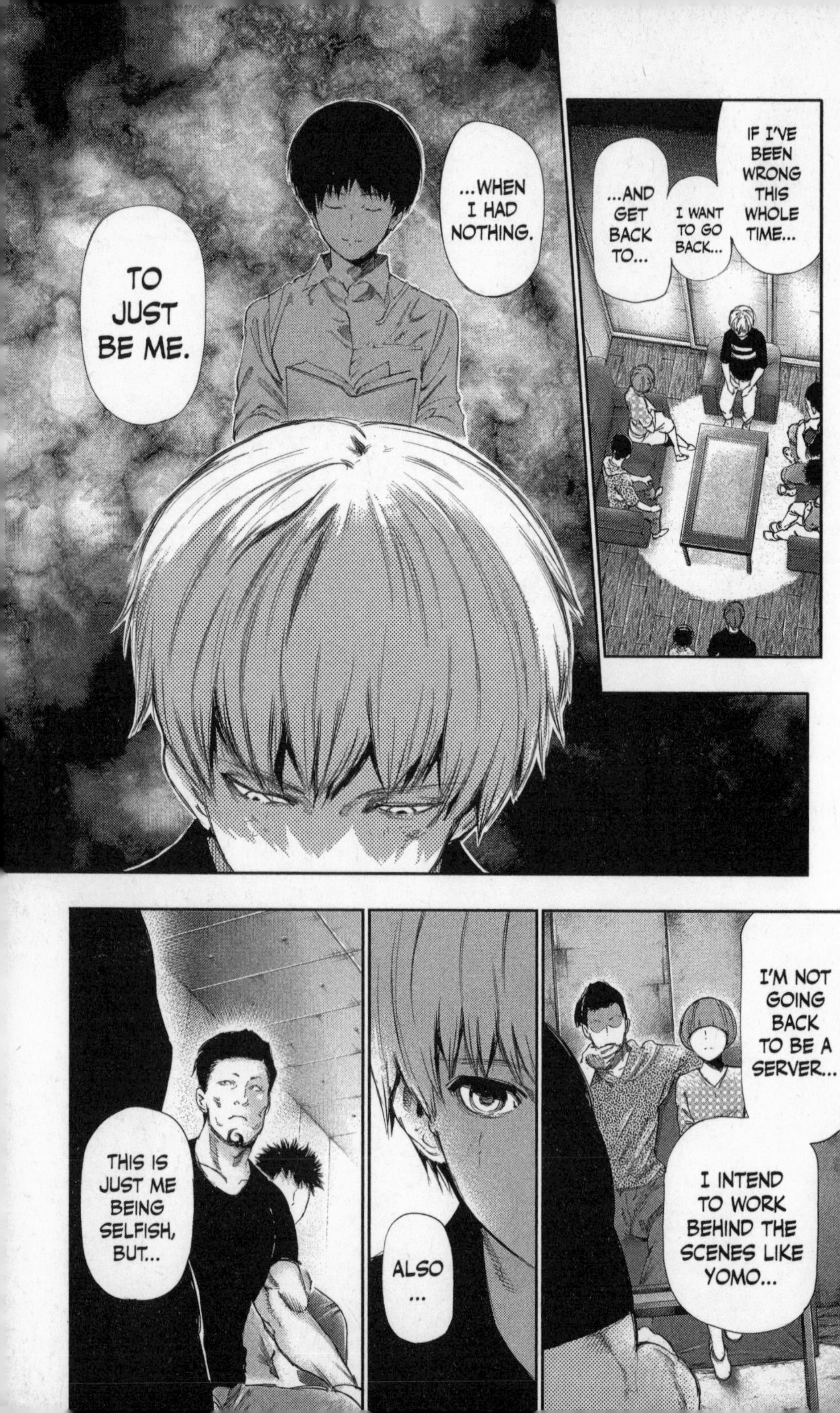
IF I'VE BEEN WRONG THIS WHOLE TIME...
I WANT TO GO BACK...
...AND GET BACK TO...
...WHEN I HAD NOTHING.
TO JUST BE ME.
I'M NOT GOING BACK TO BE A SERVER...
I INTEND TO WORK BEHIND THE SCENES LIKE YOMO...
ALSO ...
THIS IS JUST ME BEING SELFISH, BUT...

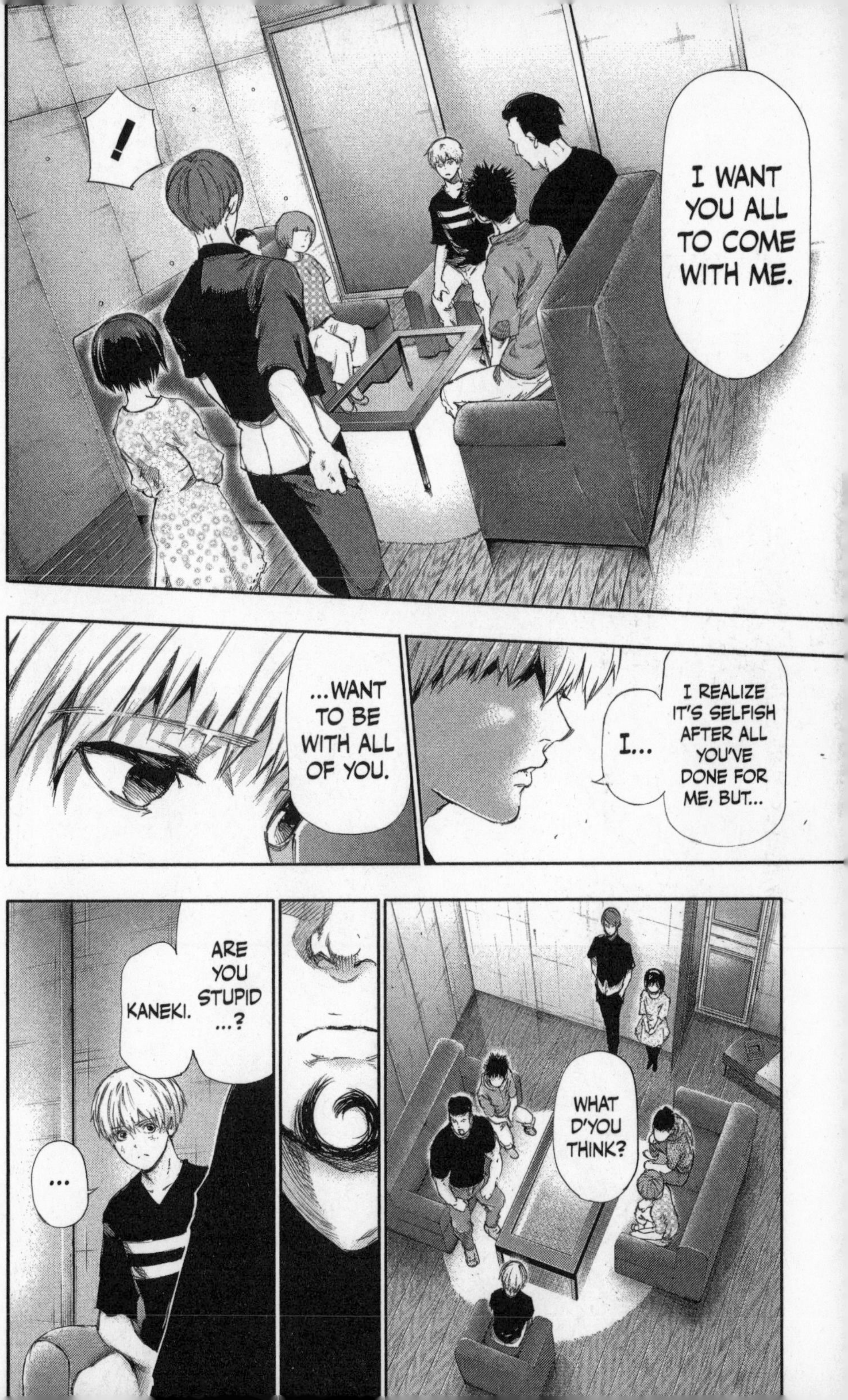
I WANT YOU ALL TO COME WITH ME.
!
I REALIZE IT'S SELFISH AFTER ALL YOU'VE DONE FOR ME, BUT...
I...
...WANT TO BE WITH ALL OF YOU.
WHAT D'YOU THINK?
ARE YOU STUPID ...?
KANEKI.
...

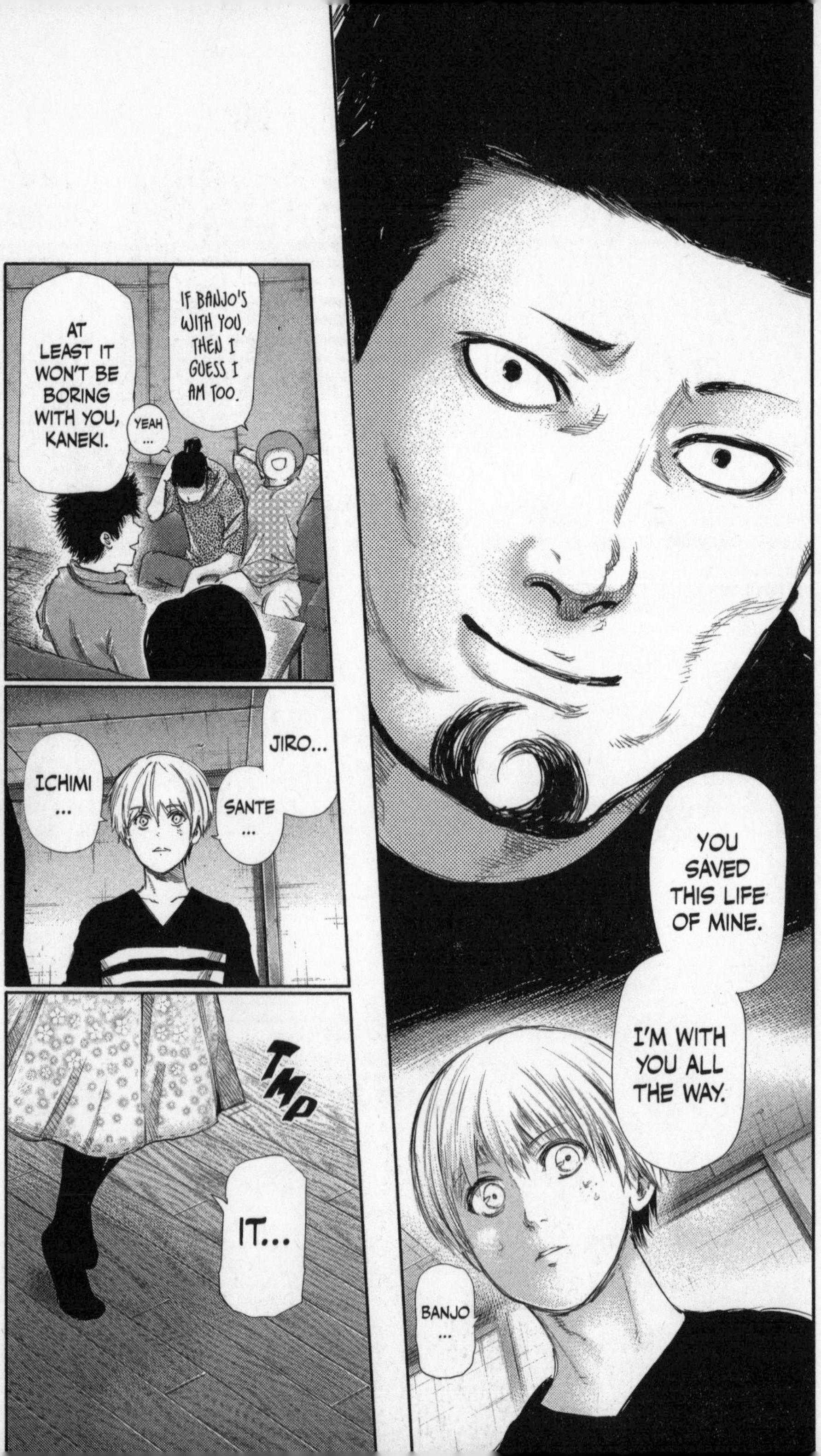
YOU SAVED THIS LIFE OF MINE.
I'M WITH YOU ALL THE WAY.
BANJO ...
IF BANJO'S WITH YOU, THEN I GUESS I AM TOO.
AT LEAST IT WON'T BE BORING WITH YOU, KANEKI.
YEAH ...
JIRO...
SANTE ...
ICHIMI ...
TMP
IT...

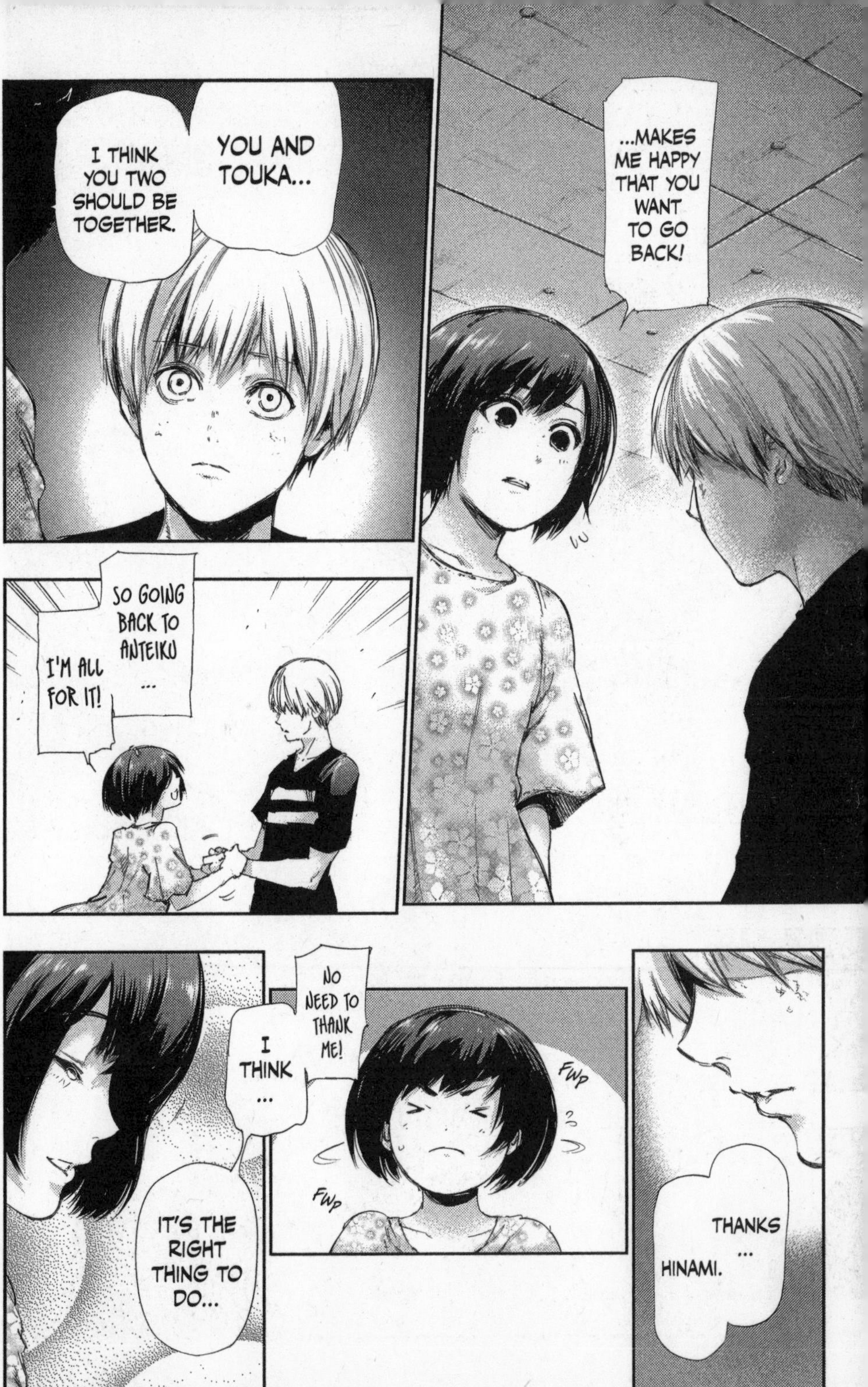
...MAKES ME HAPPY THAT YOU WANT TO GO BACK!
YOU AND TOUKA...
I THINK YOU TWO SHOULD BE TOGETHER.
SO GOING BACK TO ANTEIKU ...
I'M ALL FOR IT!
THANKS ... HINAMI.
NO NEED TO THANK ME!
FWP
FWP
I THINK ...
IT'S THE RIGHT THING TO DO...

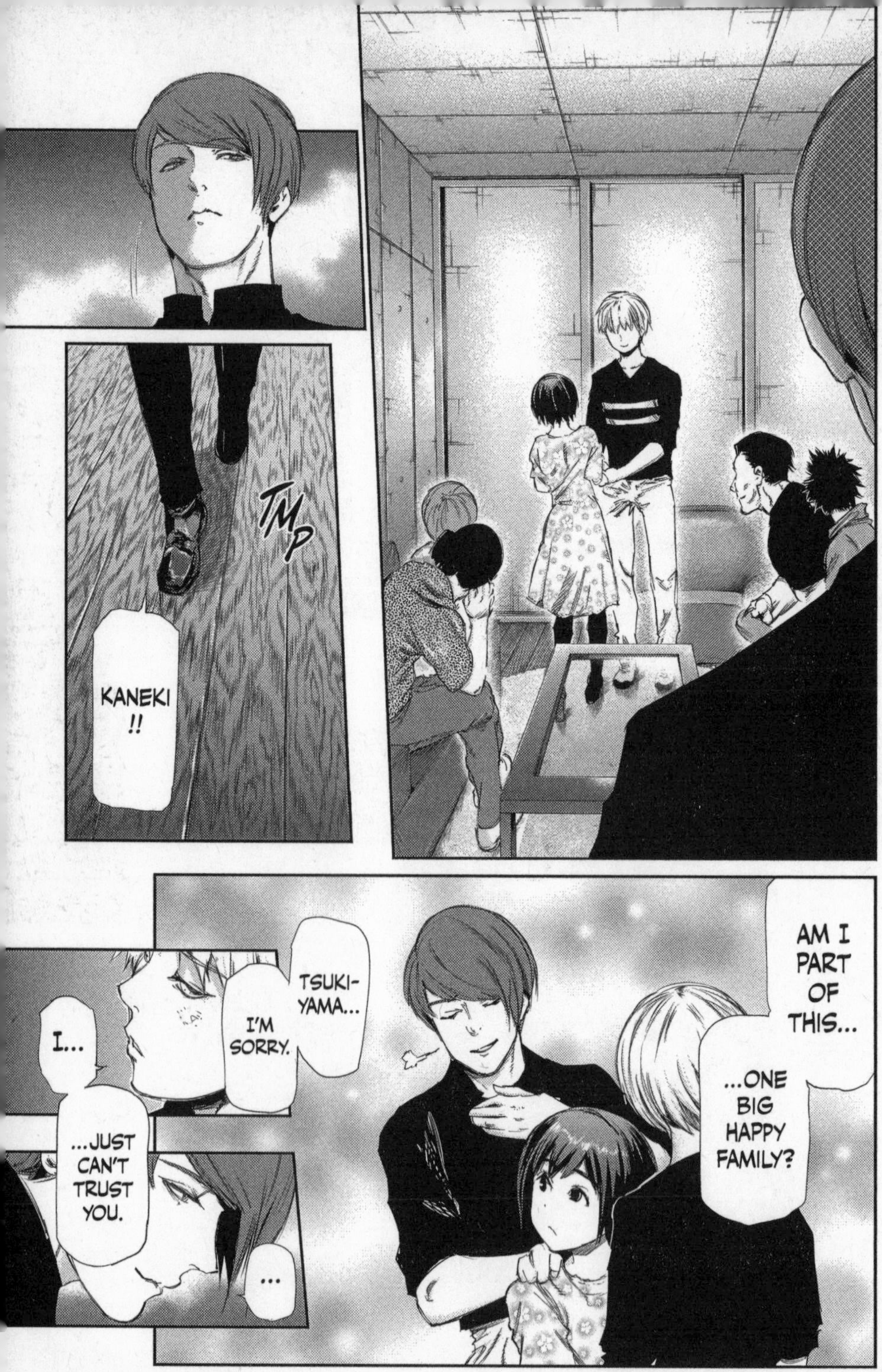
TMP
KANEKI !!
AM I PART OF THIS...
...ONE BIG HAPPY FAMILY?
TSUKI-YAMA...
I'M SORRY.
I...
...JUST CAN'T TRUST YOU.
...

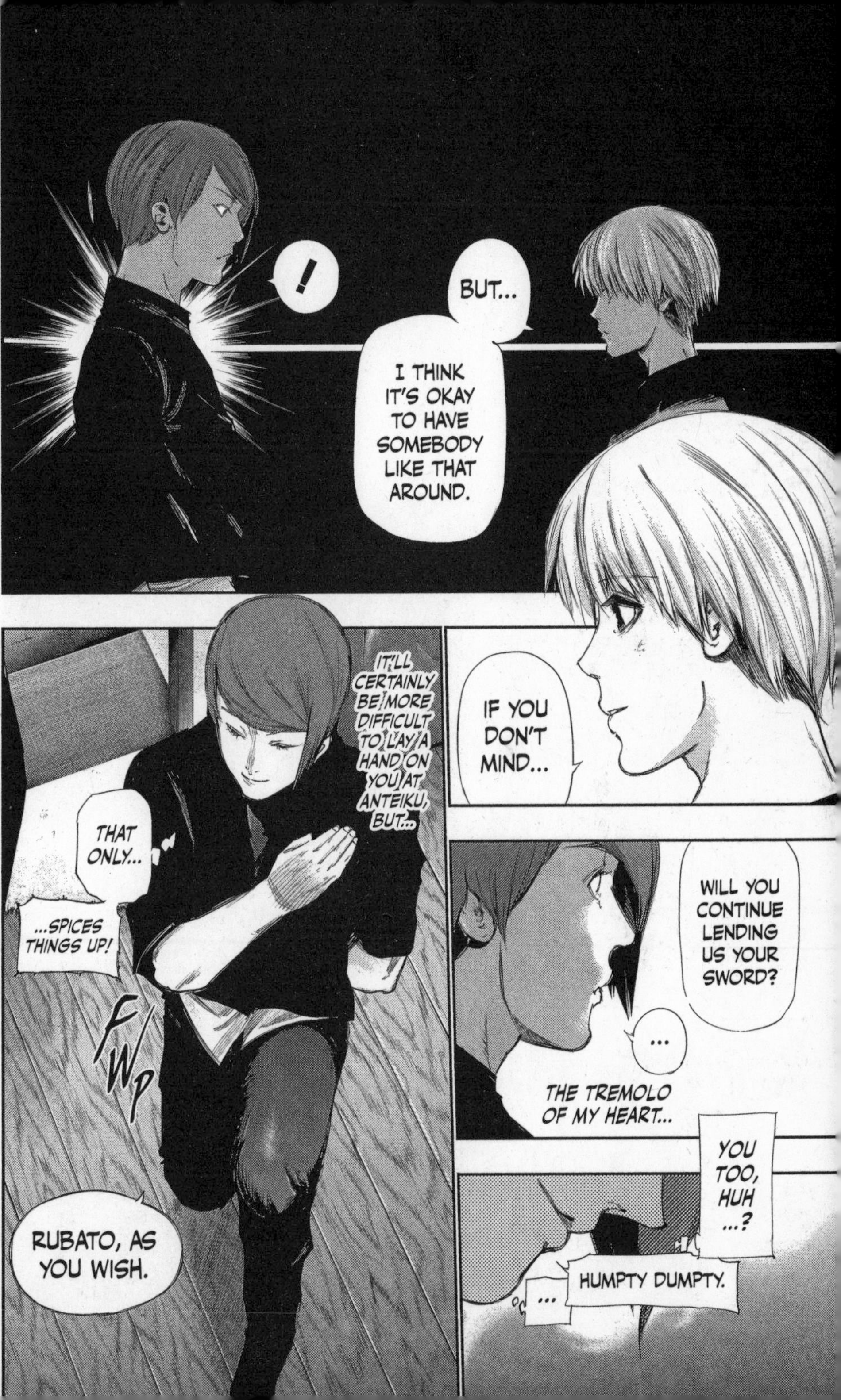
BUT...
I THINK IT'S OKAY TO HAVE SOMEBODY LIKE THAT AROUND.
!
IF YOU DON'T MIND...
WILL YOU CONTINUE LENDING US YOUR SWORD?
...
THE TREMOLO OF MY HEART...
YOU TOO, HUH ...?
HUMPTY DUMPTY.
...
IT'LL CERTAINLY BE MORE DIFFICULT TO LAY A HAND ON YOU AT ANTEIKU, BUT...
THAT ONLY...
...SPICES THINGS UP!
FWP
RUBATO, AS YOU WISH.

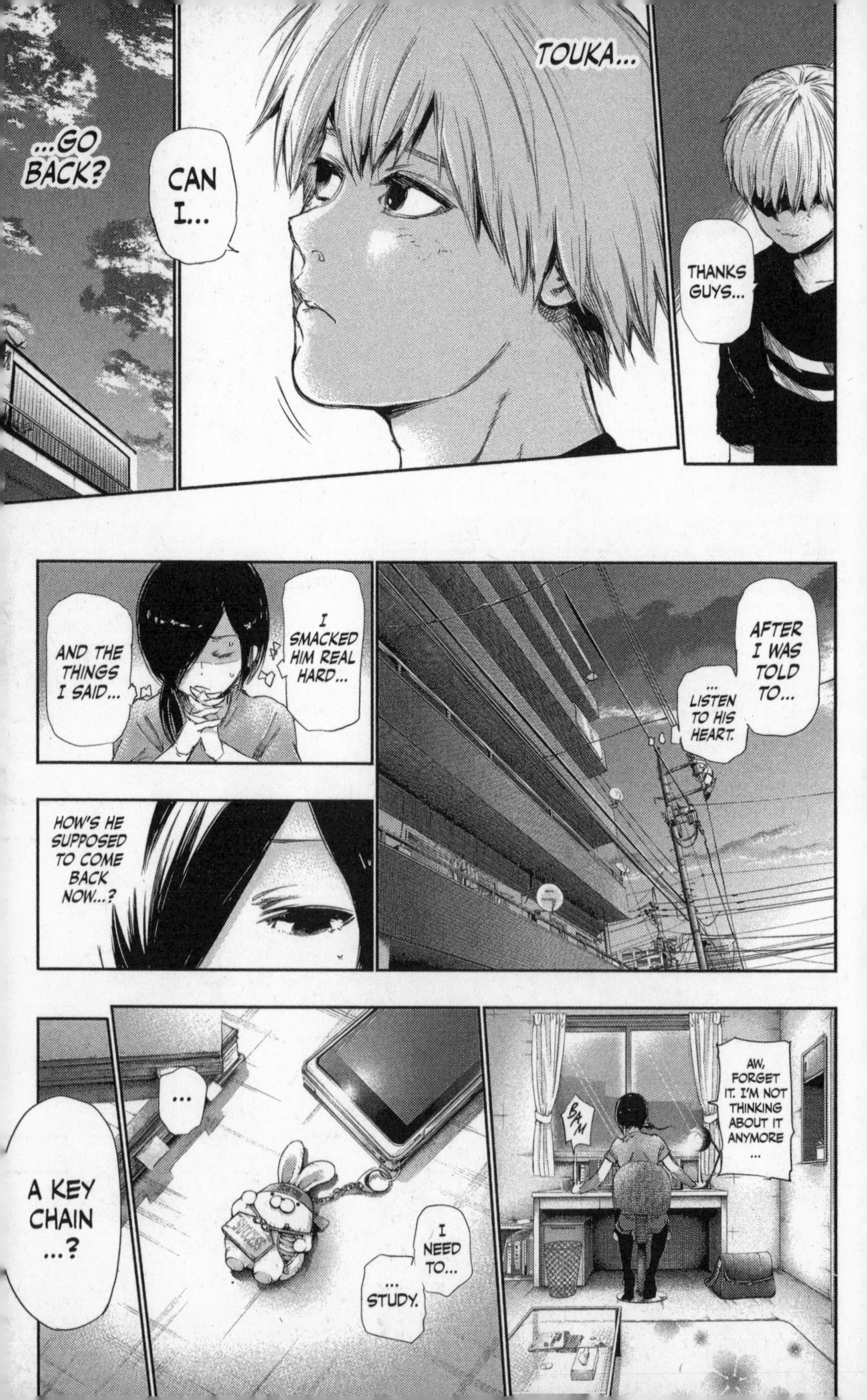
THANKS GUYS...
TOUKA...
CAN I...
...GO BACK?
AFTER I WAS TOLD TO...
... LISTEN TO HIS HEART.
I SMACKED HIM REAL HARD...
AND THE THINGS I SAID...
HOW'S HE SUPPOSED TO COME BACK NOW...?
AW, FORGET IT. I'M NOT THINKING ABOUT IT ANYMORE ...
BAM
...
I NEED TO...
... STUDY.
A KEY CHAIN ...?

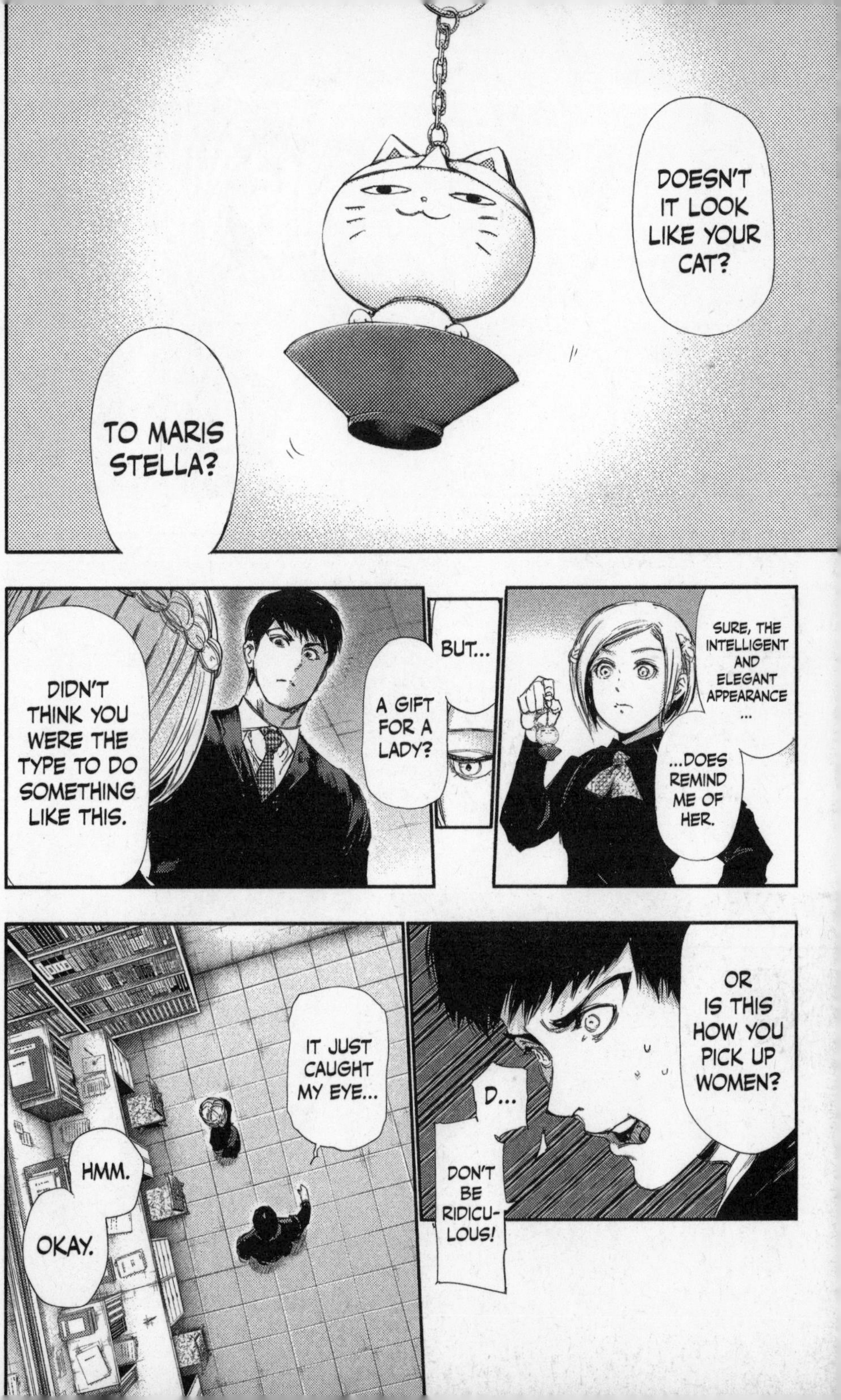
DOESN'T IT LOOK LIKE YOUR CAT?
TO MARIS STELLA?
SURE, THE INTELLIGENT AND ELEGANT APPEARANCE ...
...DOES REMIND ME OF HER.
BUT...
A GIFT FOR A LADY?
DIDN'T THINK YOU WERE THE TYPE TO DO SOMETHING LIKE THIS.
OR IS THIS HOW YOU PICK UP WOMEN?
D...
DON'T BE RIDICU-LOUS!
IT JUST CAUGHT MY EYE...
HMM.
OKAY.

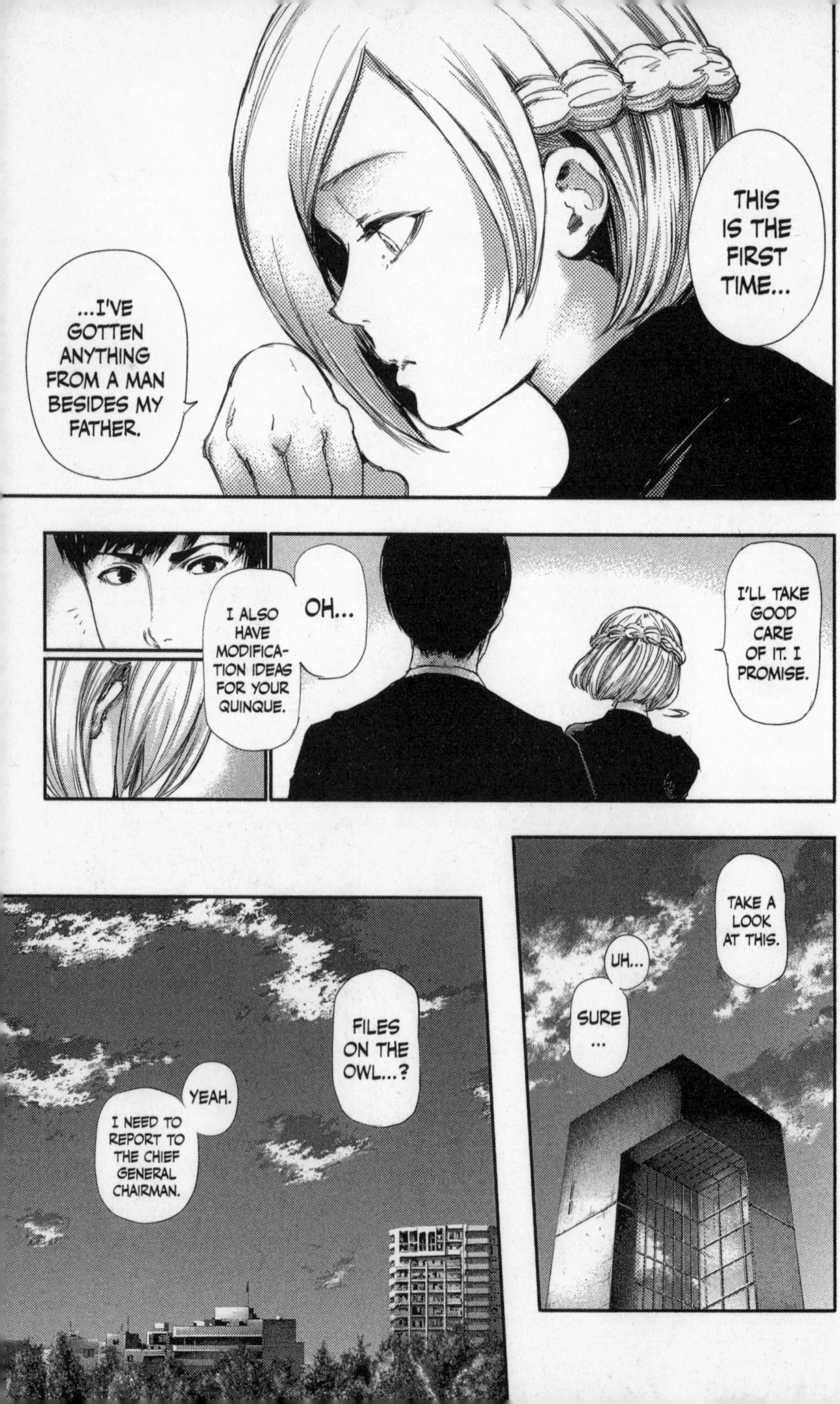
THIS IS THE FIRST TIME...
...I'VE GOTTEN ANYTHING FROM A MAN BESIDES MY FATHER.
I'LL TAKE GOOD CARE OF IT. I PROMISE.
OH...
I ALSO HAVE MODIFICA-TION IDEAS FOR YOUR QUINQUE.
TAKE A LOOK AT THIS.
UH...
SURE ...
FILES ON THE OWL...?
YEAH.
I NEED TO REPORT TO THE CHIEF GENERAL CHAIRMAN.

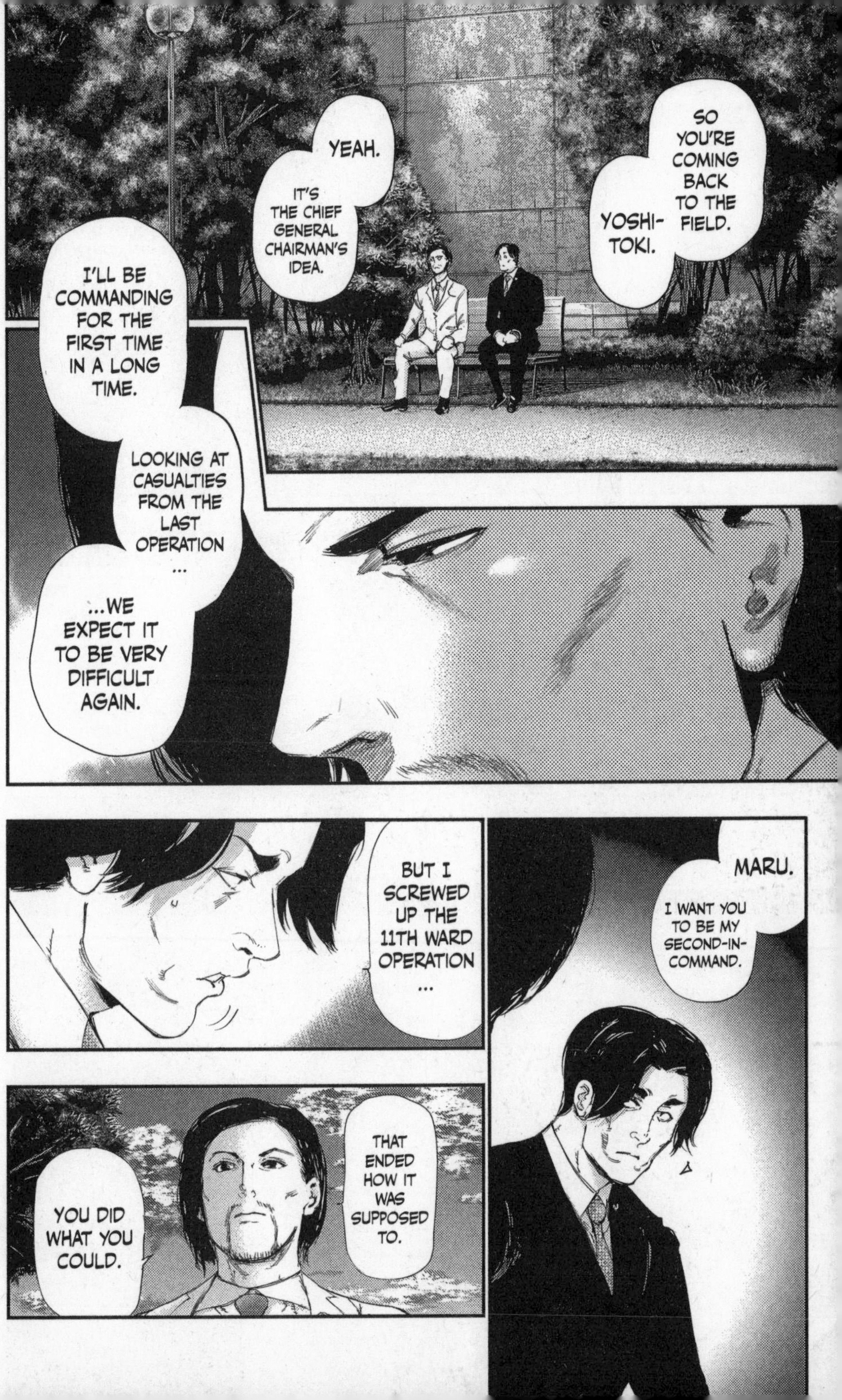
SO YOU'RE COMING BACK TO THE FIELD.
YOSHI-TOKI.
YEAH.
IT'S THE CHIEF GENERAL CHAIRMAN'S IDEA.
I'LL BE COMMANDING FOR THE FIRST TIME IN A LONG TIME.
LOOKING AT CASUALTIES FROM THE LAST OPERATION ...
...WE EXPECT IT TO BE VERY DIFFICULT AGAIN.
MARU.
I WANT YOU TO BE MY SECOND-IN-COMMAND.
BUT I SCREWED UP THE 11TH WARD OPERATION ...
THAT ENDED HOW IT WAS SUPPOSED TO.
YOU DID WHAT YOU COULD.

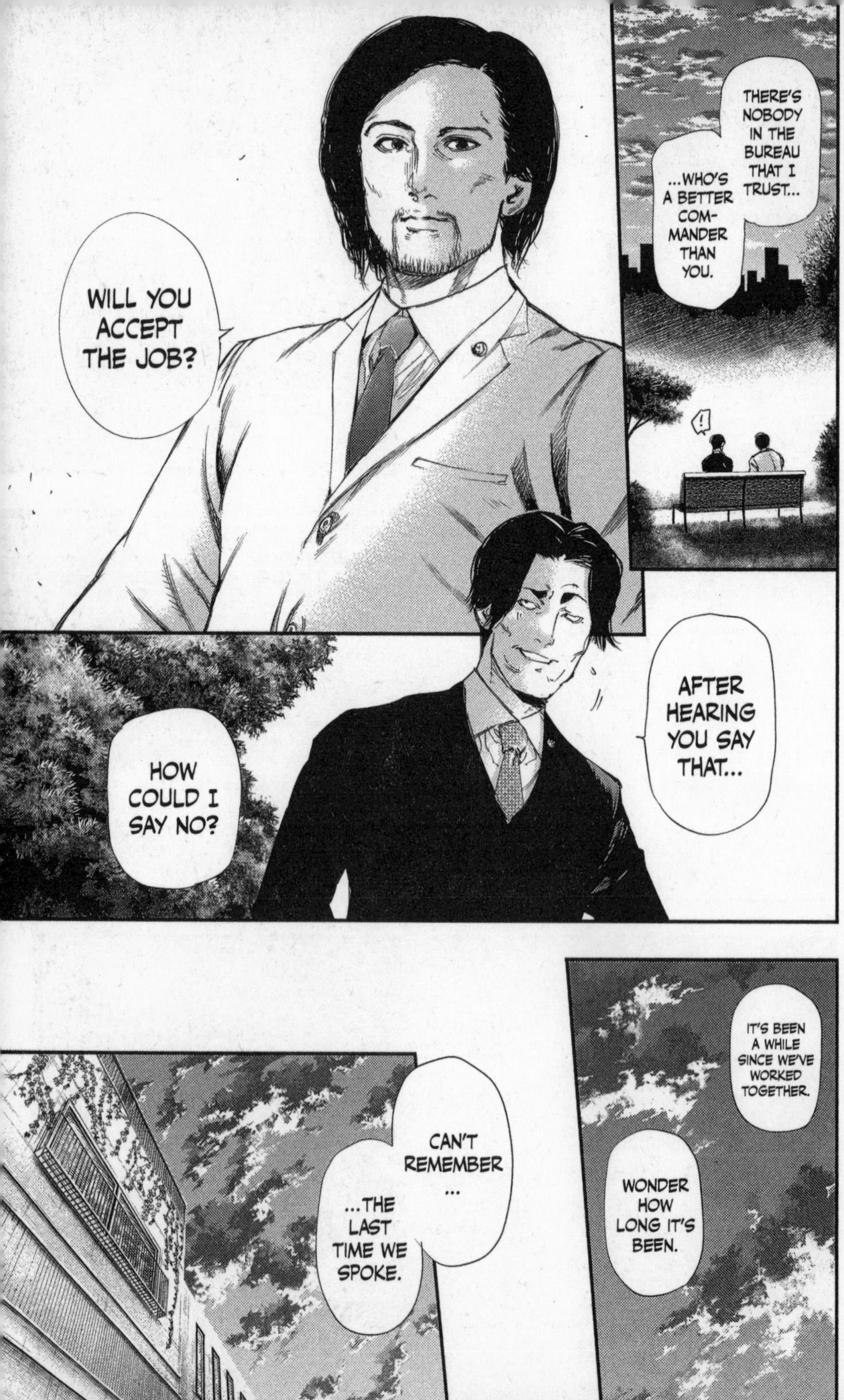
THERE'S NOBODY IN THE BUREAU THAT I TRUST...
...WHO'S A BETTER COM-MANDER THAN YOU.
!
WILL YOU ACCEPT THE JOB?
AFTER HEARING YOU SAY THAT...
HOW COULD I SAY NO?
IT'S BEEN A WHILE SINCE WE'VE WORKED TOGETHER.
WONDER HOW LONG IT'S BEEN.
CAN'T REMEMBER ...
...THE LAST TIME WE SPOKE.

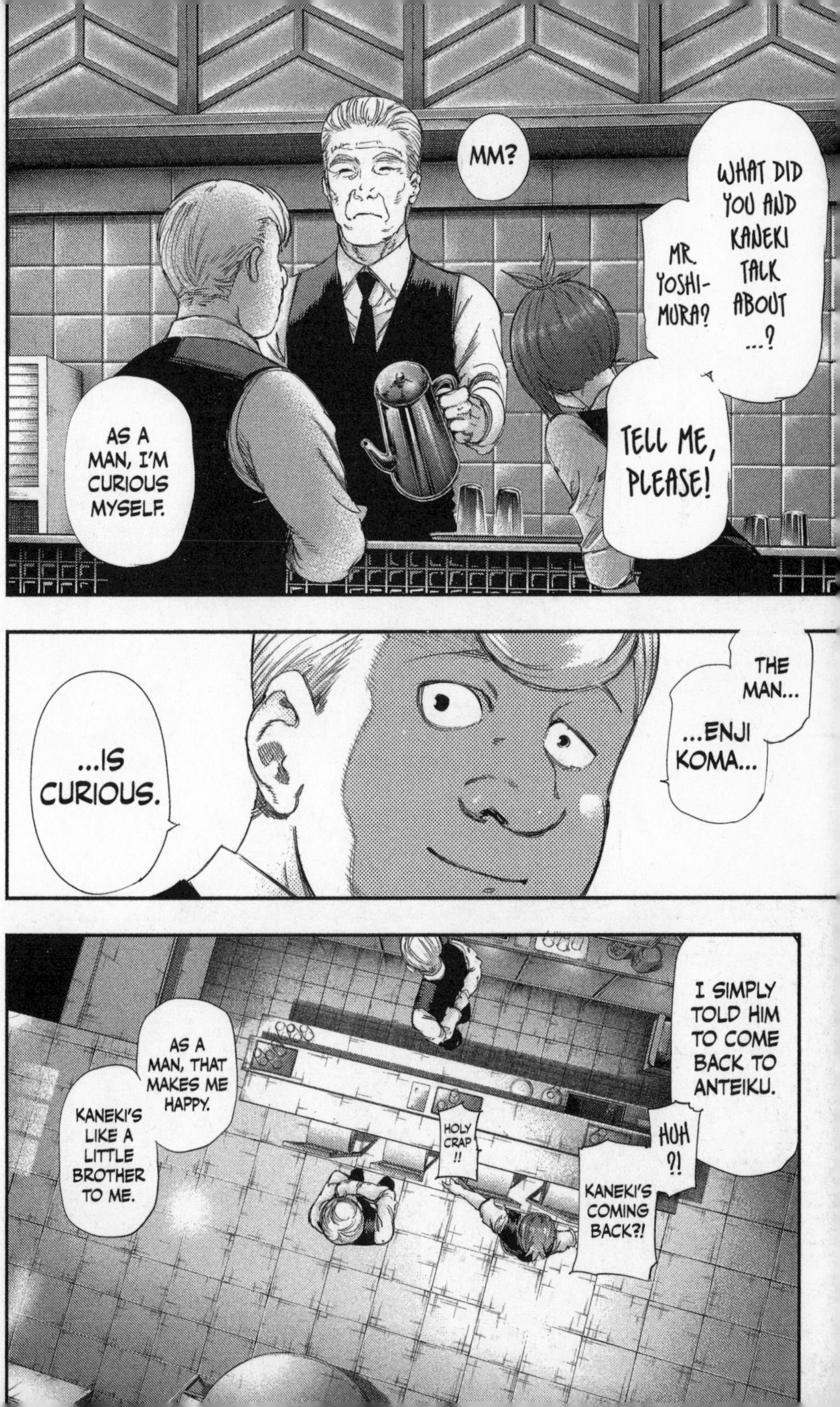
WHAT DID YOU AND KANEKI TALK ABOUT ...?
MR. YOSHI-MURA?
MM?
TELL ME, PLEASE!
AS A MAN, I'M CURIOUS MYSELF.
THE MAN...
...ENJI KOMA...
...IS CURIOUS.
I SIMPLY TOLD HIM TO COME BACK TO ANTEIKU.
HUH ?!
KANEKI'S COMING BACK?!
HOLY CRAP !!
AS A MAN, THAT MAKES ME HAPPY.
KANEKI'S LIKE A LITTLE BROTHER TO ME.

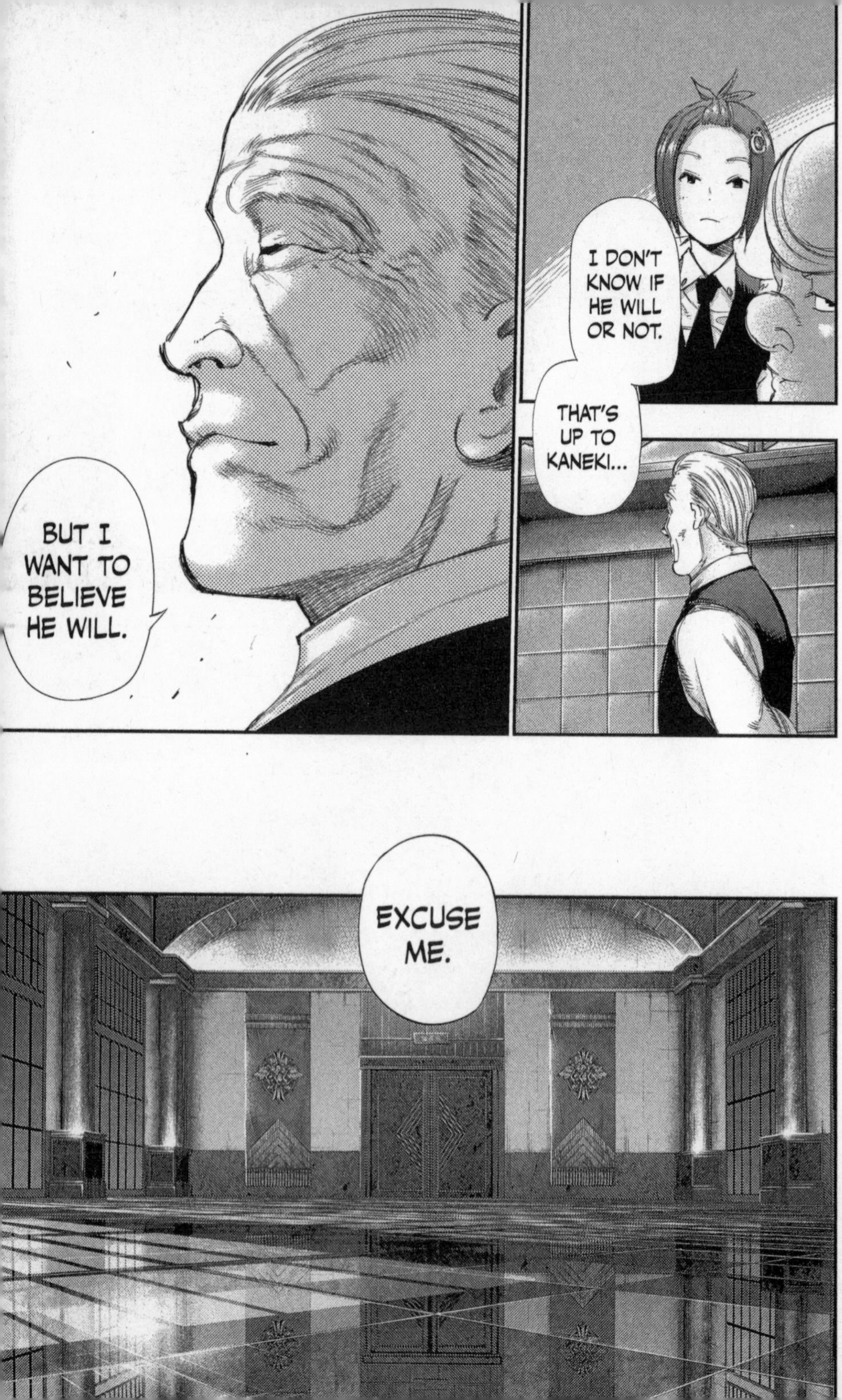
I DON'T KNOW IF HE WILL OR NOT.
THAT'S UP TO KANEKI...
BUT I WANT TO BELIEVE HE WILL.
EXCUSE ME.

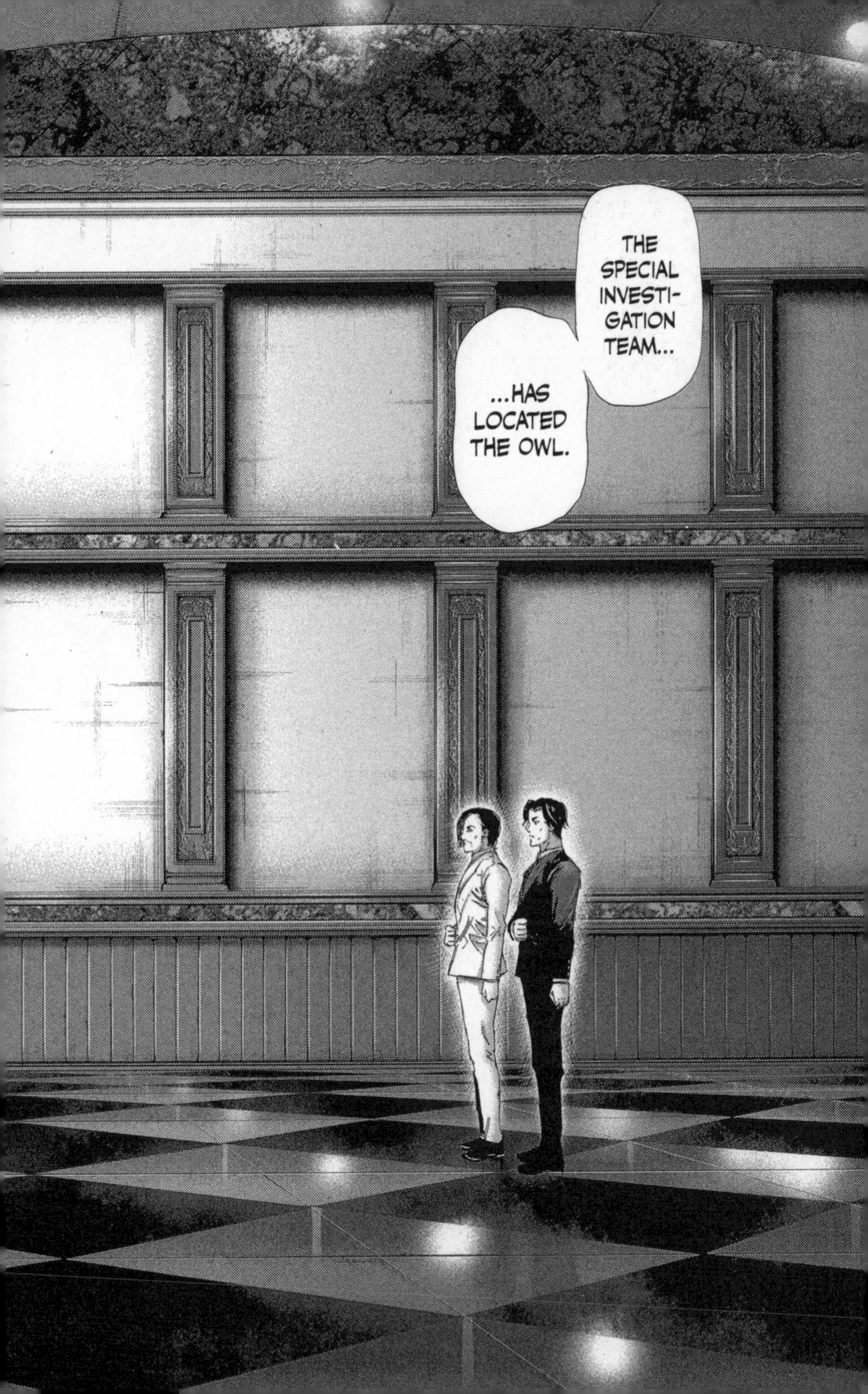
THE SPECIAL INVESTI- GATION TEAM...
...HAS LOCATED THE OWL.

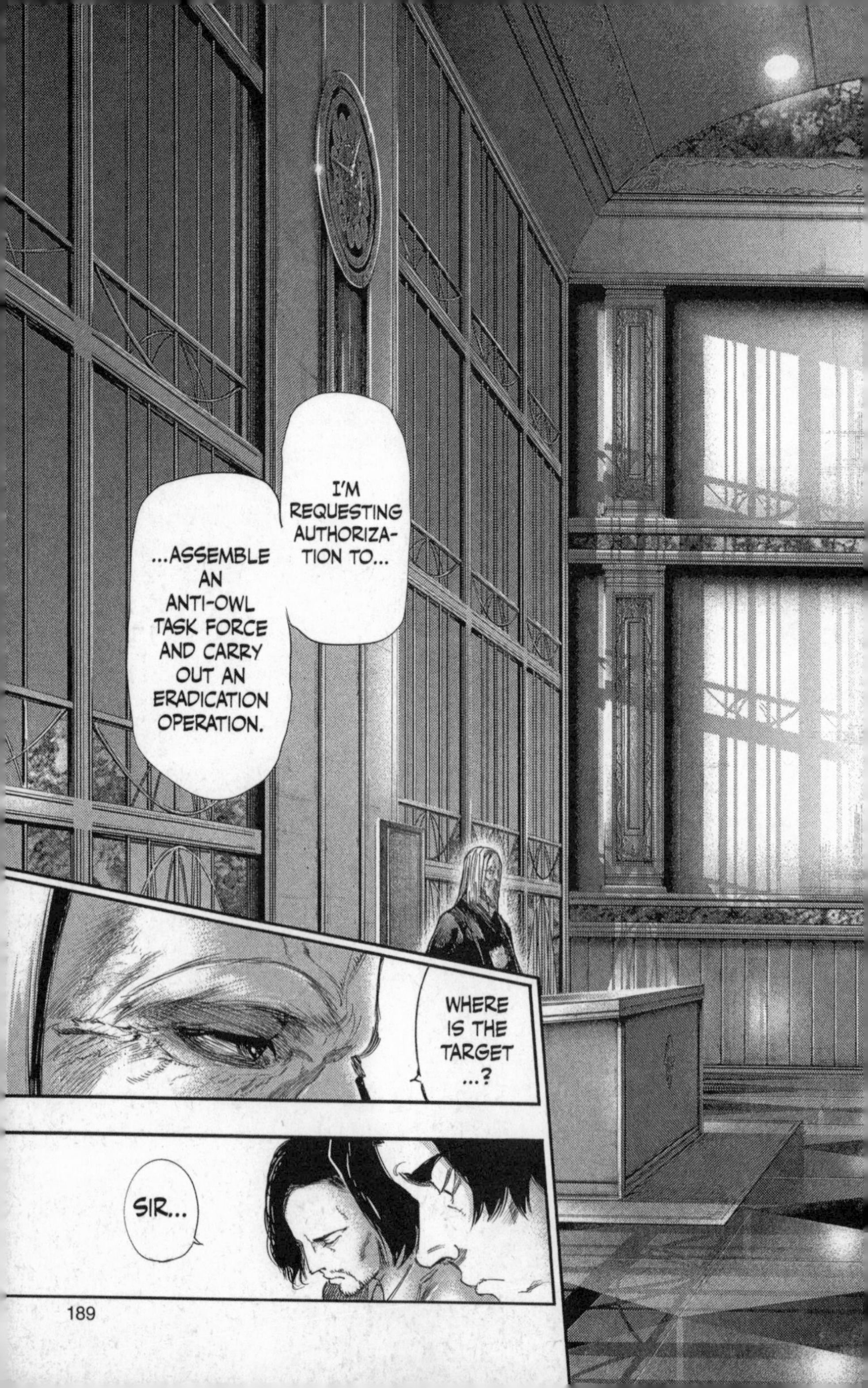
I'M REQUESTING AUTHORIZATION TO...
...ASSEMBLE AN ANTI-OWL TASK FORCE AND CARRY OUT AN ERADICATION OPERATION.
WHERE IS THE TARGET ...?
SIR...

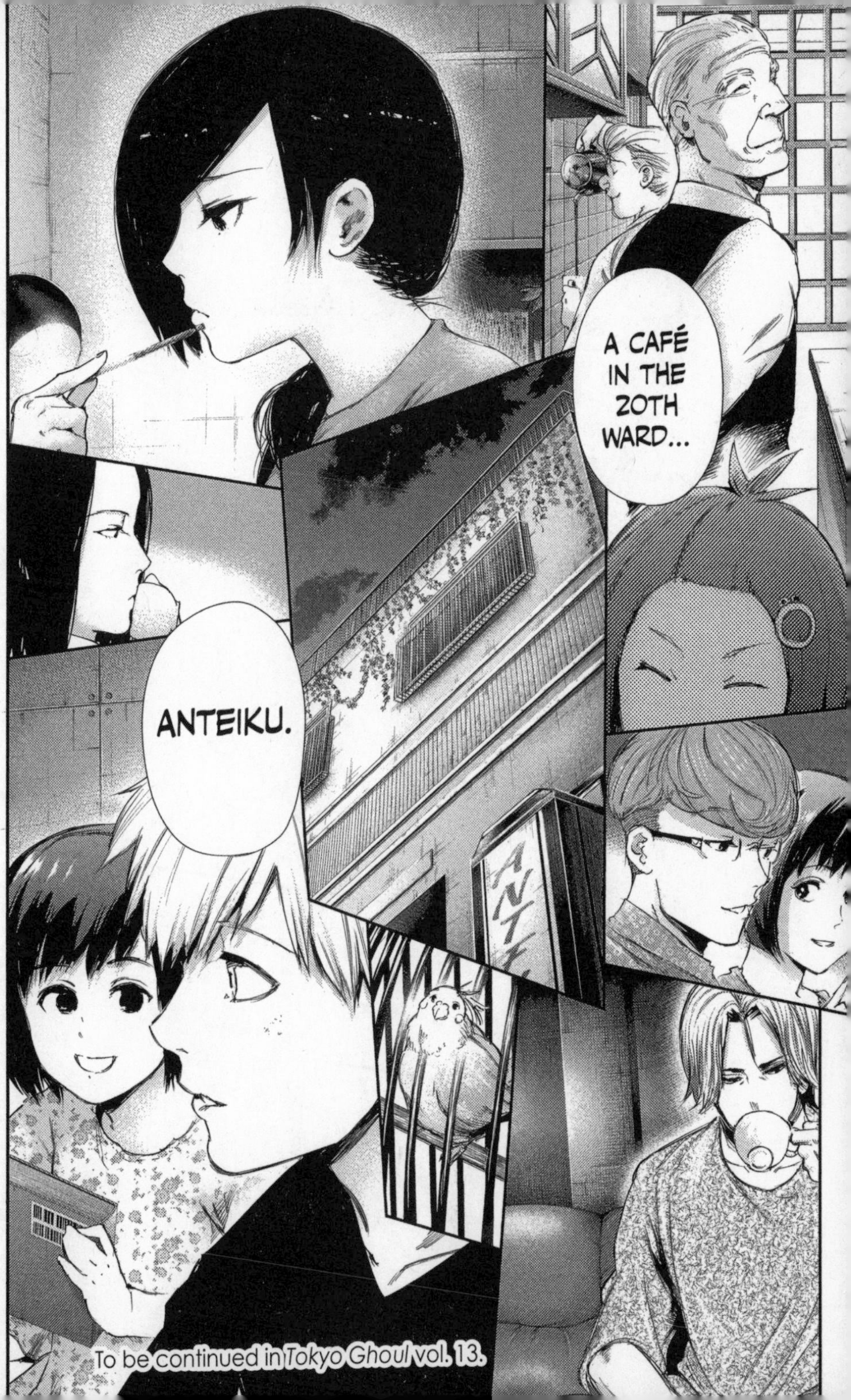
A CAFÉ IN THE 20TH WARD...
ANTEIKU.
ANT
To be continued in *Tokyo Ghoul* vol. 13.

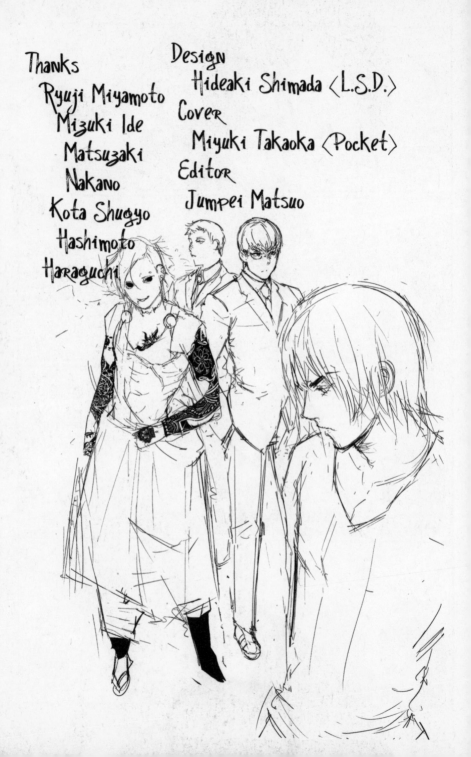

Thanks
Ryuji Miyamoto
Mizuki Ide
Matsuzaki
Nakano
Kota Shugyo
Hashimoto
Haraguchi

Design
Hideaki Shimada <L.S.D.>
Cover
Miyuki Takaoka <Pocket>
Editor
Jumpei Matsuo

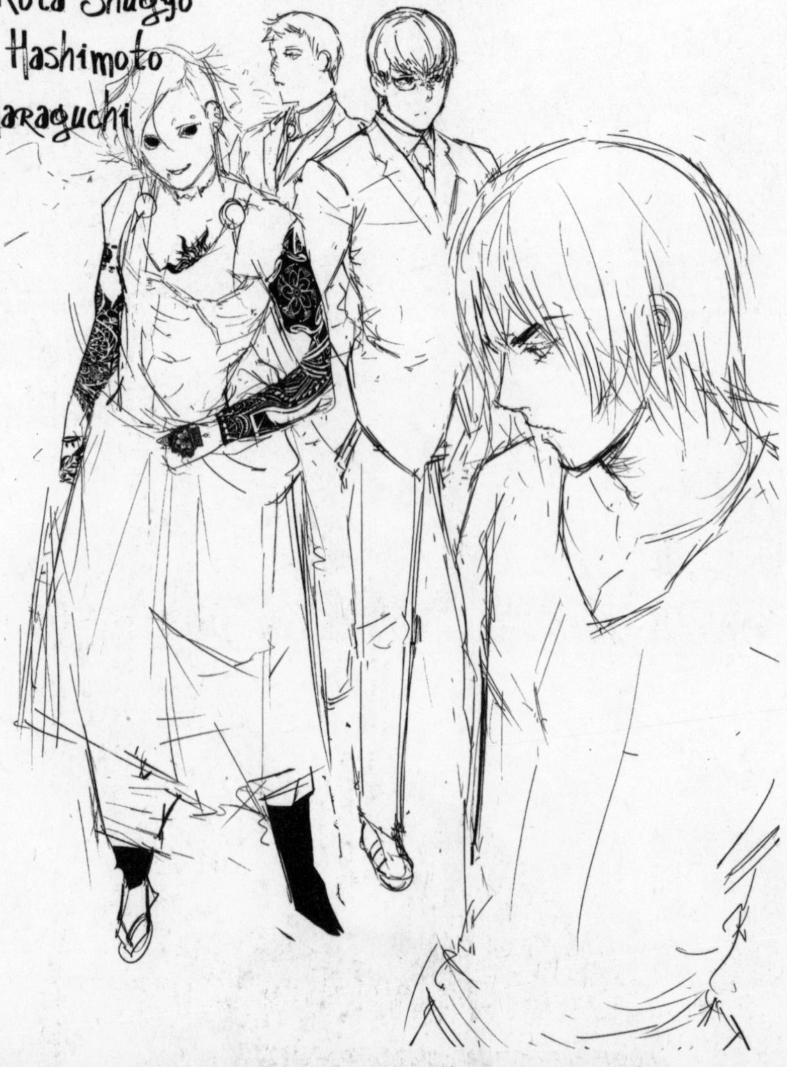

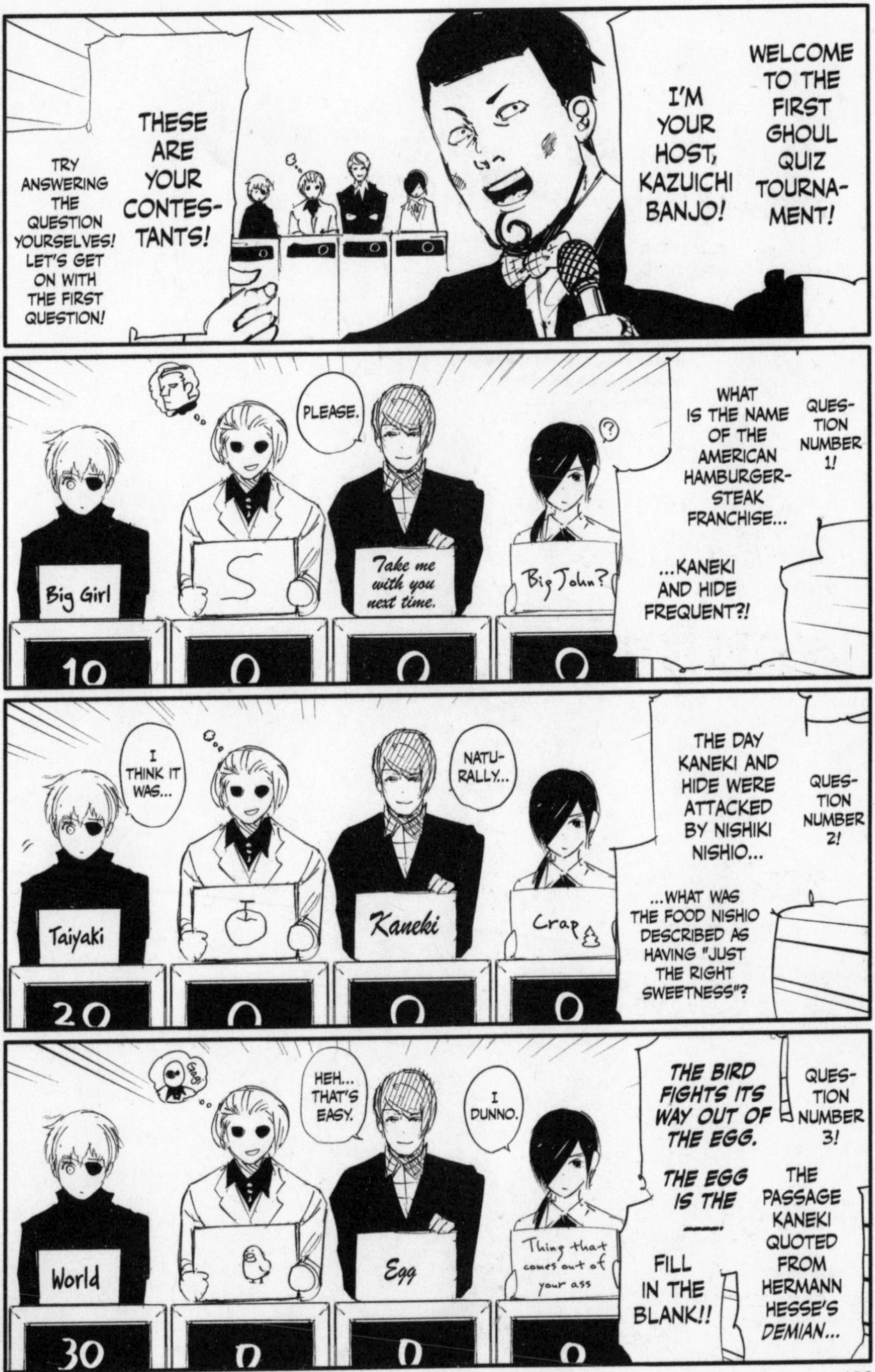
WELCOME TO THE FIRST GHOUL QUIZ TOURNAMENT!
I'M YOUR HOST, KAZUICHI BANJO!
THESE ARE YOUR CONTESTANTS!
TRY ANSWERING THE QUESTION YOURSELVES! LET'S GET ON WITH THE FIRST QUESTION!
QUESTION NUMBER 1!
WHAT IS THE NAME OF THE AMERICAN HAMBURGER-STEAK FRANCHISE...
...KANEKI AND HIDE FREQUENT?!
?
Big John?
0
PLEASE.
Take me with you next time.
0
S
0
Big Girl
10
QUESTION NUMBER 2!
THE DAY KANEKI AND HIDE WERE ATTACKED BY NISHIKI NISHIO...
...WHAT WAS THE FOOD NISHIO DESCRIBED AS HAVING "JUST THE RIGHT SWEETNESS"?
Crap
0
NATURALLY...
Kaneki
0
0
I THINK IT WAS...
Taiyaki
20
QUESTION NUMBER 3!
THE PASSAGE KANEKI QUOTED FROM HERMANN HESSE'S *DEMIAN*...
THE BIRD FIGHTS ITS WAY OUT OF THE EGG.
THE EGG IS THE ____.
FILL IN THE BLANK!!
Thing that comes out of your ass
0
I DUNNO.
Egg
0
HEH... THAT'S EASY.
0
World
30

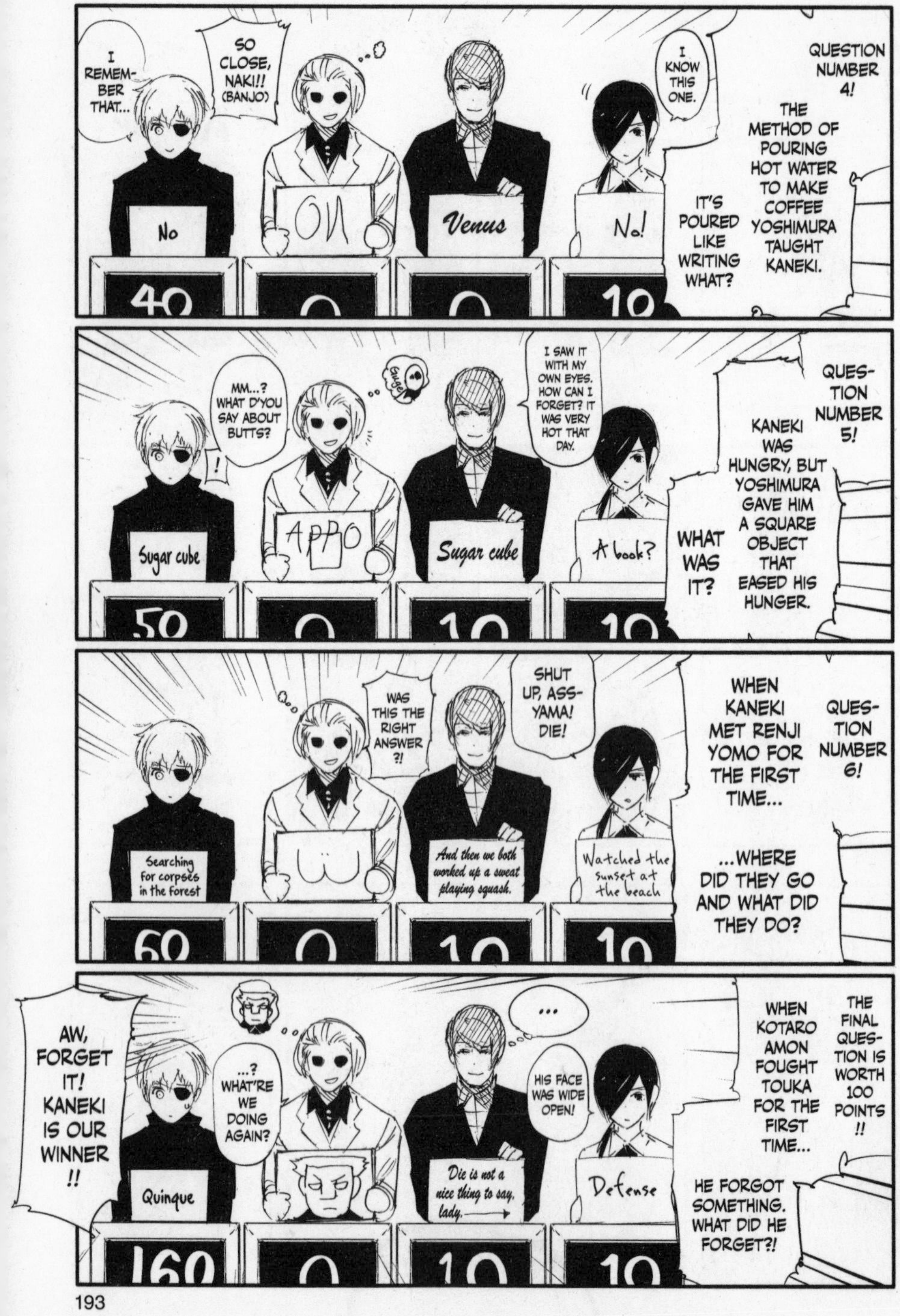
QUESTION NUMBER 4!
THE METHOD OF POURING HOT WATER TO MAKE COFFEE YOSHIMURA TAUGHT KANEKI.
IT'S POURED LIKE WRITING WHAT?
I KNOW THIS ONE.
No!
10
Venus
0
SO CLOSE, NAKI!! (BANJO)
ON
0
I REMEMBER THAT...
No
40
QUESTION NUMBER 5!
KANEKI WAS HUNGRY, BUT YOSHIMURA GAVE HIM A SQUARE OBJECT THAT EASED HIS HUNGER.
WHAT WAS IT?
I SAW IT WITH MY OWN EYES. HOW CAN I FORGET? IT WAS VERY HOT THAT DAY.
A book?
10
Sugar cube
10
MM...? WHAT D'YOU SAY ABOUT BUTTS?
APPO
0
!
Sugar cube
50
QUESTION NUMBER 6!
WHEN KANEKI MET RENJI YOMO FOR THE FIRST TIME...
...WHERE DID THEY GO AND WHAT DID THEY DO?
SHUT UP, ASS-YAMA! DIE!
Watched the sunset at the beach
10
And then we both worked up a sweat playing squash.
10
WAS THIS THE RIGHT ANSWER?!
0
Searching for corpses in the forest
60
THE FINAL QUESTION IS WORTH 100 POINTS!!
WHEN KOTARO AMON FOUGHT TOUKA FOR THE FIRST TIME...
HE FORGOT SOMETHING. WHAT DID HE FORGET?!
HIS FACE WAS WIDE OPEN!
Defense
10
...
Die is not a nice thing to say, lady.
10
...? WHAT'RE WE DOING AGAIN?
0
Quinque
160
AW, FORGET IT! KANEKI IS OUR WINNER!!

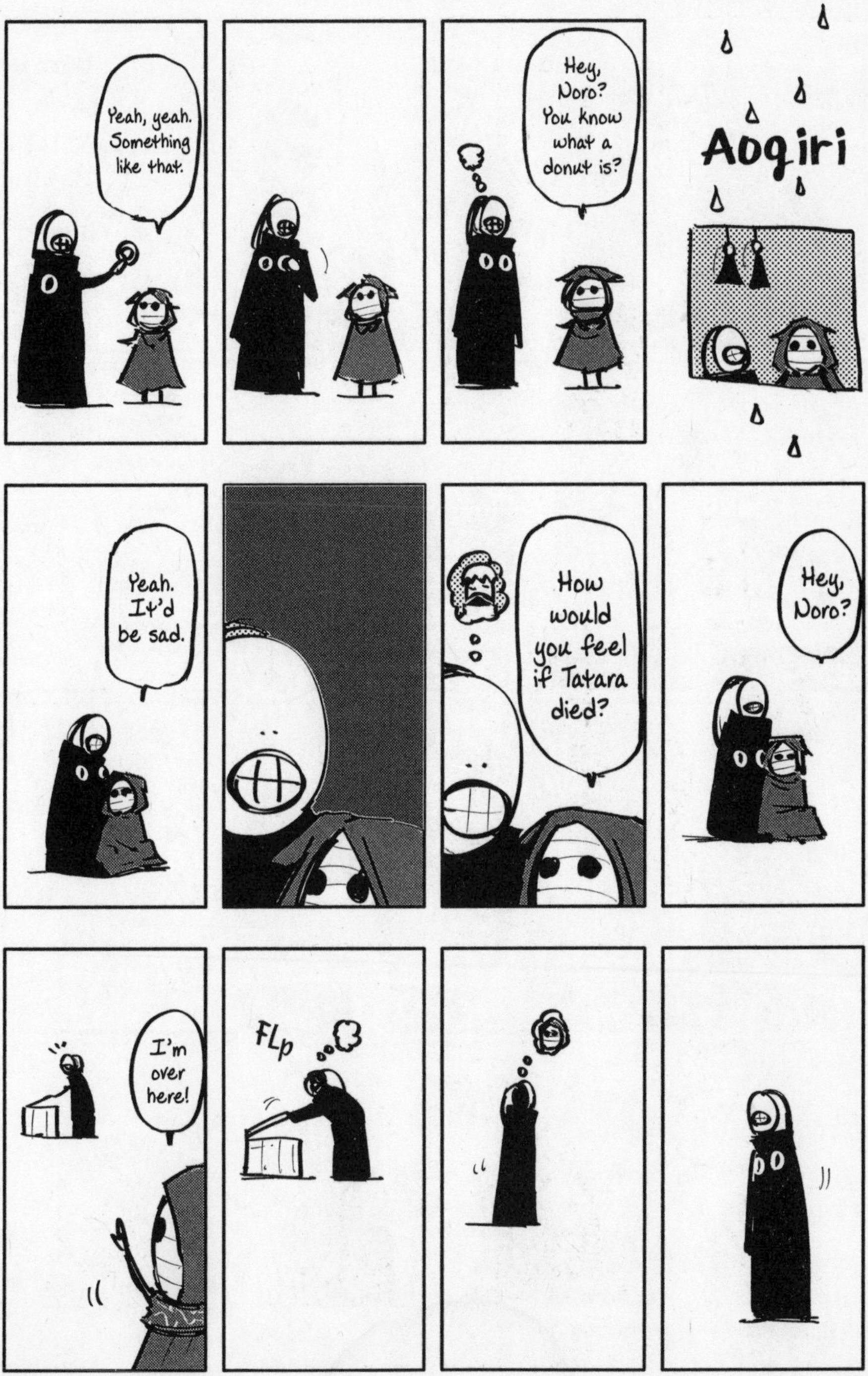
Aogiri
Hey, Noro? You know what a donut is?
Yeah, yeah. Something like that.
Hey, Noro?
How would you feel if Tatara died?
Yeah. It'd be sad.
FLp
I'm over here!

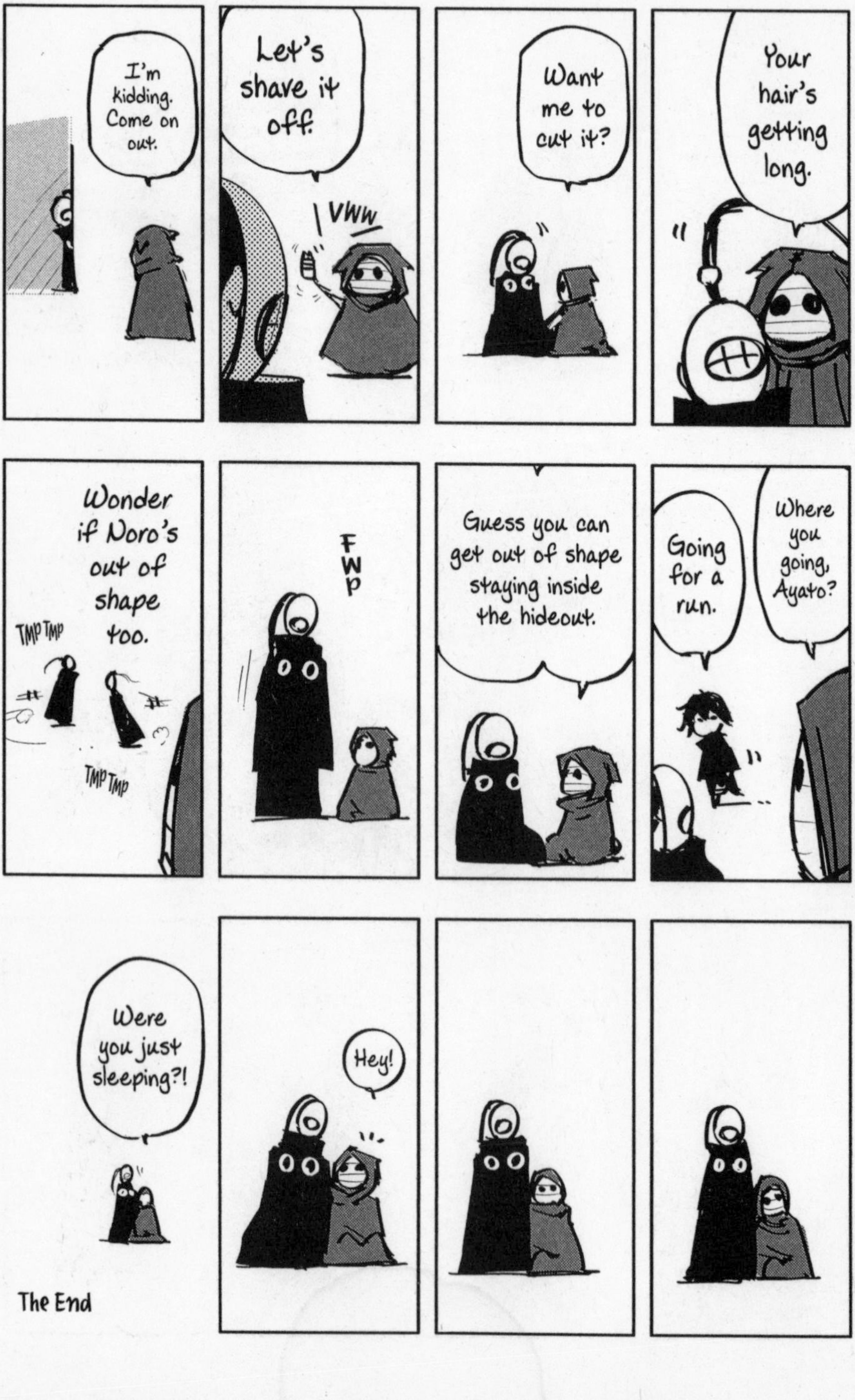
Your hair's getting long.
Want me to cut it?
VWW
Let's shave it off.
I'm kidding. Come on out.
Where you going, Ayato?
Going for a run.
Guess you can get out of shape staying inside the hideout.
FWP
Wonder if Noro's out of shape too.
TMP TMP
TMP TMP
Hey!
Were you just sleeping?!
The End

Three Adults

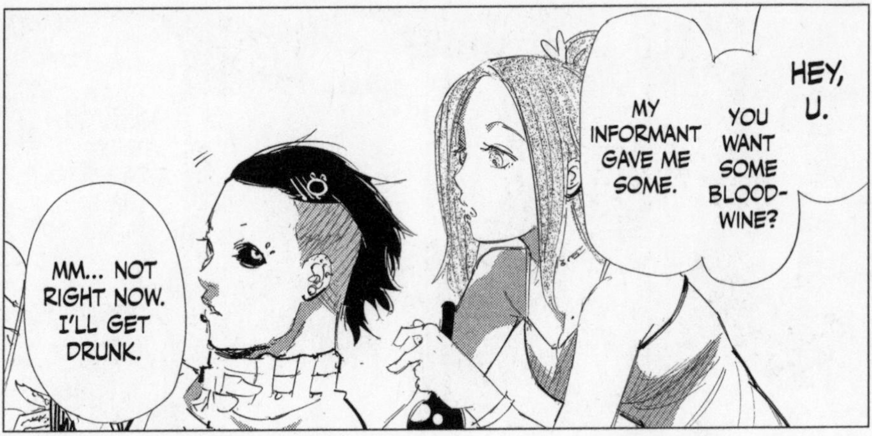
HEY, U.
YOU WANT SOME BLOOD-WINE?
MY INFORMANT GAVE ME SOME.
MM... NOT RIGHT NOW. I'LL GET DRUNK.

Letting extracted blood sit for a period of time to mature it. (In other words, rotten blood.)

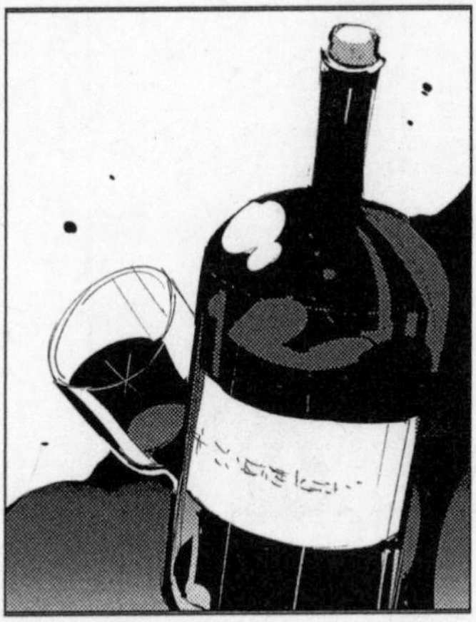

Ghouls that ingest it become inebriated.

Just like humans that consume alcohol.

Known as blood-wine or blood-liquor. Sometimes called wine because of its color.

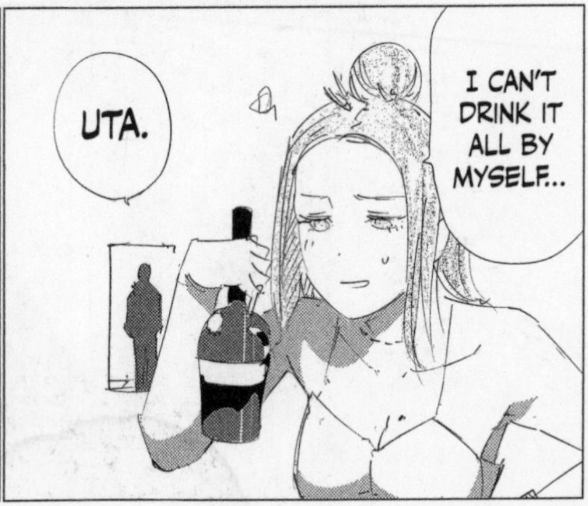
I CAN'T DRINK IT ALL BY MYSELF...
UTA.

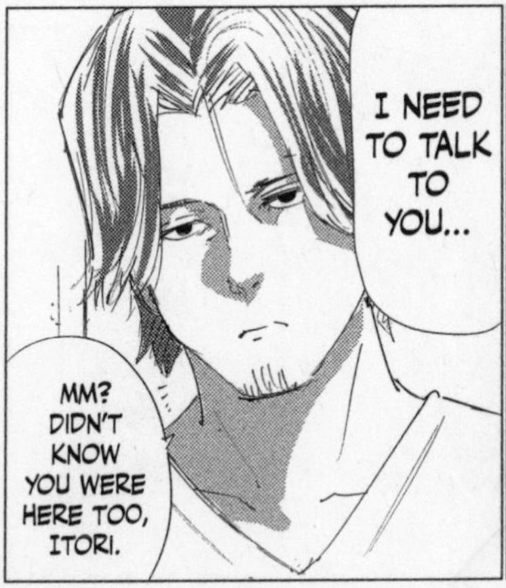
I NEED TO TALK TO YOU...
MM? DIDN'T KNOW YOU WERE HERE TOO, ITORI.

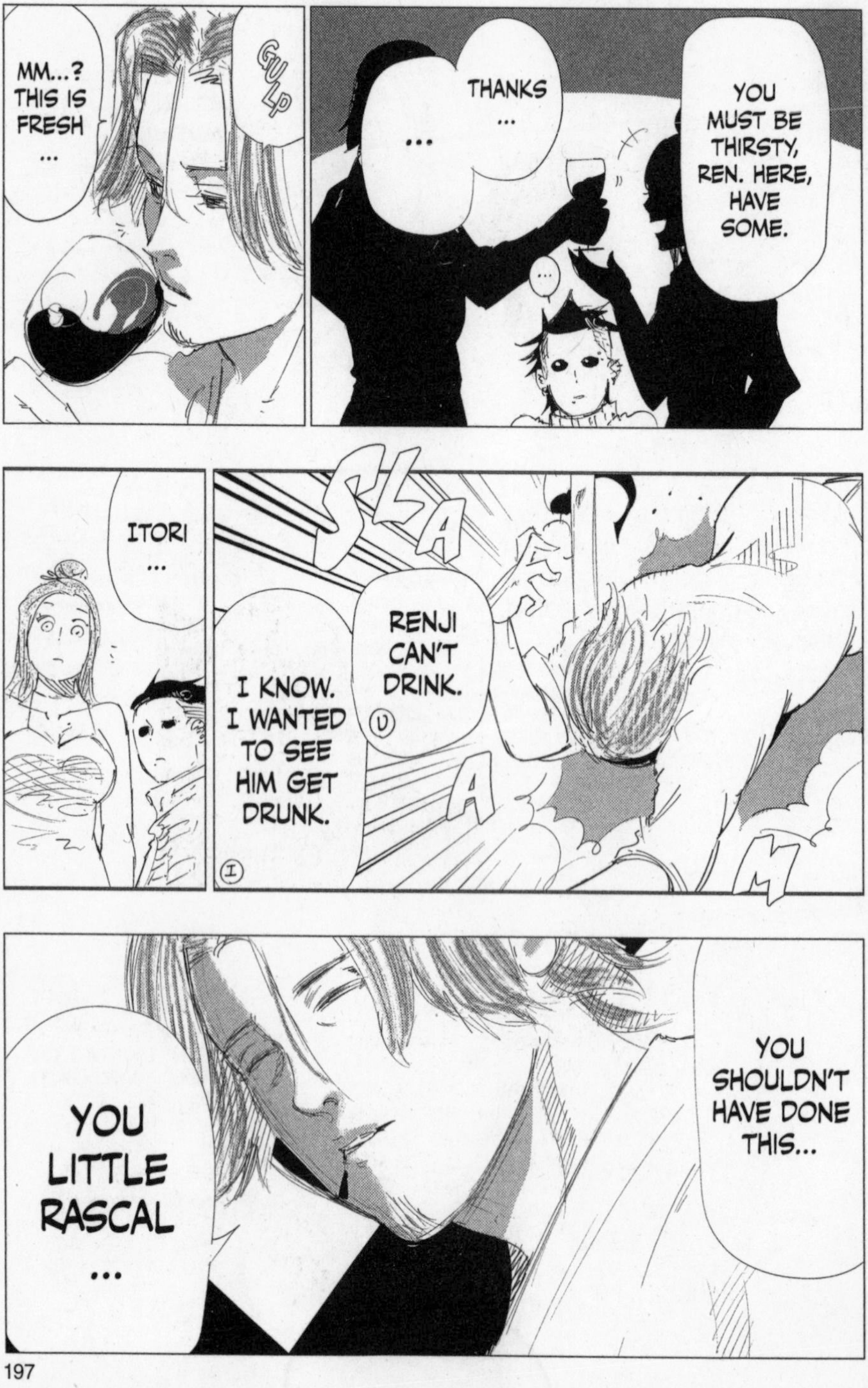
YOU MUST BE THIRSTY, REN. HERE, HAVE SOME.
THANKS ...
...
...
GULP
MM...? THIS IS FRESH ...
SLAAM
RENJI CAN'T DRINK.
I KNOW. I WANTED TO SEE HIM GET DRUNK.
ITORI ...
YOU SHOULDN'T HAVE DONE THIS...
YOU LITTLE RASCAL ...

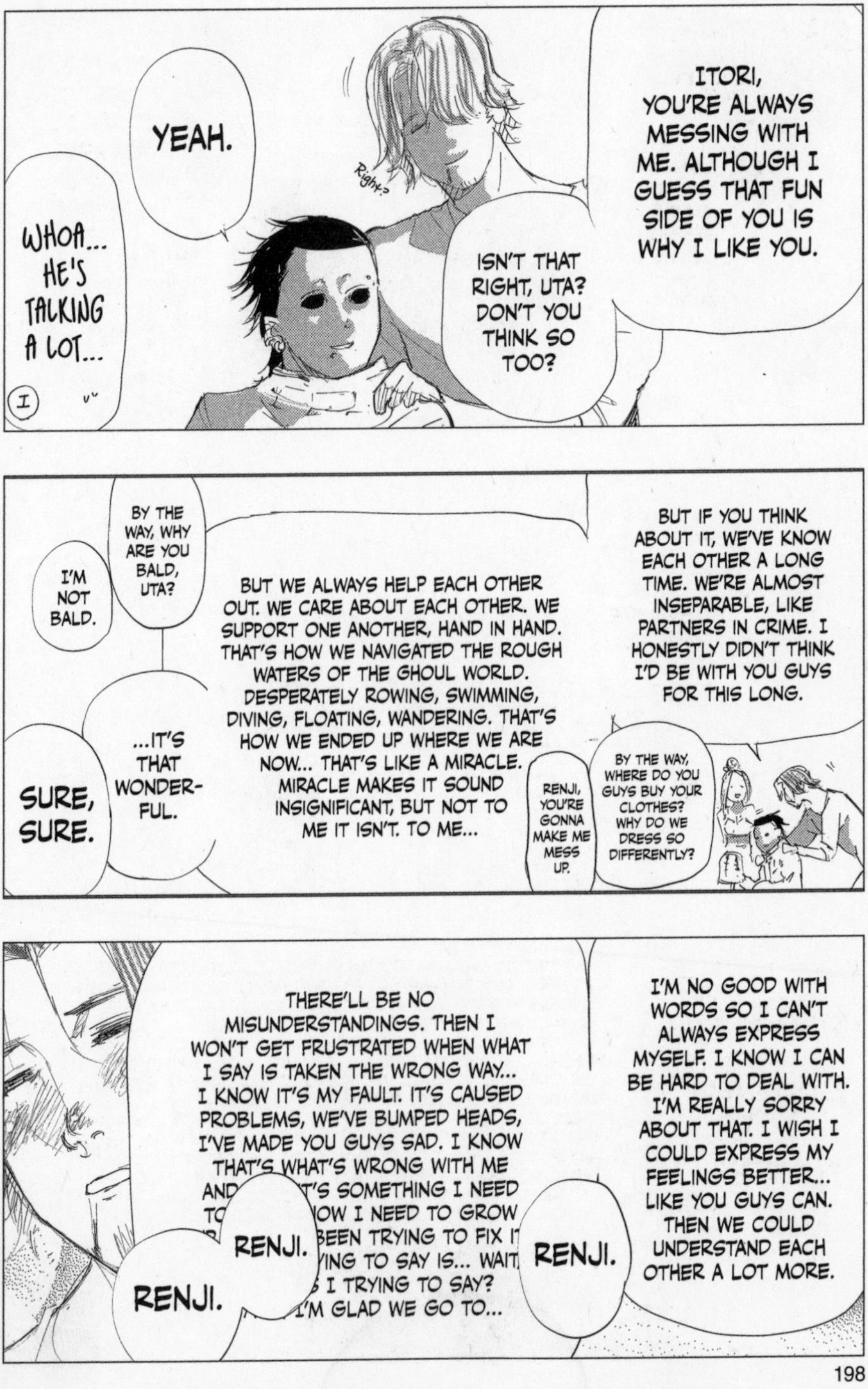
ITORI, YOU'RE ALWAYS MESSING WITH ME. ALTHOUGH I GUESS THAT FUN SIDE OF YOU IS WHY I LIKE YOU.
Right?
ISN'T THAT RIGHT, UTA? DON'T YOU THINK SO TOO?
YEAH.
WHOA... HE'S TALKING A LOT...
BUT IF YOU THINK ABOUT IT, WE'VE KNOW EACH OTHER A LONG TIME. WE'RE ALMOST INSEPARABLE, LIKE PARTNERS IN CRIME. I HONESTLY DIDN'T THINK I'D BE WITH YOU GUYS FOR THIS LONG.
BUT WE ALWAYS HELP EACH OTHER OUT. WE CARE ABOUT EACH OTHER. WE SUPPORT ONE ANOTHER, HAND IN HAND. THAT'S HOW WE NAVIGATED THE ROUGH WATERS OF THE GHOUL WORLD. DESPERATELY ROWING, SWIMMING, DIVING, FLOATING, WANDERING. THAT'S HOW WE ENDED UP WHERE WE ARE NOW... THAT'S LIKE A MIRACLE. MIRACLE MAKES IT SOUND INSIGNIFICANT, BUT NOT TO ME IT ISN'T. TO ME...
BY THE WAY, WHY ARE YOU BALD, UTA?
I'M NOT BALD.
...IT'S THAT WONDERFUL.
SURE, SURE.
BY THE WAY, WHERE DO YOU GUYS BUY YOUR CLOTHES? WHY DO WE DRESS SO DIFFERENTLY?
RENJI, YOU'RE GONNA MAKE ME MESS UP.
I'M NO GOOD WITH WORDS SO I CAN'T ALWAYS EXPRESS MYSELF. I KNOW I CAN BE HARD TO DEAL WITH. I'M REALLY SORRY ABOUT THAT. I WISH I COULD EXPRESS MY FEELINGS BETTER... LIKE YOU GUYS CAN. THEN WE COULD UNDERSTAND EACH OTHER A LOT MORE.
THERE'LL BE NO MISUNDERSTANDINGS. THEN I WON'T GET FRUSTRATED WHEN WHAT I SAY IS TAKEN THE WRONG WAY... I KNOW IT'S MY FAULT. IT'S CAUSED PROBLEMS, WE'VE BUMPED HEADS, I'VE MADE YOU GUYS SAD. I KNOW THAT'S WHAT'S WRONG WITH ME
RENJI.
RENJI.
RENJI.

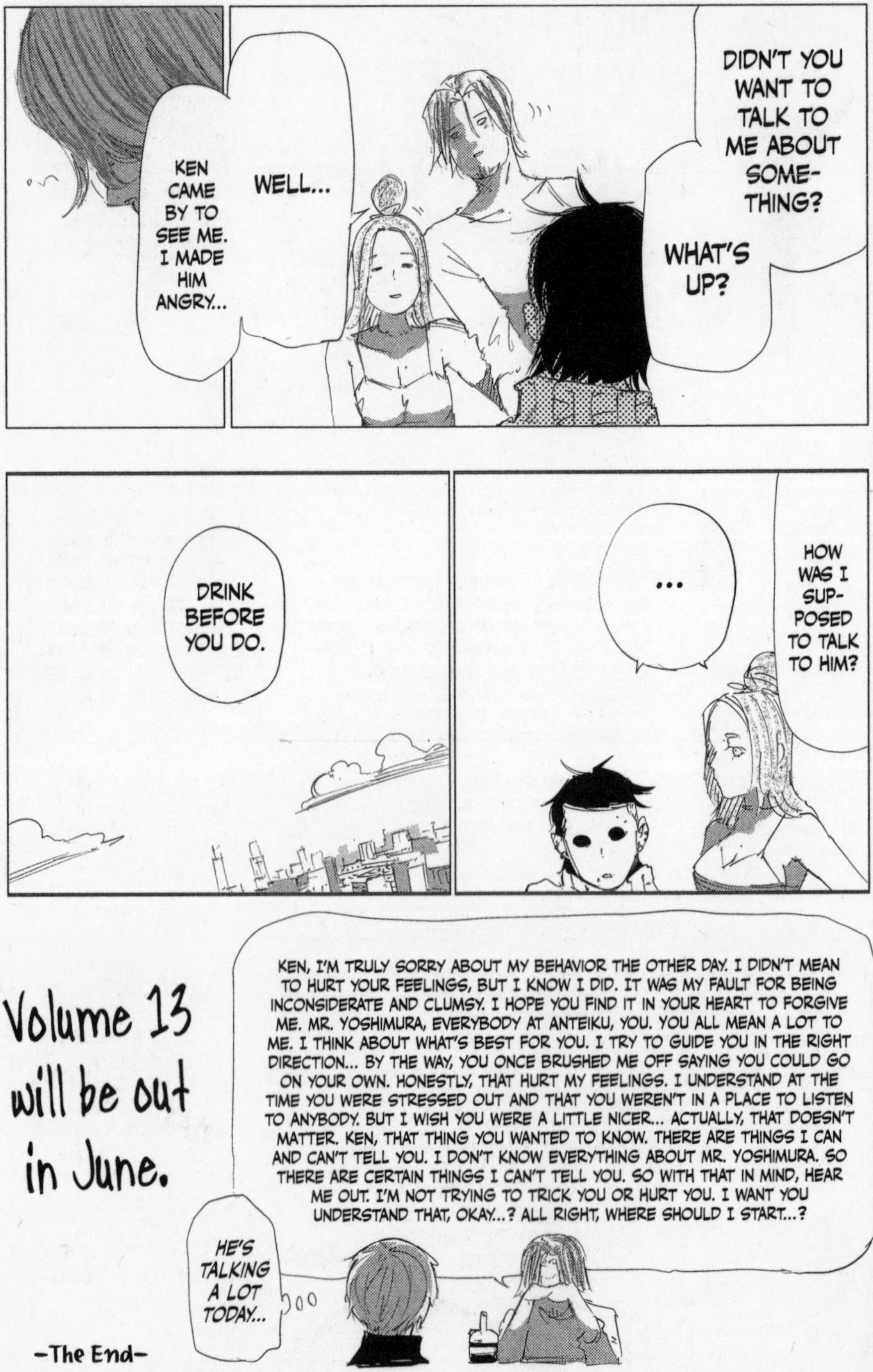
DIDN'T YOU WANT TO TALK TO ME ABOUT SOME-THING?
WHAT'S UP?
WELL...
KEN CAME BY TO SEE ME. I MADE HIM ANGRY...
HOW WAS I SUP-POSED TO TALK TO HIM?
...
DRINK BEFORE YOU DO.
KEN, I'M TRULY SORRY ABOUT MY BEHAVIOR THE OTHER DAY. I DIDN'T MEAN TO HURT YOUR FEELINGS, BUT I KNOW I DID. IT WAS MY FAULT FOR BEING INCONSIDERATE AND CLUMSY. I HOPE YOU FIND IT IN YOUR HEART TO FORGIVE ME. MR. YOSHIMURA, EVERYBODY AT ANTEIKU, YOU. YOU ALL MEAN A LOT TO ME. I THINK ABOUT WHAT'S BEST FOR YOU. I TRY TO GUIDE YOU IN THE RIGHT DIRECTION... BY THE WAY, YOU ONCE BRUSHED ME OFF SAYING YOU COULD GO ON YOUR OWN. HONESTLY, THAT HURT MY FEELINGS. I UNDERSTAND AT THE TIME YOU WERE STRESSED OUT AND THAT YOU WEREN'T IN A PLACE TO LISTEN TO ANYBODY. BUT I WISH YOU WERE A LITTLE NICER... ACTUALLY, THAT DOESN'T MATTER. KEN, THAT THING YOU WANTED TO KNOW. THERE ARE THINGS I CAN AND CAN'T TELL YOU. I DON'T KNOW EVERYTHING ABOUT MR. YOSHIMURA. SO THERE ARE CERTAIN THINGS I CAN'T TELL YOU. SO WITH THAT IN MIND, HEAR ME OUT. I'M NOT TRYING TO TRICK YOU OR HURT YOU. I WANT YOU UNDERSTAND THAT, OKAY...? ALL RIGHT, WHERE SHOULD I START...?
HE'S TALKING A LOT TODAY...
Volume 13 will be out in June.
-The End-

TOKYO GHOUL

[THIS IS THE LAST PAGE]

TOKYO GHOUL
READS
RIGHT TO LEFT

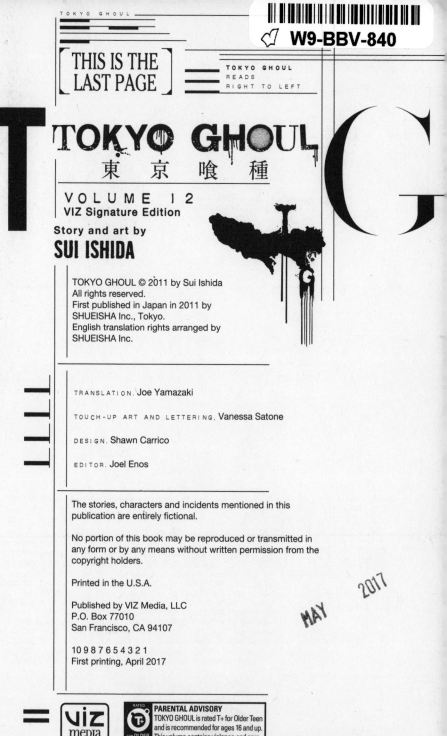

TOKYO GHOUL
東京喰種

VOLUME 12
VIZ Signature Edition

Story and art by
SUI ISHIDA

First published in Japan in 2011 by
SHUEISHA Inc., Tokyo.
English translation rights arranged by
SHUEISHA Inc.

TRANSLATION. Joe Yamazaki

TOUCH-UP ART AND LETTERING. Vanessa Satone

DESIGN. Shawn Carrico

EDITOR. Joel Enos

Printed in the U.S.A.

Published by VIZ Media, LLC
P.O. Box 77010
San Francisco, CA 94107

10 9 8 7 6 5 4 3 2 1
First printing, April 2017

viz media
www.viz.com

RATED T+ FOR OLDER TEEN
PARENTAL ADVISORY
TOKYO GHOUL is rated T+ for Older Teen and is recommended for ages 16 and up. This volume contains violence and gore.
ratings.viz.com

VIZ SIGNATURE